THE ECCLESIASTICAL HISTORY

OF

SOCRATES,

SURNAMED SCHOLASTICUS, OR THE ADVOCATE.

COMPRISING A

HISTORY OF THE CHURCH,

IN SEVEN BOOKS,

FROM THE ACCESSION OF CONSTANTINE, A. D. 305, TO
THE 38TH YEAR OF THEODOSIUS II., INCLUDING
A PERIOD OF 140 YEARS.

Translated from the Greek:

WITH SOME ACCOUNT OF THE AUTHOR, AND NOTES SELECTED
FROM VALESIUS.

LONDON:

HENRY G. BOHN, YORK STREET, COVENT GARDEN.

MDCCCLIII.

THE LIFE OF SOCRATES,

AND

AN ACCOUNT OF HIS WRITINGS.

SOCRATES, our historian, was a native of Constantinople;
for he himself states that he was born and educated in that
city, and that for this reason he has detailed principally events
which occurred there. In his youth his philological studies
were prosecuted under the direction of the grammarians Helladius and Ammonius, both of whom were idolaters; who,
having withdrawn from Alexandria about this time, had taken
up their abode at Constantinople. The reasons which induced them to migrate from Alexandria are thus explained
by Socrates himself.[1]—When the Pagan temples had been
pulled down, by the zeal and exertion of Theophilus bishop
of that city, Helladius and Ammonius (one of whom had
been a priest of Jupiter at Alexandria, and the other of
Simius) grieved at the contempt which was cast upon their
gods, quitted the scene of what they considered sacrilege,
and retired to Constantinople. These transactions took
place during the consulship of Tamasius and Promotus, according to the "Chronicon" of Marcellinus, which was the
eleventh year of the emperor Theodosius. It would therefore appear that Socrates was born about the commencement
of his reign, inasmuch as boys were generally placed under
the tuition of grammarians at ten years of age: but some date
his birth in the year 380. He afterwards studied rhetoric

[1] Book v. chap. xvi.

1

under Troïlus, a celebrated teacher of philosophy and eloquence at Constantinople. This however is rather inferred
from his frequent and honourable mention of Troïlus, than
from any direct statement of the fact. He speaks of Side
in Pamphylia as the country of Troïlus, and names Eusebius, and the bishops Silvanus and Alabius, as among the
number of his distinguished pupils; and finally[1] declares
that the Prætorian prefect Anthemius, who during the
minority of Theodosius guided the administration, was greatly
influenced by his counsels: to which he adds this eulogy of
him: "Who, in addition to his philosophical attainments, was
not inferior to Anthemius in political sagacity." On these
grounds therefore it is concluded that Troïlus taught Socrates
rhetoric.

Our author's first appearance in public life was in the
Forum at Constantinople, as a special pleader: it was from
this circumstance that the cognomen "Scholasticus" was
applied to him; which indeed was the general appellation
for advocates on their leaving the schools of the rhetoricians
to devote themselves to the duties of their profession. When
at length he resigned his legal practice, his attention was
directed to the compilation of a "History of the Church," in
seven books, from the year 309, where Eusebius ends, to the
year 445; in which he has displayed singular judgment, and
accurate as well as laborious research. He has carefully
marked the periods of remarkable events, by giving the Consulates and Olympiads; and has invested his matter with
authority, by having drawn his information from the most
authentic sources to which he could obtain access, such as
public records, pastoral and episcopal letters, acts of synods,
and the works of other ecclesiastical writers. In the composition of his "History," he has studiously adopted and
maintained simplicity and plainness of style, to the rigorous
exclusion of all oratorical ornament, in order that he might

---

[1] Book vii. chap. i.

be the more readily understood by all classes of persons, as he himself declares at the commencement of his first and third books.

His first two books were originally composed on the entire credit of Rufinus; but having afterwards discovered, from the works of Athanasius, that the principal circumstances of the persecution, which that noble defender of the Divinity of Christ suffered, had been omitted, he subsequently amended them.[1]

He however confounds Maximian with Maximin, which is surprising, considering that he chiefly lived at Constantinople. He errs also in stating that five bishops were condemned in the council of Nice for refusing to approve the confession of faith there made; for a letter of the council shows that there were but two, viz. Theonas and Secundus. Theognis and Eusebius were indeed exiled by command of the emperor Constantine; but it was at another time, and for a different reason than that assigned by Socrates, as Jerome and Philostorgus testify. His allusion to the council of Sirmium is full of obscurity; and he was evidently under the mistake of supposing that the three confessions there promulgated at three several councils, were set forth on one and the same occasion.

Socrates, moreover, in speaking of the council held at Antioch by the Arians in the year 341, seems to attach too much of *authority* to the usage which early prevailed of inviting the bishop of Rome to all ecclesiastical conventions in the West. As if he believed there was *a law* which forbad any decision in the Church without that prelate's sanction. But Julius himself, who was neither ignorant of his privileges, nor disposed to relinquish any right which pertained to his see, far from pretending to pre-eminence among his brethren, disclaimed everything beyond the courtesy of being

---

[1] See book ii. chap. i., where he states the grounds of his conduct in this respect.

[SOCRATES.] b

invited to attend, and being consulted in common with the other bishops of Italy. And although the *primacy* of that episcopate was recognised, both before and after the council of Nice, *a preference of judgment in the first instance* was neither claimed nor allowed, as the example of the council of Antioch, where Paul of Samosata was condemned without the participation of Dionysius bishop of Rome, clearly shows. In fact, the language of the bishops of Italy to those of the East, complaining of their decision in the case of Maximus and Nectarius without allowing them to take cognizance of the affair, puts the matter in a very distinct light: "Non *prærogativam* vindicamus examinis," said they, " sed *consortium* tamen debuit esse *communis* arbitrii."

With regard to his religious sentiments, Cardinal Baronius in his "Annals," and Philip Labbæus in his book "De Scriptoribus Ecclesiasticis," assert that Socrates was of the Novatian sect. Nicephorus also expresses the same opinion in the preface to his "Ecclesiastical History:" his words are, " *Socrates had indeed the appellation Catharus,* (i. e. *pure,*) *but his principles were not so.*" It must not be understood from this that his cognomen was *Catharus,* but simply that he was a Novatian; for the Novatians were accustomed to designate themselves *Cathari,* as the eighth canon of the Nicene council informs us. The same writer (book xi. chap. xiv.) speaks thus of him : " *Socrates (who from this passage clearly owns that he was not opposed to the doctrines of the Novatians) says that these things were related to him by a certain old man,*" &c. But the reasons why Socrates was by very many considered a Novatian, are neither few nor slight. For in the first place he carefully enumerates the series of Novatian prelates who governed their Church at Constantinople from the times of Constantine, noticing also the Consulates in which they severally died. In the next place he passes the highest encomiums on each of them, especially Agelius and Sisinnius, Chrysanthus and Paul, and even avers

that by the prayers of the latter a miracle was performed at
Constantinople. In short, he enters into all things relating
to the sect of the Novatians with so much interest and fidelity,
as to seem at least extremely favourable to them. Yet
if any one will candidly examine the subject, he will find
no conclusive evidence of his having himself been a Novatian. For with equal diligence he enumerates the Arian
prelates who had the administration of their church at Constantinople: he is not however on that account said to have
been an Arian. In fact he has entered as fully into all the
circumstances connected with the Arians, Eunomians, and
Macedonians at Constantinople, as with the Novatians. He
has accounted for this in book iv. chap. xxiv.: where he
states that his object more particularly was to record those
things which took place at Constantinople; as well because
he himself resided in that city, in which he had been born
and educated, as that the transactions there were of greater
importance, and more worthy of record. But if any one
should object that the Arian bishops are less commended by
Socrates than those of the Novatians, the ready answer is—
that the former were in every respect inferior to the latter;
for the Novatian Church was not only sounder in doctrines,
but at that time abounded with the most eminent clergy.
It must notwithstanding be confessed that our author generally favours the Novatians: as when he numbers the founder
of that sect among the martyrs; says that the Novatians
were attached to the Catholics by the strongest affection, and
united with them in public prayer; and commends the discourse of Sisinnius in reprobation of the expression of Chrysostom, "Even if thou hast repented a thousand times,
approach." But it is one thing to favour the Novatians,
and another to be a Novatian. Socrates might have been
favourable to them, either from being on terms of familiar
intercourse with the most distinguished among them, or
because he approved of their discipline and abstinence: for

we may gather from his writings that he was rather disposed
to austerity of habit.   Still had he identified himself with
that body, he surely would not (book ii. chap. xxxviii.) have
distinctly called the Catholics τοὺς τῆς ἐκκλησίας, *those of the
Church*, and opposed them to the Novatians, thereby acknowledging the Novatians to be without the pale of the Church.
Moreover (book vi. chap. xx. and xxiii.) he classes the Novatians among the heretics, with Arians, Macedonians, and
Eunomians ; while he styles the Church simply and absolutely the Catholic Church, so discriminating it from the
Churches of the various sects.   Again, he censures in no
ambiguous terms the abolition of a *Penitentiary Presbyter*,
on the recommendation of Nectarius : for by this means, he
observes, licence was given to transgressors, since there was
no one whose duty it was to reprove them—which is not the
language of a Novatian ; for that sect did not admit of repentance after baptism, as Socrates himself testifies.   Theodore Lector, who lived in the same city, and almost at the
same period as Socrates, viz. in the reign of Anastasius, in
an epistle prefixed to his Ecclesiastical History, denominates
Socrates, Sozomen, and Theodoret, ἄνδρας θεοφιλεῖς, *men beloved of God*.   Finally, Peter Halloxius, in his Notes on the
Life of Irenæus, (page 664,) vindicates him from the charge
of Baronius, who wrote (A. D. 159) thus respecting him :
" These things Socrates the Novatian, he himself also celebrating the passover with the Jews on the 14th day of the
month," &c.   For he remarks that, "whereas Socrates is
called a Novatian, it may be understood in two senses : in
one that he sometimes favoured the Novatians, which Bell-
arminus also affirms in his treatise 'De Scriptoribus Ecclesiasticis' (A. D. 440); in the other that he had adopted their
heretical opinions.   But in the chapter referred to he clearly
shows that he is neither a Novatian, nor favourable to their
views : on the contrary, he censures them, and exposes their
dissensions and vices in the character of an enemy rather

than a friend, or perhaps that which most became him as an historian, neither, but simply a narrator of truth."

But while we are bound to exonerate him from actual identification with a sect whom he himself (book vi. chap. xx. and xxiii.) reckons among the schismatics, we cannot so easily justify all that he has advanced respecting the Novatians; for he seems misinformed as to the state of their schism and errors. Moreover he confounds Novatian, a presbyter of the Roman Church, who really first broke the unity of the Church, with Novatus, a person who was either among the presbytery, or, as some say, was bishop of Africa, and who merely favoured that division, but was not the author of it. Cyprian, from his personal knowledge of the latter, represents him as "an unruly spirit, the enemy of peace, fond of novelties, of insatiable avarice, and inflated with insufferable pride." He further accuses him of having cast the seeds of discord among the faithful of Carthage, of having robbed the widows and orphans, and of having appropriated to his own use the property of the Church and of the poor which had been deposited in his hands. He also charges him with having suffered his father to die of hunger, and then neglected to give him the honour of sepulture, with other gross enormities. And finally, he adds, that apprehending the deposition and excommunication he had merited, he anticipated his condemnation by flight, and going to Rome, joined himself to Novatian, and committed there greater crimes than he had been guilty of at Carthage. One would not wonder so much that Socrates has not distinguished these two men, since other Greek authors have not done so, who had little need of information on Oriental affairs; had not Eusebius in book vi. of his History inserted a letter of Cornelius containing a description of the occasion of the separation of the Novatians, so very unlike his own.[1] This difference can only be attri-

[1] Socrates takes no notice whatever of the declaration of Cornelius, that Novatian separated from ecclesiastical communion through jealousy,

buted to the too great readiness with which he listened to one of these heretics at Constantinople ; who so artfully disguised the circumstances connected with the origin of the schism, as to lead him to suspect the credibility of Cornelius, as of an interested party. It is under the influence of the same principle, without doubt, that he sometimes passes such extravagant encomiums on the exterior austerity of their conduct, and the apparent sanctity of their life.

because he had not been elected bishop : that he managed to get himself ordained by three prelates whose reason had been clouded by the fumes of wine : and that the pardon granted to those who had sacrificed to idols during the persecution excited by Decius against the Church, was but a pretext for his schism.

CONTENTS.

THE

ECCLESIASTICAL HISTORY,

BY

SOCRATES SCHOLASTICUS.

BOOK I.

CHAP. I.—PREFACE.

EUSEBIUS, surnamed Pamphilus,[1] has composed a History
of the Church in ten books, brought down to the time of the
emperor Constantine, when the persecution ceased which
Diocletian had commenced against the Christians.[2] But, in
writing the Life of Constantine, this author has very slightly
treated of the Arian controversy, being evidently more intent
on a highly wrought eulogium of the emperor, than an accurate statement of facts. We therefore propose to write at
large the details of what has taken place in the Churches,
beginning with a relation of those particulars which he has
passed over, and bringing down subsequent events to our own
times : nor shall we be very solicitous to display an empty
parade of words, but to lay faithfully before the reader what
we have been able to collect from the best authenticated records, and such information as has been communicated to us

---

[1] ὁ Παμφίλου. Eusebius was so called, not, as might be at first supposed, from being the son of Pamphilus, nor as being " universally beloved," but on account of his intimacy and friendship with Pamphilus, a
presbyter of Cæsarea, who was his inseparable companion through life.
See Life of Eusebius, prefixed to the translation of his Ecclesiastical
History, in this series, p. xiv.

[2] That is, the year A. D. 309.

[SOCRATES.]   B

by those who were themselves identified with the transactions to which they bear testimony.[1] And since it has an important bearing on the matter in hand, it will be proper to enter into some account of Constantine's conversion to Christianity.

CHAP. II.—By what means the emperor Constantine became a Christian.

WHEN Diocletian and Maximian,[2] surnamed Herculius, had by mutual consent laid aside the imperial dignity, and retired into private life, Maximian, surnamed Galerius, who had been a sharer with them in the government, came into Italy and appointed two Cæsars, Maximin in the eastern division of the empire, and Severus in the Italian or western. In Britain however Constantine was proclaimed emperor, instead of his father Constantius, who died in the first year of the two hundred and seventy-first Olympiad, on the 25th of July. But at Rome Maxentius, the son of Maximian Herculius, was raised by the Prætorian soldiers to be a tyrant rather than an emperor. In this state of things Herculius, impelled by an eager desire of regaining the sovereign power, attempted to destroy his son Maxentius: but this he was prevented by the soldiery from effecting, and he soon afterwards died at Tarsus in Cilicia. Severus Cæsar was sent to Rome by Galerius Maximian, in order to seize Maxentius, but his own soldiers having betrayed him, he was slain. At length Galerius Maximian, who as senior Augustus[3] had exercised the chief authority, also died, having previously appointed as his successor, his old friend and companion in arms, Licinius, a Dacian by birth. Meanwhile Maxentius tyrannically trampled on the rights and liberties of the Roman people, shamelessly violating the wives of the nobles, putting many innocent persons to death, and perpetrating other atrocities. The emperor Constantine being informed of these things, exerted

[1] Compare the opening remarks of book iii. chap. i.

[2] Upon the way in which Socrates confounds Maximian and Maximin together, see remarks in the Life of Socrates, prefixed to this volume, p. v.

[3] For an account of the appointment of two Cæsars and two Augusti by the emperor Diocletian, together with the meaning of the titles, see Gibbon's Decline and Fall, chap. xiii. See below, chap. xxxviii.

himself to free the Romans from the slavery under which
they were groaning; and began immediately to consider by
what means he might overwhelm the tyrant. While his mind
was occupied on this subject, and he was hesitating what
³ divinity's aid he should invoke for the successful conduct of
the war, it occurred to him that Diocletian had profited but
little by the Pagan deities, whom he had so sedulously sought
to propitiate; but that his own father Constantius, who had
renounced the idolatrous worship of the Greeks, had passed
through life far more prosperously. In this state of uncer-
tainty, a preternatural vision, which transcends all description, appeared to him as he was marching at the head of his
troops : he saw, about that part of the day when the sun after
passing the meridian begins to decline towards the west, a
⁴ pillar of light in the heavens, in the form of a cross, on which
were inscribed these words, BY THIS CONQUER.¹   Struck
with amazement at the appearance of this sign, and scarcely
believing his own eyes, the emperor asked those around him
if they beheld the same spectacle; and they all declaring that
they did, the emperor's mind was strengthened by this divine
and extraordinary apparition. In his slumbers on the following night he saw Christ, who directed him to prepare a
⁵ standard according to the pattern of that which had been seen;
and to use it against his enemies as an assured trophy of victory. In obedience to this divine oracle, he caused a standard
in the form of a cross to be prepared, which is preserved in
the palace even to the present time : and proceeding in his
measures with greater confidence, he attacked the enemy and
vanquished him before the gates of Rome, near the Milvian
bridge, Maxentius himself being drowned in the river. This
victory was achieved in the seventh year of the conqueror's
reign. After this, while Licinius, who shared the government with him, and was his brother-in-law, having married
his sister Constantia, was residing in the East, the emperor
Constantine offered grateful thanksgivings to God as his
benefactor, for the signal blessings he had received, by such
actions as these :—he relieved the Christians from persecution, recalled those who were in exile, liberated such as were
imprisoned, and caused the confiscated property of the proscribed to be restored to them : he moreover rebuilt the

¹ 'Εν τούτῳ νίκα—" In hoc signo vinces."

churches, and performed all these things with the greatest
ardour.   About this time Diocletian, who had abdicated the
imperial authority, died at Salona in Dalmatia.[1]

CHAP. III.—WHILE CONSTANTINE FAVOURS THE CHRISTIANS,
LICINIUS, WHO SHARED WITH HIM THE IMPERIAL DIGNITY,
PERSECUTES THEM.

THE emperor Constantine, having thus embraced Christianity, conducted himself in a manner worthy of his profession, building churches, and enriching them with splendid
offerings: he also either closed or destroyed the idolatrous
temples, and exposed the images which were in them to popular contempt. But his colleague, Licinius, retaining his Pagan
superstitions, hated the Christians; and although for a while,
from dread of Constantine, he avoided exciting persecution
openly, yet he managed to plot against them covertly, and at
length proceeded to acts of undisguised malevolence.   This
persecution, however, was local, not extending beyond those
districts where Licinius himself was: but these and other
public outrages could not long remain concealed from Constantine, and knowing that he was indignant at his conduct,
Licinius had recourse to an apology.   Having by this obse-
quiousness propitiated him, he entered into a specious league
of friendship, pledging himself by many oaths, neither to act
again tyrannically, nor to persecute Christians.   Notwithstanding the solemn obligations under which he had bound
himself, his perjury soon became apparent ; for he ceased not
to prejudice in every possible way the interests of Constantine, and to exercise the greatest severities on Christians.
He even prohibited the bishops by law from visiting the un-
converted Pagans, lest it should be made a pretext for pro-
selyting them to the Christian faith.   Hence, while in word
he concealed the bitterness of his hostility, the reality of it
was too keenly felt to be screened from the public eye; for
those who were exposed to his persecution, suffered most
severely both in their persons and property.

[1] With this chap. compare the parallel account in Sozomen, b. i. ch. iii.

CHAP. IV.—War arises between Constantine and Licinius on account of the Christians.

By this perfidy he drew upon himself the emperor Constantine's heaviest displeasure; and the pretended treaty of friendship having been so flagrantly violated, it was not long before they took up arms against each other as declared enemies. After several engagements both by sea and land, Licinius was at last utterly defeated near Chrysopolis in Bithynia, a port of the Chalcedonians, and surrendered himself to Constantine; who having taken him alive, treated him with the utmost humanity, and would by no means put him to death, but ordered him to take up his abode and live in tranquillity at Thessalonica. He could not however remain inactive; and having in a short time managed to collect some barbarian mercenaries, he made an effort to repair his late disaster by a fresh appeal to arms: and the emperor, being made acquainted with his proceedings, directed that he should be slain. On this being carried into effect, Constantine became possessed of the sole dominion, and was accordingly proclaimed sovereign Autocrat;[1] a circumstance which secured to Christians the peaceful profession of their faith,—this monarch seeking still, in a variety of ways, to promote their welfare. But unhappily this state of repose was of short duration, owing to dissensions among themselves, the nature and origin of which I shall now endeavour to describe.

CHAP. V.—The dispute of Arius with Alexander his Bishop.

After Peter bishop of Alexandria had suffered martyrdom under Diocletian, Achilles was installed in the episcopal office, whom Alexander succeeded, during the period of peace above referred to. He, in the fearless exercise of his functions for the instruction and government of the Church, attempted one day, in the presence of the presbytery and the rest of his clergy, to explain, with perhaps too philosophical minuteness, that great theological mystery—the Unity of the Holy Trinity. A certain one of the presbyters under his jurisdiction, whose

[1] See Gibbon's Decline and Fall, chap. xiv. sub fin.

name was Arius, possessed of no inconsiderable logical acumen, imagining that the bishop entertained the same view of this subject as Sabellius the Libyan,[1] controverted his statements with excessive pertinacity, advancing another error which was directly opposed indeed to that which he supposed himself called upon to refute. "If," said he, "the Father begat the Son, he that was begotten had a beginning of existence: and from this it is evident, that there was a time when the Son was not in being. It therefore necessarily follows, that he had his existence[2] from nothing."

CHAP. VI.— DIVISION BEGINS IN THE CHURCH FROM THIS CONTROVERSY; AND ALEXANDER BISHOP OF ALEXANDRIA EX- COMMUNICATES ARIUS AND HIS ADHERENTS.

HAVING drawn this inference from his novel train of reasoning, he excited many to a consideration of the question; and thus from a little spark a large fire was kindled: for the evil which commenced in the Church at Alexandria, ran throughout all Egypt, Libya, and the Upper Thebes, and at length diffused itself over the rest of the provinces and cities. Many others also adopted the opinion of Arius; but Eusebius in particular was a zealous defender of it: not he of Cæsarea,[3] but the one who had before been bishop of the Church at Berytus, and was then in the surreptitious possession of the bishopric of Nicomedia in Bithynia. When Alexander became conscious of the spread of this leaven, both from his own observation and report, being exasperated to the highest degree, he convened a council of many prelates; and having excommunicated Arius and the abettors of his heresy, he wrote as follows to the bishops constituted in the several cities.

THE EPISTLE OF ALEXANDER BISHOP OF ALEXANDRIA.

" To our beloved and most honoured fellow-ministers of the Catholic Church everywhere, Alexander sends greeting in the Lord.

[1] So called because he was bishop of an African see.
[2] ὑπόστασιν. This word is used almost indiscriminately with the term οὐσία, as for example, in the Nicene Creed, given at length in chap. viii., where occur the words ὑποστάσεως ἢ οὐσίας. See the note in Hammond's edition of the Canons, (Oxford, 1843,) pp. 12—14.
[3] That is, Eusebius Pamphilus, the Ecclesiastical Historian.

[7] "Inasmuch as the Catholic Church is one body, and we are commanded in the Holy Scriptures to maintain the bond of unanimity and peace;[1] it consequently becomes us to write, and mutually acquaint one another with the condition of things among each of us, in order that if one member suffers or rejoices, we may either sympathize with each other, or rejoice together.[2] Know therefore that there have recently arisen in our diocese lawless and anti-christian men, teaching apostasy such as one may justly consider and denominate the forerunner of Antichrist. I wished indeed to consign this disorder to silence, that if possible the evil might be confined to the apostates alone; and lest going forth into other districts, it should contaminate the ears of some of the simple. But since Eusebius, who, after deserting his charge at Berytus, and assuming with impunity the episcopal authority over the Church at Nicomedia, seems to imagine that the affairs of the Church are under his control, has undertaken the patronage of these apostates, daring even to send commendatory letters in all directions concerning them, if by any means he might inveigle some of the ignorant into his most impious and anti-christian heresy; I felt imperatively called on to be silent no longer, knowing what is written in the law, but to inform you all of these things, that ye might understand both who the apostates are, and also the execrable character of their heresy. I am constrained at the same time to warn you to pay no attention to his communications, if Eusebius should write to you; for now wishing to renew his former malevolence, which seemed to have been buried in oblivion by time, he affects to write in their behalf; while the fact itself plainly shows that he does this for the promotion of his own purposes. These then are those who have become apostates:—Arius, Achillas, Aithales, and Carpones, another Arius, Sarmates, Euzoïus, Lucius, Julian, Menas, Helladius, and Gaius; with these also must be reckoned Secundus and Theonas, who once were called bishops. The dogmas they assert in utter contrariety to the Scriptures, and wholly of their own devising, are these: —that God was not always a father, but that there was a period when he was not a father; that the Word of God was

[1] He alludes to Eph. iv. 3.
[2] See the argument of St. Paul to the Corinthians at length, 1 Cor. xii. 12—27.

not from eternity, but was made out of nothing; for that the ever-existing God (*the I AM*—the eternal One) made him, who did not previously exist, out of nothing. Thus they conclude there was a time when he did not exist, inasmuch as, according to their philosophy, the Son is a creature and a work; that he is neither like the Father *as it regards his essence*, nor is *by nature* either the Father's true Word, or true Wisdom, but indeed one of his works and creatures, being erroneously called Word and Wisdom, since he was himself made by God's own Word and the Wisdom which is in God, whereby God both made all things and him also. 'Wherefore,' say they, 'he is as to his nature mutable and susceptible of change, as all other rational creatures are: hence the Word is alien to and other than the essence of God; and the Father is inexplicable by the Son, and invisible to him, for neither does the Son perfectly and accurately know the Father, neither can he distinctly see him. The Son knows not the nature of his own essence: for he was made on our account, in order that God might create us by him, as by an instrument; nor would he ever have existed, unless God had wished to create us.' Some one accordingly asked them whether the Word of God could be changed, as the devil has been? and they feared not to say, 'Yes, he could; for being begotten and created, he is susceptible of change.' We then, with the bishops of Egypt and Libya, being assembled together to the number of nearly a hundred, have anathematized Arius for his shameless avowal of these heresies, together with all such as have countenanced them. Yet the partisans of Eusebius have received them; endeavouring to blend falsehood with truth, and that which is impious with what is sacred. But they shall not prevail, for the truth must triumph; and light has no fellowship with darkness, nor has Christ any concord with Belial. Who ever heard such blasphemies? or what man of any piety is there now hearing them that is not horror-struck, and stops his ears, lest the filth of these expressions should pollute his sense of hearing? Who that hears John saying, 'In the beginning was the Word,' does not condemn those that dare affirm there was a period when the Word was not? or who hearing in the gospel of 'the only-begotten Son,' and that 'all things were made by him,' will not abhor those that pronounce the Son to be one of the things made? But how can He be put on a level with, or regarded as one of, the things which were made by himself? Or how can he be the only-begotten, if he is reckoned among created things? And, how could he have had his existence from non-entities, since the Father has said, 'My heart has indited a good matter' (Ps. xlv. 1); and 'I begat thee out of my bosom before the dawn' (Ps. cx. 3; see LXX. quoted from Ps. lxxii.). Or how is he unlike the Father in essence, who is 'his perfect image,' (Col. i. 15,) and 'the brightness of his glory' (Heb. i. 3); he himself also declaring, 'He that hath seen me, hath seen the Father'? Again, how is the Son the Word and Wisdom of God, if there was a period when he did not exist? for that is equivalent to their saying, that God was once destitute both of Word and Wisdom. How can he be mutable and susceptible of change, who says of himself, 'I am in the Father, and the Father in me' (John xiv. 10); and 'I and the Father are one' (John x. 30); and again by the prophet, (Mal. iii. 6,) 'Behold me because I am, and have not changed'? But if any one may also apply the expression to the Father himself, yet would it now be even more fitly said of the Word; because he was not changed by having become man, but, as the apostle says, (Heb. xiii. 8,) 'Jesus Christ, the same yesterday, to-day, and for ever.' But what could persuade them to say that he was made on our account, when Paul has expressly declared, (Heb. ii. 10,) that 'all things are for him, and by him'? One need not wonder then indeed at their blasphemous assertion, that the Son does not perfectly know the Father; for having once determined to fight against Christ, they reject even the words of the Lord himself, when he says, (John x. 15,) 'As the Father knows me, even so know I the Father.' If therefore the Father but partially knows the Son, it is manifest that the Son also knows the Father but in part. But if it would be impious to affirm this, and it be admitted that the Father perfectly knows the Son, it is evident that as the Father knows his own Word, so also does the Word know his own Father, whose Word he is. And we, by stating these things, and unfolding the divine Scriptures, have often confuted them: but again as chameleons they were changed, striving to apply to themselves that which is written, (Prov. xviii. 3; LXX.,) 'When the ungodly has ⁸ reached the depths of iniquity, he becomes contemptuous.'

Many heresies have arisen before these, which, exceeding all bounds in impious daring, have lapsed into complete infatuation : but these persons, by attempting in all their discourses to subvert the Divinity of THE WORD, as having made a nearer approach to Antichrist, have comparatively lessened the odium of former heresies.   Wherefore they have been publicly repudiated by the Church, and anathematized.   We are indeed grieved on account of the perdition of these persons, and especially so because, after having been previously instructed in the doctrines of the Church, they have now apostatized from them.   Nevertheless we are not greatly surprised at this, for Hymenæus and Philetus (2 Tim. ii. 17, 18) fell in like manner ; and before them Judas, who, though he had been a follower of the Saviour, yet afterwards deserted him and became his betrayer.   Nor were we without premonition respecting these very persons : for the Lord himself forewarned us, (Matt. xxiv. 4,) ' Take heed that no man deceive you : for many shall come in my name, saying, I am Christ : and shall deceive many' (Luke xxi. 8) ; and, ' the time is at hand ; go ye not therefore after them.'   And Paul, having learned these things from the Saviour, wrote, (1 Tim. iv. 1,) ' That in the latter times some should apostatize from the faith, giving heed to deceiving spirits, and doctrines of devils,' who pervert the truth.   Seeing then that our Lord and Saviour Jesus Christ has himself enjoined this, and has also by the apostle given us intimation respecting such men, we, having ourselves heard their impiety, have in consequence anathematized them, as we before said, and declared them to be alienated from the Catholic Church and faith.   Moreover we have intimated this to your piety, beloved and most honoured fellow-ministers, in order that ye might neither receive any of them, if they should presume to come to you, nor be induced to put confidence in Eusebius, or any other who may write to you about them.   For it is incumbent on us who are Christians, to withdraw ourselves from all those who speak or entertain a thought against Christ, as from those who are resisting God, and are destroyers of the souls of men : neither does it become us even ' to salute such men,' (2 John 10, 11,) as the blessed apostle has prohibited, ' lest we should at any time be made partakers of their sins.'   Greet the brethren which are with you : those who are with us salute you."

By Alexander's thus addressing the bishops in every city, the evil only became worse; for those to whom he made this communication were thereby excited to contention, some fully concurring in and subscribing to the sentiments expressed in this letter, while others did the reverse. But Eusebius, bishop of Nicomedia, was beyond all others incited to controversy, inasmuch as Alexander had in his letter made a personal and censorious allusion to him. Now at this juncture Eusebius possessed great influence, because the emperor resided at Nicomedia, Diocletian having a short time previously built a palace there. On this account therefore many of the bishops paid their court to Eusebius: and he himself was incessantly writing both to Alexander, that he might set aside the discussion which had been excited, and again receive Arius and his adherents into communion;[1] and also to the bishops in each city, that they might not concur in the proceedings of Alexander. By these means confusion everywhere prevailed: for one saw not only the prelates of the Churches engaged in contention, but the people also divided, some siding with one party, and some with the other. To so disgraceful an extent was this affair carried, that Christianity became a subject of popular ridicule, even in the very theatres. Those who were at Alexandria sharply disputed about the highest points of doctrine, and sent deputations to the bishops of the several dioceses; while those who were of the opposite faction created a similar disturbance.

9   With the Arians the Melitians mingled themselves, who a little while before had been separated from the Church: but who these Melitians are must now be stated.

By Peter bishop of Alexandria, who in the reign of Diocletian suffered martyrdom, an individual named Melitius, a bishop of one of the cities in Egypt, was degraded in consequence of many other charges indeed, but on this account more especially, that during the persecution he had denied the faith and sacrificed. This person, after being stripped of his dignity, had nevertheless many followers, and became the leader of the heresy of those who are now called from him Melitians throughout Egypt. And as there was no rational

---

[1] Upon the terms, conditions, and method of reconciling to the Church such presbyters as had fallen into heresy, see Bingham's Eccl. Antiq. book xvi. chap. vi. sect. 13, and book xvii. passim.

excuse for his separation from the Church, he pretended that
as an innocent man he had been unjustly dealt with, loading
Peter with calumnious reproaches. After the martyrdom of
Peter, he transferred his abuse first to Achillas, who succeeded Peter in the bishopric, and afterwards again to Alexander,
the successor of Achillas. In this state of things among them,
the discussion in relation to Arius arose; and Melitius with
his adherents took part with Arius, entering into a conspiracy
against the bishop: but as many as regarded the opinion of
Arius as untenable, justified Alexander's decision against him,
and thought that those who favoured his views were justly
condemned. Meanwhile Eusebius of Nicomedia and his partisans, with such as embraced the sentiments of Arius, demanded by letter that the sentence of excommunication which
had been pronounced against him should be rescinded; and
that those who had been excluded should be readmitted into
the Church, as they held no unsound doctrine. Thus letters
from the opposite parties were sent to the bishop of Alexandria; and Arius made a collection of those which were
favourable to himself, while Alexander did the same with
those which were adverse. This therefore afforded a plausi-
ble opportunity of defence to the sects, which are now so very
numerous, of the Arians, Eunomians, and such as receive their
name from Macedonius; who severally make use of these
epistles in vindication of their heresies.

CHAP. VII.—THE EMPEROR CONSTANTINE, BEING GRIEVED AT
THE DISTURBANCE OF THE CHURCHES, SENDS HOSIUS, A
SPANIARD, TO ALEXANDRIA, EXHORTING THE BISHOP AND
ARIUS TO UNANIMITY.

WHEN the emperor was made acquainted with these disorders, he was very deeply grieved; and regarding the matter
as his own misfortune, immediately exerted himself to extin-
guish the conflagration which had been kindled. To this end
he sent a letter to Alexander and Arius by a trustworthy person named Hosius, who was bishop of Cordova in Spain, and
whom the emperor greatly loved and held in the highest estimation. It will not be out of place to introduce here a portion of
this letter, the whole of which is given in the Life of Constantine by Eusebius.

VICTOR CONSTANTINE MAXIMUS AUGUSTUS, TO ALEXANDER
AND ARIUS.

"Your present controversy, I am informed, originated thus. When you, Alexander, inquired of your presbyters what were the sentiments of each on a certain inexplicable passage of *the written Word,* thereby mooting a subject improper for discussion ; you, Arius, rashly gave expression to a view of the matter such as ought either never to have been conceived, or if indeed it had been suggested to your mind, it became you to bury in silence. Dissension having thus been excited among you, communion has been denied ; and the most holy people being rent into two factions, have departed from the harmony of the common body. Wherefore let each, reciprocally pardoning the other, listen to the impartial exhortation of your fellow-servant. And what counsel does he offer ? It · was neither prudent at first to agitate such a question, nor to reply to such a question when proposed: for the claim of no law demands the investigation of such subjects, but the disputatious cavilling of ill-employed leisure puts them forward. And even admitting them to be calculated to exercise our natural abilities, yet ought we to confine them to our own consideration, and not incautiously bring them forth in public assemblies, nor thoughtlessly confide them to the ears of everybody. Indeed how few are capable either of adequately expounding, or even accurately understanding, the import of matters so vast and profound ! And if any one should imagine that he can satisfactorily accomplish this, how large a portion of the people would he succeed in convincing ? Or who can grapple with the subtilties of such investigations without danger of lapsing into excessive error ? It becomes us therefore on such topics to check loquacity, lest either on account of the impotence of our nature we should be incompetent to explain the subject proposed; or the dull understanding of the audience should incapacitate them for clearly apprehending what is attempted to be taught: for in the case of one or the other of these failures, the people must be necessarily involved either in blasphemy or schism. Wherefore let an unguarded question, and an inconsiderate answer, on the part of each of you, procure equal forgiveness from one another. No cause of difference has been started by you bearing on any important precept contained in the Law; nor has any new heresy been introduced by you in connexion with the worship of God; but ye both hold one and the same judgment on these points, so that nothing exists to hinder association in communion. Moreover while you thus pertinaciously contend with one another about matters of small or scarcely the least importance, and especially with such virulence of feeling, it is unsuitable for you to have charge of so many people of God: and not 10 only is it unbecoming, but it is also believed to be altogether unlawful.

" Permit me further to remind you of your duty by an example of an inferior kind. You are well aware that even the philosophers themselves, while all confederated under one sect, yet often disagree with each other on some parts of their theories: but although they may differ in their views on the very highest branches of science, yet in order to maintain the unity of their body, they still agree to coalesce. Now if this is done amongst them, how much more equitable will it be for you, who have been constituted ministers of the Most High God, to become unanimous with one another in the same religious profession. But let us examine with closer consideration, and deeper attention, what has been already stated. Is it right on account of insignificant and vain contentions between you about words, that brethren should be set in opposition against brethren; and that the venerable assembly should be distracted by unhallowed dissension, through your striving with one another respecting things so unimportant, and by no means essential? These quarrels are indeed derogatory to your character, being rather consistent with puerile thoughtlessness, than suitable to the intelligence of priests and prudent men. We should spontaneously turn aside from the temptations of the devil. The great God and Saviour of us all has extended to all the common light. Under his providence, allow me, his servant, to bring this effort of mine to a successful issue; that by my exhortation, ministry, and earnest admonition, I may lead you, his people, back to unity of assembly. For since, as I have observed, there is but one faith within you, and one sentiment respecting the heresy which prevails among you; and since the precept of the Law, in all its parts, combines all in one purpose of soul, let not this diversity of opinion, which has excited among you mutual dissension, by any means cause discord and schism, inasmuch as the cause of it touches not the force of any law. I say these things, not as compelling you all to see exactly alike on the subject of this controversy, of small moment as it is; since the dignity of the general assembly may be preserved unaffected, and the same communion with all be retained, although there should exist among you some dissimilarity of sentiment on unimportant matters. For we do not all desire the same thing in every respect; nor is there one unvarying nature, or standard of judgment, in us. Therefore in regard to Divine providence, let there be one faith, one sentiment, and one covenant of the Godhead: but respecting those minute investigations which ye enter into among yourselves with so much nicety, even if ye should not concur in one judgment, it becomes you to confine them to your own reflection, and to keep them in the secret recesses of the mind. Let then an ineffable and select bond of general friendship, with faith in the truth, reverence for God, and a devout observance of his law, remain unshaken among you. Resume the exercise of mutual friendship and grace; restore to the whole people their accustomed familiar embraces; and do ye yourselves, having purified your own souls, again recognise one another: for friendship often becomes sweeter after the removal of animosity. Return again therefore to a state of reconciliation; and by so doing give back to me tranquil days, and nights free from care; that to me also there may be some pleasure in the pure light, and that a cheerful serenity may be preserved to me during the rest of my life. But if this should not be effected, I must necessarily groan, and be wholly suffused with tears; neither will the remaining period of my earthly existence be peacefully sustained: for while the people of God (I speak of my fellow-servants) are dissevered by so unworthy and injurious a contest with one another, how is it possible for me to maintain my usual equanimity? But in order that you may have some idea of my excessive grief, on account of this unhappy difference, listen to what I am about to state. On my recent arrival at the city of Nicomedia, it was my intention immediately after to proceed into the East: but while I was hastening toward you, and had advanced a considerable distance on my way, intelligence of this affair altogether reversed my purpose, lest I should be obliged to see with my own eyes a con-

dition of things such as I could scarcely bear the report of.
Open to me therefore, by your unanimity henceforth, the way
into the East, which ye have obstructed by your contentions
against one another: and permit me speedily to behold both
you and all the rest of the people rejoicing together; and to
express my due thanks to the Divine Being, because of the
general unanimity and liberty of all parties, accompanied by
the cordial utterance of your praise."

CHAP. VIII.—Of the synod which was held at nice in
BITHYNIA, AND THE FAITH THERE PROMULGATED.[1]

SUCH was the admirable and wise counsel contained in the
emperor's letter.   But the evil had become so inveterate, that
neither the exhortations of the emperor, nor the authority of
him who was the bearer of his letter, availed any thing: for
neither was Alexander nor Arius softened by this appeal;
and moreover there was incessant strife and tumult among the
people.   But another source of disquietude had pre-existed
there, which served to trouble the Churches, though it was
confined to the eastern parts.   This arose from some desiring
to keep the Feast of the Passover, or Easter, more in accordance with the custom of the Jews; while others preferred its
mode of celebration by Christians in general throughout the
world.[2]   This difference however did not interfere with their
communion, although their mutual joy was necessarily hindered.   When therefore the emperor beheld the Church agi-

---

[1] Compare Sozomen, b. i. ch. xvii.
[2] There were great disputes in the early Church with respect to the
time at which the Paschal solemnity should be celebrated: some local
Churches observing it on a fixed day in every year; others, again, observing it with the Jews, on the 14th day of the new moon, on whatever day
of the week it happened to fall.   These disputes were especially rife in
the second century; when, a decree being issued by Pope Pius about the
year A. D. 147, commanding all Christians throughout the world to observe the Paschal Festival on a Sunday, S. Polycarp, bishop of Smyrna,
came to Rome to confer with Anicetus on the subject, alleging that the
opposite custom of the Asiatic churches had come down to them by tradition from S. John the beloved disciple and the rest of the apostles.   The
matter was finally settled at the Council of Nicæa against the practice of
the Eastern Church.   See Synodical Epistle of the Council, given at
length in chap. ix.

tated by both of these causes, he convoked a General Council,[1] summoning all the bishops by letter to meet him at Nice in Bithynia. Accordingly the bishops assembled out of the various provinces and cities; respecting whom Eusebius Pamphilus thus writes, in his third book of the Life of Constantine :[2]—

" Wherefore the most eminent of the ministers of God in all the Churches which have filled Europe, Africa, and Asia, were convened. And one sacred edifice, dilated as it were by God, contained within it on the same occasion both Syrians and Cilicians, Arabs and Palestinians, and in addition to these, Egyptians, Thebans, Libyans, and those who came from Mesopotamia. At this synod a Persian bishop was also present, neither was the Scythian absent from this assemblage. Pontus also and Galatia, Pamphylia, Cappadocia, Asia, and Phrygia, supplied those who were most distinguished among them. Besides there met there Thracians and Macedonians, Achaians and Epirots, and even those who dwelt still more distant than these. Hosius, the most celebrated of the Spaniards, took his seat among the rest. The prelate of the imperial city was absent through age; but his presbyters were present, and filled his place. Such a crown, composed as a bond of peace, the emperor Constantine alone has ever dedicated to Christ his Saviour, as a thank-offering worthy of God for victory over his enemies, having appointed this convocation among us in imitation of the apostolic assembly.[3] For among them it is said were convened 'devout men of every nation under heaven; Parthians, Medes, Elamites, and those who dwelt in Mesopotamia, Judæa, Cappadocia, Pontus, Asia, Phrygia, Pamphylia, Egypt, and the parts of Libya, strangers from Rome also, both Jews and proselytes, with Cretans and Arabs.' That congregation however was inferior in this respect, that all present were not ministers of God: whereas in this assembly the number of bishops exceeded three hundred;[4] while the number of the presbyters, deacons, and acolyths (or young priests) who attended them was almost incalculable.

---

[1] Οἰκουμενικήν, this was called the First Œcumenical Council of the Church.

[2] Chap. vii.—ix.   [3] Acts ii. 5.

[4] The exact number, as we learn elsewhere, was 318, see Evagrius, Eccl. Hist. b. iii. chap. xxxi.

Some of these ministers of God were eminent for their wisdom, some for the strictness of their life and patient endurance [13] of persecution, and others united in themselves all these distinguished characteristics; some were venerable from their advanced age, others were conspicuous for their youth and vigour of mind, and others had but recently entered on their ministerial career. For all these the emperor appointed an abundant supply of daily food to be provided." Such is Eusebius's account of those who met on this occasion. The emperor having completed the festal solemnization of his triumph over Licinius, came also in person to Nice.

There were among the bishops two of extraordinary celebrity, Paphnutius, bishop of Upper Thebes, and Spyridon, bishop of Cyprus: why I have so particularly referred to these two individuals, I shall state hereafter. Many of the laity were also present, who were practised in the art of reasoning, and each prepared to advocate the cause of his own party. Eusebius, bishop of Nicomedia, as was before said, supported the opinion of Arius, together with Theognis bishop of Nice, and Maris bishop of Chalcedon in Bithynia. These were powerfully opposed by Athanasius, a deacon of the Alexandrian Church, who was highly esteemed by Alexander his bishop, and on that account was much envied, as will be seen hereafter. For a short time previous to the general assembling of the bishops, the disputants engaged in preparatory logical contests with various opponents: and when many were attracted by the interest of their discourse, one of the laity who was a man of unsophisticated understanding, and had stood the test of persecution[1] in his confession of faith, reproved these reasoners; telling them that Christ and his apostles did not teach us the Dialectic art, nor vain subtilties, but simple-mindedness, which is preserved by faith and good works. All present admired the speaker, and assented to the justice of his remarks; and the disputants themselves, after hearing his ingenuous statement of the truth, exercised a far greater degree of moderation: thus then was the disturbance caused by these logical debates suppressed.

[1] Εἷς τις τῶν ὁμολογητῶν, "being one of the 'Confessors.'" Such was the name given to those who refused to sacrifice to idols, or to do any act of apostasy in the time of persecution. Those who apostatized under the influence of terror were called "the lapsed."

On the following day all the bishops were assembled together in one place ; the emperor arrived soon after, and on his entrance stood in their midst, declining to take his place, until the bishops by bowing intimated their desire that he should be seated : such was the respect and reverence which the emperor entertained for these men. When a silence suitable to the occasion had been observed, the emperor from his seat began to address them, entreating each to lay aside all private pique, and exhorting them to unanimity and concord. For several of them had brought accusations against one another, and many had even presented petitions to the emperor the day before. But he directing their attention to the matter before them, and on account of which they were assembled, ordered these petitions to be burnt; merely observing that Christ enjoins him who is . anxious to obtain forgiveness, to forgive his brother. When therefore he had strongly insisted on the maintenance of harmony and peace, he then sanctioned their purpose of more closely investigating the questions at issue. But it may be well to hear what Eusebius says on this subject, in his third book of the Life of Constantine.[1]   His words are these :—

" A variety of topics having been introduced by each party, and much controversy being excited from the very commencement, the emperor listened to all with patient attention, deliberately and impartially considering whatever was advanced. He in part supported the statements which were made on both sides, and gradually softened the asperity of those who contentiously opposed each other, conciliating each by his mildness and affability. Addressing them in the Greek language, with which he was well acquainted, in a manner at once interesting and persuasive, he wrought conviction on the minds of some, and prevailed on others by entreaty. Those who spoke well he applauded, and incited all to unanimity ; until at length he succeeded in bringing them into similarity of judgment, and conformity of opinion on all the controverted points : so that there was not only unity in the confession of faith, but also a general agreement as to the time for the celebration of the salutary feast of Easter. Moreover the doctrines which had thus the common consent, were confirmed by the signature of each individual."

[1] *Chap. xiii. and xiv.*

Such is the testimony respecting these things which Eusebius has left us ; and which it was thought might not unfitly
be introduced here, as an authority for the fidelity of this history.   With this end also in view, that if any one should condemn as erroneous the faith professed at this council of Nice, we
might be unaffected by it, and put no confidence in Sabinus
the Macedonian, who calls all those that were convened there
idiots and simpletons.   For this Sabinus, who was bishop of [14]
the Macedonians at Heraclea in Thrace, having made a collection of the canons published by various synods of bishops,
has treated those who composed the Nicene council in particular with contempt and derision ; not perceiving that he
thereby charges Eusebius himself with folly, who made a like
confession after the closest scrutiny.   Some things he has
wilfully passed over, others he has perverted, and on all he has
put a construction favourable to his own views.   Yet he
commends Eusebius Pamphilus as a witness worthy of credit,
and praises the emperor as capable in stating Christian
doctrines : but he still brands the faith which was declared
at Nice, as having been set forth by idiots, and such as had no
intelligence in the matter.   Thus he voluntarily contemns the
testimony of a man whom he himself pronounces a wise and
true witness : for Eusebius declares,[1] that of the ministers of
God who were present at the Nicene synod, some were
eminent for the word of wisdom, others for the strictness
of their life ; and that the emperor himself being present,
leading all into unanimity, established unity of judgment and
conformity of opinion among them.   Of Sabinus however
we shall make further mention as occasion may require.   But
the agreement of faith, assented to with loud acclamation at the
great council of Nice, is this :[2]—

[1] See his Life of Constantine, b. iii. chap. ix.
[2] This Creed is found in Greek, 1. In the Epistle of Eusebius to the
Cæsareans, of which we have four copies preserved in the works of Theodoret, Socrates, Athanasius, and Gelasius of Cyzicum. 2. In the Epistle
of Athanasius to Jovian. 3. In the 125th Epistle of Basil the Great. 4.
In the present passage of Socrates. 5. In the Epistle of Cyril of Alexandria to Anastasius. 6. In the Codex Canonum Eccl. Africanæ. 7.
In the Acts of the Council of Ephesus. 8. In Gelasius Cyzicenus, ii. 26.
9. Among the Acts of the Council of Chalcedon. 10. In the Exposition of
the Creed by Theodotus of Ancyra. 11. In the Acts of the Council of
Chalcedon, where it occurs twice.   These copies have been collated by

¹⁵ "We believe in one God, the Father Almighty, Maker of all things visible and invisible:—and in our Lord Jesus Christ, the Son of God, the only begotten of the Father, that is of the substance of the Father; God of God and Light of light; true God of true God; begotten, not made, consubstantial¹ with the 'Father: by whom all things were made, both which are in heaven and on earth: who for the sake of us men, and on account of our salvation, descended, became incarnate, and was made man; suffered, arose again the third day, and ascended into the heavens, and will come again to judge the living and the dead. We also believe in the Holy Spirit. But the holy Catholic and Apostolic Church anathematizes those who say that there was a time when the Son of God was not, and that he was not before he was begotten, and that he was made from that which did not exist; or who assert that he is of other substance or essence than the Father, or that he was created, or is susceptible of change."

This creed was recognised and acquiesced in by three hundred and eighteen bishops; and being, as Eusebius says, unanimous in expression and sentiment, they subscribed it. Five² only would not receive it, objecting to the term ὁμοού- σιος, *of the same essence,* or *consubstantial :* these were Euse- bius bishop of Nicomedia, Theognis of Nice, Maris of Chal- cedon, Thomas of Marmarica, and Secundus of Ptolemaïs. "For," said they, "that is *consubstantial* which is from another, either by partition, derivation, or germination; by

---

Walchius, and the various readings enumerated : but with the exception of those which occur in the second form in the Acts of the Council of Chalcedon, in which several of the additions of the Constantinopolitan Creed are introduced, there is not one of any consequence, or which in the least affects the sense. (Hammond, p. 12.)

¹ ὁμοούσιος. "Consubstantial with," or "of one substance with," the Father. The Latin versions are three in number, "Unius substantiæ cum Patre," "Ejusdem cum Patre substantiæ," and "Consubstantialem Pa- tri." The Semi-Arian party afterwards attempted to make a compro- mise with the orthodox, by proposing to substitute the word ὁμοιούσιος, i. e. "of *like* substance." See below, b. ii. ch. xvi. and xx.

² It would seem that Socrates is mistaken here in stating that five bishops were condemned by the council of Nice, for refusing to subscribe to its doctrinal decision, and the orthodox confession of faith. Two only, namely Theonas and Secundus, were actually so condemned, as appears from a letter of the council. See below, ch. ix., and the Life of Socrates prefixed to this volume.

germination, as a shoot from the roots; by derivation, as children from their parents; by division, as two or three vessels of gold from a mass." But they contended that the Son is from the Father by none of these modes: wherefore they declared themselves unable to assent to this creed; and having scoffed at the word *consubstantial*, they would not subscribe 16 to the condemnation of Arius. Upon this the synod anathematized Arius, and all who adhered to his opinions, prohibiting him at the same time from entering into Alexandria. By an edict of the emperor also, Arius himself was sent into exile, together with Eusebius and Theognis; but the two latter, a short time after their banishment, tendered a written declaration of their change of sentiment, and concurrence in the faith of the *consubstantiality* of the Son with the Father, as we shall show as we proceed. At the same time Eusebius surnamed Pamphilus, bishop of Cæsarea in Palestine, who had withheld his assent in the synod after mature consideration whether he ought to receive this form of faith, at length acquiesced in it, and subscribed it with all the rest: he also sent to the people under his charge a copy of the Creed, with an explanation of the word ὁμοούσιος, that no one might impugn his motives on account of his previous hesitation. His address to them was as follows:—"You have probably had some intimation, beloved, of the transactions of the great council convened at Nice, in relation to the faith of the Church, inasmuch as rumour generally outruns an accurate statement of that which has really taken place. But lest from such report alone you might form an incorrect estimate of the matter, we have deemed it necessary to submit to you, in the first place, an exposition of the faith propounded by us; and then a second which has been promulgated, consisting of certain additions to the expression of ours. The declaration of faith set forth by us, and which, when read in the presence of our most pious emperor, seemed to meet with universal approbation, was thus expressed:—

"'According as we received from the bishops who preceded us, both at our initiation [1] into the knowledge of the truth, and when we were baptized; as also we have ourselves learned

---

[1] ἐν τῇ κατηχήσει. Upon the gradual initiation of catechumens into the mysteries of the faith, as preparatory to the reception of baptism, see Bingham, Eccl. Antiq. b. x. ch. i. and ii. See below, b. vii. ch. xvii.

from the sacred Scriptures; and in accordance with what we
have both believed and taught while discharging the duties of
presbyter and the episcopal office itself, so now believing, we
п present to you the distinct avowal of our faith. It is this:—
  "'We believe in one God, the Father Almighty, Maker of
all things visible and invisible:—and in one Lord, Jesus Christ,
the Word of God, God of God, Light of light, Life of life, the
only-begotten Son, born before all creation,[1] begotten of God
the Father, before all ages; by whom also all things were
made; who on account of our salvation became incarnate, and
lived among men; and who having suffered and risen again
on the third day, ascended to the Father, and shall come again
in glory to judge the living and the dead. We believe also in
one Holy Spirit. We believe in the existence and subsistence
of each of these persons: that the Father is truly Father, the
Son truly Son, and the Holy Spirit truly Holy Spirit; even
as our Lord also, when he sent forth his disciples to preach
the gospel, said, (Matt. xxviii. 19,) 'Go and teach all nations,
baptizing them in the name of the Father, and of the Son, and
of the Holy Spirit.' These doctrines we thus stedfastly
maintain, and avow our full confidence in truth of them; such
also have been our sentiments hitherto, and such we shall
continue to hold until death: and in an unshaken adherence
to this faith, we anathematize every impious heresy. In the
presence of God Almighty, and of our Lord Jesus Christ, we
testify, that thus we have believed and thought from our
heart and soul, since we were capable of forming a judgment
on the matter, and have possessed a right estimate of ourselves; and that we now think and speak what is perfectly in
accordance with the truth. We are moreover prepared to
prove to you by undeniable evidences, and to convince you
that in time past we have thus believed, and so preached.'
  "When these articles of faith were proposed, they were received without opposition: nay, our most pious emperor himself was the first to admit that they were perfectly orthodox,
and that he precisely concurred in the sentiments contained
in them; exhorting all present to give them their assent,

[1] Πρωτότοκον πάσης κτίσεως. These words are taken from Col. i. 15,
where they are rendered erroneously, "The first-born of every creature."
The word πρῶτος however is frequently used for πρότερος, e. g. St. John
i. 15, ὅτι πρῶτός μου ἦν. See also St. Luke ii. 2.

and subscribe to these very articles, thus agreeing in an unanimous profession of them.   It was suggested however that
the word ὁμοούσιος (consubstantial) should be introduced, an
expression which the emperor himself explained, as not indicating corporeal affections or properties; and consequently
that the Son did not subsist from the Father either by division
or abscission: for, said he, a nature which is immaterial and
incorporeal cannot possibly be subject to any corporeal affection; hence our apprehension of such things can only be expressed in divine and mysterious terms.   Such was the philosophical view of the subject taken by our most wise and
pious sovereign; and the bishops, on account of the word
ὁμοούσιος, drew up this formula of faith.

"THE CREED.

"'We believe in one God, the Father Almighty, Maker
of all things visible and invisible:—and in one Lord Jesus
Christ, the Son of God, the only-begotten of the Father,
that is of the substance of the Father; God of God, Light
of light, true God of true God; begotten not made, consubstantial with the Father; by whom all things were made both
which are in heaven and on earth; who for the sake of us
men, and on account of our salvation, descended, became incarnate, suffered, and rose again on the third day; he ascended
into the heavens, and will come to judge the living and the
dead.   We believe also in the Holy Spirit.   But those who
say that there was a time when he was not, or that he did not
exist before he was begotten, or that he was made of nothing,
or assert that he is of other substance or essence than the
Father, or that the Son of God is created, or mutable, or
susceptible of change, the catholic and apostolic church of
God anathematizes.'

"In forming this declaration of faith, we did not neglect to
investigate the distinct sense of the expressions *of the substance of the Father*, and *consubstantial with the Father*.
Whereupon much discussion arose, and the meaning of these
terms was clearly defined; when it was generally admitted
that οὐσίας (of the essence or substance) simply implied that
the Son is of the Father indeed, but not as a part of the
Father.   To this interpretation of the sacred doctrine, which
declares that the Son is of the Father, but is not a part of

his substance, it seemed right to us to assent. We ourselves therefore concurred in this exposition : nor do we cavil at the word ὁμοούσιος, having regard as well to peace, as dreading lest we should lose a right understanding of the matter. On the same grounds we admitted also the expression *begotten, not made:* 'for *made,*' said they, 'is a term which is applied to all the creatures which were made by the Son, to whom the Son has no resemblance. Consequently he is no creature like those which were made by him, but is of a substance far excelling any creature ; which substance the sacred Oracles teach us was begotten of the Father by such a mode of generation as can neither be apprehended nor explained by any creature.' Thus also the declaration that *the Son is consubstantial with the Father* having been discussed, it was agreed that this must not be understood in a corporeal sense, or in any way analogous to mortal creatures ; inasmuch as it is neither by division of substance, nor by abscision, nor by any change of the Father's substance and power, since the underived nature of the Father is inconsistent with all these things. That he is consubstantial with the Father then simply implies, that the Son of God has no resemblance to created things, but is in every respect like the Father only who begat him ; and that he is of no other substance or essence but of the Father. To which doctrine, explained in this way, it appeared right to assent, especially since we knew that some eminent bishops and learned writers among the ancients have used the term ὁμοούσιος in their theological discourses concerning the nature of the Father and the Son. Such is what I have to state to you in reference to the articles of faith which have been recently promulgated ; and in which we have all concurred, not without due examination, but according to the senses assigned, which were investigated in the presence of our most religious emperor, and for the reasons mentioned approved. We have also unhesitatingly acquiesced in the anathema pronounced by them after the declaration of faith ; because it prohibits the use of terms which do not occur in Scripture, and from which almost all the distraction and commotion of the churches have arisen. Accordingly, since no divinely-inspired [1] Scripture contains the expressions, *of things which do not exist,* and

[1] Θεόπνευστος. The same word occurs in a similar sense in 2 Tim. iii. 16.

there was a time when he was not, and such other phrases
as are therein subjoined, it seemed unwarrantable to utter
and teach them : and moreover this decision received our
sanction the rather from the consideration that we have never
heretofore been accustomed to employ these terms.   We
deemed it incumbent on us, beloved, to acquaint you with the
caution which has characterized our examination of these
things, as well as with what deliberateness our assent has been
given, and on what justifiable grounds we resisted the introduction of certain objectionable expressions ; and finally, that
it was only after mature consideration of the full import of
some points to which we demurred at first, that we were induced to withdraw our opposition, perceiving them in fact to be
quite accordant with what we had originally proposed as a
sound confession of faith."

Such was the letter addressed by Eusebius Pamphilus to
the Christians at Cæsarea in Palestine.   The synod itself
also, with one accord, wrote the following epistle to the Church
of the Alexandrians, and to the believers in Egypt, Libya, and
Pentapolis.

CHAP. IX.—The epistle of the synod, relative to its
DECISIONS : AND THE CONDEMNATION OF ARIUS, WITH ALL
THOSE WHO HELD HIS OPINIONS.

" To the holy, by the grace of God, and great Church of the
Alexandrians, and to our beloved brethren throughout Egypt,
Libya, and Pentapolis, the bishops assembled at Nice, consti-
tuting the great and holy synod, send greeting in the Lord.

" Since, by the grace of God, a great and holy synod has
been convened at Nice, our most pious sovereign Constantine
having summoned us out of various cities and provinces for
that purpose, it appeared to us indispensably necessary that a
letter should be written to you on the part of the sacred
synod ; in order that ye may know what subjects were
brought under consideration, what rigidly investigated, and
also what was eventually determined on and decreed.   In the
first place then the impiety and guilt of Arius and his adherents were examined into, in the presence of our most religious emperor Constantine : and it was unanimously decided

that his impious opinion should be anathematized, with all the blasphemous expressions he has uttered, in affirming that *the Son of God sprang from nothing,* and that *there was a time when he was not;* saying moreover that *the Son of God was possessed of free-will, so as to be capable either of vice or virtue;* and calling him a creature and a work. All these sentiments the holy synod has anathematized, having scarcely patience to endure the hearing of such an impious or rather bewildered opinion, and such abominable blasphemies. But the conclusion of our proceedings against him you must either have been informed of already or will soon be apprized of; for we would not seem to trample on a man who has received the chastisement which his crime deserved. Yet so contagious has his pestilential error proved, as to involve in the same perdition Theonas bishop of Marmarica, and Secundus of Ptolemaïs;[1] for they have suffered the same condemnation as himself. But when, by the grace of God, we were delivered from those execrable dogmas, with all their impiety and blasphemy, and from those persons who had dared to cause discord and division among a people previously at peace, there still remained the contumacy of Melitius to be dealt with, and those who had been ordained by him; and we shall now state to you, beloved brethren, what resolution the synod came to on this point. Acting with more clemency towards Melitius, [18] although strictly speaking he was wholly undeserving of favour, the council permitted him to remain in his own city, but decreed that he should exercise no authority either to ordain or nominate for ordination; and that he should appear in no other district or city on this pretence, but simply retain a nominal dignity. That those who had received appoint- [19] ments from him, after having been confirmed by a more [20] legitimate ordination, should be admitted to communion on these conditions:—that they should continue to hold their rank and ministry, but regard themselves as inferior in every respect to all those who had been previously ordained and established in each place and church by our most honoured fellow-minister Alexander. In addition to these things, they shall have no authority to propose or nominate whom they please, or to do anything at all without the concurrence of some bishop of the catholic church who is one of Alexander's

---

[1] See above, note on chap. viii.

suffragans. Let such as by the grace of God and your prayers
have been found in no schism, but have continued in the
catholic church blameless, have authority to nominate and ordain those who are worthy of the sacred office,[1] and to act in
all things according to ecclesiastical law and usage.   When it
may happen that any of those holding preferments in the
Church die, then let such as have been recently admitted into
orders be preferred to the dignity of the deceased, provided
that they should appear worthy, and that the people should
elect them, the bishop of Alexandria also ratifying their
choice.   This privilege is conceded to all the others indeed,
but to Melitius personally we by no means grant the same ²¹
licence, on account of his former disorderly conduct; and because of the rashness and levity of his character, he is deprived of all authority and jurisdiction, as a man liable again
to create similar disturbances.   These are the things which
specially affect Egypt, and the most holy Church of the Alexandrians: and if any other canon or ordinance should be
established, our lord and most honoured fellow-minister and
brother Alexander being present with us, will on his return
to you enter into more minute details, inasmuch as he is not
only a participator in whatever is transacted, but has the
principal direction of it.   We have also gratifying intelligence
to communicate to you relative to unity of judgment on the
subject of the most holy feast of Easter:[2] for this point also
has been happily settled through your prayers; so that all the
brethren in the East who have heretofore kept this festival
when the Jews did, will henceforth conform to the Romans
and to us, and to all who from the earliest time have observed our period of celebrating Easter.   Rejoicing therefore
in this most desirable conclusion, and in the general unanimity
and peace, as well as in the extirpation of all heresy, receive
with the greater honour and more abundant love our fellow-
minister and your bishop Alexander; who has greatly delighted us by his presence, and even at his advanced age has
undergone extraordinary exertions in order that peace might
be re-established among you.   Pray on behalf of us all, that
the decisions to which we have so justly come may be in-

[1] Κλήρου. On the origin of the application of this name to the clergy
see Bingham's Eccl. Antiq. b. i. ch. v.
[2] See above, note on chap. viii., sub init.

violably maintained through Almighty God, and our Lord
Jesus Christ, together with the Holy Spirit; to whom be
glory for ever. Amen."

From this epistle of the synod it is manifest, that they not
only anathematized Arius and his adherents, but the very expressions of his tenets; and that, having agreed among themselves respecting the celebration of Easter, they readmitted
the schismatic Melitius into communion, suffering him to retain
his episcopal rank, but divesting him of all authority to act as
a bishop. It is for this reason I suppose that even at the
present time the Melitians in Egypt are separated from the
Church, because the synod deprived Melitius of all power. It
should be observed moreover that Arius had written a treatise
on his own opinion which he entitled *Thalia;* but the character of the book was loose and dissolute, its style and metres
not being very unlike the songs of Sotades the obscene
Maronite.[1] This production also the synod condemned at
the same time. Nor was it a matter of anxiety to the synod
only that letters should be written to the Churches announcing
the restoration of peace, but the emperor Constantine himself
also wrote to the same effect, and sent the following address
to the Church of the Alexandrians.

THE EMPEROR'S LETTER.

" Constantine Augustus, to the Catholic Church of the
Alexandrians. Beloved brethren, we send you greeting!
We have received from Divine Providence the inestimable
blessing of being relieved from all error, and united in the
acknowledgment of one and the same faith. The devil will
no longer have any power against us, since all that which he
had malignantly devised for our destruction has been entirely
overthrown. The splendour of truth has dissipated at the
command of God those dissensions, schisms, tumults, and, so
to speak, deadly poisons of discord. Wherefore we all worship
the one true God, and believe that he is. But in order that
this might be done, by divine admonition I assembled at the
city of Nice most of the bishops; with whom I myself also,
who am but one of you, and who rejoice exceedingly in being
your fellow-servant, undertook the investigation of the truth.

[1] For an account of the doctrines of the Maronites, see Gibbon's Decline and Fall, ch. xlvii. sect. 3.

Accordingly all points which seemed in consequence of ambiguity to furnish any pretext for dissension, have been discussed and accurately examined. And may the Divine Majesty pardon the fearful enormity of the blasphemies which some have shamelessly uttered concerning the mighty Saviour, our life and hope; declaring and confessing that they believe things contrary to the divinely-inspired Scriptures. While more than three hundred bishops, remarkable for their moderation and intellectual superiority, were unanimous in their confirmation of one and the same faith, which, according to the truth and legitimate construction of the law of God, can only be *the* faith; Arius, beguiled by the subtlety of the devil, was regarded as the sole disseminator of this mischief, first among you, and afterwards with unhallowed purposes among others also. Let us therefore embrace that doctrine which the Almighty has presented to us: let us return to our beloved brethren from whom this irreverent agent of the devil has separated us: let us go with all speed to the common body and our own natural members. For this is becoming your penetration, faith, and sanctity; that since he has been convicted of error who has been proved to be an enemy to the truth, ye should return to the Divine favour. For that which has commended itself to the judgment of three hundred bishops cannot be other than the doctrine of God; seeing that the Holy Spirit dwelling in the minds of so many dignified persons has effectually enlightened them respecting the Divine will. Wherefore let no one vacillate or linger, but let all with alacrity return to the undoubted path of duty; that when I shall arrive among you, which will be as soon as possible, I may with you return due thanks to God, the inspector of all things, because, having revealed the pure faith, he has also restored to you that love for which ye have prayed. May God protect you, beloved brethren."

Thus wrote the emperor to the Christians of Alexandria, to assure them that the exposition of the faith was neither made rashly nor inconsiderately, but that it was dictated with much research, and after strict investigation: and not that some things were spoken of, while others were suppressed in silence; but that whatever could be fittingly advanced in support of any opinion was fully stated. That nothing indeed was precipitately determined, but all was previously discussed with minute accuracy; so that every point which seemed to furnish a pretext for ambiguity of meaning, or difference of opinion, was thoroughly sifted, and its difficulties removed. In short, he terms the decision of all those who were assembled there the will of God; and does not doubt that the unanimity of so many eminent bishops was effected by the Holy Spirit. Sabinus, however, the chief of the Macedonian heresy, wilfully rejects these authorities, and calls those who were convened there simpletons and illiterate persons; nay, he almost accuses Eusebius of Cæsarea himself of ignorance: nor does he reflect, that even if those who constituted that synod were idiots, yet, as being illuminated by God and the grace of the Holy Spirit, they were utterly unable to err from the truth.[1] Nevertheless, hear further what the emperor decreed both against Arius and those who held his opinions, sending in all directions to the bishops and people.

ANOTHER EPISTLE OF CONSTANTINE.

" Victor Constantine Maximus Augustus, to the bishops and people. — Since Arius has imitated wicked and impious persons, it is just that he should undergo the like ignominy. Wherefore as Porphyry,[2] that enemy of piety, for having composed licentious treatises against religion, found a suitable recompence, and such as thenceforth branded him with infamy, overwhelming him with deserved reproach, his impious writings also having been destroyed; so now it seems fit both that Arius and such as hold his sentiments should be denominated Porphyrians, that they may take their appellation from those whose conduct they have imitated. And in addition to this, if any treatise composed by Arius should be discovered, let it be consigned to the flames, in order that not only his depraved doctrine may be suppressed, but also that no memorial of him may be by any means left. This therefore I decree, that if any one shall be detected in concealing a book compiled by Arius, and shall not instantly bring it forward and burn it, the penalty for this offence shall be death; for immediately after conviction the criminal shall suffer capital punishment.   May God preserve you!"

[1] This shows the light in which the decision of an ecumenical council was regarded by the faithful in the 4th century. Compare Concil. Trid.
[2] For further account of Porphyry and his writings, see below, b. iii. ch. xxiii.

ANOTHER EPISTLE.

" Constantine Augustus, to the Churches.

" Having experienced from the flourishing condition of
public affairs, how great has been the grace of divine power,
I judged this to be an object above all things claiming my
care, that one faith, sincere love, and uniform piety toward
Almighty God should be maintained amongst the most blessed
assemblies of the Catholic Church. But I perceived this
could not be firmly and permanently established, unless all,
or at least the greatest part, of the bishops could be convened
in the same place, and every point of our most holy religion
should be discussed by them in council. For this reason as
many as possible were assembled, and I myself also as one of
you was present; for I will not deny what I especially rejoice
in, that I am your fellow-servant. All points were then minutely investigated, until a decision acceptable to Him who
is the inspector of all things was published for the promotion
of uniformity of judgment and practice; so that nothing
might be henceforth left for dissension or controversy in matters of faith. There also the question having been considered
relative to the most holy day of Easter, it was determined by
common consent that it would be proper that all should celebrate it on one and the same day everywhere. For what can
be more appropriate, or what more solemn, than that this
feast, from which we have received the hope of immortality,
should be invariably kept in one order, and for an obvious
reason among all? And in the first place, it seemed very unsuitable in the celebration of this sacred feast, that we should
follow the custom of the Jews; a people who, having imbrued 23
their hands in a most heinous outrage, and thus polluted their
souls, are deservedly blind. Having therefore cast aside their
usage, it becomes us to take care that the celebration of this
observance should occur in future in the more correct order
which we have kept from the first day of the Passion until
the present time. Let us then have nothing in common with
that most hostile people the Jews.[1] We have received from
the Saviour another way; for there is set before us both a

[1] For an account of the light in which the Jews were regarded by the
early Church, see Bingham's Christian Antiq. vi. 4; viii. 11; xvi. 6;
xxii. 2.

legitimate and accurate course in our holy·religion : unanimously pursuing this, let us, most honoured brethren, withdraw ourselves from that detestable association. How truly absurd it is for them to boast that we are incapable of rightly observing these things without their instruction ! For on what subject will they themselves be competent to form a correct judgment, who after that murder of their Lord, having been bereft of their senses, are led not by any rational motive, but by an ungovernable impulse, wherever their innate fury may drive them? Thence it is, therefore, that even in this particular they do not perceive the truth, so that they, constantly erring in the utmost degree, instead of making a suitable correction, celebrate the Feast of Passover a second time in the same year. Why then should we follow the example of those who are acknowledged to be infected with grievous error ? Surely we should never suffer Easter to be kept twice in one and the same year ! But even if these considerations were not laid before you, it became your prudence at all times to take heed, both by diligence and prayer, that the purity of your soul should in nothing have communion, or seem to have accordance, with the customs of men so utterly depraved. Moreover this should also be considered, that in a matter so important and of such religious significancy, the slightest disagreement is to be deprecated. For our Saviour left us but one day to be observed in commemoration of our deliverance, that is, the day of his most holy Passion : he also wished his Catholic Church to be one ; the members of which, however much they may be scattered in various places, are notwithstanding cherished by one Spirit, that is, by the will of God. Let the prudence consistent with your sacred character consider how grievous and indecorous it is, that on the same days some should be observant of fasts, while others are celebrating feasts ; and especially that this should be the case on the days immediately after Easter. On this account therefore Divine ˙Providence directed that an appropriate correction should be effected, and uniformity of practice established, as I suppose you are all aware.

" Since then it was desirable that this should be so amended that we should have nothing in common with that nation of parricides, and of those who slew their Lord ; and since the order is a becoming one which is observed by all the churches

of the western, southern, and northern parts, and by some also in
the eastern; from these considerations all have on the present
occasion thought it to be expedient, and I pledged myself that
it would be satisfactory to your prudent penetration, that what
is observed with such general unanimity of sentiment in the
city of Rome, throughout Italy, Africa, all Egypt, Spain, France,
Britain, Libya, the whole of Greece, and the dioceses of Asia,
Pontus, and Cilicia, your intelligence also would readily concur
in.   Reflect too, that not only is there a greater number of
churches in the places before-mentioned, but also that this in
particular is a most sacred obligation, that all should in common
desire whatever strict reason seems to demand, and which has
no communion with the perjury of the Jews.   But to sum up
matters briefly, it was determined by common consent that the
most holy festival of Easter should be solemnized on one and
the same day; for in such a hallowed solemnity any difference
is unseemly: and it is more commendable to adopt that opinion
in which there will be no intermixture of strange error, or
deviation from what is right.   These things therefore being
thus ordered, do you gladly receive this heavenly and truly
divine command: for whatever is done in the sacred assemblies
of the bishops is referable to the Divine will.   Wherefore
when ye have indicated the things which have been prescribed
to all our beloved brethren, it behoves you both to assent to the
reasoning which has been adduced, and to establish this observance of the most holy day: that when I arrive at
the long and earnestly desired view of your order, I may be
able to celebrate the sacred festival with you on one and the
same day; and may rejoice with you for all things, in seeing
Satanic cruelty frustrated by Divine power through our efforts,
while your faith, peace, and concord are everywhere flourishing.   May God preserve you, beloved brethren."

ANOTHER EPISTLE, TO EUSEBIUS.[1]

"Victor Constantine Maximus Augustus, to Eusebius.

"Since an impious purpose and tyranny have even to the
present time persecuted the servants of God our Saviour, I
have been credibly informed and am fully persuaded, most

---

[1] Valesius considers this letter misplaced, as having been written before the council of Nice.   The allusion to the death of Licinius, as a
recent event, would fix the date of this letter in the year A. D. 315 or 316.

. beloved brother, that all our sacred edifices have either by
⁹ neglect gone to decay, or from dread of impending danger
have not been adorned with becoming dignity. But now that
liberty has been restored, and that persecuting dragon Licinius
has, by the providence of the Most High God, and our instru-
mentality, been removed from the administration of public
affairs, I imagine that the Divine power has been made manifest to all; and trust that those who either through fear or
unbelief fell into any sins, having acknowledged the living
God, will come to the true and right course of life. Wherefore enjoin the churches over which you yourself preside, as
well as the other bishops presiding in various places, together
with the presbyters and deacons whom you know, to be diligent about the sacred edifices, either by repairing those which
remain standing, or enlarging them, or by erecting new ones
wherever it may be requisite. And do you yourself ask, and
the rest through you, the necessary supplies both from the
⁵ governors of the provinces and the officers of the Prætorian
Prefecture: for directions have been given to them to be
strictly attentive to the orders of your Holiness. May God
preserve you, beloved brother."

Similar instructions concerning the building of churches
were sent by the emperor to the bishops in every province:
but what he wrote to Eusebius of Palestine respecting the
preparation of some copies of the Scriptures, we may ascertain from the letters themselves :—

"Victor Constantine Maximus Augustus, to Eusebius of
Cæsarea.

"In the city which derives its name from us, a very great
multitude of persons, through the assisting providence of our
Saviour God, have united themselves to the most holy Church,
so that it has received much increase there. It is therefore
requisite that more churches should be provided in that
place : wherefore do you most cordially enter into the purpose
which I have conceived. I have thought fit to intimate this
to your prudence, that you should order to be transcribed on
well-prepared parchment, by competent writers accurately
acquainted with their art, fifty copies of the Sacred Scriptures,
both legibly described, and of a portable size, the provision
and use of which you know to be needful for the instruction
of the Church. Letters have also been despatched from our

clemency, to the Vicar-general[1] of the Diocese, in order that [27] he may take care to provide all things necessary for the preparation of them. Let this task be your responsibility, that these copies may be got ready as quickly as possible : and you are authorized, on the warrant of this our letter, to use two of the public carriages for their conveyance ; for thus the copies which are most satisfactorily transcribed, may be easily conveyed for our inspection. Charge one of the deacons of your church with this commission, who when he has reached us shall experience our bounty. May God preserve you, beloved brother."

ANOTHER EPISTLE, TO MACARIUS.

"Victor Constantine, Maximus Augustus, to Macarius of Jerusalem.—Such is the grace of our Saviour, that no supply of words seems to be adequate to the expression of its present manifestation. For that the monument[2] of his most holy passion, long since hidden under the earth, should have lain concealed for a period of so many years, until, through the destruction of the common enemy of all, it should shine forth [28] to his own servants after their having regained their freedom, exceeds all admiration. Surely if all those who throughout the whole habitable earth are accounted wise, should be convened in one and the same place, desiring to say something worthy of this miracle, they would fall infinitely short of the least part of it ; for the apprehension of this wonder as far transcends every nature capable of human reasoning, as heavenly things are mightier than human. Hence, therefore, this is always my especial aim, that as the credibility of the truth daily demonstrates itself by fresh miracles, so the souls of us all should become more anxious respecting the holy law, with modesty and unanimous ardour. But I desire that you should be fully aware of what I conceive is pretty generally known, that it is now my chief care, that we should adorn with magnificent structures that hallowed spot, which by God's appointment I [29] have disencumbered of a most disgusting appendage[3] of an

[1] Διοικήσεως καθολικὸν. There is no word exactly corresponding to this term in the Western Church : we give that which most nearly corresponds to it.

[2] Γνώρισμα. Our Saviour's sepulchre, close by Mount Calvary, is here meant.

[3] A temple of Venus, built on Mount Calvary by the emperor Adrian.

idol, as of some grievous burden; which was consecrated indeed from the beginning in the purpose of God, but has been
more manifestly sanctified since he has brought to light the
evidence of the Saviour's passion. Wherefore it is becoming
your prudence both to make such arrangements, and provision
of every thing necessary, that not only the church[1] itself may
be superior to any elsewhere, but that the rest of its parts also
may be such that all the most splendid edifices in every city
may be excelled by this. With regard to the workmanship
and chaste execution of the walls, know that we have intrusted
the care of these things to our friend Dracilian, deputy to the
most excellent the prefects of the prætorium, and to the governor of the province: for our piety has ordered that artificers
and workmen, and whatever other things they may be informed from your sagacity to be necessary for the structure,
shall through their care be immediately sent. Respecting the
columns or the marbles, and whatever you may judge to be
more precious and useful, do you yourself, after having inspected the model, take care to write to us; that when we
shall understand from your letter how many things and of
what kind there may be need of, these may be conveyed to
you from all quarters: for it is but reasonable that the most
wonderful place in the world should be adorned in accordance
with its dignity. But I wish to know from you, whether you
consider that the inner roof of the Temple should be arched,
or constructed on some other plan: for if it is to be arched, it
can also be decorated with gold. It remains that your Holiness should inform the officers before-mentioned, as soon as
possible, how many workmen and artificers, and what money
for expenses you will want: and hasten to report to me
speedily, not only concerning the marbles and columns, but
also concerning the arched roof, if indeed you should decide
this to be the more beautiful. May God preserve you, beloved brother."

The emperor having also written other letters of a more
oratorical character against Arius and his adherents, caused
them to be everywhere published throughout the cities, exposing him to ridicule, and taunting him with the keenest

---

[1] Βασιλικήν. So called because the ancient Roman basilicas were frequently turned into Christian churches. See Bloxam on Gothic Architecture, chap. i.

irony. Moreover, writing to the Nicomedians against Eusebius and Theognis, he censures the misconduct of Eusebius,
not only on account of his Arianism, but because also, having
formerly been well-affected to the tyrant,[1] he had traitorously
conspired against his affairs. He then exhorts them to elect
another bishop instead of him. But I thought it would be
superfluous to insert here the letters respecting these things,
because of their length: those who may wish to see them, will
be readily able to find them elsewhere and give them a perusal.
This is sufficient notice of these transactions.

CHAP. X.—THE EMPEROR SUMMONS TO THE SYNOD ACESIUS
ALSO, BISHOP OF THE NOVATIANS.

THE emperor's diligence induces me to mention another
circumstance expressive of his mind, and serving to show how
much he desired peace: for aiming at ecclesiastical harmony,
he summoned to the council Acesius also, a bishop of the
Novatian sect.[2] When therefore the synod had written out
and subscribed a declaration of faith, the emperor asked
Acesius whether he would also assent to this creed, and acquiesce in the settlement of the day on which Easter should be
observed. He replied, "The synod has determined nothing
new, my prince: for thus heretofore, even from the commencement and times of the apostles, I traditionally receive the definition of the faith, and the time of the celebration of Easter."
When therefore the emperor further asked him, "For what
reason then do you separate yourself from communion with the
rest of the Church?" he related what had taken place during
the persecution under Decius; and referred to the rigidness of
that austere canon which declares, that it is right to account
unworthy of participation in the divine mysteries persons who
after baptism have committed a sin, which the sacred Scriptures denominate "a sin unto death" (1 John v. 16): that
they should indeed be exhorted to repentance, but were not

---

[1] The emperor himself is meant by this term.
[2] Upon the suspicion which attaches to Socrates as a person infected
with the Novatian heresy, see some remarks in his Life, prefixed to this
volume.

to expect remission from the priests, but from God, who is alone able and has authority to forgive sins. When Acesius had thus spoken, the emperor said to him, "Place a ladder, Acesius, and climb alone into heaven." Neither Eusebius Pamphilus nor any other has ever mentioned these things: but I heard them from a man who was by no means prone to falsehood, and who simply stated what had taken place in the council in his presence. From which I conjecture that those who have passed by this occurrence in silence, were actuated by motives which have influenced many other historians; for they frequently suppress important facts, either from prejudice against some, or partiality towards others.

CHAP. XI.—Of the bishop paphnutius.

As we have before pledged ourselves to make some mention of Paphnutius and Spyridon, it will be seasonable to speak of them here. Paphnutius then was bishop of one of the cities in Upper Thebes: he was a man of such eminent piety, that extraordinary miracles were done by him. In the time of the persecution he had been deprived of one of his eyes. The emperor honoured this man exceedingly, and often sent for him to the palace, and kissed the part where the eye had been torn out. So devout was the emperor Constantine. Having noticed this circumstance respecting Paphnutius, I shall explain another thing which was wisely ordered in consequence of his advice, both for the good of the Church and the honour of the clergy. It seemed fit to the bishops to introduce a new law into the Church, that those who were in holy orders, I speak of bishops, presbyters, and deacons, should have no conjugal intercourse with the wives which they had married prior to their ordination.[1] And when it was proposed to deliberate on this matter, Paphnutius, having arisen in the midst of the assembly of bishops, earnestly entreated them not to impose so heavy a yoke on the ministers of religion: asserting

---

[1] Upon the voluntary celibacy of the clergy, and how far it was encouraged in the early Church, see Bingham's Christian Antiq. b. iv. 5. Compare Canon 10 of the Council of Ancyra; Canon 1 of Neocæsarea; Apostolical Canons, 5, 17, 26, 51.

that "marriage is honourable among all, and the nuptial bed [33] undefiled;" so that they ought not to injure the Church by too stringent restrictions. "For all men," said he, "cannot bear the practice of rigid continence; neither perhaps would the chastity of each of their wives be preserved." He termed the intercourse of a man with his lawful wife chastity. It would be sufficient, he thought, that such as had previously entered on their sacred calling should abjure matrimony, according to the ancient tradition of the Church: but that none should be separated from her to whom, while yet unordained, he had been legally united. And these sentiments he expressed, although himself without experience of marriage, and, to speak plainly, without ever having known a woman: for from a boy he had been brought up in a monastery, and was specially renowned above all men for his chastity. The whole assembly of the clergy assented to the reasoning of Paphnutius: wherefore they silenced all further debate on this point, leaving it to those who were husbands to exercise their own discretion in reference to their wives.

CHAP. XII.—OF SPYRIDON, BISHOP OF THE CYPRIANS.

WITH respect to Spyridon, so great was his sanctity while a shepherd, that he was thought worthy of being made a pastor of men; and having been assigned the bishopric of one of the cities in Cyprus named Trimithuntis, on account of his extreme humility he continued to feed his sheep during his prelacy. Many extraordinary things are related of him: I shall however record but one or two, lest I should seem to wander from my subject. Once about midnight, thieves, having clandestinely entered his sheepfold, attempted to carry off the sheep. But God, who protected the shepherd, preserved his sheep also; for the thieves were by an invisible power bound to the folds. At day-break, when he came to the sheep and found the men with their hands tied behind them, he understood what was done; and after having prayed he liberated the thieves, earnestly admonishing and exhorting them to support themselves by honest labour, and not to take anything unjustly. He then gave them a ram, and sent them away, jocosely adding, " that ye may not appear to have watched all night in vain." This is one of Spyridon's miracles. Another was of this kind. He had a virgin daughter named Irene, who was a partaker of her father's piety. An acquaintance intrusted to her keeping an ornament of considerable value : she, to guard it more securely, hid what had been deposited with her in the ground, and soon afterwards died. Subsequently the owner of the property came to claim it ; and not finding the virgin, he implicated the father in the transaction, sometimes accusing him of an attempt to defraud him, and then again beseeching him to restore the deposit. The old man regarding this person's loss as his own misfortune, went to the tomb of his daughter, and called upon God to show him in anticipation the promised resurrection. Nor was he disappointed in his hope ; for the virgin again reviving appeared to her father, and having pointed out to him the spot where she had hidden the ornament, she once more departed. Such characters as these adorned the Church in the time of the emperor Constantine. These details were communicated to me by many of the inhabitants of Cyprus ; and moreover I found them recorded in a treatise composed in Latin by the presbyter Rufinus, from which I have collected these and some other things which will be hereafter adduced.[1]

CHAP. XIII.—OF EUTYCHIAN THE MONK.

I HAVE heard extraordinary things also of Eutychian, a devout person who flourished about the same time ; who, although of the Novatian Church, yet was venerated for the performance of miracles similar to those just mentioned. I shall unequivocally state my authority for this narrative, nor will I attempt to conceal it, though I expect it will give umbrage to some parties. It was Auxanon, a very aged presbyter of the Novatian Church ; who when quite a youth accompanied Acesius to the synod at Nice, and related to me what I have said concerning him. His life extended from that period to the

[1] Upon the extent to which Socrates is indebted to Rufinus, see some observations in the Life of Socrates prefixed to this volume, p. v. That he does not, however, servilely follow his authority, is clear from the remarks which occur at the opening of book ii. chap. i.

reign of Theodosius the Younger; and while I was a mere stripling he recounted to me the acts of Eutychian, enlarging much on the divine grace which was manifested in him: but one circumstance he alluded to, which occurred in the reign of Constantine, peculiarly worthy of mention.   One of those military attendants,[1] whom the emperor calls his domestic or body-guards, having been suspected of treasonable practices, sought his safety in flight.   The indignant monarch ordered that he should be put to death, wherever he might be found: who having been arrested on the Bithynian Olympus, was heavily ironed and incarcerated near those parts of Olympus where Eutychian was leading a solitary life, and healing both the bodies and souls of many. The venerable Auxanon, being then very young, was with him, and was initiated by him into the discipline of the monastic life. Many persons came to this Eutychian, entreating him to procure the release of the prisoner by interceding for him with the emperor, who had been informed of the miracles done by Eutychian. The saint readily promised to go to his sovereign; but as the chains inflicted intolerable suffering, those who interested themselves on his behalf declared that it was to be feared death, accelerated by the effect of his chains, would both anticipate the emperor's vengeance, and render nugatory any intercession that might be made for the prisoner. Accordingly Eutychian sent to the jailors, requesting them to release the man; but they having answered that they should bring themselves into danger by liberating a criminal, he went himself to the prison attended by Auxanon; and on their refusal to admit him, the grace which rested on Eutychian was rendered more conspicuous: for the gates of the prison opened of their own accord, while the jailors had the keys in their custody. As soon as Eutychian together with Auxanon had entered the prison, to the great astonishment of all then present the fetters spontaneously fell from the prisoner's limbs. He then proceeded with Auxanon to the city which was anciently called Byzantium, but afterwards Constantinople, where having been ushered into the Imperial palace, he obtained remission of the sentence of death for the prisoner; for the emperor, entertaining great

---

[1] Δορυφόρων, spearmen or lancers. The use of the word in this sense of a royal body-guard, is strictly classical. See Herod. i. 59, 98, &c.; ii. 168; Xen. Cyrop. vii. 5, 84, &c.

veneration for Eutychian, readily granted his request. This indeed occurred some time after the period to which this part of our history refers.

The bishops who were convened at the council of Nice, after having drawn up and enrolled certain other ecclesiastical regulations which they are accustomed to term canons,[1] again departed to their respective cities: and as I conceive it will be appreciated by lovers of history, I shall here subjoin the names of such as were present, as far as I have been able to ascertain them, with the province and city over which they severally presided, and likewise the date at which this assembly took place. Hosius was, I believe, bishop of Cordova in Spain, as I have before stated ; Vito and Vicentius, presbyters of Rome ; Alexander, bishop of Egypt ; Eustathius, of Antiochia Magna ; Macarius, of Jerusalem ; and Harpocration, of Cynopolis : the names of the rest are fully reported in *The Synodicon* of Athanasius bishop of Alexandria. This synod was convened (as we have discovered from the notation of the date prefixed to the record of the synod) in the consulate of Paulinus and Julian, on the 20th day of May, and in the 636th year from the reign of Alexander the Macedonian. And when the council was dissolved, the emperor went into the western parts of the empire.

CHAP. XIV.—EUSEBIUS BISHOP OF NICOMEDIA, AND THEOGNIS BISHOP OF NICE, WHO HAD BEEN BANISHED ON ACCOUNT OF THEIR CONCURRING IN OPINION WITH ARIUS, HAVING PUBLISHED THEIR RECANTATION, AND AGREED TO THE EXPOSITION OF THE FAITH, ARE REINSTATED IN THEIR SEES.

EUSEBIUS[2] and Theognis having sent a penitential confession to the principal bishops, were by an imperial edict recalled from exile and restored to their own churches, those who had been ordained in their places being removed ; Eusebius displacing Amphion, and Theognis, Chrestus. This is a copy of their written retractation :—

[1] See the Canons given at length in Hammond's "Canons of the Church," p. 15, &c. (Oxford, 1843.)
[2] Chronological order has been somewhat disregarded here ; for this occurred A. D. 328.

"We having been sometime since condemned by your piety, without our cause having been pleaded, ought to bear in [37] silence the decisions of your sacred adjudication.   But since it is unreasonable that we by silence should countenance calumniators against ourselves, we on this account declare that we entirely concur with you in the faith; and also that, after having closely considered the import of the term *consubstantial*, we have been wholly studious of peace, having never followed any heresy.   After suggesting whatever entered our thought for the security of the churches, and fully assuring those under our influence, we subscribed the declaration of faith, but did not subscribe the anathematizing; not as objecting to the creed, but as disbelieving the party accused to be such as was represented, having been satisfied on this point, both from his own letters to us, as well as from his discourses in our presence.   But if your holy council was convinced, we not opposing but concurring in your decisions, by this statement give them our full assent and confirmation : and this we do, not as wearied with our exile, but to avoid the suspicion of heresy.   If therefore ye should now think fit to restore us to your presence, ye will have us on all points conformable, and acquiescent in your decrees.   For since it has seemed good to your piety to deal tenderly with and recall even him who was primarily accused ; it would be absurd for us to be silent, and thus submit to presumptive evidence against ourselves, when the one who was arraigned has been permitted to clear himself from the charges brought against him.   Vouchsafe then, as is consistent with that piety of yours, dear to Christ, to remind our most religious emperor, to present our petitions, and to determine speedily concerning us in a way becoming yourselves."

Such was the language of the recantation[1] of Eusebius and Theognis; from which I infer that they had subscribed the articles of faith which had been set forth, but would not become parties to the condemnation of Arius.   It appears also that Arius was recalled before them ; but, although this may be true, yet he had been forbidden to enter Alexandria.   This is evident from the fact that he afterwards devised a way of return for himself, both into the Church and into Alexandria,

---

[1] Παλινῳδίας βιβλίον, (πάλιν and ᾠδή from ἀείδω,) re-cantatio. Plato, Alc. II. 142, D.

by having made a fictitious repentance, as we shall show in
its proper place.

CHAP. XV.—AFTER THE SYNOD, ON THE DEATH OF ALEXANDER,
ATHANASIUS IS CONSTITUTED BISHOP OF ALEXANDRIA.

ALEXANDER, bishop of Alexandria, having died a little
after this, Athanasius was immediately set over that Church.
Rufinus relates, that this person, when quite a boy, played
with others of his own age at a sacred game: this was an
imitation of the priesthood and the order of consecrated persons. In this game therefore Athanasius was allotted the
episcopal dignity, and each of the other lads personated either
a presbyter or a deacon. The children engaged in this sport
on the day in which the memory of the martyr and bishop
Peter was celebrated; and at that time Alexander, bishop of
Alexandria, happening to pass by, observed the play in which
they were engaged, and, having sent for the children, inquired
from them the part each had been assigned in the game, conceiving that something might be portended by that which
had been done. He then gave directions that the children
should be educated for the Church, and instructed in learning,
but especially Athanasius; and having afterwards ordained
him deacon on his becoming of adult age, he brought him to
Nice to assist him in the disputations there when the synod
was convened. Rufinus in his writings has given this account
of Athanasius; nor is it improbable that it took place, for
many transactions of this kind have often occurred.

CHAP. XVI.—THE EMPEROR CONSTANTINE HAVING ENLARGED
THE ANCIENT BYZANTIUM, CALLS IT CONSTANTINOPLE.

AFTER the synod the emperor spent some time in recre-
ation, and after the public celebration of his Vicennalia, (i. e.
the completion of the twentieth year of his reign,) he immediately devoted himself to the reparation of the churches.
This he carried into effect in other cities as well as in the city
named after him, which, being previously called Byzantium,

he enlarged, surrounded with massive walls, and adorned with various edifices; and having rendered it equal to imperial Rome, he named it Constantinople, establishing by law that it should be designated New Rome. This law was engraven on a pillar of stone erected in public view in the Strategium,[1] near the emperor's equestrian statue.[2] He built also in the same city two churches, one of which he named *Irene* (Peace), and the other that of *The Apostles*. Nor did he only improve the affairs of the Christians, as I have said, but he also destroyed the superstitions of the heathens;[3] for he brought forth their images into public view to ornament the city of Constantinople, and set up the Delphic tripods publicly in the Hippodrome. It seems now indeed superfluous to mention these things, since they are seen before they are heard of. But at that time the Christian cause received its greatest augmentation; for Divine Providence reserved this among other things for the times of the emperor Constantine. Eusebius Pamphilus has in magnificent terms recorded the praises of the emperor;[4] and I considered it would not be ill-timed to advert thus to them as concisely as possible.

CHAP. XVII.—THE EMPEROR'S MOTHER HELEN HAVING ARRIVED AT JERUSALEM, FINDS THE CROSS OF CHRIST WHICH SHE HAD LONG SOUGHT, AND BUILDS A CHURCH.

HELEN the emperor's mother, (from whose name Drepanum, once a village, having been made a city by the emperor, was called Helenopolis,) being divinely directed by dreams, went to Jerusalem. Finding that which was once Jerusalem, desolate *as a preserve*[5] *for autumnal fruits*, according to the

---

[1] A public edifice for the two principal magistrates.
[2] The city was solemnly dedicated as the seat of empire in the year A. D. 330.
[3] τῶν Ἑλλήνων. The heathen were generally understood by this term in writers of the Eastern Church, as was naturally the case.
[4] See the Life of Constantine by Eusebius, book iii. ch. 48, and his Oration in praise of Constantine.
[5] Ὀπωροφυλάκιον, to which ἐν σικυηράτῳ is added in LXX., which in the authorized version is "a lodge in a garden of cucumbers," according to the Hebrew.

prophet, she sought carefully the sepulchre of Christ, from
which he arose after his burial ; and after much difficulty, by
God's help she discovered it. What the cause of the difficulty
was I will explain in few words. Those who embraced the
Christian faith, after the period of His passion, greatly venerated this tomb ; but those who hated Christianity, having
covered the spot with a mound of earth, erected on it a temple
to Venus, and set up her image [1] there, endeavouring to abolish the recollection of the place. This succeeded for a long
time ; but it at length became known to the emperor's mother,
who, having caused the statue [2] to be thrown down, the earth
to be removed, and the ground entirely cleared, found three
crosses in the sepulchre : one of these was that blessed cross
on which Christ had hung, the other two were those on which
the two thieves that were crucified with him had died. With
these was also found the tablet of Pilate, on which he had inscribed in various characters, that the Christ who was crucified was king of the Jews. Since however it was doubtful
which was the cross they were in search of, the emperor's
mother was not a little distressed ; but from this trouble she
was shortly relieved by Macarius bishop of Jerusalem, whose
faith solved the doubt, for he sought a sign from God and
obtained it. The sign was this :—a certain woman of the
neighbourhood, who had been long afflicted with disease, was
now just at the point of death ; the bishop therefore ordered
that each of the crosses should be applied to the dying woman,
believing that she would be healed on being touched by the
precious cross. Nor was he disappointed in his expectation :
for the two crosses having been applied which were not the
Lord's, the woman still continued in a dying state ; but when
the third, which was the true cross, touched her, she was
immediately healed, and recovered her former strength. In
this manner then was the genuine cross discovered. The
emperor's mother erected over the place of the sepulchre a
magnificent church, and named it *New Jerusalem*, having
built it opposite to that old and deserted city. There she left
a portion of the cross, enclosed in a silver case, as a memorial to those who might wish to see it : the other part she

[1] ἄγαλμα. See above in chap. ix., The Epistle of Constantine to Macarius.
[2] Ξόανον (from ξέω to polish).

sent to the emperor, who, being persuaded that the city would
be perfectly secure where that relic should be preserved, privately enclosed it in his own statue, which stands on a large
column of porphyry in the forum called Constantine's at Con- 40
stantinople.   I have written this from report indeed ; but almost all the inhabitants of Constantinople affirm that it is
true.   Moreover Constantine caused the nails with which
Christ's hands were fastened to the cross (for his mother
having found these also in the sepulchre had sent them) to be
converted into bridle-bits and a helmet, which he used in his
military expeditions.   The emperor supplied all materials for
the construction of the churches, and wrote to Macarius the
bishop to expedite these edifices.   When the emperor's mother
had completed the *New Jerusalem*, she reared another church
not at all inferior, over the cave at Bethlehem where Christ
was born according to the flesh : nor did she stop here, but
built a third on the mount of his Ascension.   So devoutly
was she affected in these matters, that she would pray in the
company of women ; and inviting the virgins enrolled in the
register[1] of the churches to a repast, serving them herself,
she brought the dishes to table.   She was also very munificent
to the churches and to the poor ; and having completed a life
of piety, she died when about eighty years old.   Her remains
were conveyed to New Rome, and deposited in the imperial
sepulchres.

CHAP. XVIII.—THE EMPEROR CONSTANTINE ABOLISHES PA-
GANISM AND ERECTS MANY CHURCHES IN DIFFERENT PLACES.

AFTER this the emperor became increasingly attentive to
the interests of Christianity, and turned with disgust from the
heathen superstitions.   He abolished the combats of the gladi-

---

[1] ἐν τῷ κανόνι.   Here we see the beginning of the conventual life of
women, as afterwards developed in the succeeding centuries.   Thus we
read of deaconesses and even presbyteresses (πρεσβύτιδες).   St. Paul
gives the name of διάκονος to Phœbe, thereby doubtless intimating that
she was a deaconess of the church in Cenchrea. (See Rom. xvi. 1.)   The
corresponding word in Latin was " ministra," by which name Pliny says
that the female servants of the Church were called. (See Ep. x. 97.) A full
account of all the particulars of their office, and of the manner of their
ordination, is given in Bingham's Christian Antiq. book ii. ch. xxii.

ators, and set up his own statues in the temples. And as the heathens affirmed that it was Serapis who brought up the Nile for the purpose of irrigating Egypt, because a cubit was " usually carried into his temple, he directed Alexander to transfer the cubit to the church.[1] It was then asserted that the Nile would not overflow because of the displeasure of Serapis ; nevertheless there was an inundation in the following year, and has been every subsequent one : thus it was proved by fact that the rising of the Nile was not in consequence of their superstition, but by reason of the decrees of Providence. About the same time those barbarians the Sarmatians and Goths made incursions on the Roman territory ; yet the emperor's earnestness respecting the churches was by no means abated, but he made suitable provision for both these matters. Placing his confidence in the Christian banner, he completely vanquished his enemies, so as even to cast off the tribute of gold which preceding emperors were accustomed to pay the barbarians : while they themselves, being terror-struck at their unexpected defeat, then for the first time embraced the Christian religion, by means of which Constantine had been protected. Again he built other churches, one of which was erected near the Oak of Mamre, under which the sacred oracles declare that Abraham entertained angels. For the emperor having been informed that altars had been reared under that oak, and that Pagan sacrifices were performed there, severely censured by letter Eusebius bishop of Cæsarea, and ordered that the altars should be demolished, and a house of prayer erected beside the oak. He also directed that another church should be constructed in Heliopolis in Phœnicia, for this reason. Who originally legislated for the inhabitants of this city I am unable to state, but his character and morals may be judged of from the practice of that city ; for the laws of the country ordered the women among them to be common, and therefore the children born there were of doubtful descent, so that there was no distinction of fathers and their offspring. Their virgins also were presented for prostitution to the strangers who resorted thither. The emperor undertook the correction of these impure and disgraceful customs, which had long prevailed among them, by the establishment of a solemn law of chastity, which

---

[1] See below, note on b. v. ch. xiv.

[SOCRATES.]   E

provided for the mutual recognition of families: and when churches had been built there, he took care that a bishop and sacred clergy should be ordained, by whose means the corrupt manners of the people of Heliopolis might be reformed. He likewise demolished the temple of Venus at Aphaca on Mount Libanus, and abolished the obscene mysteries which were there celebrated. Why need I describe his expulsion of the Pythonic demon from Cilicia, by commanding the mansion in which he was lurking to be razed from its foundations? So great was the emperor's devotion to Christianity, that when he was about to enter on a war with Persia, he prepared a tabernacle formed of embroidered linen on the model of a church, just as Moses had done in the wilderness;[1] and this he adapted to conveyance from place to place, in order that he might have a house of prayer even in the most desert regions. But the war was suppressed at that time, being prevented through dread of the emperor. It would, I conceive, be out of place here to describe the emperor's diligence in rebuilding cities and converting many villages into cities; as for example Drepane, to which he gave his mother's name, and Constantia in Palestine, so called from his sister: for my purpose is to confine my narration of the emperor's actions chiefly to such as are connected with Christianity, and especially those which relate to the churches. Wherefore I leave to others more competent to detail such matters, the emperor's glorious achievements, inasmuch as they belong to a different subject, and require a distinct treatise. But I myself should have been silent, if the Church had remained undisturbed by divisions: for where the subject does not supply matter for relation, there is no necessity for a narrator. Since, however, the apostolic faith of Christianity has been disturbed and at the same time frittered away by a vain and subtle mode of disputation, I thought it desirable to record these things, in order that the transactions of the Churches might not be lost in obscurity. Accurate information on these points, while it procures celebrity among the many, renders him who is acquainted with them more secure from error, and instructs him not to be agitated by any empty sound of sophistical argumentation which he may chance to hear.

[1] See Exod. chap. xxxv.—xl.

CHAP. XIX.—By what means, in the time of Constantine, the nations in the interior of India were Christianized.

a. We must now mention by what means the profession of
Christianity was extended in this emperor's reign : for it was
in his time that the nations both of the Indians in the interior,
and of the Iberians, first embraced the Christian faith. But
it may be needful briefly to explain why the expression *in the
interior* is appended. When the apostles went forth by lot
among the nations, Thomas received the apostleship of the
Parthians ; Matthew was allotted Ethiopia ; and Bartholomew
the part of India contiguous to that country : [1] but the interior
of India, which was inhabited by many barbarous nations using
different languages, was not enlightened by Christian doctrine
before the time of Constantine. I now come to speak of the
cause which led them to become converts to Christianity.
Meropius, a Tyrian philosopher, determined to visit the country
of the Indians, being stimulated to this by the example of the
philosopher Metrodorus, who had previously travelled through
that region. Having taken with him therefore two youths to
whom he was related, who were by no means ignorant of the
Greek language, Meropius arrived at that country by ship ; and
when he had inspected whatever he wished, he touched at a
certain place which had a safe harbour, for the purpose of pro-
curing some necessaries. It so happened that the treaty between the Romans and Indians had been violated a little before
his arrival. The Indians therefore, having seized the philosopher and those who sailed with him, killed them all except
his two young kinsmen ; but sparing them from compassion
for their tender age, they sent them as a gift to the king of the
Indians. He being pleased with the personal appearance of
the youths, constituted one of them, whose name was Edesius,.
cup-bearer at his table ; to the other, named Frumentius, he in-

[1] See Euseb. Eccl. Hist. v. 10, who says that Pantænus in the second
century found in India a copy of St. Matthew's Gospel, which had been
left there by the apostle Bartholomew. Compare Burton's Lectures,
especially xi. and xxi., and Cave's Lives of the Apostles. For further information of a very interesting character upon the early introduction of
Christianity into India, the general reader is referred to a recent publication entitled " The Jesuit in India."

trusted the care of the royal records. The king, dying soon after, left them free, the government devolving on his wife and infant son ; and the queen, seeing her son thus left in his minority, begged the young men to undertake the charge of him, until he should become of adult age. They therefore accepted this commission, and entered on the administration of the kingdom ; but the chief authority was in the hands of Frumentius, who began anxiously to inquire whether among the Roman merchants trafficking with that country, there were any Christians to be found : and having discovered some, he informed them who he was, and exhorted them to select some appropriate places for the celebration of Christian worship. In the course of a little while he built a house of prayer ; and having instructed some of the Indians in the principles of Christianity, they were admitted to participation in the worship. On the young king's reaching maturity, Frumentius resigned to him the administration of public affairs, in the management of which he had honourably acquitted himself, and besought permission to return to his own country. Both the king and his mother entreated him to remain ; but he being desirous of revisiting his native place, could not be prevailed on, and consequently they both departed. Edesius hastened to Tyre to see his parents and kindred : but Frumentius arriving at Alexandria, relates his whole story to Athanasius the bishop, who had but recently been invested with that dignity; and acquainting him with the particulars of his residence abroad, expressed a hope that measures would be taken to convert the Indians to Christianity. He also begged him to send a bishop and clergy there, and by no means to neglect those who might thus be brought to the knowledge of salvation. Athanasius, having considered how this could be most profitably effected, requested Frumentius himself to accept the bishopric, declaring that he could appoint no one more suitable than he. He was accordingly ordained, and again returning to India with episcopal authority, became there a preacher of the gospel, and built several *Oratories:*[1] being aided also by Divine grace, he performed various miracles, healing diseases both of the souls and bodies of many. Rufinus assures us that he heard these facts from Edesius, who was afterwards inducted into the sacred office at Tyre.

[1] Εὐκτήρια, called also οἶκοι εὐκτήριοι, above ch. xviii.

CHAP. XX.—By what means the Iberians were con-
VERTED TO CHRISTIANITY.

It is now proper to relate how the Iberians,[1] about the
⊄same time, became proselytes to the faith.   A certain woman
distinguished by her devout and chaste life, was, in the providential ordering of God, taken captive by the Iberians, who
dwell near the Euxine Sea, and are a·colony of the Iberians
of Spain.   She accordingly in her captivity exercised[2] herself among the barbarians in the practice of virtue : for
she not only maintained the most rigid continence, but spent
much time in fastings and prayers ; which extraordinary
conduct the barbarians observing, were very greatly astonished
at. The king's son, then a mere babe, happening to be attacked
with disease, the queen, according to the custom of the country, sent the child to other women to be cured, in the hope that
their experience would supply a remedy.   After the infant had
been carried around by its nurse without obtaining relief from
any of the women, he was at length brought to this captive.
She, having no knowledge of the medical art, applied no
material remedy ; but taking the child and laying it on her
bed, which was made of horse-cloth, in the presence of other
females, she simply said, "Christ, who healed many, will heal
this child also :" then having prayed in addition to this expression of faith, and called upon God, the boy was immediately restored, and continued well from that period.   The
report of this miracle spread itself far and wide among the
barbarian women, and soon reached the queen, so that the
captive became very celebrated.   Not long afterwards the
queen herself, having fallen sick, sent for this woman, who being a person of modest and retiring manners, excused herself
from going ; on which the queen was conveyed to her, and
received relief in like manner as her son had, for the disease
was at once removed.   But when the queen thanked the
stranger, she replied, "This work is not mine, but Christ's,

[1] The country of Iberia is situated on the east of the Euxine Sea, and is
now called Georgia.   It is, of course, far more probable that the name
passed from that part into Spain, than that a country so far to the east
should have been colonized from Spain, as asserted by our author here.
[2] Ἐφιλοσόφει (this sense was adopted by later writers).

who is the Son of God that made the world:" she therefore exhorted her to call upon him, and acknowledge the true God. Amazed at his wife's sudden restoration to health, the king of the Iberians wished to requite her with gifts whom he had understood to be the means of effecting these cures : she however declined their acceptance, telling him that she needed not riches, inasmuch as she possessed abundance in the consolations of religion ; but that she would regard as the greatest present he could offer her, his recognition of the God whom she worshipped and declared. This answer the king treasured up in his mind, and going forth to the chase the next day, the following circumstance occurred : a mist and thick darkness covered the mountain-tops and forests where he was hunting, so that their sport was embarrassed, and their path became inextricable. In this perplexity the prince earnestly invoked the gods whom he worshipped, but finding that it profited him nothing, he at last determined to implore the assistance of the captive's God ; when scarcely had he begun to pray, ere the darkness arising from the mist was completely dissipated. Wondering at that which was done, he returned to his palace rejoicing ; and relating to his wife what had happened, he immediately sent for the captive stranger, and begged her to inform him who that God was whom she adored. The woman on her arrival caused the king of the Iberians to become a preacher of the gospel : for having believed in Christ through the faithfulness of this devoted woman, he convened all the Iberians who were under his authority ; and when he had declared to them what had taken place in reference to the cure of his wife and child, as well as the circumstances connected with the chase, he exhorted them to worship the God of the captive. Thus therefore both the king and queen were made preachers of Christ, the one addressing their male, and the other their female subjects. Moreover the king, having ascertained from his prisoner the plan on which churches were constructed among the Romans, ordered an Oratory to be built, providing all things necessary for its immediate erection ; and the edifice was accordingly commenced. But when they came to set up the pillars, Divine Providence interposed for the confirmation of the inhabitants in the faith, for one of the columns remained immovable ; and the workmen, disheartened by the fracture of their ropes

and machinery, at length gave up all further effort.   Then
was proved the reality of the captive's faith in the following
manner : going to the place at night without the knowledge
of any one, she spent the whole time in prayer ; and the
power of God was manifested by the pillar's being raised,
and caused to stand erect in the air above its base, yet so as
not to touch it.   At day-break the king, who was an intelligent
person, came himself to inspect the work, and seeing the pillar
suspended in this position without support, both he and his
attendants were amazed ; but shortly after, while they stood
gazing on this wonder, the pillar descended on its own pedestal
and there remained fixed.   Upon this the people shouted, attesting the truth of the king's faith and hymning the praise
of the God of the captive.   Their belief being thus established,
the rest of the columns were easily reared, and the whole building was soon completed.   An embassy was afterwards sent to
the emperor Constantine, requesting that henceforth they
might be in alliance with the Romans, and receive from them a
bishop and consecrated clergy, since they sincerely believed
in Christ.   Rufinus says that he learnt these facts from Bacurius, formerly one of the petty princes of the Iberians, who
subsequently went over to the Romans, and was made a
captain of the military force in Palestine : being at length intrusted with the supreme command in the war against the
tyrant Maximus, he greatly assisted the emperor Theodosius.
In this way then, during the reign of Constantine, were the
Iberians converted to Christianity.

CHAP. XXI.—Of ANTONY THE MONK.

WHAT sort of a character the monk Antony was, who lived
in the same age, in the Egyptian desert, it would be superfluous for us to describe ; and how he openly contended with
devils, clearly detecting their devices and wily modes of war-
fare ; or to enumerate the many miracles he did: for Athanasius bishop of Alexandria has anticipated us, having devoted
an entire book to his biography.[1]   The mention of his name

[1] See the Life of St. Anthony by Athanasius, given in the Benedictine
edition of that Father's works.

among others, will however serve to show the abundance of
good men that flourished contemporaneously with the emperor
Constantine.

CHAP. XXII.—Of MANES THE RINGLEADER OF THE MANI-
CHÆAN HERESY, AND WHENCE HIS ORIGIN.

BUT amidst the good corn tares are accustomed to spring
up ; for Satan's envy loves to plot insidiously against the good.
Hence it was that a little while before the time of Constantine
a species of heathenish Christianity made its appearance together with that which was real : just as false prophets and
false apostles heretofore insinuated themselves amongst those
who were constituted of God.   For at that time a dogma of
Empedocles, the heathen philosopher, was by Manichæus attempted to be amalgamated with Christian doctrine.   Eusebius
Pamphilus indeed has mentioned this person in the seventh
book of his Ecclesiastical History :[1] but since he did not
enter into minute details concerning him, I deem it incumbent
on me to supply some particulars which he has left unnoticed :
thus it will be known who this Manichæus was, whence he
came, and what was the nature of his presumptuous daring.
A Saracen named Scythian having married a captive from
the Upper Thebes, dwelt on her account in Egypt, where,
after studying the learning of the Egyptians, he introduced
the theory of Empedocles and Pythagoras among the doctrines
of the Christian faith.   Asserting that there were two natures,
a good and an evil one, he termed, as Empedocles had done,
the latter *Discord,* and the former *Friendship.*   Of this Scythian, Buddas, who had been previously called Terebinthus,
became a disciple ; and he having proceeded to Babylon, which
the Persians inhabit, made many extravagant statements respecting himself, declaring that he was born of a virgin, and
brought up in the mountains.   The same man afterwards composed four books ; one he entitled *The Mysteries,* another *The
Gospel,* a third *The Treasure,* and the fourth *Heads :* but
pretending to perform some mystic rites, he was hurled down
a precipice by the devil, and so perished.   He was buried by

[1] A full account of the Manichæan heresy will be found in chap. xxxi.
of that book.

a woman at whose house he had lodged, who taking possession of his property, bought a boy about seven years old whose name was Cubricus: this lad she enfranchised, and having given him a liberal education, she soon after died, leaving him all that belonged to Terebinthus, including the books he had written on the principles inculcated by Scythian. Cubricus, now free, taking these things with him travelled into Persia, where he changed his name, calling himself Manes; and disseminated the books of Buddas or Terebinthus among his deluded followers, as his own. Now the contents of these treatises are apparently accordant with Christianity in expression, but thoroughly Pagan in sentiment: for Manichæus, being an impious person, incited his disciples to acknowledge a plurality of gods, and taught them to worship the sun. He also introduced *Fatalism*, taking away human free-will; and distinctly affirmed a transmutation of bodies, a notion which closely approximates to, and was doubtless borrowed from, the opinions of Empedocles, Pythagoras, and the Egyptians, respecting the transmigration of souls. He denied that Christ existed in the flesh, asserting that he was an unsubstantial apparition;[1] and rejected moreover the Law and the Prophets, calling himself the *Comforter:*[2]—all of which dogmas are totally repugnant to the orthodox faith of the Church. In his epistles he even dared to assume the title of Apostle; but a pretension so unfounded brought upon him merited retribution in the following manner. The son of the Persian monarch having been attacked with disease, his father became anxious for his recovery, and left no stone unturned in order to effect it; and as he had heard of the specious deceptions of Manichæus, under the impression that these miracles were real, he sent for him as an apostle, trusting that through him his son might be restored. The impostor accordingly presented himself at court, and with well-dissembled mysticism of manner undertook the cure of the young prince: the child however died under his hands, and the king seeing his hope thus painfully frustrated, shut up the deceiver in prison, with intent to put him to death. Manichæus contriving to escape, fled into Mesopotamia, and so for a time saved himself; but

---

[1] In this error identifying himself with the ancient heretics, the Docetæ, who were a branch of the early Gnostics; their founder was Simon Magus.
[2] τὸν Παράκλητον. See St. John xiv. 16, &c.

tho king of Persia having discovered where he was secreted, caused him to be brought thence by force, and after having flayed him alive, he stuffed his skin with chaff, and suspended it in front of the gate of the city. These are no fabrications of ours, but facts which we collected from a book entitled "The disputation of Archelaus bishop of Cascharum" (one 45 of the cities of Mesopotamia); in which the author states that he disputed with Manichæus face to face, and mentions the circumstances connected with his life to which we have now alluded. The envy of Satan thus delights, as we before remarked, to be insidiously at work in the midst of a prosperous condition of affairs. But for what reason the goodness of God permits this to be done, whether he wishes thereby to bring into activity the excellence of the principles of the Church, and to utterly break down the self-importance which is wont to unite itself with faith; or for what other cause, is too difficult a question for present discussion. Nor would it be consistent with the object here proposed, which is neither to examine the soundness of doctrinal views, nor to analyse the mysterious purposes of the providential arrangements of God; but to detail as faithfully as possible the transactions which have taken place in the Churches. Having then described the way in which the corrupt superstition of the Manichæans sprang up a little before the time of Constantine, we will return to the series of events which are the proper subjects of this history.

CHAP. XXIII.—Eusebius bishop of Nicomedia, and Theognis bishop of Nice, having resumed courage, endeavour to subvert the Nicene Creed, by plotting against Athanasius.

On the return of Eusebius and Theognis from their exile, they were reinstated in their churches, having expelled, as we observed, those who had been ordained in their stead. Moreover they came into great consideration with the emperor, who honoured them exceedingly, as those who had returned from damnable error to the orthodox faith. They however abused the licence thus afforded them, by exciting greater commotions in the world than they had done before; being instigated to this by two causes—the Arian heresy with which they had been previously infected on the one hand, and bitter animosity against Athanasius on the other, because he had so vigorously withstood them in the synod while the articles of faith were under discussion. And in the first place they objected to his ordination, as a person unworthy of the prelacy, alleging that he had been elected by disqualified persons. But when Athanasius had shown himself superior to this calumny, and possessing the confidence of the Church of Alexandria, ardently contended for the Nicene creed, then Eusebius exerted himself to the utmost in insidious plots against him, and efforts to bring Arius back to Alexandria: for he thought that thus only could the doctrine of consubstantiality be eradicated, and Arianism introduced. Eusebius therefore wrote to Athanasius, desiring him to re-admit Arius and his adherents into the Church: the tone of his letter indeed being that of entreaty, while openly he menaced him. When Athanasius would by no means accede to this, he endeavoured to induce the emperor to give Arius an audience, and then permit him to return to Alexandria: but by what means he attained his object, I shall mention in its proper place. Before however this was effected, another commotion was raised in the Church, her peace being again disturbed by her own children. Eusebius Pamphilus says, that immediately after the synod, Egypt became agitated by intestine divisions: but as he does not assign the reason for this, some have accused him of disingenuousness, and have even attributed his avoiding to specify the causes of these dissensions, to a determination on his part not to give his sanction to the proceedings at Nice. Yet, as we ourselves have discovered from various letters which the bishops wrote to one another after the synod, the term ὁμοούσιος troubled some of them. But while they occupied themselves in a too minute investigation of its import, the discussion assumed a polemical character, though it seemed not unlike a contest in the dark; for neither party appeared to understand distinctly the grounds on which they calumniated one another. Those who objected to the word *consubstantial*, conceived that those who approved it, favoured the opinion of Sabellius[1] and Montanus;[2] they

---

[1] Upon the heresy of Sabellius, see Euseb. Eccl. Hist. book vii. ch. 6.
[2] See Euseb. Eccl. Hist. v. ch. 16.

therefore called them blasphemers, as subverters of the existence of the Son of God. And again the advocates of this term, charging their opponents with polytheism, inveighed against them as introducers of heathen superstitions. Eustathius, bishop of Antioch, accuses Eusebius Pamphilus of perverting the Nicene creed: but Eusebius denies that he violates that exposition of the faith, and recriminates, saying that Eustathius was a defender of the opinion of Sabellius. In consequence of these misunderstandings, each of them wrote volumes as if contending against adversaries: and although it was admitted on both sides that the Son of God has a distinct person and existence, and all acknowledged that there is one God in a Trinity of Persons, yet, from what cause I am unable to divine, they could not agree among themselves, and therefore were never at peace.

CHAP. XXIV.—OF THE SYNOD HELD AT ANTIOCH, WHICH DEPOSED EUSTATHIUS BISHOP OF ANTIOCH, ON WHOSE ACCOUNT A SEDITION WAS EXCITED WHICH ALMOST RUINED THE CITY.

HAVING therefore convened a synod at Antioch, they degrade Eustathius, as a supporter of the Sabellian heresy, rather than the tenets which had been recognised at the council of Nice. There are some who affirm that his deposition arose from less justifiable motives, though none other have been openly assigned: but this is a matter of common occurrence, for the bishops frequently load with opprobrious epithets, and pronounce impious those whom they depose, without explaining their warrant for so doing. George bishop of Laodicea in Syria, one of the number of those who abominated the term *consubstantial*, assures us in his *Encomium of Eusebius Emisenus*, that they deposed Eustathius as a favourer of Sabellianism, on the impeachment of Cyrus bishop of Berœa. Of Eusebius Emisenus we shall speak elsewhere in due order:[1] but there seems to be something contradictory in the report which George has given of Eustathius; for after asserting that he was accused by Cyrus of maintaining the heresy of

[1] He refers to book ii. ch. ix.

Sabellius, he tells us again that Cyrus himself was convicted of the same error, and degraded for it. Now how could it happen that Cyrus should be the accuser of Eustathius as a Sabellian, when he entertained similar opinions? It appears likely therefore that Eustathius must have been condemned on other grounds. That circumstance however gave rise to a dangerous sedition at Antioch : for when they proceeded to the election of a successor, so fierce a dissension was kindled, as to threaten the whole city with destruction. The populace was divided into two factions, one of which vehemently contended for the translation of Eusebius Pamphilus from Cæsarea in Palestine to Antioch ; the other equally insisted on the reinstatement of Eustathius. And as all the citizens were infected with the spirit of partisanship in this quarrel among the Christians, a military force was arrayed on both sides with hostile intent, so that a bloody collision would have taken place, had not God and the dread of the emperor repressed the violence of the multitude. But the emperor's letters, together with the refusal of Eusebius to accept the bishopric, served to allay the ferment : on which account that prelate was exceedingly admired by the emperor, who wrote to him commending his prudent determination, and congratulating him as one who was considered worthy of being bishop not of one city merely, but of almost the whole world. It is said that the episcopal ^achair of the church at Antioch was vacant for eight years after this period ; but at length, by the exertions of those who aimed at the subversion of the Nicene creed, Euphronius was duly installed. This is the amount of my information respecting the synod held at Antioch on account of Eustathius. Immediately after these events Eusebius, who had long before left Berytus, and was at that time presiding over the church at Nicomedia, strenuously exerted himself in connexion with those of his party, to bring back Arius to Alexandria. But how they managed to effect this, and by what means the emperor was prevailed on to admit both Arius and Euzoïus into his presence, must now be related.

CHAP. XXV.—Of the presbyter who exerted himself
that arius might be recalled.

The emperor Constantine had a sister named Constantia,
formerly the wife of Licinius, who, after having for some time
shared the imperial dignity with Constantine, was put to death
in consequence of his tyranny and ambition.   This princess
maintained in her household establishment a certain confidential presbyter, tinctured with the dogmas of Arianism;
who being prompted by Eusebius and others, took occasion in
his familiar conversations with Constantia, to insinuate that
the synod had done Arius injustice, and that his sentiments
were greatly misrepresented.   Constantia gave full credence
to the presbyter's assertions, but durst not report them to the
emperor; until at length she became dangerously ill, which
caused her brother to visit her daily.   When the disease had
reduced her to such a state that her speedy dissolution seemed
inevitable, she commended this presbyter to the emperor, testifying to his diligence and piety, as well as his devoted loyalty
to his sovereign.   On her death, which occurred soon after,
the presbyter became one of the most confidential persons
about the emperor; and having gradually increased in freedom of speech, he repeated to the emperor what he had before
stated to his sister, affirming that the opinions of Arius were
perfectly accordant with the sentiments avowed by the synod;
and that if he were admitted to the imperial presence, he would
give his full assent to what the synod had decreed: he added
moreover that he had been falsely accused without the slightest reason.   The emperor was astonished at the presbyter's
discourse, and replied, "If Arius subscribes to the synod's
determination, and his views correspond with that, I will both
give him an audience, and send him back to Alexandria with
honour."   Having thus said, he immediately wrote to him in
these words :—

"VICTOR CONSTANTINE MAXIMUS AUGUSTUS, TO ARIUS.

"It was intimated to your reverence[1] some time since, that
you might come to my court, in order to your being admitted

[1] Στερρότητί σου. This is so *harsh* an *epithet*, as to make a perfect
barbarism in English, if more literally rendered.

to the enjoyment of our presence. We are not a little surprised that you did not immediately avail yourself of this permission. Wherefore having at once mounted a public vehicle,
hasten to arrive at our court ; that when you have experienced our clemency and regard for you, you may return to
your own country. May God protect you, beloved."
   This letter was dated the twenty-fifth of November. And
one cannot but be struck with the ardent zeal which this
prince manifested for religion : for it appears from this document that he had often before exhorted Arius to retract his
opinions, inasmuch as he censures his delaying to return to
the truth, although he had himself written frequently to him.
Not long after the receipt of this letter, Arius came to Constantinople accompanied by Euzoïus, whom Alexander had
divested of his deaconship when Arius and his adherents were
excommunicated. The emperor accordingly admitted them to
his presence, and asked them whether they would agree to the
Nicene creed? And when they readily gave their assent, he
ordered them to deliver to him a written statement of their
faith.

CHAP. XXVI.—ARIUS, ON BEING RECALLED, PRESENTS HIS
   RECANTATION TO THE EMPEROR, AND PRETENDS TO ACKNOW-
   LEDGE THE NICENE CREED.

   THEY having drawn up a declaration to the following
effect, presented it to the emperor.
   " Arius and Euzoïus, to our Most Religious and Pious
Lord the Emperor Constantine.
   " In accordance with the command of your devout piety,
sovereign lord, we declare our faith, and before God profess
in writing, that we and our adherents believe as follows :—
   " We believe in one God the Father Almighty : and in the
Lord Jesus Christ his Son, who was made[1] of him before all
ages, God the Word by whom all things were made which
are in the heavens and upon the earth ; who descended, became incarnate, suffered, rose again, ascended into the heavens, and will again come to judge the living and the dead.
We believe also in the Holy Spirit, in the resurrection of the
flesh, in the life of the coming age, in the kingdom of the ·

---

[1] Γεγενημένον, not γεγεννημένον, begotten.

heavens, and in one Catholic Church of God, extending over the whole earth.

"This faith we have received from the holy Gospels, the Lord therein saying to his disciples: ' Go and teach all nations, baptizing them in the name of the Father, and of the Son, and of the Holy Spirit.' If we do not so believe and truly receive the Father, the Son, and the Holy Spirit, as the whole Catholic Church and the Holy Scriptures teach, (in which we place implicit faith,) God is our judge both now, and in the coming judgment. Wherefore we beseech your piety, most devout emperor, that we who are persons consecrated to the ministry, and holding the faith and sentiments of the Church and of the Holy Scriptures, may by your pacific and devoted piety be reunited to our mother the Church, all superfluous questions and disputings being avoided : that so both we and the whole Church, being at peace, may in common offer our accustomed prayers for your tranquil reign, and on behalf of your whole family."

CHAP. XXVII.—ARIUS HAVING RETURNED TO ALEXANDRIA WITH THE EMPEROR'S CONSENT, AND NOT BEING RECEIVED BY ATHANASIUS, THE PARTISANS OF EUSEBIUS LAY MANY CHARGES BEFORE THE EMPEROR AGAINST ATHANASIUS.

ARIUS having thus satisfied the emperor, returned to Alexandria. But his artifice for suppressing the truth did not succeed ; for Athanasius would not receive him on his arrival at Alexandria, having turned away from him as a pest: he therefore attempted to excite a fresh commotion in that city by disseminating his heresy. Then indeed both Eusebius himself wrote, and prevailed on the emperor also to write, in order that Arius and his partisans might be readmitted into the Church. Athanasius nevertheless wholly refused to receive them, informing the emperor in reply, that it was impossible for those who had once rejected the faith, and had been anathematized, to be again received into communion on their return. But the emperor, provoked at this answer, menaced Athanasius in these terms: " Since you have been apprized of my will, afford unhindered access into the Church to all those who are desirous of entering it. For if it shall be intimated to me that you have prohibited any of those claiming to be reunited to the Church, or have hindered their admission, I will forthwith send some one who at my command shall depose you, and drive you into exile."

The emperor wrote thus sternly from a desire of promoting the public good, and to prevent division in the Church ; for he laboured earnestly to bring them all into unanimity. Then indeed the partisans of Eusebius, who were most malicious against Athanasius, imagining they had found a seasonable opportunity, availed themselves of the emperor's displeasure as subsidiary to their own purpose : they therefore raised a great disturbance, endeavouring to eject him from his bishopric ; for they had not the slightest hope of the prevalence of Arian doctrine, until they could effect his removal. The chief conspirators against him were Eusebius bishop of Nicomedia, Theognis of Nice, Maris of Chalcedon, Ursacius of Singidunum in Upper Mœsia, and Valens of Mursa in Upper Pannonia. These persons suborn by bribes certain of the Meletian heresy to fabricate various charges against Athanasius; and first they accuse him through the Meletians Ision, Eudæmon, and Callinicus, of having ordered the Egyptians to pay a linen garment as tribute to the Church at Alexandria. But this calumny was immediately refuted by Alypius and Macarius, presbyters of the Alexandrian Church, who then happened to be at Nicomedia ; and they convinced the emperor that these statements to the prejudice of Athanasius were false. Wherefore the emperor by letter severely censured his accusers, but desired Athanasius to come to him. The Eusebian faction, anticipating his arrival, impute to him another crime of a still more serious nature than the former ; charging Athanasius with plotting against his sovereign, and with having sent for treasonable purposes a chest full of gold to one Philumenus. When however the emperor had himself investigated this matter at Psamathia, which is in the suburbs of Nicomedia, and had found Athanasius innocent, he dismissed him with honour ; and wrote with his own hand to the Church at Alexandria to assure them that their bishop had been falsely accused. It would indeed have been both proper and desirable to have passed over in silence the subsequent attacks which the Eusebians made upon Athanasius, lest from these circumstances the

[SOCRATES.]   F

Church of Christ should be judged unfavourably of by those
who are adverse to its interests. But since, by having been
already committed to writing, they have become known to
everybody, I have on that account deemed it necessary to make
a cursory allusion to these things, the particulars of which
would require a special treatise. Whence these accusations
originated, and the character of those who devised them, I shall
now therefore compendiously state. Mareotis is a district of [50]
Alexandria, containing very many villages, and an abundant
population, with numerous splendid churches, which are all
under the jurisdiction of the bishop of Alexandria, and are
subject to his city as parishes.[1] There was in this region a
person named Ischyras,[2] who had been guilty of an act deserving of many deaths; for although he had never been admitted
to holy orders, he had the audacity to assume the title of presbyter, and to exercise the sacred functions. But having been
detected in his sacrilegious career, he made his escape thence
and sought refuge in Nicomedia, where he implored the protection of Eusebius; who from his hatred to Athanasius, not
only received him as a presbyter, but even promised to confer
upon him the dignity of the prelacy, if he would frame an accusation against Athanasius, listening as a pretext for this to
whatever stories Ischyras had invented. For he spread a report that he had suffered dreadfully from an assault made on
him by Macarius, who (he affirmed) rushing furiously toward
the altar, had overturned the table, and broken the mystical
cup: he added also that he had burnt the sacred books. As
a reward for this accusation, the Eusebian faction, as I have
said, promised him a bishopric; foreseeing that if the charges
against Macarius could be sustained, the onus would equally
fall on Athanasius, under whose orders he would seem to have
acted. But before they brought this forward, they devised
another calumny full of the bitterest malignity, to which I

---

[1] παροικίαι (παρα and οἶκος). Lat. parochia, or parœcia; and French,
paroisse; whence "parish." Upon the antiquity of the parochial system,
see Selden's History of Tithes, ch. vi. sect. 3. In early ages the terms
"parish" and "diocese" are frequently confounded, and, indeed, most
probably meant originally the same thing.

[2] Concerning the discipline exercised upon the clergy in the way of deposition from their sacred office, see Bingham's Christian Antiq. b. xviii.
chap. ii. sect. 3—5. For the subsequent history of Ischyras himself, see
below, b. ii. chap. xx.

shall now advert. Having by some means, I know not what, obtained a man's hand; whether they themselves had murdered any one, and cut off his hand, or had severed it from some dead body, God knows both the mode, and the authors of the deed: but be that as it may, they publicly exposed it, as the hand of Arsenius a Meletian bishop, though they kept the alleged owner of it concealed. This hand, they asserted, had been made use of by Athanasius in the performance of certain magic arts; and therefore it was made the gravest ground of accusation which these calumniators had concerted against him: but as it generally happens, all those who entertained any pique against Athanasius, came forward at the same time with a variety of other charges. When the emperor was informed of these proceedings, he wrote to his nephew Dalmatius the censor, who then had his residence at Antioch in Syria, directing him to order the accused parties to be brought before him, and after due investigation, to inflict punishment on such as might be convicted. He also sent thither Eusebius and Theognis, that the case might be tried in their presence. When Athanasius knew that he was to be summoned before the censor, he sent into Egypt to make a strict search after Arsenius; for he ascertained that he was secreted there, although he was unable to apprehend him, because he often changed his place of concealment. Meanwhile the emperor suppressed the trial which was to have been held before the censor, on the following account.

CHAP. XXVIII.—On account of the charges against Athanasius, the emperor directs a synod of bishops to be held at Tyre.

The emperor had ordered a synod of bishops to be present at the consecration of the church which he had erected at Jerusalem. He therefore directed that before they met there, they should on their way first assemble at Tyre, to examine into the charges against Athanasius; in order that all cause of contention being by this means removed, they might the more peacefully perform the solemnities[1] of religion in the dedication

[1] Ἐπιβατήρια. In classical authors this is the common expression de-

of the church of God. It was in the thirtieth year of Constantine's reign, that sixty bishops were thus convened at Tyre from various places on the summons of Dionysius the consul Macarius the presbyter was conducted from Alexander in chains, under a military escort. But Athanasius was indeed unwilling to go thither, not so much from a dread of the charges preferred against him, because he was conscious of his own innocence ; as that he feared lest any innovations should be made on the decisions of the council of Nice : he was however constrained to be present by the menacing letters of the emperor, in which he was told that if he did not come voluntarily, he should be brought by force.

CHAP. XXIX.—OF ARSENIUS, AND HIS HAND WHICH WAS SAID TO HAVE BEEN CUT OFF.

THE special providence of God drove Arsenius also to Tyre : for, disregarding the injunctions he had received from the accusers by whom he had been bribed, he went thither disguised, to see what would be done. It by some means happened that the servants of Archelaus, the governor of the province, heard some persons at an inn affirm, that Arsenius, who was reported to have been murdered, was at that very time concealed in the house of one of the citizens. Having marked the individuals by whom this statement was made, they communicated the circumstance to their master, who, causing strict search to be made for the man immediately, discovered and properly secured him ; after which he gave notice to Athanasius that he need not be under any alarm, inasmuch as Arsenius was alive and there present. Arsenius, on being apprehended, at first denied that he was the person supposed ; but Paul bishop of Tyre, who had formerly known him, soon established his identity. Divine providence having thus disposed matters, Athanasius was shortly after summoned by the synod : and as soon as he presented himself, his traducers exhibited the hand, and pressed their charge. Managing the affair with great prudence, he simply inquired

noting the sacrifices made on embarkation upon a voyage. It is here used metaphorically.

of those present, as well as his accusers, whether any of them knew Arsenius? and several having answered in the affirmative, he caused Arsenius to be introduced, having his hands covered by his cloak. Then he again asked them, is this the person who has lost a hand? All were astonished at the strangeness of this procedure, except those who knew whence the hand had been cut off; for the rest thought that Arsenius was really deficient of a hand, and expected that the accused would make his defence in some other way. But Athanasius turning back the cloak of Arsenius on one side shows one of the man's hands: again, while some were supposing that the other hand was wanting, after permitting them to remain a short time in doubt, he turned back the cloak on the other side and exposed the other hand. Then addressing himself to those present he said, "Arsenius, as you see, is found to have two hands: let my accusers show the place whence the third was cut off."

CHAP. XXX.—The accusers betake themselves to flight, when Athanasius is found innocent of what was first laid to his charge.

Matters having been brought to this issue with regard to Arsenius, the contrivers of this imposture were reduced to the utmost perplexity; and Achab, who was also called John, one of the principal accusers, having slipped out of court, effected his escape in the tumult. Thus Athanasius cleared himself from this charge, without having recourse to any pleading; for he was confident that the sight only of Arsenius alive would confound his calumniators.

CHAP. XXXI.—When the bishops will not admit his defence on the second charge, Athanasius flees to the emperor.

But in refuting the false allegations against Macarius, he took legal exception to Eusebius and his party, as his enemies; protesting against the inequitableness of any man's being tried by his adversaries. He next insisted on its being proved, that his accuser Ischyras had really obtained the dignity of presbyter; for so he had been designated in the indictment. But when the judges would not allow any of these objections, and the case of Macarius was entered into, on the informers being found deficient of proofs, the hearing of the matter was postponed, until some person should have gone into Mareotis, in order that they might on the spot examine into all doubtful points. Athanasius, seeing that those very individuals were to be sent to whom he had taken exception, (for the investigation was committed to Theognis, Maris, Theodorus, Macedonius, Valens, and Ursacius,) exclaimed that their procedure was both treacherous and fraudulent; for that it was unjust that the presbyter Macarius should be detained in bonds, while the accuser, together with the judges who were his adversaries, were permitted to go, in order that evidence of the facts might be obtained on one side of the question only. Having made this protest before the whole synod, and Dionysius the governor of the province, but finding his appeal wholly disregarded, he privately withdrew. Those therefore who were sent to Mareotis, having registered such circumstances only as might serve to countenance the charges of the accuser, returned to Tyre.

CHAP. XXXII.—ON THE DEPARTURE OF ATHANASIUS, THOSE WHO COMPOSED THE SYNOD VOTE HIS DEPOSITION.

ᾱ. ATHANASIUS, on his departure, hastened immediately to the emperor. But the synod meanwhile condemned him in his absence, in the first place for deserting his cause; and when the result of the inquiry which had been instituted at Mareotis was presented, they passed sentence of deposition against him; loading him with opprobrious epithets in their record of this act, but being wholly silent respecting the disgraceful defeat of his calumniators in the fictitious case of Arsenius. And having received into communion him who was reported to have been murdered, he who had formerly been a bishop of the Meletian heresy, was allowed to subscribe to the deposition of Athanasius as bishop of the city of Hypselis. Thus, by an extraordinary course of circumstances, the alleged victim of assassination by Athanasius was found alive to assist in degrading him.

CHAP. XXXIII.—THE SYNOD PROCEED FROM TYRE TO JERUSA-
LEM, AND HAVING KEPT THE FEAST OF DEDICATION OF THE
" NEW JERUSALEM," RECEIVE ARIUS AND HIS FOLLOWERS AGAIN
INTO COMMUNION.

LETTERS in the mean time were brought from the emperor directing those who composed the synod to hasten to the *New Jerusalem:*[1] having therefore immediately left Tyre, they set forward with all despatch thither, where, after completing the ceremony of the consecration of the place, they re-admitted Arius and his adherents into communion, in obedience, as they said, to the wishes of the emperor, who had signified in his communication to them, that he was fully satisfied respecting the faith of Arius and Euzoïus. They moreover wrote to the Church at Alexandria, stating that all envy being now banished, the affairs of the Church were established in peace : and that since Arius had by his recantation acknowledged the truth, it was but just that he should henceforward be received by them as a member of the Church. No other allusion was made to the deposition of Athanasius, than what was obscurely couched in their assurance that all envy was now banished. At the same time they sent information of what had been done to the emperor, in terms nearly to the same effect. But whilst the bishops were engaged in these transactions, other letters came most unexpectedly from the emperor, intimating that Athanasius had fled to him for protection ; and that it was necessary for them on his account to come to Constantinople. This unanticipated communication from the emperor was as follows :—

[1] See above, chap. xvii.

CHAP. XXXIV.—THE EMPEROR SUMMONS THE SYNOD TO HIM-
SELF BY LETTER, IN ORDER THAT THE CHARGES AGAINST
ATHANASIUS MIGHT BE MINUTELY INVESTIGATED BEFORE HIM.

" VICTOR Constantine Maximus Augustus, to the bishops
convened at Tyre.

" I am indeed ignorant of the decisions which have been
made by your Council with so much turbulence and commotion :
but the truth seems to have been perverted by some tumultuous
and disorderly proceedings ; while, in your mutual love of contention, which you seem desirous of perpetuating, you disregard the consideration of those things which are acceptable to
God.   It will however, I trust, be the work of Divine Providence to utterly dissipate the mischiefs resulting from this spirit
of jealous rivalry, as soon as they shall have been clearly
detected ; and to make it apparent to us, how much regard ye
who have been convened have had to truth, and whether
your decisions on the subjects which have been submitted to
your judgment have been made apart from partiality or prejudice.   Wherefore it is indispensable that you should all
without delay attend upon my Piety,[1] that you may yourselves
give a strict account of your transactions.   The reasons
which have induced me to write thus, and to summon you
before me, you will learn from what follows.   As I was making my entry on horseback into the city which bears our
name, in this our most flourishing country, suddenly the Bishop
Athanasius, with certain ecclesiastics whom he had around him,
presented himself so unexpectedly in our path, as to produce
a degree of consternation.   For the Omniscient Being is my
witness, that at first sight I did not recognise him, until some
of my attendants, in answer to my inquiry, informed me very
properly both who he was, and what injustice he had suffered.
At that time indeed I neither conversed nor held any communication with him : but when he entreated an audience,
and I had not only refused it, but even ordered that he should
be removed from my presence, he said with greater boldness,
that he petitioned for nothing more than that you might be

---

[1] πρὸς τὴν ἐμὴν εὐσεβείαν. The term denotes merely a title of courtesy, like " his Grace," " his Majesty," in English.

summoned hither, in order that in our presence, he, driven
by necessity to such a course, might have a fair opportunity
afforded him of deprecating his wrongs. This request seemed
so reasonable, and so consistent with the equity of my government, that I willingly gave instructions for writing these things
to you.   My command therefore is, that all, as many as composed the synod convened at Tyre, should forthwith hasten to
the Court of our Piety, in order that from the facts themselves
the purity and integrity of your decision may be made apparent in my presence, whom you cannot but own to be a true
servant of God.   It is in consequence of the acts of my religious service towards the Deity that peace is everywhere
reigning; and that the name of God is devoutly had in reverence even among the barbarians themselves, who until
now were ignorant of the gospel.   Now it is evident that he
who knows not the truth cannot possibly acknowledge God:
yet, as I before said, even the barbarians on my account, who
am a faithful servant of God, have acknowledged and learned
to worship him, by whose provident care they perceive that I
am everywhere protected.   So that from dread of us chiefly,
they have been thus brought to the knowledge of the true
God, whom they now worship. Nevertheless, we who pretend
to have a religious veneration for (I will not say who guard)
the holy mysteries of his Church, we, I say, do little else
than what tends to discord and animosity, and to speak
plainly, to the destruction of the human race.   Come therefore
all of you to us as speedily as possible: and be assured that
I shall endeavour with all my power to cause that what is
contained in the Divine Law may be preserved inviolate, on
which neither stigma nor reproach shall be able to be affixed.
This however can only be effected by dispersing, crushing to ·
pieces, and utterly destroying its enemies, who under covert
of the sacred profession introduce numerous and diversified
blasphemies."

CHAP. XXXV.—THE SYNOD NOT HAVING COME TO THE EM-
PEROR, THE PARTISANS OF EUSEBIUS ACCUSE ATHANASIUS OF
HAVING THREATENED TO WITHHOLD THE CORN WHICH IS
SUPPLIED TO CONSTANTINOPLE FROM ALEXANDRIA: ON WHICH
ACCOUNT THE EMPEROR, BEING EXASPERATED, SENDS ATHA-
NASIUS AWAY INTO EXILE, ORDERING HIM TO REMAIN IN THE
GALLIAS.[1]

THIS letter created so much alarm in the minds of those
who constituted the synod, that most of them, instead of obey-
ing the emperor, returned to their respective cities. But Eusebius, Theognis, Maris, Patrophilus, Ursacius, and Valens,
having gone to Constantinople, would not permit any
further inquiry to be instituted concerning the broken cup,
the overturned communion table, and the murder of Arsenius;
but they had recourse to another calumny, informing the emperor that Athanasius had threatened to prohibit the sending
of the corn which was usually conveyed from Alexandria to
Constantinople. They affirmed also that these menaces were
uttered by Athanasius in the hearing of the bishops Adamantius, Anubion, Arbathion, and Peter: for slander is most prevalent when the assertor of it appears to be a person worthy
of credit. The emperor being deceived and excited to indignation against Athanasius by this charge, at once condemned
him to exile, ordering him to reside in the Gallias.[2] Some
affirm that the emperor came to this decision with a view to
the establishment of unity in the Church, since Athanasius was
inexorable in his refusal to hold any communion with Arius
and his adherents. He accordingly took up his abode at
Treves, a city of Gaul.[3]

[1] Comp. Theodoret, b. i. ch. xxxi.
[2] The ancient Gallia included considerably more than what is now
known by the name of France. Besides France itself, it contained all
that which is now included in Belgium, as well as Lombardy and the
kingdom of Sardinia: it was divided into three parts, Belgica, Gallia
Cisalpina, and Transalpina.
[3] See Theodoret, b. i. ch. xxxi.

CHAP. XXXVI.—Of MARCELLUS BISHOP OF ANCYRA, AND
ASTERIUS THE SOPHIST.

THE bishops assembled at Constantinople deposed also Marcellus bishop of Ancyra, a city of Galatia Minor, on this account.   A certain rhetorician of Cappadocia named Asterius
having abandoned his art, and professed himself a convert to
Christianity, undertook the composition of some treatises,
which are still extant, in which he maintained the dogmas of
Arius : asserting that Christ is the power of God, in the same
sense that the locust and the palmer-worm are said by Moses
to be the power of God, with other similar blasphemies.   This
man was in constant association with the bishops, and especially
with those of their number who did not discountenance the
Arian doctrine : he also frequently attended their synods, in
the hope of insinuating himself into the bishopric of some
city : but he failed even to obtain ordination, in consequence
of having sacrificed during the persecution.[1]   Going therefore throughout the cities of Syria, he read in public the books
which he had composed.   Marcellus being informed of this,
and wishing to counteract his influence, in his over-anxiety to
confute him, fell into the opposite error ; for he dared to say,
as Paul of Samosata had done, that Christ was a mere man.
When the bishops then convened at Jerusalem had intelligence
of these things, they took no notice of Asterius, because he
was not enrolled in the catalogue of those who had been admitted to holy orders ; but they insisted that Marcellus, as a
priest, should give an account of the book which he had written.   Finding that he entertained Paul of Samosata's sentiments, they required him to retract his opinion ; and he being
ashamed of the position into which he had brought himself,
promised to burn his book.   But the convention of bishops
being hastily dissolved by the emperor's summoning them to
Constantinople, the Eusebians, on their arrival at that city,

---

[1] As to the punishment inflicted upon the clergy and laity who "lapsed,"
that is to say, who sacrificed to idols, during the persecutions of the early
Church, see Bingham's Christian Antiq. b. xvi. ch. iv., and compare the
canons of the Council of Ancyra, (A. D. 315,) Nos. 1—9. A great distinction was always made by the Church between those who sacrificed by
actual compulsion and those who did so through mere fear. See St. Cyprian, Ep. 55, (al. 52,) ad Antonian, p. 106.

again took the case of Marcellus into consideration; and on his refusal to fulfil his promise of burning his impious book, the assembled bishops deposed him, and sent Basil into Ancyra in his stead. Moreover Eusebius wrote a refutation of this work in three books, in which he fully exposed its erroneous doctrine. Marcellus however was afterwards reinstated in his bishopric by the synod at Sardis, on his assurance that his book had been misunderstood, and that therefore he was supposed to favour Paul of Samosata's views. But of this we shall speak more fully in its proper place.

CHAP. XXXVII.—After the banishment of Athanasius, Arius, having been sent for from Alexandria by the emperor, excites commotions against Alexander bishop of Constantinople.

While these things were taking place, the thirtieth year of Constantine's reign was completed. But Arius and his adherents having returned to Alexandria, again caused a general disturbance; for the people were exceedingly indignant, both at the restoration of this incorrigible heretic with his partisans, and also at the exile of their bishop Athanasius. When the emperor was apprized of the perverse disposition and conduct of Arius, he once more ordered him to repair to Constantinople, to give an account of the commotions he had afresh endeavoured to excite. The Church at Constantinople was then presided over by Alexander, who had some time before succeeded Metrophanes. That this prelate was a man of devoted piety was distinctly manifested by the conflict upon which he entered with Arius; upon whose arrival the whole city was thrown into confusion by the renewal of factious divisions: some insisting that the Nicene creed should be by no means infringed on, while others contended that the opinion of Arius was consonant to reason. In this distracted state of affairs, Alexander felt most painfully the difficulties of his position: more especially since Eusebius of Nicomedia had violently threatened that he would cause him to be immediately deposed, unless he admitted Arius and his followers to communion. Alexander however was far less troubled at the thought of his own degradation, than fearful of the subversion of the principles of the faith, which they were so anxious to effect : and regarding himself as the constituted guardian of the doctrines recognised and the decisions made by the council at Nice, he exerted himself to the utmost to prevent their being violated or depraved.   Reduced to the last extremity, he bade farewell to all logical resources, and made God his refuge, devoting himself to continued fasting and prayer. Communicating his purpose to no one, he shut himself up alone in the church called Irene : there going up to the altar, and prostrating himself on the ground beneath the holy communion table, he poured forth his fervent intercessions mingled with tears ; and this he ceased not to do for several successive nights and days.   What he thus earnestly asked from God, he received : for his petition was, that if the opinion of Arius were correct, he might not be permitted to see the day appointed for its discussion ; but that if he himself held the true faith, Arius, as the author of all these evils, might suffer the punishment due to his impiety.

CHAP. XXXVIII.—THE DEATH OF ARIUS.

SUCH was the supplication of Alexander.   Meanwhile the emperor, being desirous of personally examining Arius, sent for him to the palace, and asked him whether he would assent to the determinations of the Nicene synod.   He without hesitation replied in the affirmative, and subscribed the declaration of the faith in the emperor's presence, acting with duplicity all the while. The emperor, surprised at his ready compliance, obliged him to confirm his signature by an oath.   This also he did with equal promptitude and dissimulation : for it is affirmed that he wrote his own opinion on paper, and placed it under his arm, so that he then swore truly to his really holding the sentiments he had written.   It must however be owned that this statement of his having so acted is grounded on hearsay alone ; but that he added an oath to his subscription, I have myself ascertained, from an examination of the emperor's own letters.   The emperor being thus convinced, ordered that he should be received into communion by Alex-

ander bishop of Constantinople. It was then Saturday,[1] and
Arius was expecting to assemble with the church on the day
following: but Divine retribution overtook his daring crimin-
alities. For going out of the imperial palace, attended by a
crowd of Eusebian partisans like guards, he paraded proudly
through the midst of the city, attracting the notice of all the
people. On approaching the place called Constantine's Forum,
where the column of porphyry is erected, a terror arising
from the consciousness of his wickedness seized him, accompanied by violent relaxation of the bowels : he therefore inquired whether there was a convenient place near, and being
directed to the back of Constantine's Forum, he hastened
thither. Soon after a faintness came over him, and together
with the evacuations his bowels protruded, followed by a
copious hæmorrhage, and the descent of the smaller intes-
tines: moreover portions of his spleen and liver were brought
off in the effusion of blood, so that he almost immediately
died. The scene of this catastrophe still exists at Constantinople, behind the shambles in the piazza, in the situation already described : and by persons going by pointing the finger
at the place, there is a perpetual remembrance preserved of
this extraordinary kind of death. So disastrous an occurrence
filled with dread and alarm the party of Eusebius bishop of
Nicomedia ; and the report of it quickly spread itself over the
city and throughout the whole world. The verity of the
Nicene faith being thus miraculously confirmed by the testimony of God himself, the emperor adhered still more zealously
to Christianity. He was also glad at what had happened, not
only because of its effect on the Church, but on account of the
influence such an event was calculated to have on the minds of
his three sons, whom he had already proclaimed Cæsars ;[1] one
of each of them having been created at every successive De-
cennalia of his reign. To the eldest, whom he called Constantine, after his own name, he assigned the government of

---

[1] Σαββάτου ἡμέρα. On the observance of Saturday, the old Jewish
sabbath in the early Christian Church, as a weekly festival in the Eastern
Church, and as a fast in the greater part of the Western Church, consult
Bingham's Christian Antiq. b. xx. ch. iii.   See also No. 66 of the Apostolical Canons.

[2] See above, note on ch. ii., and Gibbon's Decl. and Fall, ch. xiii.

the Western parts of the empire, on the completion of his first decade.   His second son, Constantius, who bore his grandfather's name, was constituted Cæsar in the Eastern division, when the second decade had been completed.   And Constans, the youngest, was invested with a similar dignity, when his father had reached the thirtieth year of his empire.

CHAP. XXXIX.—THE EMPEROR, HAVING FALLEN INTO
DISEASE, DIES.

IN the following year, the emperor Constantine, having just entered the sixty-fifth year of his age, was attacked with a dangerous malady ; he therefore left Constantinople, and made a voyage to Helenopolis, that he might try the effect of the medicinal hot springs which are found in the vicinity of that city.   Perceiving however that his illness increased, he deferred the use of the baths ; and removing from Helenopolis to Nicomedia, he took up his residence in the suburbs, and there received Christian baptism.[1] After this he became cheerful and resigned ; and making his will, appointed his three sons heirs to the empire, allotting to each one of them his portion, in accordance with his previous arrangements.   He also granted many privileges to the cities of Rome and Constantinople ; and intrusting the custody of his will to that presbyter by whose means Arius had been recalled, and of whom mention has been already made, he charged him to deliver it into no one's hand, except that of his son Constantius, to whom he had given the sovereignty of the East.   He survived but a few days after the execution of this document, and died in the absence of all his sons.   A courier was therefore immediately despatched into the East, to inform Constantius of his father's decease.

[1] Upon the common practice of deferring baptism to a death-bed, called clinical baptism, together with the reasons for its frequent adoption, and the disabilities which it involved in case of subsequent recovery, see Bingham's Eccl. Antiq. iv. 3, and xi. 11.   Compare also the case of Theodosius mentioned below, b. v. ch. vi.

CHAP. XL.—THE FUNERAL OBSEQUIES OF THE EMPEROR CONSTANTINE.

THE body of the emperor was placed in a coffin of gold, and then conveyed to Constantinople, where it was laid out on an elevated bed of state in the palace, surrounded by a guard, and treated with the same respect as when he was alive, until the arrival of one of his sons. When Constantius was come out of the eastern parts of the empire, it was honoured with an imperial sepulture, and deposited in the church called that of *The Apostles:* for therein he had caused magnificent tombs to be constructed for the emperors and prelates, in order that they might receive a degree of veneration but little inferior to that which was paid to the relics of the apostles. The emperor Constantine lived sixty-five years, and reigned thirty-one. He died in the consulate of Felician and Titian, on the twenty-second of May, in the second year of the 278th Olympiad. This book therefore embraces a period of thirty-one years.

BOOK II.

CHAP. I.—THE PREFACE, IN WHICH THE REASON IS ASSIGNED FOR THE AUTHOR'S REVISION OF HIS FIRST AND SECOND BOOKS.

RUFINUS,[1] who wrote an Ecclesiastical History in Latin, has committed many chronological errors. For he supposes that what was done against Athanasius occurred after the death of the emperor Constantine: he was also ignorant of his exile to the Gallias, and of various other circumstances. We originally wrote the first two books of our History from the testimony of this author; but from the third to the seventh, some facts have been collected from Rufinus,

[1] See note on b. i. ch. xii., sub fin., and Life of Socrates prefixed to this volume.

others from different authors, and the rest from the narration of individuals still surviving. When however we had perused the writings of Athanasius, wherein he depicts his own sufferings and exile through the calumnies of the Eusebian faction, we judged that more credit was due to him who had suffered, and to those who were witnesses of the things they describe, than to such as have been dependent on conjecture, and were therefore liable to err. Moreover, having obtained several letters of persons eminent at that period, we have availed ourselves of their assistance also in tracing out the truth. On this account it became necessary to revise the first and second Book of this History, without however discarding the testimony of Rufinus where it is evident that he could not be mistaken. It should also be observed, that in our former edition, neither the sentence of deposition which was passed upon Arius, nor the emperor's letters, were inserted ; having restricted myself to a simple narration of facts, to avoid wearying the reader with tedious matters of detail. But in the present edition, such alterations and additions have been made for your sake, O sacred man of God, Theodore,[1] as might serve to make you fully acquainted with the emperors' proceedings by their letters, as well as the decisions of the bishops in their various synods, wherein they continually altered the confession of faith. Having adopted this course in the first Book, we shall endeavour to do the same in the consecutive portion of our History on which we are about to enter.

CHAP. II.—Eusebius bishop of Nicomedia and his party, by again endeavouring to introduce the Arian heresy, create disturbances in the churches.

AFTER the death of the emperor Constantine, Eusebius bishop of Nicomedia, and Theognis of Nice, imagining that a favourable opportunity had arisen, used their utmost efforts to abolish the doctrine[2] of *Consubstantiality*, and to introduce Arianism. They nevertheless despaired of effecting this, if Athanasius should return to Alexandria : in order therefore

---

[1] See below, Preface to b. vi., and the concluding words of b. vii.

[2] Ὁμοουσίου πίστιν. See below, ch. xvi.

[SOCRATES.]   G

to accomplish their designs, they sought the assistance of that presbyter by whose means Arius had been recalled from exile a little before. Their plan of operation shall now be described. The presbyter in question having been intrusted with Constantine's will at that emperor's death, presented it to his son Constantius; who finding those dispositions in it which he was most desirous of, for the empire of the East was by his father's will apportioned to him, treated the presbyter with great consideration, loaded him with favours, and ordered that free access should be given him both to the palace and to himself. This licence soon obtained for him familiar intercourse with the empress, as well as with her eunuchs. The chief eunuch of the imperial bed-chamber at that time was named Eusebius, who, under the influence of the presbyter, was induced to embrace the Arian doctrine; after which the rest of the eunuchs were also prevailed on to adopt the same sentiments. Through the combined persuasives of these eunuchs and the presbyter, the empress became favourable to the tenets of Arius; and not long after the subject was introduced to the emperor himself. Thus it became gradually diffused throughout the court, and among the officers of the imperial household and guards, until at length it spread itself over the whole population of the city. The chamberlains in the palace discussed this doctrine with the women; and in the family of every citizen there was a war of dialectics. Moreover the mischief quickly extended to other provinces and cities, the controversy, like a spark, insignificant at first, exciting in the auditors a spirit of contention: for every one who inquired the cause of the tumult, found an immediate occasion for disputing, and determined to take part in the strife at the moment of making the inquiry. By general altercation of this kind all order was subverted: the agitation however was confined to the cities of the East, those of Illyricum and the western parts of the empire meanwhile being perfectly tranquil, because they would not annul the decisions of the council of Nice. As this disorderly state of things continued to increase, Eusebius of Nicomedia and his party calculated on profiting by the popular ferment, so as to be enabled to constitute some one who held their own sentiments bishop of Alexandria. But the return of Athanasius at that time defeated their purpose, for he came thither fortified by a letter

³³ from one of the Augusti, which the younger Constantine, who bore his father's name, addressed to the people of Alexandria, from Treves, a city in Gaul. A copy of this epistle is here subjoined.

CHAP. III.—ATHANASIUS, CONFIDING IN THE LETTER OF CON- · STANTINE THE YOUNGER, RETURNS TO ALEXANDRIA.

" CONSTANTINE Cæsar to the members of the Catholic Church of the Alexandrians.

" It cannot, I conceive, have escaped the knowledge of your devout minds, that Athanasius, the expositor of.the venerated law, was sent for a while into the Gallias, lest he should sustain some irreparable injury from the perverseness of his blood-thirsty adversaries, whose ferocity continually endangered his sacred life. To rescue him therefore from the hands of those who sought to destroy him, he was sent into a city under my jurisdiction, where, as long as it was his appointed residence, he has been abundantly supplied with every necessary : although his distinguished virtue, sustained by Divine aid, would have made light of the pressure of a more rigorous fortune. And since our sovereign, my father, Constantine Augustus of blessed memory, was prevented by death from accomplishing his purpose of restoring this bishop to his see, and to your most sanctified piety, it devolves on me, his heir, to carry his wishes into effect. With how great veneration he has been regarded by us, ye will learn on his arrival among you :. nor need any one be surprised at the honour I have put upon him, since I have been alike influenced by a sense of what was due to so excellent a personage, and the knowledge of your affectionate solicitude respecting him. May Divine Providence preserve you, beloved brethren."

Relying on this letter, Athanasius came to Alexandria, and was most joyfully received by the people. Nevertheless, as many as had embraced Arianism, combining together, entered into a conspiracy against him : by which means frequent seditions were excited, affording a pretext to the Eusebians for accusing him to the emperor of having taken possession of the Alexandrian Church on his own responsibility, without the permission of a general council of bishops. So far indeed

did they succeed in pressing their charges, that the emperor
became exasperated against him, and banished him from
Alexandria. How his enemies managed to effect this I shall
hereafter explain.

CHAP. IV.—ON THE DEATH OF EUSEBIUS PAMPHILUS, ACACIUS SUCCEEDS TO THE BISHOPRIC OF CÆSAREA.

AT this time Eusebius, who was bishop of Cæsarea in
Palestine, and had the surname of Pamphilus, having died,
his disciple Acacius succeeded him in the bishopric. This
individual published several books, and among others a bio-
graphical sketch of his master.

CHAP. V.—THE DEATH OF CONSTANTINE THE YOUNGER.

NOT long after this the brother of the emperor Constantius,
Constantine the younger, who bore his father's name, having
invaded those parts of the empire which were under the government of his younger brother Constans,[1] was slain in a conflict with his brother's soldiery. This took place under the
consulship of Acindynus and Proclus.

CHAP. VI.—ALEXANDER BISHOP OF CONSTANTINOPLE, AT HIS DEATH, PROPOSES THE ELECTION EITHER OF PAUL OR MACE-DONIUS AS HIS SUCCESSOR.

ABOUT the same time, another disturbance in addition to
those we have recorded, was raised at Constantinople on the
following account. Alexander, who had presided over the
churches in that city for twenty-three years, and had strenuously opposed Arius, departed this life at the age of ninety-
eight, without having ordained any one to succeed him. But
he had enjoined those in whose hands the elective power was,
to choose one of the two whom he named : telling them that
if they desired one who was competent to teach, and of eminent

[1] See Gibbon's Decline and Fall, ch. xviii.

piety, they must elect Paul, whom he had himself ordained presbyter, a man young indeed in years, but of advanced intelligence and prudence ; but if they would be content with one possessed of a venerable aspect, and an external show only of sanctity, they might appoint the aged Macedonius, who had long been a deacon among them.   Hence there arose a great contest respecting the choice of a bishop, which troubled the Church exceedingly ; the people being divided into two parties, one of which favoured the tenets of Arius, while the other adhered to the decrees of the Nicene synod. Those who held the doctrine of consubstantiality always had the advantage during the life of Alexander, the Arians disagreeing among themselves and perpetually conflicting in opinion.   But after the death of that prelate, the issue of the struggle became doubtful, the defenders of the orthodox faith insisting on the ordination of Paul, and all the Arian party espousing the cause of Macedonius.   Paul however was ⁵⁵ ordained bishop in the church called Irene, which is situated near the great church of Sophia ;¹ which election was undoubtedly sanctioned by the suffrage of the deceased Alexander.

CHAP. VII.—The emperor Constantius ejects Paul after his election to the prelacy, and sending for Eusebius of Nicomedia, invests him with the bishopric of Constantinople.

The emperor having arrived at Constantinople shortly after, was highly incensed at the consecration of Paul; and having convened an assembly of the bishops of Arian sentiments, he divested Paul of his dignity, translating Eusebius from the see of Nicomedia to the now vacant one of Constantinople.   This being done, the emperor proceeded to Antioch.

CHAP. VIII.—Eusebius having convened another synod at Antioch in Syria, causes a new form of faith to be promulgated.

Eusebius however could by no means remain quiet, but, as the saying is, *left no stone unturned,* in order to effect the pur-

¹ Σοφίας, wisdom.   See below, note on ch. xvi.

pose he had in view.   He therefore causes a synod [1] to be convened at Antioch in Syria, under pretence of dedicating a
church which Constantine, the father of the Augusti, had commenced, and which had been completed by his son Constantius
in the tenth year after its foundations were laid : but his real
motive was the subversion of the doctrine of consubstantiality.
There were present at this synod ninety bishops from various
cities.   Nevertheless Maximus bishop of Jerusalem, who had
succeeded Macarius, declined attending there, from the recollection of the fraudulent means by which he had been induced
to subscribe the deposition of Athanasius.   Neither was
Julius bishop of Ancient [2] Rome there, nor did he indeed send
a representative ; although the ecclesiastical canon expressly
commands that the Churches shall not make any ordinances,
without the sanction of the bishop of Rome.[3]   This synod
assembled at Antioch, in the consulate of Marcellus and Pro-
binus, which was the fifth year after the death of Constantine,
father of the Augusti, the emperor Constantius being present.
Placitus, otherwise called Flaccillus, successor to Euphronius,
at that time presided over the Church at Antioch.   The confederates of Eusebius were chiefly intent on calumniating Athanasius ; accusing him in the first place of having acted contrary to a canon which they then constituted, in resuming his
episcopal authority without the licence of a general council of
bishops, inasmuch as on his return from exile he had on his
own responsibility taken possession of the Church.   In the
next place, that a tumult having been excited on his entrance,
many were killed in the riot : and that some had been scourged
by him, and others brought before the tribunals.   Besides, they
failed not to bring forward what had been determined against
Athanasius at Tyre.

[1] For the reasons why the decisions of this synod were invalid, see below, ch. xvii.
[2] So called in opposition to the city of Constantinople, which was
called New Rome, as being the place to which Constantine endeavoured
to transfer the seat of supreme government.   See Council of Chalcedon,
Canon xxviii.
[3] No such canon as that referred to here by Socrates is known to be in
existence as a written document; and consequently our author must be
understood to refer here to a principle, or unwritten law, existing, and universally acknowledged as existing, prior to all positive enactment on the
subject.

CHAP. IX.—OF EUSEBIUS EMISENUS.

ON the ground of such charges as these, they proposed another bishop for the Alexandrian Church, and first indeed Eusebius surnamed Emisenus. Who this person was, George bishop of Laodicea, who was present on this occasion, informs us. For he says, in the book which he has composed on his life, that he was descended from a noble family of Edessa in "Mesopotamia, and that from a child he had studied the Holy Scriptures; that he was afterwards instructed in Greek literature by a master resident at Edessa; and finally, that the sacred books were expounded to him by Patrophilus and Eusebius, the latter of whom presided over the Church at Cæsarea, and the former over that at Scythopolis. Having afterwards gone to Antioch, about the time that Eustathius was deposed on the accusation of Cyrus of Bercœa for holding the tenets of Sabellius, he lived on terms of familiar intercourse with Euphronius, that prelate's successor. When however a bishopric was offered him, he retired to Alexandria to avoid the intended honour, and there devoted himself to the study of philosophy. On his return to Antioch, he formed an intimate acquaintance with Placitus or Flaccillus, the successor of Euphronius. At length he was ordained bishop of Alexandria, by Eusebius bishop of Constantinople, but did not go thither in consequence of the attachment of the people of that city to Athanasius. He was therefore sent to Emisa, where the inhabitants excited a sedition on account of his appointment, for they reproached him with the study and practice of judicial astrology; whereupon he fled to Laodicea, and abode with George, who has given so many historical details of him. George, having taken him to Antioch, procured his being again brought back to Emisa by Flaccillus and Narcissus; but he was afterwards charged with holding the Sabellian heresy. His ordination is elaborately described by the same writer, who adds at the close that the emperor took him with him in his expedition against the barbarians, and that miracles were wrought by his hand.

CHAP. X.—THE BISHOPS ASSEMBLED AT ANTIOCH, ON THE
REFUSAL OF EUSEBIUS EMISENUS TO ACCEPT THE BISHOPRIC
OF ALEXANDRIA, ORDAIN GREGORY, AND CHANGE THE EX-
PRESSION OF THE NICENE CREED.

WHEN Eusebius durst not go to Alexandria, to the see of
which he had been appointed by the synod at Antioch, Gregory was designated bishop of that Church. This being done,
they alter the creed ; not as condemning anything in that
which was set forth at Nice, but in fact with a determination
to subvert the doctrine of consubstantiality by means of frequent councils, and the publication of various expositions of
the faith, so as gradually to establish the Arian views.   The
course of our history will unfold the measures to which they
resorted for the accomplishment of their purpose ; but the
epistle then circulated respecting the faith was as follows :—
   " We have neither become followers of Arius, for it would
be absurd to suppose that we who are bishops should be
guided by a presbyter ; nor have we embraced any other faith
than that which was set forth from the beginning. But being
constituted examiners and judges of his sentiments, we admit
their soundness, rather than adopt them from him : this you
will readily perceive from what we are about to state.   We
have learned from the beginning to believe in one God of the
Universe, the Creator and Preserver of all things both intelligent and sensible : and in one only-begotten Son of God, subsisting before all ages, and co-existing with the Father who
begat him, by whom also all things visible and invisible were
made ; who in the last days, according to the Father's good
pleasure, descended, and assumed flesh from the holy virgin,
and having fully accomplished his Father's will, suffered, was
raised, ascended into the heavens, and sits at the right hand
of the Father ; and is coming to judge the living and the dead,
continuing King and God for ever.   We believe also in the
Holy Spirit.   And if it is necessary to add this, we believe
in the resurrection of the flesh, and the life everlasting."
   Having thus written in their first epistle, they sent it to
the bishops of every city.   But after remaining some time at
Antioch, they published another letter in these words, as if
to condemn the former.

ANOTHER EXPOSITION OF THE FAITH.

" In conformity with evangelic and apostolic tradition, we believe in one God the Father Almighty, the Creator and Framer of the universe.   And in one Lord Jesus Christ, his Son, God the only-begotten, by whom all things were made : begotten of the Father before all ages, God of God, Whole of Whole, Only of Only, Perfect of Perfect, King of King, Lord of Lord ; the living Word, the Wisdom, the Life, the True Light, the Way of Truth, the Resurrection, the Shepherd, the Gate ; immutable and inconvertible ; the unalterable image of the Divinity, Substance, Power, Counsel, and Glory of the Father ; born before all creation ; who was in the beginning with God, God the Word, according as it is declared in the Gospel, (John i. 1,) and the Word was God, by whom all things were made, and in whom all things have subsisted : who in the last days came down from above, and was born of the virgin according to the Scriptures ; and was made man, the Mediator between God and men, the Apostle of our Faith, and the Prince of Life, as he says, (John vi. 38,) 'I came down from heaven, not to do mine own will, but the will of him that sent me.'   Who suffered on our behalf, rose again for us on the third day, ascended into the heavens, and is seated at the right hand of the Father ; and will come again with glory and power to judge the living and the dead.   We believe also in the Holy Spirit, who is given to believers for their consolation, sanctification, and perfection ; even as our Lord Jesus Christ commanded his disciples, saying, (Matt. xxviii. 19,) ' Go and teach all nations, baptizing them in the name of the Father, and of the Son, and of the Holy Spirit ;' that is to say, of the Father who is truly the Father, of the Son who is truly the Son, and of the Holy Spirit who is truly the Holy Spirit, these epithets not being simply or insignificantly applied, but accurately expressing the proper person,[1] glory, and order of each of these who are named : so that there are three in person, but one in concordance.   Holding therefore this faith in the presence of God and of Christ, we anathematize all heretical and false doctrine.   And if. any one shall teach contrary to the sound and right faith of the Scriptures, affirming that there is or was a period or an age before the Son

[1] Ἰδίαν ὑπόστασιν.   See above, note on b. i. ch. v.

of God existed, let him be accursed. And if any one shall say that the Son is a creature as one of the creatures, or that he is *a branch*[1] as one of the *branches*, and shall not hold each of the aforesaid doctrines as the Divine Scriptures have delivered them to us; or if any one shall teach or preach any other doctrine contrary to that which we have received, let him be accursed. For we truly believe and follow all things handed down to us from the sacred Scriptures by the prophets and apostles."

Such was the exposition of the faith published by those then assembled at Antioch, to which Gregory subscribed as bishop of Alexandria, although he had not yet entered that city. The synod having done these things, and framed some other canons, was dissolved. At the same time also it happened that public affairs were disturbed, both by the incursion of the nation called Franks into the Roman territories in Gaul, as well as by most violent earthquakes in the East, but especially at Antioch, which continued to suffer concussions during a whole year.

CHAP. XI.—ON THE ARRIVAL OF GREGORY AT ALEXANDRIA, GUARDED BY A MILITARY FORCE, ATHANASIUS FLEES.

AFTER these things, Syrian, a military commander, conducted Gregory to Alexandria under an escort of 5000 heavy-armed soldiers; and such of the citizens as were of Arian sentiments combined with them. But it will be proper here to relate by what means Athanasius escaped the hands of those who wished to apprehend him, after his expulsion from the church. It was evening, and the people were congregated there, a service[2] being expected, when the commander arrived, and posted his forces in order of battle on every side of the church. Athanasius having observed what was done, considered with himself how he might prevent the people's suffering in any degree on his account: he accordingly directed the deacon to give notice of prayer, and after that ordered the recitation of a psalm; and when the melodious chant of the psalm arose, all went out through one of the church doors.

[1] Γέννημα, literally a thing begotten, offspring.
[2] Συνάξεως, literally a congregation or gathering, from συνάγω.

While this was doing, the troops remained inactive spectators, and Athanasius thus escaped unhurt in the midst of those who were chanting the psalm, and immediately hastened to Rome. Gregory was then installed in the church: but the people of Alexandria being indignant at this procedure, set the church called that of Dionysius on fire.   Eusebius having thus far [57] obtained his object, sent a deputation. to Julius bishop of Rome, begging that he would himself take cognizance of the charges against Athanasius, and order a judicial investigation to be made in his presence.[1]

CHAP. XII.—THE PEOPLE OF CONSTANTINOPLE RESTORE PAUL TO HIS SEE AFTER THE DEATH OF EUSEBIUS, WHILE THE ARIANS ELECT MACEDONIUS.

But Eusebius was prevented from knowing the decision of Julius concerning Athanasius, for he died a short time after that synod was held.   Whereupon the people introduce Paul again into the Church of Constantinople: the Arians however ordain Macedonius at the same time, in the church dedicated to Paul. This was done by those who had formerly lent their aid to Eusebius, (that disturber of the public peace,) but who then had assumed all his authority: viz. Theognis bishop of Nice, Maris of Chalcedon, Theodore of Heraclea in Thrace, Ursacius of Singidunum in Upper Mysia, and Valens of Mursa in Upper Pannonia.   Ursacius and Valens indeed afterward altered their opinions, and presented a written recantation of them to Bishop Julius,[2] so that on subscribing the doctrine of consubstantiality they were again admitted to communion: but at that time they warmly supported the Arian error, and were instigators of the most violent commotions in the Churches, one of which was connected with Macedonius at Constantinople.   By this intestine war among the Christians, that city was kept in a state of perpetual turbulence, and the most atrocious outrages were perpetrated, whereby many lives were sacrificed.

[1] Upon the ancient recognised prerogatives of the Roman see, their extent and limit, consult Hammond's Canons of the Church, notes on the Canons of Nicæa.   [2] See note on preceding chapter.

CHAP. XIII.—PAUL IS AGAIN EJECTED FROM THE CHURCH BY
CONSTANTIUS, IN CONSEQUENCE OF THE SLAUGHTER OF HER-
MOGENES HIS GENERAL.

WHEN intelligence of these proceedings reached the emperor Constantius, whose residence was then at Antioch, he
ordered his general Hermogenes, who had been despatched to
Thrace, to pass through Constantinople on his way, and expel
Paul from the Church. He accordingly went to Constantinople, but in endeavouring to execute his commission, threw the
whole city into confusion; for the people, in their eagerness
to defend the bishop, were reckless of all subordination. And
when Hermogenes persisted in his efforts to drive out Paul by
means of his military force, the people became exasperated as
is usual in such cases; and making a desperate attack upon
him, they set his house on fire, and after dragging him by the
feet through the city, they at last put him to death. This took
place in the consulate of the two Augusti, Constantius being
a third, and Constans a second time consul: at which time the
latter having subdued the Franks, admitted them to an allied
confederacy with the Romans. The emperor Constantius, on
being informed of the assassination of Hermogenes, set off on
horseback from Antioch, and arriving at Constantinople he
immediately expelled Paul, and then punished the inhabitants
by withdrawing from them more than 40,000 measures of the
daily allowance of wheat which his father had granted for
gratuitous distribution among them: for prior to this catastrophe, nearly 80,000 measures[1] of wheat brought from Alexandria had been bestowed on the citizens. He hesitated however to ratify[2] the appointment of Macedonius to the bishopric
of that city, being irritated against him not only because he
had been ordained without his consent; but also on account of
the contests in which he had been engaged with Paul, which
had eventually caused the death of Hermogenes his general,
and that of many other persons. But having given him permission to assemble the people in the church in which he had
been consecrated, he returned to Antioch.

[1] Σιτηρεσίου . . . ἡμερησίου, rations of bread.
[2] Upon the control which the emperor occasionally held in this and
succeeding centuries over the appointment of bishops, see Bingham, b.
iv. ch. xi. sect. 19.

CHAP. XIV.—THE ARIANS REMOVE GREGÓRY FROM THE SEE
OF ALEXANDRIA, AND APPOINT GEORGE IN HIS PLACE.

[58] ABOUT the same time the Arians eject Gregory from the see
of Alexandria, who had rendered himself extremely unpopular
by setting a church[1] on fire, and not manifesting sufficient
zeal in promoting the interests of their party. They therefore
inducted George into his see, who was a native of Cappadocia,
and had acquired the reputation of being an able advocate of
their tenets.

CHAP. XV.—ATHANASIUS AND PAUL GOING TO ROME, AND
BEING FORTIFIED BY THE LETTERS OF BISHOP JULIUS, RE-
COVER THEIR RESPECTIVE DIOCESES.

AFTER experiencing considerable difficulties, Athanasius at
last reached Italy.   The whole western division of the empire
was then under the power. of Constans, the youngest of Constantine's sons, his brother Constantine having been slain by
[59] the soldiery, as was before stated.   At the same time also Paul
bishop of Constantinople, Asclepas of Gaza, Marcellus of
Ancyra a city of Galatia Minor, and Lucius of Adrianople,
having been expelled from their several churches on various
charges, arrived at the imperial city.   There each laid his case
before Julius bishop of Rome,[2] who sent them back again into
the East, restoring them to their respective sees by virtue of
his letters, in the exercise of the Church of Rome's peculiar
privilege ; and at the same time in the liberty of that prerogative, sharply rebuking those by whom they had been deposed.
Relying on the authority of these documents, the bishops depart from Rome, and again take possession of their own
churches, forwarding the letters to the parties to whom they
were addressed.   These persons considering themselves treated
with indignity by the reproaches of Julius, assemble themselves in council at Antioch, and dictate a reply to his letters
as the expression of the unanimous feeling of the whole synod.
It was not his province, they said, to take cognizance of their

[1] That of Dionysius.   See above, chap. xi.
[2] See below, chap. xxiv.

decisions in reference to the expulsion of any bishops from
their churches; seeing that they had not opposed themselves
to him, when Novatus was ejected from the church. Such
was the tenor of the Eastern bishops' disclaimer of the right of
interference of Julius bishop of Rome. But sedition was
excited by the partisans of George the Arian, on the entry of
Athanasius into Alexandria, in consequence of which, it is
affirmed, many persons were killed; and since the Arians
endeavour to throw the whole odium of this transaction on
Athanasius as the author of it, it behoves us to make a few
remarks on the subject. God the Judge of all only knows the
true causes of these disorders; but no one of any experience
can be ignorant of the fact, that such fatal accidents are the
frequent concomitants of the factious movements of the populace. It is in vain therefore for the calumniators of Athanasius
to attribute the blame to him; and especially Sabinus,[1] bishop
of the Macedonian heresy. For had the latter reflected on
the number and magnitude of the wrongs which Athanasius,
in conjunction with the rest who hold the doctrine of consubstantiality, has suffered from the Arians; or on the many
complaints made of these things by the synods convened on
account of Athanasius; or, in short, on what that arch-heretic
Macedonius himself has done throughout all the churches, he
would either have been wholly silent, or, if constrained to
speak, would have highly commended Athanasius, instead of
loading him with reproaches. But intentionally overlooking
all these things, he wilfully misrepresents his character and
conduct; without however trusting himself to speak at all of
Macedonius, lest he should betray the gross enormities of
which he knew him to be guilty. And what is still more
extraordinary, he has not said one word to the disadvantage of
the Arians, although he was far from entertaining their sentiments. The ordination of Macedonius, whose heretical views
he had adopted, he has also passed over in silence; for had he
mentioned it, he must necessarily have recorded his impieties,
which were most distinctly manifested on that occasion.

---

[1] He alludes to his " Collection of Synodical Transactions," mentioned
below, chap. xvii.

CHAP. XVI.—The emperor Constantius sends an order
· to Philip the prætorian prefect, that Paul should be
exiled and Macedonius installed in his see.

When the intelligence of Paul's having resumed his
episcopal functions reached Antioch, where the emperor
Constantius then held his court, he was excessively enraged
at his presumption. A written order was therefore despatched to Philip the Prætorian Prefect, whose power exceeded
that of the other governors of provinces, and who was styled
the second person from the emperor,[1] to drive Paul out of the
church again, and introduce Macedonius into it in his place.
The prefect, dreading an insurrectionary movement among
the people, used artifice to entrap the bishop : keeping therefore the emperor's mandate secret, he went to the public
bath called Xeuxippus, and on pretence of attending to some ·
public affairs, sent to Paul with every demonstration of respect, requesting his attendance there, as his presence was
indispensable. On his arrival in obedience to this summons,
the prefect immediately shows him the emperor's order ; to
which the bishop patiently submitted, notwithstanding his
being thus condemned without having had his cause heard.
But as Philip was afraid of the violence of the multitude, who
had gathered round the building in great numbers to see what
would take place, for their suspicions had been aroused by
current reports, he commands one of the bath doors to be
opened which communicated with the imperial palace, and
through that Paul was carried off, put on board a vessel provided for the purpose, and so sent into exile. The prefect
directed him to go to Thessalonica, the metropolis of Macedonia,
whence he had derived his origin from his ancestors ; commanding him to reside in that city, but granting him permission to visit other cities of Illyricum, while he strictly
forbad his passing into any portion of the Eastern empire.
Thus was Paul, contrary to his expectation, at once expelled
from the church, and from the city, and again hurried off into
exile. Philip the imperial prefect, leaving the bath, imme-

---

[1] δεύτερος μετὰ βασιλέα, next from, or to, the emperor, his right-hand
man. The same phrase occurs even in classical Latin. Thus Virgil,
(Ecl. v. 49,) "alter ab illo;" and again, (Ecl. viii. 39,) "alter ab undecimo
annus;" and Juvenal, (Sat. x. 125,) "volveris a primâ quæ proxima."

diately proceeded to the church, accompanied by Macedonius, whose appearance was as sudden as if he had been thrown there by an engine. He was exposed to open view seated with the prefect in his chariot, which was environed by a military guard with drawn swords. The multitude was completely overawed by this spectacle, and both Arians and Homoousians[1] hastened to the church, every one endeavouring to secure an entrance there. On the approach of the prefect with Macedonius, the crowd and the soldiery seemed alike seized with an irrational panic : for the assemblage was so numerous that there was insufficient room to admit the passage of the prefect and Macedonius, and the soldiers therefore attempted to thrust aside the people by force. But the confined space into which they were crowded together rendering it impossible to recede, the soldiers imagined that resistance was offered, and that the populace intentionally stopped the passage; they accordingly began to use their naked swords, and to cut down those that stood in their way. It is affirmed that upwards of 3150 persons were massacred on this occasion ; of whom the greater part fell under the weapons of the military, and the rest were crushed to death by the desperate efforts of the multitude to escape their violence. After such distinguished achievements, Macedonius was seated in the episcopal chair by the prefect, rather than by the ecclesiastical canon, as if he had not been the author of any calamity, but was altogether guiltless of what had been perpetrated. These were the sanguinary means by which Macedonius and the Arians grasped the supremacy in the churches. About this period the emperor built the great church called *Sophia*,[1] adjoining to that named *Irene,* which being originally of small dimensions, the emperor's father had considerably enlarged and adorned. In the present day both are seen within one enclosure, and have but one appellation.

CHAP. XVII.—ATHANASIUS, AFRAID OF THE EMPEROR'S MENACES, RETURNS TO ROME AGAIN.

ANOTHER accusation was now framed against Athanasius by the Arians, who invented this pretext for it. The father of

---

[1] Οἵ τε τῆς ὁμοουσίου πίστεως, the defenders of the doctrine of consubstantiality. See above, ch. ii. of this book.
[2] See above, ch. vi.

the Augusti had long before granted an allowance of corn to the Church of the Alexandrians for the relief of the indigent. This they asserted had usually been sold by Athanasius, and the proceeds converted to his own advantage. The emperor giving credence to this slanderous report, threatened to put Athanasius to death; who becoming alarmed at the intimation of this threat, consulted his safety by flight, and kept himself concealed. When Julius bishop of Rome was apprized of these fresh machinations of the Arians against Athanasius, and had also received the letter of the then deceased Eusebius, he invited the persecuted prelate to come to him, having ascertained where he was secreted. The epistle of the bishops who had been some time before assembled at Antioch, just then reached him, together with others from several bishops in Egypt, assuring him that the entire charge against Athanasius was a fabrication. On the receipt of these contradictory communications, Julius first replied to the bishops who had written to him from Antioch, complaining of the acrimonious feeling they had evinced in their letter, and charging them ⁶⁰ with a violation of the canons, in neglecting to request his attendance at the council, seeing that by ecclesiastical law, no decisions of the Churches are valid unless sanctioned by the bishop of Rome:[1] he then censured them with great severity for clandestinely attempting to pervert the faith. In allusion to their former proceedings at Tyre, he characterized their acts as fraudulent, from the attestation of what had taken place at Mareotis being on one side of the question only; nor did he fail to remind them of the palpable evidence which had been afforded of their malevolence, in the imputed murder of Arsenius. Such was the nature of his answer to the bishops convened at Antioch, which we should have inserted here at length, as well as those letters which were addressed to Julius, did not their prolixity interfere with our purpose. But Sabinus, the favourer of the Macedonian heresy, of whom we have before spoken, has not taken the least notice of the letters of Julius in his *Collection of Synodical Transactions*;[2] although he has not omitted that which the bishops at Antioch sent to Julius. This however is the unfair course generally pursued by Sabinus, who carefully introduces such letters as make no reference to, or wholly repudiate, the term

---

[1] See above, note on ch. viii.   [2] See above, ch. xv.

[SOCRATES.]   H

consubstantial; while he invariably passes over in silence those of a contrary tendency. Not long after this, Paul pretending to make a journey from Thessalonica to Corinth, arrived in Italy: upon which both the bishops[1] made an appeal to the emperor of those parts, laying their respective cases before him.

CHAP. XVIII.—THE EMPEROR OF THE WEST REQUESTS HIS BROTHER TO SEND HIM SUCH PERSONS AS COULD GIVE AN ACCOUNT OF THE DEPOSITION OF ATHANASIUS AND PAUL. THOSE WHO ARE SENT PUBLISH ANOTHER FORM OF THE CREED.

WHEN the Western emperor[2] was informed of the unjust treatment to which Paul and Athanasius had been subjected, he sympathized with their sufferings; and wrote to his brother Constantius, begging him to send three bishops to explain to him the reason of their deposition. In compliance with this request, Narcissus the Cilician, Theodore the Thracian, Maris of Chalcedony, and Mark the Syrian, were deputed to execute this commission; who on their arrival refused to hold any communication with Athanasius, but, suppressing the creed which had been promulgated at Antioch, presented to the emperor Constans another declaration of faith composed by themselves, in the following terms:—

ANOTHER EXPOSITION OF THE FAITH.

" We believe in one God, the Father Almighty, the Creator and Maker of all things, of whom the whole family in heaven and upon earth is named (Eph. iii. 15); and in his only-begotten Son, our Lord Jesus Christ, begotten of the Father before all ages; God of God; Light of Light; by whom all things in the heavens and upon the earth, both visible and invisible, were made; who is the Word, Wisdom, Power, Life, and true Light: who in the last days for our sake was made man, and was born of the holy virgin; was crucified, and died; was buried, arose again from the dead on the third day, ascended into the heavens, is seated at the right hand of the

---

[1] i. e. Athanasius and Paul.
[2] Constantine the younger, who had succeeded to that portion of his father's empire.

Father, and shall come at the consummation of the ages, to judge the living and the dead, and to render to every one according to his works: whose kingdom being perpetual, shall continue to infinite ages; for he shall sit at the right hand of the Father, not only in this age, but also in that which is to come. We believe in the Holy Spirit, that is, in the Comforter, whom the Lord, according to his promise, sent to his apostles after his ascension into the heavens, to teach them, and bring all things to their remembrance: by whom also the souls of those who have sincerely believed on him shall be sanctified. But the catholic Church accounts as aliens those who assert that the Son was made of things which are not, or of another substance, and not of God, or that there was ever a time when he did not exist."

Having delivered this creed to the emperor, and exhibited it to many others also, they departed without attending to any thing besides. But while there was yet an inseparable communion between the Western and Eastern churches, there sprang up another heresy at Sirmium, a city of Illyricum: for Photinus, who presided over the churches in that district, a native of Galatia Minor, and a disciple of that Marcellus who had been deposed, adopting his master's sentiments, asserted that the Son of God was a mere man. We shall however enter into this matter more fully in its proper place.[1]

CHAP. XIX.—An elaborate exposition of the faith.

AFTER the lapse of about three years from the events above recorded, the Eastern bishops again assembled a synod, and having composed another form of faith, they transmitted it to those in Italy by the hands of Eudoxius, at that time bishop of Germanicia, Martyrius, and Macedonius, who was bishop of Mopsuestia in Cilicia. This expression of the Creed, entering into more minute details of doctrine, contained many additions to those which had preceded it, and was set forth in these words:—

" We believe in one God, the Father Almighty, the Creator and Maker of all things, of whom the whole family in heaven

[1] See below, ch. xxix.

and upon earth is named; and in his only-begotten Son, Jesus
Christ our Lord, begotten of the Father before all ages; God
of God; Light of Light; by whom all things in the heavens
and upon the earth, both visible and invisible, were made;
who is the Word, Wisdom, Power, Life, and true Light: who
in the last days for our sake was made man, and was born of
the holy virgin; was crucified, and died; was buried, arose
again from the dead on the third day, ascended into heaven, is
seated at the right hand of the Father, and shall come at the
consummation of the ages, to judge the living and the dead,
and to render to every one according to his works: whose
kingdom being perpetual, shall continue to infinite ages; for
he sits at the right hand of the Father, not only in this age,
but also in that which is to come.   We believe in the Holy
Spirit, that is in the Comforter, whom the Lord according to
his promise sent to his apostles after his ascension into heaven,
to teach them and bring all things to their remembrance: by
whom also the souls of those who have sincerely believed on
him are sanctified.   But the holy catholic Church accounts as
aliens those who assert that the Son was made of things not
in being, or of another substance, and not of God, or that
there was ever a time or age when he did not exist.[1]   The
holy and catholic Church likewise anathematizes those also
who say that there are three Gods, or that Christ is not God
before all ages, or that he is neither Christ, nor the Son of
God, or that the same person is Father, Son, and Holy Spirit,
or that the Son was not begotten, or that the Father begat
not the Son by his own voluntary will.   Neither is it safe to
affirm that the Son had his existence from things that were [62]
not, since this is nowhere declared concerning him in the
divinely-inspired Scriptures.   Nor are we taught that he had
his being from any other pre-existing substance besides the
Father, but that he was truly begotten of God alone: for the
Divine word teaches that there is one unbegotten principle
without beginning, the Father of Christ.   But those who,
unauthorized by Scripture, rashly assert that there was a time
when he was not, ought not to preconceive any antecedent
interval of time, but God only who without time begat him:
for both times and ages were made by him.   Yet it must not

---

[1] Here the former Creed terminates, the present being thus far almost
literally identical with it.

be thought that the Son is co-inoriginate, or co-unbegotten[1]
with the Father : for this could not be predicated where such
a relationship exists.   But we know that the Father alone
being inoriginate and incomprehensible, has ineffably and in-
comprehensibly to all begotten, and that the Son was begotten
before the ages, but is not unbegotten like the Father, but has
a beginning, viz. the Father who begat him, for 'the head of
Christ is God' (1 Cor. xi. 3).   Now although according to
the Scriptures we acknowledge three things or persons, viz.
that of the Father, and of the Son, and of the Holy Spirit, we
do not on that account make three Gods : since we know that
there is but one God perfect in himself, unbegotten, inoriginate,
and invisible, the God and Father of the only-begotten, who
alone has 'existence from himself, and alone affords existence
abundantly to all other things.   But while we assert that
there is one God, the Father of our Lord Jesus Christ, the
only unbegotten, we do not therefore deny that Christ is God
before the ages, as the followers of Paul of Samosata do, who
affirm that after his incarnation he was by exaltation deified,
in that he was by nature a mere man.   We know indeed that
he was subject to his God and Father: nevertheless he was
begotten of God, and is by nature true and perfect God, and
was not afterwards made God out of man; but was for our
sake made man out of God, and has never ceased to be God.
Moreover we execrate and anathematize those who falsely style
him the mere unsubstantial[2] word of God, having existence
only in another, either as the word to which utterance is
given, or as the word conceived in the mind : and who pretend
that before the ages he was neither the Christ, the Son of God,
the Mediator, nor the Image of God ; but that he became the
Christ, and the Son of God, from the time he took our flesh
from the virgin, about 400 years ago.   For they assert that
Christ had the beginning of his kingdom from that time, and
that it shall have an end after the consummation of all things
and the judgment.   Such persons as these are the followers of
Marcellus and Photinus, the Ancyro-Galatians, who under
pretext of *establishing his sovereignty,* like the Jews set aside
the eternal existence and deity of Christ, and the perpetuity
of his kingdom.   But we know him to be not simply the word

[1] Συνάναρχον ἢ συναγέννητον.
[2] 'Ανύπαρκτον, not existing, imaginary, ideal.

of God by utterance or mental conception, but God the Word living and subsisting of himself; and Son of God and Christ; and who co-existed and was conversant with his Father before the ages not by prescience only, and ministered to him at the creation of all things, whether visible or invisible: but that he is the substantial Word of the Father, and God of God; for this is he to whom the Father said,[1] 'Let us make man in our image, and according to our likeness:' who in his own person[2] appeared to the fathers, gave the law, and spake by the prophets; and being at last made man, he manifested his Father to all men, and reigns to endless ages.   Christ has not attained any new dignity; but we believe that he was perfect from the beginning, and like his Father in all things.   We also deservedly expel from the Church those who say that the Father, Son, and Holy Spirit are the same person, impiously supposing the three names to refer to one and the same thing and person: because by an incarnation they render the Father, who is incomprehensible and insusceptible of suffering, subject to comprehension and suffering.   These heretics are denominated Patropassians among the Romans, but by us, Sabellians. For we know that the Father who sent, remained in the proper nature of his own immutable deity; but that Christ who was sent, has fulfilled the economy of the incarnation.   In like manner we regard as most impious and strangers to the truth, those who irreverently affirm that Christ was begotten not by the will and pleasure of his Father; thus attributing to God an involuntary and reluctant necessity, as if he begat the Son by constraint: because they have dared to determine such things respecting him as are inconsistent with our common notions of God, and are contrary indeed to the sense of the divinely-inspired Scripture.   For knowing that God is self-dependent and Lord of himself, we devoutly maintain that of his own volition and pleasure he begat the Son.   And while we reverentially believe what is spoken concerning him (Prov. viii. 22),[3] 'The Lord created me the beginning of his

---

[1] Gen. i. 26.

[2] αὐτοπροσώπως.   See this explained below, chap. xxx.

[3] The Eastern bishops have here quoted the very words of the Septuagint: Κύριος ἔκτισέ με ἀρχὴν ὁδῶν αὐτοῦ εἰς ἔργα αὐτοῦ.   But the English version exactly follows the Hebrew: יְהֹוָה קָנָנִי רֵאשִׁית דַּרְכּוֹ קֶדֶם מִפְעָלָיו מֵאָז   "The Lord possessed me in the beginning of his way, before his works of old."

ways on account of his works,' yet we do not suppose that
he was made similarly to the creatures or works made by him.
For it is impious and repugnant to the ecclesiastic faith to
compare the Creator with the works created by him; or to
imagine that he had the same manner of generation as things
of a nature totally different from himself: although the sacred
Scriptures teach us that the alone only-begotten Son was absolutely and truly begotten.   And when we say that the Son
is of himself, and lives and subsists in like manner to the
Father; we do not therefore separate him from the Father, as
if we supposed them dissociated by the intervention of material space.   For we believe that they are united without
medium or interval, and that they are incapable of separation
from each other: the whole Father embosoming the Son; and
the whole Son attached to and eternally reposing in the
Father's bosom.   Believing therefore in the altogether perfect and most holy Trinity, (Τριάδα,) and asserting that the
Father is God, and that the Son also is God, we do not
acknowledge two Gods, but one only, on account of the majesty of the Deity, and the perfect blending and union of the
kingdoms: the Father ruling over all things universally, and
even over the Son himself; the Son being subject to the
Father, but except him, ruling over all things which were
made after him and by him; and by the Father's will bestowing abundantly on the saints the grace of the Holy Spirit.
For the sacred oracles inform us that in this consists the
character of the sovereignty which Christ exercises.

"We have been under the necessity of giving this more
ample exposition of the creed, since the publication of our
former epitome; not to gratify a vain ambition, but to clear
ourselves from all strange suspicion respecting our faith which
may exist among those who are ignorant of our real sentiments.   And that the inhabitants of the West may both be
aware of the shameless misrepresentations of the heterodox
party; and also know the ecclesiastical opinion of the Eastern
bishops concerning Christ, confirmed by the unwrested testimony of the divinely-inspired Scriptures, among all those of
unperverted minds."

CHAP. XX.—OF THE SYNOD AT SARDICA.[1]

THE Western prelates, on account of their being of another language, and not understanding this exposition, would not admit of it ; saying that the Nicene creed was sufficient, and that anything beyond it was a work of supererogation. But when the emperor had again written to insist on the re-establishment of Paul and Athanasius in their respective sees, but without effect in consequence of the continual agitation of the people, these two bishops demanded that another synod should be convened, both for the determination of their case, as well as for the settlement of other questions in relation to the faith: for they made it obvious that their deposition arose from no other cause than that the faith might be the more easily perverted. Another general council was therefore summoned to meet at Sardica, a city of Illyricum, by the joint authority of the two emperors ; the one requesting by letter that it might be so, and the other of the East readily acquiescing in it. This synod was convened at Sardica, in the eleventh year after the death of the father of the two Augusti, during the consulship of Rufinus and Eusebius. Athanasius states that about 300 bishops from the western parts of the empire were[66] present ; but Sabinus says there came only seventy from the eastern parts, among whom was Ischyras[2] of Mareotis, who had been ordained bishop of that country by those who deposed Athanasius. Of the rest, some pretended infirmity of body ; others complained of the shortness of the notice given, casting the blame of it on Julius bishop of Rome, although a year and a half had elapsed from the time of its having been summoned : in which interval Athanasius remained at Rome awaiting the assembling of the synod. When at last they were convened at Sardica, the Eastern prelates refused either to meet or to enter into any conference with those of the West, unless Athanasius and Paul were excluded from the convention. But Protogenes bishop of Sardica, and Hosius bishop of Cordova in Spain, would by no means permit them to be absent ; on which the Eastern bishops immediately withdrew, and returning to Philippolis in Thrace, held a separate coun-

---

[1] See Theodoret, b. ii. ch. vii.
[2] See above, b. i. ch. xxvii.

cil, wherein they openly anathematized the term *consubstan-*
tial: and having introduced the Anomoian [1] opinion into their
epistles, they sent them in all directions. On the other hand,
those who remained at Sardica, condemning in the first place
their departure, afterwards divested the accusers of Athanasius
of their dignity : then confirming the Nicene creed, and rejecting the term ἀνόμοιος, they more distinctly recognised the doctrine of consubstantiality in epistles addressed to all the
Churches. Both parties believed they had acted rightly : those
of the East conceived themselves justified, because the Western bishops had countenanced those whom they had deposed ;
and these again were satisfied with the course they had taken,
in consequence not only of the retirement of those who had
deposed them before the matter had been examined into, but
also because they themselves were the defenders of the Nicene
faith, which the other party had dared to adulterate. They
therefore reinstated Paul and Athanasius in their sees, and
also Marcellus of Ancyra in Galatia Minor, who had been deposed long before, as we have stated in the former Book.[2]
This person at that time exerted himself to the utmost to procure the revocation of the sentence pronounced against him,
declaring that his being suspected of entertaining the error of
Paul of Samosata, arose from a misunderstanding of some expressions in his book. It must however be noticed that Eusebius Pamphilus wrote three entire books against Marcellus,
in which he quotes that author's own words to prove that he
asserts, with Sabellius the Libyan, and Paul of Samosata, that
the Lord Jesus was a mere man.

CHAP. XXI.—DEFENCE OF EUSEBIUS PAMPHILUS.

BUT since some have attempted to stigmatize Eusebius
Pamphilus as having favoured the Arian views in his works, it
may not be irrelevant here to make a few remarks respecting
him. In the first place, then, he was present at the council of
Nice, and gave his assent to what was there determined in reference to the consubstantiality of the Son with the Father.

[1] ἀνόμοιος—dissimilis, different, unlike. See book i. ch. viii., note.
[2] He refers to b. i. chaps. xxxv. and xxxvi.

And in the third book of the Life of Constantine, he thus expressed himself:—" The emperor incited all to unanimity, until he had rendered them united in judgment on those points on which they were previously at variance: so that they were quite agreed at Nice in matters of faith."   Since therefore Eusebius, in mentioning the Nicene synod, says that all differences were composed, and that unanimity of sentiment prevailed, what ground is there for assuming that he was himself an Arian? The Arians are certainly deceived in supposing him to be a favourer of their tenets.   But some one will perhaps say, that in his discourses he seems to have adopted the opinions of Arius, because of his frequently saying *by Christ*. Our answer is, that ecclesiastical writers often use [68] this mode of expression, and others of a similar kind, ·denoting the *economy* of our Saviour's humanity: and that before all these the apostle (1 Cor. i.) made use of such expressions, without ever being accounted a teacher of false doctrine.   Moreover, inasmuch as Arius has dared to say that the Son is a creature, as one of the others, observe what Eusebius says on this subject, in his first book against Marcellus:—

" He alone, and no other, has been declared to be, and is, the only-begotten Son of God; whence any one would justly censure those who have presumed to affirm that he is a Creature made of nothing, like the rest of the creatures: for how then would he be a Son? and how could he be God's only-begotten, were he assigned the same nature as the other creatures, and were he one of the many created things, seeing that he, like them, would in that case be partaker of a creation from nothing?   The sacred Scriptures do not thus instruct us concerning these things." He again adds a little afterwards:—" Whoever then determines that the Son is made of things that are not, and that he is a creature produced from nothing pre-existing, forgets that while he concedes the name of Son, he denies him to be so in reality. For he that is made of nothing, cannot truly be the Son of God, any more than the other things which have been made: but the true Son of God, forasmuch as he is begotten of the Father, is properly denominated the only-begotten and beloved of the Father. For this reason also, he himself is God: for what can the offspring of God be, but the perfect resemblance of him who

begat him? A sovereign indeed builds (κτίζει) a city, but
does not beget it; and is said to beget a son, not to build one.
An artificer may be called the framer (κτιστής), but not the
father of his work; while he could by no means be styled
the framer of him whom he had begotten. So also the God
of the Universe is the Father of the Son; but would be fitly
termed the Framer and Maker of the world. And although
it is once said in Scripture, (Prov. viii. 22,) ' The Lord created
(ἔκτισε) me the beginning of his ways on account of his
works,' yet it becomes us to consider the import of this phrase,
which I shall hereafter explain; and not, as Marcellus has
done, from a single passage to subvert one of the most important doctrines of the Church."

These and many other such expressions are found in the
first book of •Eusebius Pamphilus against Marcellus; and in
his third book, declaring in what sense the term *creature*
(κτίσμα) is to be taken, he says:—

"Accordingly, these things being established, it follows that
in the same sense as that which preceded, these words also are
to be understood, ' The Lord created me the beginning of his
ways on account of his works.' For although he says that he
was created, it is not as if he should say that he had arrived
at existence from what was not, nor that he himself also was
made of nothing like the rest of the creatures, which some
have erroneously supposed: but as subsisting, living, pre-
existing, and being before the constitution of the whole world;
and having been appointed to rule the.universe by his Lord
and Father: the word *created* being here used instead of *ordained* or *constituted*. Certainly the apostle (1 Pet. ii. 13, 14)
expressly called the rulers and governors among men *creature*,
when he said, ' Submit yourselves to every human creature
(ἀνθρωπίνῃ κτίσει) for the Lord's sake; whether to the king as
supreme, or to governors as those sent by him.' The prophet
also (Amos iv. 12, 13) does not use the word *created* (ἔκτισεν)
in the sense of *made of that which had no previous existence*,
when he says, ' Prepare, Israel, to invoke[1] thy God. For
behold, he who confirms the thunder, creates the Spirit, and
announces his Christ unto men:' for God did not then create
the Spirit, when he declared his Christ to all men, since

---

[1] 'Ἐπικαλεῖσθαι. Eusebius quotes from the Septuagint, omitting ἐγώ,
which greatly differs from the Hebrew.

(Eccles. i. 9) ' There is nothing new under the sun ;' but the
Spirit was, and subsisted before : but he was sent at what
time the apostles were gathered together, when, like thunder,
' There came a sound from heaven as of a rushing mighty
wind : and they were filled with the Holy Spirit' (Acts ii.
2, 4). And thus they declared unto all men the Christ of
God, in accordance with that prophecy which says, (Amos iv.
13,) ' Behold, he who confirms the thunder, creates the Spirit,
and announces his Christ unto men :' the word *creates* (κτίζει)
being used instead of *sends down*, or *appoints ;* and *thunder*
in a similar way implying *the preaching of the gospel.* Again,
he that says, ' Create in me a clean heart, O God,' (Psal. li.
10,) said not this as if he had no heart ; but prayed that his
mind might be purified. Thus also it is said, (Eph. ii. 15,)
' That he might create the two into one new man,' instead of
unite. Consider also whether this passage is not of the same
kind, (Eph. iv. 24,) ' Clothe yourselves with the new man,
which is created according to God :' and this, (2 Cor. v. 17,)
' If therefore any one be in Christ, he is a new creature'
(κτίσις) : and whatever other expressions of a similar nature
any one may find who shall carefully search the divinely-
inspired Scripture. Wherefore one should not be surprised
if in this passage, ' The Lord created me the beginning of his
ways,' the term *created* is used metaphorically, instead of *appointed*, or *constituted*."

These quotations from the books of Eusebius against Marcellus, have been adduced to confute those who have slander-
ously attempted to traduce and criminate him. Neither can
they prove that Eusebius attributes a beginning of subsistence
to the Son of God, although they may find him often using
the expressions of dispensation : and especially so, because he
was an emulator and admirer of the works of Origen, in which
those who are able to comprehend that author's writings, will
perceive it to be everywhere stated that the Son was begotten
of the Father. These remarks have been made in passing, in
order to refute those who have misrepresented Eusebius.

CHAP. XXII.—THE SYNOD OF SARDICA RESTORES PAUL AND
ATHANASIUS TO THEIR SEES; AND ON THE EASTERN EMPE-
ROR'S REFUSAL TO ADMIT THEM, THE EMPEROR OF THE WEST
THREATENS HIM WITH WAR.

WHEN those convened at Sardica, as well as those who
had formed a separate council at Philippolis in Thrace, had
severally performed what they deemed requisite, they returned
to their respective cities. From that time therefore the Western Church was severed from the Eastern :[1] and the boundary
of communion between them was the mountain called Soucis,
which divides the Illyrians from the Thracians. As far as
this mountain there was indiscriminate communion, although
there was a difference of faith; but beyond it they did not
communicate with one another. Such was the perturbed condition of the Churches at that period. Soon after these transactions, the emperor of the Western parts informs his brother
Constantius of what had taken place at Sardica, and begs him
to ratify the restoration of Paul and Athanasius to their sees.
But as Constantius delayed to carry this matter into effect,
the emperor of the West again wrote to him, giving him the
choice either of re-establishing Paul and Athanasius in their
former dignity, and restoring their churches to them; or on
his failing to do this, of regarding him as his enemy, and immediately expecting war. The letter which he addressed to
his brother was as follows :—

" Athanasius and Paul are here with me : and I am quite
satisfied, after strict investigation, that their piety alone has
drawn persecution upon them. If therefore you will pledge
yourself to reinstate them in their sees, and to punish those
who have so unjustly injured them, I will send them to you :
but should you refuse to execute my wishes, be assured of
this, that I will myself come thither, and restore them to their
own sees, in spite of your opposition."

---

[1] Such temporary suspensions of outward communion as this were not
uncommon in early ages. There is however a clear and well-marked line
of distinction to be observed between them and a formal and lasting schism.
See Bingham, b. xvi. ch. i., &c.

CHAP. XXIII.—CONSTANTIUS BEING AFRAID OF HIS BROTHER'S MENACES, BY LETTER RECALLS ATHANASIUS, AND SENDS HIM TO ALEXANDRIA.

THIS communication placed the emperor of the East in the utmost difficulty; and immediately sending for the greater part of the Eastern bishops, he acquainted them with the choice his brother had submitted to him, and asked what ought to be done. They replied, it was better to concede the churches to Athanasius, than to undertake a civil war. Accordingly the emperor, urged by necessity, summoned Athanasius to his presence. Meanwhile the emperor of the West sends Paul to Constantinople, with two bishops and other honourable attendance, having fortified him with his own letters, together with those of the synod. But while Athanasius was still apprehensive, and hesitated to go to him, dreading the treachery of his calumniators, the emperor of the East not once only, but even a second and a third time, invited him to come to him: this is evident from his letters, of which I shall here give a translation from the Latin tongue.

EPISTLE OF CONSTANTIUS TO ATHANASIUS.

" Constantius Victor Augustus to Athanasius the bishop.
" Our compassionate clemency cannot permit you to be any longer tossed and disquieted as it were by the boisterous waves of the sea. Our unwearied piety has not been unmindful of you driven from your native home, despoiled of your property, and wandering in pathless solitudes. And although we have too long deferred acquainting you by letter with the purpose of our mind, in the expectation of your coming to us of your own accord to seek a remedy for your troubles; yet since fear perhaps has hindered the execution of your wishes, we therefore have sent to your reverence letters full of indulgence, in order that you may fearlessly hasten to appear in our presence, whereby, after experiencing our benevolence, you may attain your desire, and be re-established in your proper position. For this reason we have requested our Lord and brother Constans Victor Augustus, to grant you permission to come, to the end that you may be restored to your country by the consent of us both, having this assurance of our favour."

ANOTHER EPISTLE TO ATHANASIUS.

"Constantius Victor Augustus to the bishop Athanasius.

"Although we have abundantly intimated in a former letter that you might securely come to our court,[1] as we are extremely anxious to reinstate you in your proper place, yet we have again addressed your reverence. We therefore desire you will, without any distrust or apprehension, take a public vehicle and hasten to us, in order that you may realize your wishes."

ANOTHER EPISTLE TO ATHANASIUS.

"Constantius Victor Augustus to the bishop Athanasius.

"While we made our residence at Edessa, where your presbyters were present, it pleased us to send one of them to you, for the purpose of hastening your arrival at our court, in order that, after having been introduced to our presence, you might forthwith proceed to Alexandria. But inasmuch as a considerable time has elapsed since your receipt of our letter, and you have not yet come; we now therefore again exhort you to speedily present yourself before us, that so you may be able to be restored to your country, and obtain your desire. For the more ample assurance of our intention, we have despatched to you Achetas the deacon, from whom you will learn both our mind in regard to you, as well as our readiness to facilitate the objects you have in view."

When Athanasius had received these letters at Aquileia, where he abode after his departure from Sardica, he immediately hastened to Rome; and having shown these communications to Julius the bishop, there was the greatest joy in the Roman Church. For they concluded that the emperor of the East had recognised their faith, since he had recalled Athanasius. Julius then wrote to the clergy and laity of Alexandria on behalf of Athanasius.

EPISTLE OF JULIUS BISHOP OF ROME, TO THOSE AT ALEXANDRIA.

"Julius the bishop, to the presbyters, deacons, and people inhabiting Alexandria, brethren beloved, salutations in the Lord.

---

[1] Κομιτάτον, a Grecised form of the Latin word "comitatus." So in the New Test. we have κῆνσος, κουστωδία, σπεκουλάτωρ, &c. &c.

"I also rejoice with you, beloved brethren, because you at length see before your eyes the fruit of your faith. For that this is really so, any one may perceive in reference to our brother and fellow-prelate Athanasius; whom God has restored to you both on account of his purity of life, and in answer to your prayers. It is therefore evident that your supplications to God have unceasingly been offered pure and abounding with love; and that mindful of the Divine promises and of the charity connected with them, which ye learned from the instruction of our brother, ye knew assuredly, and according to the sound faith which is in you clearly foresaw, that your bishop would not be separated from you for ever, whom ye had in your devout hearts as though he were ever present. Wherefore it is unnecessary for me to use many words in addressing you, for your faith has already anticipated whatever I could have said: and the common prayer of you all has been fulfilled according to the grace of Christ. I therefore rejoice with you; and repeat it, because ye have preserved your souls invincible in the faith. Nor do I the less rejoice with my brother Athanasius; because, while suffering many afflictions, he was never unmindful of your love and desire: for although he seemed to be withdrawn from you in person for a season, yet was he always present with you in spirit. And I am convinced, beloved, that every trial which he has endured has not been inglorious; since both your faith and his has thus been tested and made manifest to all. But had not so many troubles happened to him, who would have believed, either that you had so great a value and love for this eminent prelate, or that he was endowed with such distinguished virtues, on account of which also he will by no means be defrauded of his hope in the heavens? He has accordingly obtained a testimony of confession in every way glorious, both in the present age and in that which is to come. After having suffered so many and diversified trials both by land and by sea, he has trampled on every machination of the Arian heresy; and though often exposed to danger in consequence of envy, he despised death, being protected by Almighty God and our Lord Jesus Christ, ever trusting that he should not only escape the treachery of his adversaries, but also be restored for your consolation, and bring back to you at the same time greater trophies from your own conscience. By which means his fame has been extended

even to the ends of the whole earth, his worth having been
approved by the purity of his life, the firmness of his purpose,
and his stedfastness in the heavenly doctrine, all being attested
by your unchanging esteem and love. He therefore returns to
you, more distinguished now than when he departed from you.
For if the fire tries the precious metals (I speak of gold and
silver) for purification, what can be said of so excellent a man
proportionate to his worth, who, after having overcome the fire
of so many calamities and dangers, is now restored to you,
being declared innocent not only by us, but also by the whole
synod? Receive therefore with godly honour and joy, beloved
brethren, your bishop Athanasius, together with those who
have been his companions in tribulation. And rejoice in
having attained the object of your prayers, who have supplied
with meat and drink, by your supporting letters, your pastor
hungering and thirsting, so to speak, for your spiritual welfare.
Ye were a comfort to him while he was sojourning in a
strange land; and ye cherished him in your most faithful
affections when he was exposed to treachery and persecution. It
makes me happy even to picture to myself in imagination the
universal delight that will be manifested on his return, the
pious greetings of the populace, the glorious festivity of those
assembled to meet him, and indeed what the entire aspect of
that day will be, when my brother shall be brought back to you
again : past troubles will then be at an end, and his prized and
longed-for return will unite all hearts in the warmest expression of joy. This feeling will in a very high degree extend
to us, who regard it as a token of Divine favour, that we
should have been privileged to become acquainted with so
eminent a person. It becomes us therefore to close this epistle
with prayer. May God Almighty, and his Son our Lord and
Saviour Jesus Christ, afford you this grace continually, thus
rewarding the admirable faith which ye have manifested in .
reference to your bishop by an illustrious testimony : that the
things more excellent, which 'eye has not seen, nor ear heard,
neither have entered into the heart of man; even the things
which God has prepared for them that love him,' (1 Cor. ii. 9,)
may await you and yours in the world to come, through our
Lord Jesus Christ, by whom glory be to Almighty God for
ever and ever. Amen. I pray that ye may be strengthened,
beloved brethren."

[SOCRATES.]   I·

Athanasius relying on these letters went back to the East. The emperor Constantius did not at that time receive him with any marked hostility of feeling ; nevertheless, at the instigation of the Arians, he endeavoured to circumvent him, addressing him in these words: "You have been reinstated in your see in accordance with the decree of the synod, and with our consent. But inasmuch as some of the people of Alexandria refuse to hold communion with you, permit them to have one church in the city." To this demand Athanasius at once replied: "You have the power, my sovereign, both to 'order, and to carry into effect, whatever you may please. I also therefore would beg you to grant me a favour." The emperor having readily promised to acquiesce, Athanasius immediately added, that he desired the same thing might be conceded to him, which the emperor had exacted from him, viz. that in every city one church should be assigned to those who might refuse to hold communion with the Arians. That party perceiving the purpose of Athanasius to be inimical to their interests, said that this affair might be postponed to another time: but they suffered the emperor to act as he pleased.   He therefore restored Athanasius, Paul, and Marcellus to their respective sees ; as also Asclepas bishop of Gaza, and Lucius of Adrianople.   For these too had been received by the council of Sardica: Asclepas, on his exhibiting records from which it appeared that Eusebius Pamphilus, in conjunction with several others, after having investigated his case, had restored him to his former rank ; and Lucius, because his accusers had fled.   Hereupon the emperor's edicts were despatched to their respective cities, enjoining the inhabitants to receive them readily.   At Ancyra indeed, when Basil was ejected, and Marcellus was introduced in his stead, there was a considerable tumult made, which afforded his enemies an occasion of calumniating him : but the people of Gaza willingly admitted Asclepas.   Macedonius, at Constantinople, for a short time gave place to Paul, convening assemblies by himself separately, in a private church of that city.   Moreover the emperor wrote on behalf of Athanasius to the bishops, clergy, and laity, to receive him cheerfully: and at the same time he ordered by other letters, that whatever had been enacted against him in the judicial courts should be abrogated.   The communications respecting both these matters were as follows:—

THE EPISTLE OF CONSTANTIUS IN BEHALF OF ATHANASIUS.

" Victor Constantius Maximus Augustus, to the bishops and presbyters of the Catholic Church.

The most reverend bishop Athanasius has not been for-saken by the grace of God. But although he was for a short time subjected to trial according to men, yet has he obtained from an omniscient providence the sentence which was due to him ; having been restored by the will of God, and our deci-sion, both to his country and to the Church over which by Divine permission he presided. It was therefore suitable that what is in accordance with this should be duly attended to by our clemency : so that all things which have been heretofore determined against those who held communion with him should now be rescinded ; that all suspicion against him should henceforward cease; and that the immunity which those clergymen who are with him formerly enjoyed, should be, as it is meet, confirmed to them. Moreover we thought it just to add this to our grace toward him, that the whole ecclesiastical body should understand that protection is ex-tended to all who have adhered to him, whether bishops or clerics ; and union with him shall be a sufficient evidence of each person's right intention. Wherefore we have ordered, according to the similitude of the previous providence, that as many as have the wisdom to adopt the sounder judgment, and to join themselves to his communion, shall enjoy that indul-gence which we have now granted in accordance with the will of God."

ANOTHER EPISTLE, ADDRESSED TO THE ALEXANDRIANS.

" Victor Constantius Maximus Augustus, to the laity of the Catholic Church at Alexandria.

" Aiming at your good order in all respects, and knowing that you have long since been bereft of episcopal oversight, we thought it just to send back to you again Athanasius your bishop, a man known to all by the integrity and sanctity of his life and manners. Having received him with your usual courtesy, and constituted him the assistant of your prayers to God, exert yourselves to maintain at all times, according to the ecclesiastical canon, concord and peace, which will be

alike honourable to yourselves and grateful to us.   For it is
unreasonable that any dissension or faction should be excited
among you, contrary to the felicity of our times; and we trust
that such a misfortune will be wholly removed from you. We
exhort you therefore to assiduously persevere in your accustomed devotions, by the assistance of this prelate, as we before
said: so that when this resolution of yours shall become
generally known, even the Pagans who are still enslaved in
the ignorance of idolatrous worship, may eagerly seek the
knowledge of our sacred religion.   Wherefore, most beloved
Alexandrians, give heed to these things: heartily welcome
your bishop, as one appointed you by the will of God and my
decree; and esteem him worthy of being embraced with all
the affections of your souls, for this becomes you, and is consistent with our clemency.   But in order to check all tendency to seditions and tumult in persons of a factious disposition, orders have been issued to our judges to exercise the
utmost severity of the laws on all who expose themselves to
their operation.   Respecting then both our and God's determination, with the anxiety we feel to secure harmony
among you, and remembering also the punishment that will be
inflicted on the disorderly, make it your especial care to act
agreeably to the sanctions of our sacred religion, with all
reverence honouring your bishop; that so in conjunction with
him you may present your supplications to the God and
Father of the universe, both for yourselves, and for the
orderly government of the whole human race."

AN EPISTLE RESPECTING THE ABROGATION OF THE ENACT-
MENTS AGAINST ATHANASIUS.

"Victor Constantius Augustus to Nestorius, and in the
same terms to the Governors of Augustamnica, Thebaïs, and
Libya.

"If it be found that at any time previously enactments
have been passed prejudicial and derogatory to those who
hold communion with Athanasius the bishop, our pleasure is
that they should now be wholly abrogated; and that his clergy
should again enjoy the same immunity which was granted to
them formerly.   We enjoin strict obedience to this command,
to the intent that since this prelate has been restored to his
Church, all who hold communion with him may possess the

same privileges as they had before, and such as other ecclesiastics now enjoy; that so, their affairs being happily arranged,
they also may share in the general prosperity."

CHAP. XXIV.—ATHANASIUS PASSING THROUGH JERUSALEM IN
HIS RETURN TO ALEXANDRIA, IS RECEIVED INTO COMMUNION
BY MAXIMUS: AND A SYNOD OF BISHOPS BEING CONVENED IN
THAT CITY, THE NICENE CREED IS CONFIRMED.

ATHANASIUS the bishop, being fortified with these letters,
passed through Syria, and came into Palestine. On arriving at
Jerusalem he acquainted Maximus the bishop both with what
had been done in the council of Sardica, and also that the
emperor Constantius had confirmed its decision: he then
proposed that a synod of bishops should be held there. Maximus therefore at once sent for certain of the prelates of Syria
and Palestine, who having assembled in council, restored
Athanasius to communion, and to his former dignity. After
¹ which they communicated by letter to the Alexandrians, and
to all the bishops of Egypt and Libya, what had been determined respecting Athanasius.   On this the adversaries of
Athanasius exceedingly derided Maximus, because, having before assisted in the deposition of that prelate, he had suddenly
changed his mind, and, as if nothing had previously taken
place, had promoted his restoration to communion and rank.
When these things became known, Ursacius and Valens,
who had been fiery partisans of Arianism, condemning their
former zeal, proceeded to Rome,¹ where they presented their
recantation to Julius the bishop, and gave their assent to the
doctrine of consubstantiality: they then wrote to Athanasius,
and expressed their readiness to hold communion with him in
future.   Thus did the prosperity of Athanasius so subdue
Ursacius and Valens, as to induce them to recognise the orthodox faith.   Athanasius, passing through Pelusium on his
way to Alexandria, admonished the inhabitants of every city
to beware of the Arians, and to receive those only that professed the Homoöusian faith.   In some of the churches also
³ he performed ordination; which afforded another ground of

¹ See above, note on chap. viii., and compare chap. xv.

accusation against him, because of his undertaking to ordain in the dioceses of others. Such was the condition of things at that period in reference to Athanasius.

CHAP. XXV.—OF THE TYRANTS MAGNENTIUS AND VETRANIO.

ABOUT this time a terrible commotion shook the whole state, of which it is needful to give a summary account of the principal heads. We mentioned in our first Book, that after the death of the founder of Constantinople, his three sons succeeded him in the empire: it must now be also stated, that their kinsman Dalmatius, so named from his father, shared with them the imperial authority. This person, after being associated with them in the sovereignty for a very little while, was slain by the soldiery, Constantius having neither commanded his destruction, nor forbidden it. The manner in which Constantine the younger was killed by the soldiers on his invading that division of the empire which belonged to his brother, has already been recorded.[1] After his death, a Persian war was raised against the Romans, in which Constantius did nothing prosperously: for in a battle fought by night on the frontiers of both parties, the Persians had to some slight extent the advantage. Meanwhile the affairs of Christians became no less unsettled, there being great disturbance throughout the churches on account of Athanasius, and the term *consubstantial*. During this general agitation, there sprang up a tyrant in the western parts called Magnentius;[2] who by treachery slew Constans, the emperor of that division of the empire, at that time residing in the Gallias. In the furious civil war which thence arose, this usurper made himself master of all Italy, reduced Africa and Libya under his power, and even obtained possession of the Gallias. But at the city of Sirmium in Illyricum, the military set up another tyrant whose name was Vetranio; while a fresh trouble threw Rome itself into commotion: for Nepotian, Constantine's sister's son, supported by a body of gladiators, there

[1] See above, b. ii. ch. v.
[2] He was governor of the provinces of Rhœtia, and assassinated his sovereign in his bed.

assumed the sovereignty.   He was however slain by some of
the officers of Magnentius, who himself invaded the western
provinces, and spread desolation in every direction.

CHAP. XXVI.—After the death of Constans the western
emperor, Paul and Athanasius are again ejected from
their sees: the former after being carried into exile is
slain; but the latter escapes by flight.

A conflux of these disastrous events occurred at nearly
one and the same time; for they happened in the fourth year
after the council at Sardica, during the consulate of Sergius
and Nigrinian.   Under these circumstances the entire sovereignty of the empire seemed to devolve on Constantius
alone; who being accordingly proclaimed in the East sole
Autocrat, made the most vigorous preparations against the
tyrants.   Hereupon the adversaries of Athanasius, thinking a
favourable crisis had arisen, again framed the most calumnious
charges against him, before his arrival at Alexandria; assuring the emperor Constantius that all Egypt and Libya was in
danger of being subverted by him.   And his having undertaken to ordain out of the limits of his own diocese,[1] tended
not a little to accredit the accusations against him.   Amidst
such unhappy excitement, Athanasius entered Alexandria;
and having convened a council of the bishops in Egypt, they
confirmed by their unanimous vote, what had been determined
in the synod at Sardica, and that assembled at Jerusalem by
Maximus.   But the emperor, who had been long since imbued
with Arian doctrine, reversed all the indulgent proceedings he
had so recently resolved on.   He began by ordering that
Paul, bishop of Constantinople, should be sent into exile;
whom those who conducted him strangled, at Cucusus in
Cappadocia.   Marcellus was also ejected, and Basil again
made ruler of the Church at Ancyra.   Lucius of Adrianople,
being loaded with chains, died in prison.   The reports which
were made concerning Athanasius so wrought on the emperor's mind, that in an ungovernable fury he commanded him

[1] See Apost. Canons, No. xxxv. "Let not a bishop dare to ordain beyond his own limits, in cities and places not subject to him."

to be put to death wherever he might be found : he moreover
included Theodulus and Olympius, who presided over churches
in Thrace, in the same proscription. Athanasius, having
obtained intelligence of the peril to which these mandates exposed him, once more had recourse to flight, and so escaped
the emperor's menaces. The Arians denounced his retreat
as criminal, particularly Narcissus bishop of Neroniades in
Cilicia, George of Laodicæa, and Leontius who then had the
oversight of the Church at Antioch. This last person, when a
presbyter, had been divested of his rank,[1] because in order to
remove all suspicion of illicit intercourse with a woman named
Eustolium, with whom he spent a considerable portion of his
time, he had castrated himself, and thenceforward lived more
unreservedly with her, when there could be no longer any
ground for evil surmises. Afterwards however, at the earnest
desire of the emperor Constantius, he was created bishop of
the Church at Antioch, after Stephen, the successor of Flaccillus.

CHAP. XXVII.—MACEDONIUS, HAVING POSSESSED HIMSELF OF
THE SEE OF CONSTANTINOPLE, DOES MUCH MISCHIEF TO THOSE
WHO DIFFER FROM HIM IN OPINION.

PAUL having been removed, in the manner described,
Macedonius then became ruler of the churches in Constantinople, and acquiring very great ascendancy over the emperor,
stirred up a war among Christians, of a no less grievous kind
than that which the tyrants themselves were waging. For
having prevailed on his sovereign to co-operate with him in
devastating the churches, he procured the sanction of law for
whatever pernicious measures he determined to pursue.
Throughout the several cities, therefore, an edict was proclaimed, and a military force appointed to carry the imperial
decrees into effect. Hence those who acknowledged the

---

[1] " If any one in good health has mutilated himself so, (by castration,)
it is right that, if he be enrolled among the clergy, he should cease from his
ministrations. . . . . . This is said with reference to those who dare to
mutilate themselves."—*Canon* I. *of the Council of Nice.* Compare also
Apostolical Canons 22 and 23, which enjoin the sentence of deposition on
all clerics for such a crime.

doctrine of consubstantiality were not only expelled from the churches, but also from the cities. But although expulsion at first satisfied them, they soon proceeded to the worse extremity of inducing compulsory communion with them; caring but little for such a desecration of the churches. Their violence indeed was scarcely less intolerable than that of those who had formerly obliged the Christians to worship idols; for they resorted to all kinds of scourgings, a variety of tortures, and confiscation of property. Many were punished with exile; some died under the torture; and others were put to death while being driven from their country. These atrocities were exercised throughout all the eastern cities, but especially at Constantinople; the internal persecution, which was but slight before, being thus savagely increased by Macedonius, as soon as he obtained the bishopric. The cities of Achaia and Illyricum, with those of the western parts, still enjoyed tranquillity; inasmuch as they preserved unanimity of judgment among themselves, and continued to adhere to the rule of faith promulgated by the council of Nice.

CHAP. XXVIII.—ATHANASIUS'S ACCOUNT OF THE VIOLENCES COMMITTED AT ALEXANDRIA BY GEORGE THE ARIAN.

WHAT cruelties were perpetrated at Alexandria by George at the same time, may be learnt from the narration of Athanasius, who was not only a spectator of the scenes he describes, but also a sufferer in them. In his "Vindication of his flight," speaking of these transactions, he thus expresses himself:—"Moreover they came to Alexandria, again seeking to destroy me: and on this occasion their proceedings were worse than before; for the soldiery having suddenly surrounded the church, there arose the din of war instead of the voice of prayer. Afterwards, on the arrival of George during Lent,[1] the mischief for which he had been trained by those who had sent him from Cappadocia, was greatly augmented. When Easter week[2] was past, the virgins were cast into prison, the bishops led in chains by the military, and the dwellings even

---

[1] Τεσσαρακοστῇ, the forty days' fast.
[2] Ἑβδομα τοῦ Πάσχα, the octave of Easter.

of orphans and widows forcibly entered and pillaged. Christians were interred by night; houses were set a mark upon; and the relatives of the clergy were endangered on their account. Even these outrages were dreadful ; but the persecutors soon proceeded to such as were still more so. For in the week after the holy Pentecost, the people, having fasted, went forth to a cemetery to pray, because all were averse to communion with George: that brutal persecutor being informed of this, instigated against them Sebastian, an officer who was a Manichæan. At the head of a body of troops armed with drawn swords, bows, and darts, he marched out to attack the people, although it was the Lord's day: finding but few at prayers, as the most part had retired because of the lateness of the hour, he performed such exploits as might be expected from savage barbarians. Having kindled a fire, he set the virgins near it, in order to compel them to say that they were of the Arian faith; but seeing they were not to be overcome, and that they despised the fire, he then stript them, and so beat them on the face, that for a long time afterwards they could scarcely be recognised. Seizing also about forty men, he flogged them in an extraordinary manner: for he so lacerated their backs with rods fresh cut from the palm-tree, which still had their thorns on, that some were obliged to procure surgical aid in order to have the thorns extracted from their flesh; while others, unable to bear the agony, died under its infliction. All the survivors with one virgin he banished to the Great Oasis. The bodies of the dead were not at first suffered to be claimed by their relatives, but being denied the rites of sepulture were concealed as the authors of these barbarities thought fit, that the evidences of their cruelty might not appear. Such was the blindness with which these madmen acted: for while the friends of the deceased rejoiced on account of their confession, but mourned because of their bodies being uninterred, the impious inhumanity of these acts became more distinctly conspicuous. Soon after this they sent into exile out of Egypt and the two Libyas the following bishops, Ammonius, Thmuis, Caïus, Philo, Hermes, Pliny, Psenosiris, Nilammon, Agatho, Anagamphus, a second Ammonius, Mark, Dracontius, Adelphius, a third Ammonius, another Mark, and Athenodorus, and the presbyters Hierax and Discorus. And so harshly were they treated by those who had the charge of conducting them, that some expired while on their journey, and others in the very place of banishment. In this way more than thirty bishops were got rid of: for the anxious desire of the Arians, like Ahab's, was to exterminate the truth if possible."

Such is the statement Athanasius has given of the atrocities perpetrated by George at Alexandria. The emperor meanwhile led his army into Illyricum, where the urgency of public affairs demanded his presence; for Vetranio had been there proclaimed emperor by the military. On arriving at Sirmium, a truce being made, he came to a conference with Vetranio; and so managed, that the soldiers who had previously declared for his rival, now deserted him, and saluted Constantius alone as Augustus and sovereign Autocrat. Vetranio, perceiving himself to be abandoned, immediately threw himself at the feet of the emperor; who, after taking from him his imperial crown and purple, treated him with great clemency, and recommended him to pass the rest of his days tranquilly in the condition of a private citizen; observing that a life of repose at his advanced age was far more suitable than a dignity which entailed anxieties and care. Vetranio's affairs having come to this issue, he was assigned a liberal provision out of the public revenue: and writing frequently to the emperor during his residence at Prusa in Bithynia, he assured him that he had conferred the greatest blessing on him, by liberating him from the disquietudes which are the inseparable concomitants of sovereign power; adding that he himself did not act wisely in depriving himself of that happiness in retirement which he had bestowed upon him. After these things, the emperor Constantius, having created Gallus his kinsman Cæsar, and given him his own name, sent him to Antioch in Syria to guard the eastern parts. When Gallus 75 was entering this city, the Saviour's sign appeared in the East:[1] for a pillar in the form of a cross was seen in the heavens, to the great amazement of the spectators. Other generals were despatched by the emperor against Magnentius with considerable forces, while he himself remained at Sirmium, awaiting the course of events.

[1] Comp. b. i. ch. ii.

CHAP. XXIX.—OF THE HERESIARCH PHOTINUS.

IN the interim, Photinus, who then presided over the Church in that city, having more openly avowed his sentiments, and a tumult being made in consequence, the emperor ordered a synod of bishops to be assembled at Sirmium. There were [76] accordingly convened there of the Oriental prelates, Mark of [77] Arethusa, George of Alexandria, whom the Arians, as we have before said, had placed over that see on the removal of Gregory, Basil who presided over the Church at·Ancyra, Marcellus having been ejected, Pancratius of Pelusium, and Hypatian of Heraclea. Of the Western bishops there were present Valens of Mursa, and the celebrated Hosius of Cordova in Spain, who attended much against his will. These met at Sirmium, after the consulate of Sergius and Nigrinian, in which year no consul celebrated the customary inaugural [1] solemnities, in consequence of the martial preparations; and it being ascertained that Photinus held the heresy of Sabellius the Libyan and Paul of Samotasa, they immediately deposed him. This decision was both at that time and afterwards universally commended as honourable and just; but those who continued there subsequently acted in a way which was by no means so generally approved.

CHAP. XXX.—FORMS OF THE CREED PUBLISHED AT SIRMIUM, IN PRESENCE OF THE EMPEROR CONSTANTIUS.

As if they would rescind their former determinations respecting the faith, they published anew other expositions of the creed, viz.—one in Greek, which Mark of Arethusa composed; and two others in Latin, which harmonized with one another neither in expression nor in sentiment, nor with that

---

[1] The " *Ludi Circenses,*" consisting of the five games, leaping, wrestling, boxing, racing, and hurling, (called in Greek πέντἀθλον,) with scenic representations, and spectacles of wild beasts at the amphitheatre; with which the consuls entertained the people at their entrance on the consulate. The Circensian games are alluded to by Juvenal, Sat. x. l. 81; and Tacit. Ann. i. 2.

dictated by the bishop of Arethusa. I shall here subjoin one
of those drawn up in Latin, to that prepared in Greek by
Mark: the other, which was afterwards recited at Rimini,
will be given when we describe what was done at that place.
It must be understood however, that both the Latin forms
were translated into Greek. The declaration of faith set forth
by Mark, was as follows :—

[78] "We believe in one God the Father Almighty, the Creator
and Maker of all things, of whom the whole family in heaven
and on earth is named (Eph. iii. 15): and in his only-begotten
Son, our Lord Jesus Christ, who was begotten of his Father
before all ages, God of God, Light of Light, by whom all
things visible and invisible, which are in the heavens and
upon the earth, were made; who is the Word, the Wisdom,
the true Light, and the Life; who in the last days for our
sake was made man and born of the holy virgin, was crucified
and died, was buried, and arose again from the dead on the
third day, was received up into heaven, sits at the right hand
of the Father, and is coming at the completion of the age to
judge the living and the dead, and to requite every one according to his works: whose kingdom being everlasting, en-
dures into endless ages; for he will be seated at the Father's
right hand, not only in the present age, but also in that which
is to come. We believe in the Holy Spirit, that is to say, the
Comforter, whom our Lord according to his promise sent to
his apostles after his ascension into the heavens, to teach them,
and bring all things to their remembrance; by whom also the
souls of those who have sincerely believed in him are sanctified. But those who affirm that the Son is of things which
are not, or of another substance, and not of God, and that
there was a time or an age when he was not, the holy and
catholic Church declares to be aliens. We therefore again
say, if any one affirms that the Father and Son are two Gods,
let him be anathema. And if any one admits that Christ is
God and the Son of God before the ages, but does not confess that he ministered to the Father in the formation of all
things, let him be anathema. If any one shall dare to assert
that the Unbegotten, or a part of him, was born of Mary,
let him be anathema. If any one says that the Son was of
Mary according to foreknowledge, and that he was not with
God, begotten of the Father before the ages, and that all

things were not made by him, let him be anathema. If any one affirms the essence of God to be dilated or contracted, let him be anathema. If any one says that the dilated essence of God makes the Son, or shall term the Son the dilatation of his essence, let him be anathema. If any one asserts that the internal or uttered word is Son of God, let him be anathema. If any one declares that the Son that was born of Mary was man only, let him be anathema. If any man, affirming him that was born of Mary to be God and man, shall imply the unbegotten God himself, let him be anathema. If any one shall understand the text, ' I am the first, and I am the last, and besides me there is no God,' (Isa. xliv. 6,) which was spoken for the destruction of idols and false gods, in the sense the Jews do, as if it were said for the subversion of the only-begotten of God before the ages, let him be anathema. If any one hearing (John i. 14) ' the Word was made flesh,' should imagine that the Word was changed into flesh, or that he underwent any change in assuming flesh, let him be anathema. If any one, hearing that the only-begotten Son of God was crucified, should say that his divinity[1] underwent any corruption, or suffering, or change, or diminution, or destruction, let him be anathema. If any one should affirm that the Father said not to the Son, ' Let us make man,' (Gen. i. 26,) but that God spoke to himself, let him be anathema. If any one says that it was not the Son of God that was seen by Abraham, but the unbegotten God, or a part of him, let him be anathema.[2] If any one says that it was not the Son that as man wrestled with Jacob, but the unbegotten God, or a part of him, let him be anathema. If any one shall understand the words, (Gen. xix. 24,) ' The Lord rained from the Lord,'[3] not in relation to the Father and the Son, but shall say that God rained from himself, let him be anathema: for the Lord the Son rained from the Lord the Father. If any one, hearing *the Lord the Father, and the Lord the Son*, shall term both the Father and the Son Lord, and saying *the Lord from the Lord*

---

[1] Τὴν θεότητα αὐτοῦ occurs in the Allat. MS. and in Athanasius, " Lib. de Synodis."   [2] See above, chap. xix.
[3] The original has יהוה in both cases. The Authorized Version has it, " Then the Lord rained . . . . . . brimstone and fire from the Lord out of heaven."

79 shall assert that there are two Gods, let him be anathema. For we rank not the Son with the Father, but conceive him to be subordinate to the Father. For he neither came down to Sodom[1] without his Father's will; nor did he rain from himself, but from the Lord (i. e. the Father) who exercises supreme authority: nor does he sit at the Father's right hand of himself, but in obedience to the Father, saying, 'Sit thou at my right hand' (Psal. cx. 1). If any one should say that the Father, Son, and Holy Spirit are one person, (πρόσωπον,) let him be anathema. If any one speaking of the Holy Spirit the Comforter, shall call him the begotten God, let him be anathema. If any one asserts that the Comforter is none other than the Son, when he has himself said, 'the Father, whom I will ask, shall send you another Comforter,' (John xiv. 16,) let him be anathema. If any one affirm that the Spirit is part of the Father and of the Son, let him be anathema. If any one say that the Father, Son, and Holy Spirit are three Gods, let him be anathema. If any one say that the Son of God was made as one of the creatures by the will of God, let him be anathema. If any one shall say that the Son was begotten against the Father's will, let him be anathema: for the Father did not, as compelled by any natural necessity, beget the Son at a time when he was unwilling; but as soon as it pleased him, he has declared that of himself, without time and without passion, he begat him. Should any one say that the Son is unbegotten, and without beginning, intimating that there are two without beginning, and unbegotten, so making two Gods, let him be anathema: for the Son is the head and beginning of all things; but 'the head of Christ is God' (1 Cor. xi. 3). Thus we devoutly trace up all things by the Son to one source of all things who is without beginning. Moreover to give an accurate conception of Christian doctrine, we again say, that if any one shall not declare Christ Jesus to have been the Son of God before all ages, and to have ministered to the Father in the creation of all things; but shall affirm that from the time only when he was born of Mary was he called the Son and Christ, and that he then received the commencement of his Divinity, let him be anathema, as the Samosatan."[2]

---

[1] Athanasius has ἐπὶ Σόδομα, not εἰς σῶμα.

[2] He alludes to Paul of Samosata, see Euseb. Eccl. Hist. b. vii. chaps. 29 and 30.

ANOTHER EXPOSITION OF THE FAITH SET FORTH AT SIR-
MIUM IN LATIN, AND AFTERWARDS TRANSLATED INTO
GREEK.

" Since there appears to have been some misunderstanding [80]
respecting the faith, all points have been carefully investigated and discussed at Sirmium, in presence of Valens, Ursacius, Germinius, and others.   It is evident that there is one
God, the Father Almighty, according as it is declared over
the whole word; and his only-begotten Son Jesus Christ, our
Lord, God, and Saviour, begotten of him before the ages.
But we ought not to say that there are two Gods, since the
Lord himself has said, (John xx. 17,) 'I go unto my Father
and your Father, and unto my God and your God.'   Therefore he is God even of all, as the apostle also taught, (Rom.
iii. 29, 30,) 'Is he the God of the Jews only? Is he not also
of the Gentiles? Yea of the Gentiles also; seeing that it is
one God who shall justify the circumcision by faith.'   And
in all other matters there is agreement, nor is there any ambiguity.   But since very many have been troubled about that
which is termed *substantia* in Latin, and οὐσία in Greek;
that is to say, in order to mark the sense more accurately, of
the *same* substance, (ὁμοούσιον,) or of *like* substance, (ὁμοιού-
σιον,) it is altogether desirable that none of these terms should
be mentioned: nor should they be preached on in the church,
for this reason, that nothing is recorded concerning them in
the Holy Scriptures; and because these things are above the
knowledge of mankind and human capacity, and that no one
can explain the Son's generation, of which it is written, (Isa.
liii. 8.) 'And who shall declare his generation?'   It is manifest that the Father only knows in what way he begat the
Son; and again, the Son, how he was begotten by the Father.
But no one can doubt that the Father is greater in honour,
dignity, and Divinity, and in the very name of Father; the
Son himself testifying, (John xiv. 28,) 'My Father is greater
than I.'   And no one is ignorant of this catholic doctrine,
that there are two persons of the Father and Son, and that
the Father is the greater: but that the Son is subject, together with all things which the Father has subjected to him.
That the Father had no beginning, and is invisible, immortal,
and impassible: but that the Son was begotten of the Father,

God of God, Light of Light; and that no one comprehends his generation, as was before said, but the Father alone. That the Son himself, our Lord and God, took flesh or a body, that is to say human nature, according as the angel brought glad tidings of : and as the whole Scriptures teach, and especially the apostle who was the great teacher of the Gentiles, Christ assumed the human nature through which he suffered, from the Virgin Mary. But the summary and confirmation of the entire faith is, that the doctrine of the Trinity should be always maintained, according as we read in the Gospel, (Matt. xxviii. 19,) 'Go ye and disciple all nations, baptizing them in the name of the Father, and of the Son, and of the Holy Spirit.' Thus the number of the Trinity is complete and perfect. Now the Holy Spirit, the Comforter sent by the Son, came according to his promise, in order to sanctify and instruct the apostles and all believers."

They endeavoured to induce Photinus, even after his deposition, to assent to and subscribe these things, promising to restore him his bishopric, if by recantation he would anathematize the dogma he had invented, and adopt their opinion. But instead of accepting their proposal, he challenged them to a disputation : and a day being appointed by the emperor's arrangement, the bishops who were there present assembled, and not a few of the senators, whom the emperor had directed to attend the discussion. In their presence, Basil, who at that time presided over the church at Ancyra, opposed Photinus, notaries writing down their respective speeches. The conflict of arguments on both sides was extremely severe ; but Photinus having been worsted, was condemned, and spent the rest of his life in exile, during which time he composed a treatise in both languages [1] (for he was not unskilled in Latin) against all heresies, and in favour of his own views. But the bishops who were convened at Sirmium, were afterwards dissatisfied with that form of the creed which had been promulgated by them in Latin : for after its publication, it appeared to them to contain many contradictions. They therefore endeavoured to get it back again from the transcribers; but inasmuch as many secreted it, the emperor by his edicts commanded that all the copies of it should be sought for, threatening punishment to any one who should be detected concealing

[1] i. e. both in Greek and Latin.

them. These menaces however were incapable of suppressing what had already fallen into the hands of many.

CHAP. XXXI.—OF HOSIUS BISHOP OF CORDOVA.

SINCE we have observed that Hosius the Spaniard was present at the council of Sirmium against his will, it is necessary to give some further account of him.   This prelate had but a short time before been sent into exile by the intrigues of the Arians: but at the earnest solicitation of those convened at Sirmium, the emperor summoned him thither, with the design either of influencing him by persuasion, or of compelling him by force, to give his sanction to their proceedings; for if this could be effected, they considered it would give great authority to their sentiments.   On this occasion therefore he was most unwillingly obliged to be present: and when he refused to concur with them, stripes and tortures were inflicted on the old man, until they had constrained him to acquiesce in and subscribe their exposition of the faith.   Such was the issue of affairs at that time transacted at Sirmium. But the emperor Constantius after these things still continued to reside at that place, awaiting there the result of the operations against Magnentius.

CHAP. XXXII.—OVERTHROW OF THE TYRANT MAGNENTIUS.

MAGNENTIUS in the interim having made himself master of the imperial city Rome, put to death many of the senatorial order, as well as of the populace.   But as soon as the commanders under Constantius had collected an army of Romans, and commenced their march against him, he left Rome, and retired into the Gallias.   There several battles were fought, sometimes to the advantage of one party, and sometimes to that of the other; but at last Magnentius having been defeated near Mursa, a fortress of the Gallias, was there closely besieged.   In this place the following remarkable incident is said to have occurred.   Magnentius, desiring to arouse the courage of his soldiers, who were disheartened by their late overthrow, ascended a lofty tribunal for this purpose. They wishing to receive him with such acclamations as emperors are usually greeted with, contrary to their intention, simultaneously shouted the name, not of Magnentius, but of Constantius Augustus. Regarding this as an omen wholly unfavourable to himself, Magnentius immediately withdrew from the fortress, and retreated to the remotest parts of Gaul, whither he was closely pursued by the generals of Constantius. An engagement having again taken place near Mount Seleucus,[1] Magnentius was totally routed, and fled alone to Lyons, a city of Gaul, which is distant three days' journey from the fortress at Myrsa. Magnentius having reached this city, first slew his own mother; then having killed his brother also, whom he had created Cæsar, he at last committed suicide by falling on his own sword. This happened in the sixth consulate of Constantius, and the second of Constantius Gallus, on the fifteenth[2] day of August. Not long after, another brother of Magnentius, named Decentius, put an end to his own life by hanging himself. Such was the issue of the ambitious enterprises of Magnentius, whose death however did not restore the affairs of the empire to perfect tranquillity; for soon after this another tyrant arose, whose name was Silvanus; but the generals of Constantius speedily destroyed him, whilst raising disturbances in Gaul.

CHAP. XXXIII.—Of the Jews inhabiting Dio Cæsarea in Palestine.

About the same time there arose another intestine commotion in the East: for the Jews who inhabited Dio Cæsarea in Palestine having taken arms against the Romans, began to ravage the adjacent places. But Gallus, who was also called Constantius, whom the emperor, after creating Cæsar, had sent into the East, despatched an army against them, whereby they were completely vanquished: after which their city Dio Cæsarea was by his order totally destroyed.

[1] Μιλτοσέλευκος: in the Allat. MS. Μοντοσέλευκος.
[2] The date is different in Idatius.

K 2

CHAP. XXXIV.—Of gallus cæsar.

GALLUS, having accomplished these things, was unable to bear his success with moderation; but forthwith attempted innovations on the authority of him who had constituted him Cæsar, himself aspiring to the sovereign power. His purpose was however soon detected by Constantius: for he had dared to put to death on his own responsibility Domitian, at that time Prætorian præfect of the East, and Magnus the quæstor, because they had disclosed his designs to the emperor. Constantius, extremely incensed at this conduct, summoned Gallus to his presence, who being in great terror went very reluctantly; and when he arrived in the western parts, and had reached the island of Flanona, Constantius ordered him to be slain. But not long after he created Julian, the brother of Gallus, Cæsar, and sent him against the barbarians in Gaul. It was in the seventh consulate of the emperor Constantius that Gallus was slain, when he himself was a third time consul: and Julian, of whom we shall make further mention in the next Book,[1] was created Cæsar on the 6th of November in the following year, when Arbetion and Lollian were consuls. When Constantius was thus relieved from the disquietudes which had occupied him, his attention was again directed to ecclesiastical contentions. Going therefore from Sirmium to the imperial city Rome, he again appointed a synod of bishops, summoning some of the Eastern prelates to hasten into Italy,[2] and commanding those of the West to meet them there. While preparations were making for this purpose, Julius bishop of Rome died, after having presided over the Church in that place fifteen years, and was succeeded in the episcopal dignity by Liberius.

CHAP. XXXV.—Of aëtius the syrian, master of eunomius.

AT Antioch in Syria another heresiarch sprang up, Aëtius surnamed Atheus. He agreed in doctrine with Arius, and

[1] See below, b. iii. chap. i.
[2] The text has Γαλλίαν, but in the codex of Leon Allatius it is rightly Ἰταλίαν, as is evident from the context.

maintained the same opinions; but separated himself from the Arian party, because they had admitted Arius into communion. For Arius, as we have before related, entertaining one opinion in his heart, professed another with his lips; having both hypocritically assented to and subscribed the form of faith set forth at the council of Nice, in order to deceive the reigning emperor. On this account therefore Aëtius separated himself from the Arians, although he had previously been a heretic, and a zealous advocate of Arian views. After receiving some very scanty instruction at Alexandria, on his return from thence, and arrival at Antioch in Syria, which was his native place, he was ordained deacon by Leontius, who was then bishop of that city. Upon this he began to astonish his auditors by the singularity of his discourses, which were constructed in dependence on the precepts of Aristotle's Categories, a book the scope of which he neither himself perceived, nor had been enlightened on by intercourse with learned persons; so that he was little aware that he was framing fallacious arguments to perplex and deceive himself. For Aristotle had composed this work to exercise the ingenuity of his young disciples, and to confound by subtile arguments the sophists who affected to deride phi-
83 losophy. Wherefore the Ephectic academicians [1] who expound the writings of Plato and Photius, censure the vain subtilty which Aristotle has displayed in that book: but Aëtius, who never had the advantage of an academical preceptor, adhered to the sophisms of the Categories. For this reason he was unable to comprehend how there could be generation without a beginning, and how that which was begotten can be co-eternal with him who begat. In fact Aëtius was a man of very superficial attainments, very little acquainted with the sacred Scriptures, and extremely fond of cavilling, a thing which any clown might do. Nor had he ever carefully studied those ancient writers who have interpreted the Christian oracles; wholly rejecting Clemens, Africanus, and Origen, men eminent for their information in every department of literature and science. But he composed epistles both to the emperor Constantius, and to some other persons, wherein he interwove tedious disputes for the purpose of displaying his

---

[1] Not the *Dogmatici*, but the *Sceptics*, who doubted everything.

sophisms. He has therefore been surnamed Atheus.[1] But
although his doctrinal statements were similar to those of the
Arians, yet from the abstruse nature of his syllogisms, which
they were unable to comprehend, they pronounced him a
heretic. Being for that reason expelled from their Church,
he pretended to have separated himself from their communion.
Even in the present day there are to be found some who from
him were formerly named Aëtians, but now Eunomians. For
Eunomius, who had been his secretary, having been instructed
by his master in this heretical mode of reasoning, afterwards
became the head of that sect. But of Eunomius we shall
speak more fully in the proper place.

CHAP. XXXVI.—OF THE SYNOD AT MILAN.

WHEN the bishops met in Italy, very few from the East
were present, most of them being hindered from coming either
by the infirmities of age, or by the distance ; but of the West
there were more than three hundred. Being assembled at [84]
Milan, according to the emperor's order, the Eastern prelates
opened the synod by calling upon those convened to pass an
unanimous sentence of condemnation against Athanasius ;
with this object in view, that he might thenceforward be utterly shut out from Alexandria. But Paulinus bishop of
Treves in Gaul, Dionysius of Alba, the metropolis of Italy, [85]
and Eusebius of Verceil, a city of Liguria in Italy, perceiving
that the Eastern bishops, by demanding a ratification of the
sentence against Athanasius, were intent on subverting the
faith, arose and loudly exclaimed that this proposition indicated a covert plot against the principles of Christian truth.
For they insisted that the charges against Athanasius were
unfounded, and merely invented by his accusers as a means of
corrupting the faith. Having made this protest with much
vehemence of manner, the congress of bishops was then dissolved.

[1] ἄθεος, the atheist.

CHAP. XXXVII.—OF THE SYNOD AT RIMINI, AND THE CREED THERE PUBLISHED.[1]

THE emperor, on being apprized of what had taken place, sent these three bishops into exile; and determined to convene a general council, that by drawing all the Eastern bishops into the West, he might, if possible, bring them all to unity of judgment. But when, on consideration, the length of the journey seemed to present serious obstacles, he directed that the synod should consist of two divisions; permitting those present at Milan to meet at Rimini in Italy; but the Eastern bishops were instructed by his letters to assemble at Nicomedia in Bithynia. The emperor's object in these arrangements was to effect a general coincidence of opinion; but the issue was contrary to his expectation. For neither of the synods was in harmony with itself, but each was divided into opposing factions: those convened at Rimini could not agree with one another; and the Eastern bishops assembled at Seleucia in Isauria made another schism. The details of what took place in both will be given in the course of our history, but we shall first make a few observations on Eudoxius. About that time Leontius died, who had ordained the heretic Aëtius deacon: and Eudoxius bishop of Germanicia in Syria, who was then at Rome, thinking no time was to be lost, speciously represented to the emperor that the city over which he presided was in need of his counsel and care, and requested permission to return there immediately. This the emperor readily acceded to, having no suspicion of a clandestine purpose: and Eudoxius, having obtained some of the principal officers of the emperor's bed-chamber to assist him, deserted his own diocese, and fraudulently installed himself in the see of Antioch. His first act there was an attempt to restore Aëtius to his office of deacon, of which he had been divested; and he accordingly convened a council of bishops for that purpose. But his wishes in this respect were baffled, for the odium with which Aëtius was regarded, was more prevalent than the exertions of Eudoxius in his favour. When the bishops were assembled at Rimini, those from the East declared that they were willing to forego all reference to the

[1] Compare the parallel history given by Theodoret, b. ii. ch. xviii.

case of Athanasius : a resolution that was zealously supported
by Ursacius and Valens, who had formerly maintained the
tenets of Arius ; but their disposition being always to identify
themselves with the strongest side, they had afterwards presented a recantation of their opinion to the bishop of Rome,
and publicly avowed their assent to the doctrine of consubstantiality.   Germinius, Auxentius, Demophilus, and Gaïus
made the same declaration in reference to Athanasius.   When
therefore some endeavoured to propose one thing in the convocation of bishops, and some another, Ursacius and Valens
said that all former draughts of the creed ought to be considered as set aside, and the last alone, which had been prepared at their late convention at Sirmium, regarded as authorized.   They then caused to be read a schedule which they held
in their hands, containing another form of the creed : this had
indeed been drawn up at Sirmium, but had been kept concealed, as we have before observed, until their present publication of it at Rimini.   Its contents, translated from the Latin
into Greek, were these :—   87

    " The catholic faith was expounded at Sirmium in presence
of our lord Constantius, in the consulate of the most illustrious 88
Flavius Eusebius, and Hypatius, on the twenty-third May.

    " We believe in one only and true God, the Father Almighty,
the Creator and Framer of all things : and in one only-begotten
Son of God, begotten without passion, before all ages, before
all beginning, before all conceivable time, and before all com-
prehensible thought : by whom the ages were framed, and all
things made : who was begotten the only-begotten of the
Father, only of only, God of God, like to the Father who
begat him, according to the Scriptures : whose generation no
one knows, but the Father only who begat him.   We know
that this his only-begotten Son came down from the heavens
by his Father's appointment for the putting away of sin, was
born of the Virgin Mary, conversed with his disciples, and
fulfilled every dispensation according to the Father's will : was
crucified and died, and descended into the lower parts[1] of
the earth, and disposed matters there ; at the sight of whom
the door-keepers of Hades trembled : having arisen on the
third day, he again conversed with his disciples, and after forty

    [1] Καταχθόνια.   The word καταχθονίων seems to be used in Phil. ii.
10, to denote *departed souls.*

days were completed he ascended into the heavens, and is
seated at the Father's right hand; and at the last day he
will come in his Father's glory, to render to every one according to his works.   We believe also in the Holy Spirit, whom
the only-begotten Son of God Jesus Christ himself promised
to send to the human race as the Comforter, according to that
which is written : 'I go away to my Father, and will ask him,
and he will send you another Comforter, the Spirit of truth.
He shall receive of mine, and shall teach you, and bring all
things to your remembrance.'   As for the term *substance*,
which was used by our fathers for the sake of greater simplicity, but not being understood by the people has caused
offence on account of its not being contained in the Scriptures ;
it seemed desirable that it should be wholly abolished, and that
in future no mention should be made of substance in reference
to God, since the divine Scriptures have nowhere spoken concerning the substance of the Father and the Son.   But we
say that the Son is in all things *like* the Father, as the Holy
Scriptures affirm and teach."

These statements having been read, those who were dissatisfied with them rose and said : " We came not hither
because we were in want of a creed ; for we preserve inviolate
that which we received from the beginning : but we are here
met to repress any innovation upon it which may have been
made.   If therefore what has been recited introduces no novelties, now openly anathematize the Arian heresy, in the same
manner as the ancient canon of the Church has rejected all
heresies as blasphemous : for it is evident to the whole world
that the impious dogma of Arius has excited the disturbances
of the Church, and the troubles which exist until now."   This
proposition not being acceded to by Ursacius, Valens, Germinius, Auxentius, Demophilus, and Gaïus, the Church was rent
asunder by a complete division : for these prelates adhered to
what had then been recited in the synod of Rimini ; while
the others again confirmed the Nicene creed.   The inscription
at the head of the creed that had been read was greatly derided, and especially by Athanasius in a letter which he sent
to his friends, wherein he thus expresses himself:—

" What point of doctrine was wanting to the piety of the
Catholic Church, that they should now make an investigation
respecting the faith, and prefix moreover the consulate of the

present times to their published exposition of it? For Ursacius, Valens, and Germinius have done what was neither done nor even heard of at any time before among Christians: having composed a creed such as they themselves are willing to believe, they preface it with the consulate, month, and day of the present time, in order to prove to all discerning persons that theirs is not the ancient faith, but such as was originated under the reign of the present emperor Constantius.[1]   Moreover they have written all things with a view to their own heresy: and besides this, affecting to write respecting the Lord, they name another Lord as theirs, even Constantius, who has countenanced their impiety, so that those who deny the Son to be eternal, have styled him eternal emperor. Thus are they proved to be the enemies of Christ by their profanity. But perhaps the holy prophets' record of time afforded them a precedent for noticing the consulate! Now should they presume to make this pretext, they would most glaringly expose their own ignorance.   The prophecies of these holy men do indeed mark the times.   Isaiah and Hosea lived in the days of Uzziah, Joatham, Ahaz, and Hezekiah (Isa. i. 2; Hos. i. 1); Jeremiah in the time of Josiah (Jer. i. 2); Ezekiel and Daniel in the reign of Cyrus and Darius; and others uttered their predictions in other times: but they did not then lay the foundations of religion.   That was in existence before them, and always was, even before the creation of the world, God having prepared it for us in Christ.   Nor did they designate the commencement of their own faith; for they were themselves men of faith previously: but they signify the times of the promises given through them. Now the promises primarily referred to our Saviour's advent; and all that was foretold respecting the course of future events in relation to Israel and the Gentiles was merely collateral and subordinate. Hence the periods mentioned indicated not the beginning of their faith, as I before observed, but the times in which these prophets lived and foretold such things.   But these sages of our day, who neither compile histories, nor predict future events, after writing *The Catholic Faith was published*, immediately add the Consulate, with the month and the day:

---

[1] This appeal to antiquity, as the test of truth, is very common with the earlier Fathers, who always brand strange doctrines with the stamp of heresy.

and as the holy prophets wrote the date of their records and
of their own ministration, so these men intimate the era of
their own faith.   And would that they had written concerning *their own* faith only, since they have now begun to believe, and had not undertaken to write respecting the *Catholic*
faith.   For they have not written *Thus we believe;* but *The
Catholic Faith was published.*   The temerity of purpose
herein manifested argues their impiety; while the novelty of
expression found in the document they have concocted assimi-
lates it with the Arian heresy.   By writing in this manner
they have declared when they themselves began to believe,
and from what time they wish it to be understood their faith
was first preached.   And just as when the evangelist Luke
says, 'A decree of enrolment[1] was published,' he speaks of
an edict which was not in existence before, but came into
operation at that time, and was published by him who had
written it; so these men by writing *The faith has now been
published,* have declared that the tenets of their heresy are of
modern invention, and did not exist in former times.   But
since they apply the term *Catholic* to it, they seem to have
unconsciously fallen into the extravagant assumption of the
Cataphrygians, asserting even as they did, that *the Christian
faith was first revealed to us, and commenced with us.*   And
as those termed Maximilla and Montanus, so these styled
Constantius their Lord, instead of Christ.   But if, according
to them, the faith had its beginning from the present consulate, what will the fathers and the blessed martyrs do?   Moreover what will they themselves do with those who were instructed in religious principles by them, and died before this
consulate?   By what means will they recall them to life, in
order to obliterate from their minds what they seemed to have
taught them, and to implant in its stead those new discoveries
of theirs?   So 'stupid are they as to be only capable of framing pretences, and these such as are presumptuous and unreasonable, and carry with them their own refutation."

Athanasius wrote thus to his friends: and the learned who
may read through his whole epistle will perceive how powerfully he treats the subject; but for brevity's sake we have
here inserted a part only.   Valens, Ursacius, Auxentius, Germinius, Gaïus, and Demophilus, were deposed by the synod,

---

[1] 'Απογραφῆς δόγμα, edictum de censu.

for refusing to anathematize the Arian doctrine; who being
very indignant at their deposition, hastened directly to the
emperor, carrying with them the exposition of faith which
had been read in the synod.   The council also acquainted the
emperor with their determinations in a communication which,
translated from the Latin into Greek, was to the following
effect:—

EPISTLE[1] OF THE SYNOD OF RIMINI TO THE EMPEROR CON-
STANTIUS.

" We believe that it was by the appointment of God, as [89]
well as at the command of your piety, that we, the bishops of
the West, came out of various districts to Rimini, in order
that the faith of the Catholic Church might be made manifest
to all, and that heretics might be detected.   For on a con-
siderate review by us of all points, our decision has been to
adhere to the ancient faith which we have received from the
prophets, the Gospels, the apostles, from God himself, and our
Lord Jesus Christ, the guardian of your empire, and the pro-
tector of your person, which faith also we have always maintained.   We conceived that it would be unwarrantable and
impious to mutilate any of those things which have been
justly and solemnly ratified, by those who sat in the Nicene
council with Constantine of glorious memory, the father of
your piety.   What was then determined has been made public, and infused into the minds of the people; and it is found
to be so powerfully opposed to the Arian heresy which then
sprang up, as to subdue not it only, but also all others.   Should
therefore any thing be taken away from what was at that
time established, a passage would be opened to the poisonous
doctrine of heretics.
" These matters having been strictly investigated and the
creed drawn up in the presence of Constantine, who, after
being baptized, departed to God's rest in the faith of it; we
regard as an abomination any infringement thereon, or any
attempt to invalidate the authority of so many saints, confessors, and successors of the martyrs, who assisted at that council, and themselves preserved inviolate all the determinations
of the ancient writers of the Catholic Church: whose faith

[1] We have here followed Valesius, who gives from Hilary the original
Latin copy, from which the Greek version differs considerably.

has remained unto these times in which your piety has received from God the Father, through Jesus Christ our God
and Lord, the power of ruling the world.

" Ursacius and Valens being heretofore suspected of entertaining Arian sentiments, were suspended from communion :
but on making an apology, as their written recantation attests,
they obtained pardon from the council of Milan, at which the
legates of the Church of Rome were present.   Yet have
these infatuated beings, endued with an unhappy disposition,
again had the temerity to declare themselves the propagators
of false doctrine ; and even now they endeavour to shake
what has been in great wisdom established.   For when the
letters of your piety had ordered us to assemble for the examination of the faith, these troublers of the Churches, supported by Germinius, Auxentius, and Gaïus, presented for
consideration a new creed, containing much unsound doctrine.
But when the exposition they thus publicly brought forward
in the council met with general disapprobation, they thought
it should be otherwise expressed : and indeed it is notorious
that they have often changed their sentiments within a short
time.   Lest therefore the Churches should be more frequently
disturbed, it was decreed that the ancient sanctions should be
ratified and maintained inviolable ; and moreover that the
aforesaid persons should be excommunicated.   We have accordingly directed our legates to inform your clemency of these
things, and to present our letter in which the decisions of the
council are announced.   To them also this special charge
has been given, that they should not otherwise execute their
commission, than that the ancient ordinances should continue
firmly established ; and also to assure your wisdom that peace
could not be secured by some slight alteration, such as Valens,
Ursacius, Germinius, and Gaïus subsequently proposed.   For
how can peace be preserved by those who are ever seeking to
subvert it? or by men who have filled all regions, and especially the Church of Rome, with confusion ?   Wherefore we
beseech your clemency propitiously to regard and favourably
to listen to our deputies ; and not to permit anything to be
reversed to the prejudice of the ancient faith, but to cause
that those truths may remain unimpaired which we have received from our ancestors, whom we know to have been prudent men, and who did not act otherwise than in subjection

to the Holy Spirit of God. Because not only are the believing people distracted by these novel doctrines, but infidels also are turned aside from embracing the faith. We further entreat you to order that the bishops who are detained at Rimini, among whom are many that are wasted by age and poverty, may return to their several provinces; lest the members of their Churches should suffer from the absence of their bishops. But we pray still more earnestly that no innovation may be made on the faith, and nothing abstracted; but that those principles may continue unvitiated which were recognised in the times of the father of your sacred piety, and have been transmitted to your own religious age. Let not your holy prudence suffer us in future to be exhausted by fatigue, and torn from our sees: but permit the bishops to dwell with their people free from contentions, that they may uninterruptedly offer up supplications for the safety of your person, for the prosperity of your reign, and for peace, which may the Deity grant, according to your merits, to be profound and perpetual. Our legates will present your sacred and religious prudence another document, containing the names and signatures of all the bishops or their deputies."

The synod having thus written, sent their communications to the emperor by the bishops selected for that purpose. But Ursacius and Valens having arrived before them, did their utmost to calumniate the council, exhibiting the exposition of the faith which they had brought with them: and as the mind of this prince had long been infected with Arian sentiments, he became extremely exasperated against the synod, but conferred great honour on Valens and Ursacius. Those deputed by the council were consequently detained a considerable time, without being able to obtain an answer: at length however the emperor replied through those who had come to him, in manner following:—

"Constantius Victor and Triumphator Augustus to all the bishops convened at Rimini.

"That our especial care is ever exercised respecting the divine and venerated law even your sanctity is not ignorant. Nevertheless we have hitherto been unable to give an audience to the twenty bishops who undertook the part of a deputation from you, inasmuch as preparations for an expedition against the barbarians have wholly engrossed our attention.

And since, as you will admit, matters relative to the divine law ought to be entered on with a mind free from all anxiety, I have therefore ordered these prelates to await our return to Adrianople; that when public business shall have been duly attended to, we may then give our consideration to what they shall propose. In the interim, let it not seem troublesome to your gravity to wait for their return; since when they shall convey to you our resolution, you will be prepared to carry into effect such measures as may be most advantageous to the welfare of the.Catholic Church."

The bishops on the receipt of this letter wrote thus in reply :—

" We have received your clemency's letter, sovereign lord most beloved of God, in which you inform us that the exigences of state affairs have hitherto prevented your admitting our legates to your presence; and you bid us await their return, until your piety shall have learnt from them what has been determined on by us in conformity with the tradition of our ancestors. But we again protest by this letter that we can by no means depart from our, primary resolution; and this also we have commissioned our deputies to state. We beseech you therefore, both with unruffled countenance to order this present epistle of our modesty to be read, and also to listen benignantly to the reprsentations with which our legates have been charged. Your mildness doubtless perceives, as well as we, to how great an extent grief and sadness prevail, because of so many Churches being bereft of their bishops in these most blessed times of yours. Again therefore we entreat your clemency, sovereign lord most dear to God, to command us to return to our Churches, if it please your piety, before the rigour of winter; in order that we may be enabled, in conjunction with the people, to offer up our solemn prayers to Almighty God, and to our Lord and Saviour Jesus Christ, his only-begotten Son, for the prosperity of your reign, as we have always done, and now desire to do."

The bishops having waited together some time after this letter had been despatched, without the emperor's deigning to reply, departed to their respective cities. Now it had long before been the emperor's intention to disseminate Arian doctrine throughout the Churches; which he then being anxious to accomplish so as to give it pre-eminence, pretended their

departure was an act of contumely, declaring they had treated
him with contempt by dissolving the council in opposition to
his wishes. He therefore gave the partisans of Ursacius unbounded licence of acting as they pleased in regard to the
Churches : and directed that the form of creed which had been
read at Rimini, should be sent to the Churches throughout
Italy ; ordering that whoever would not subscribe it should
be ejected from their sees, and others substituted in their.
place.[1] Liberius bishop of Rome, having refused his assent
to that creed, was the first who was sent into-exile ; the adherents of Ursacius appointed Felix to succeed him, who had
been a deacon in that Church, but on embracing the Arian heresy
was elevated to the episcopate. Some however assert that he
was not favourable to that opinion, but was constrained by
force to receive the ordination of bishop. After this all parts
of the West were filled with agitation and tumult, some being
ejected and banished, and others established in their stead ;
these things being effected by violence, on the authority of the
imperial edicts, which were also sent into the eastern parts.
Not long after indeed Liberius was recalled, and reinstated in
his see ; for the people of Rome having raised a sedition, and
expelled Felix from their Church, Constantius deemed it inexpedient to further provoke the popular fury. The Ursacian
faction quitting Italy, passed through the eastern parts ; and
arriving at Nice a city of Thrace, they there held another
synod, where after translating the form of faith which was
read at Rimini into Greek, they confirmed and published it
afresh, as the one that had been dictated at the general council. In this way they attempted to deceive the more simple.
by the similarity of names, and to impose upon them as the
creed promulgated at Nice in Bithynia, that which they had
prepared at Nice[2] in Thrace. But this artifice was of little
advantage to them ; for being soon detected, it exposed them
to the contempt and derision of all men. With this we close
our account of the transactions which took place in the West :
we shall now proceed to state what was done in the East.

[1] Compare Theodoret, ii. 16.
[2] The name of the former place is correctly written Nicæa, that of the
latter, Nice.

CHAP. XXXVIII.—CRUELTY OF MACEDONIUS, AND TUMULTS
RAISED BY HIM.

THE bishops of the Arian party assumed greater assurance
from the imperial edicts. For what reason they undertook to
convene a synod, we will explain, after having briefly mentioned a few of their acts previously. Acacius and Patrophilus having ejected Maximus bishop of Jerusalem, installed
Cyril in his see. Macedonius subverted the order of things
in the cities and provinces adjacent to Constantinople, promoting to ecclesiastical honours the assistants of his machinations against the Churches. He ordained Eleusius bishop of
Cyzicum, and Marathonius bishop of Nicomedia: the latter
had before been a deacon under Macedonius himself, and had
been very active in founding monasteries both of men and
women. But we shall now mention in what way Macedonius,
after having again possessed himself of the prelacy by the
means before stated, desolated the Churches around Constantinople, and inflicted innumerable calamities on such as were
unwilling to adopt his views. His persecutions were not confined to those who were recognised as members of the Catholic
Church, but extended to the Novatians also,[1] inasmuch as
they maintained the doctrine of *consubstantiality;* they therefore with the others underwent the most intolerable sufferings,
but Angelius their bishop effected his escape by flight.
Many persons eminent for their piety were seized and tortured, because they refused to communicate with him : and
after being subjected to the torture, they were forcibly constrained to be partakers of the holy mysteries, their mouths
being forced open with a piece of wood, and then the consecrated elements thrust into them. Those who were so treated
regarded this as a punishment far more grievous than all

---

[1] From the manner in which Socrates here contrasts the Novatians
with the Catholic Church, it is quite clear that, however much disposed he
may have been to view the peculiar tenets of that sect with leniency, and
even with favour, he never united himself to their body. Indeed in b. vi.
chaps. xx. and xxiii., he classes the Novatians among heretics, together
with the Arians, Macedonians, and Eunomians. Bellarmine is therefore
probably right, in affirming, (as he does in his treatise " de Scriptoribus
Ecclesiasticis,") that he favoured the Novatians. Of more than this there
is no proof.

[SOCRATES.]   L

others. Moreover, they laid hold of women and children, and
compelled them to be initiated by baptism: and if any one
resisted or otherwise spoke against it, stripes immediately followed, with bonds, imprisonment, and other violent measures.
I shall here relate an instance or two whereby the reader may
form some idea of the extent of the barbarity exercised by
Macedonius and those who were then in power. They first
pressed in a box, and then sawed off, the breasts of such
women as were unwilling to communicate with them. The
same parts of the persons of other women they burnt, partly
with iron, and partly with eggs intensely heated in the fire:
a mode of torture which was never practised, even among the
heathen, but was invented by those who professed to be
Christians. These facts were related to me by the aged
Auxano, the presbyter in the Novatian Church of whom I
spoke in the first Book. He said also that he had himself endured great severities from the Arians, prior to his receiving
the dignity of presbyter; having been thrown into prison and
beaten with many stripes, together with Alexander Paphlagon,
his companion in the monastic life. He added that he was
himself enabled to sustain these tortures, but that Alexander
died in prison from the effects of their infliction. His tomb
is still visible on the right of those sailing into the bay of
Constantinople which is called Ceras, close by the rivers,
where there is a church of the Novatians bearing Alexander's
name. Moreover the Arians, at the instigation of Macedonius, demolished, with many other churches in various cities,
that of the Novatians at Constantinople near Pelargus. Why
I particularly mention this church, will be seen from the extraordinary circumstances connected with it, as testified by
the same venerable informant. The emperor's edict and the
violence of Macedonius had doomed to destruction the churches
of those who maintained the doctrine of consubstantiality; and
not only was the ruin of this church threatened, but those also
who were charged with the execution of the mandate were at
hand to carry it into effect. The zeal displayed by the Novatians on this occasion, as well as the sympathy they experienced from those whom the Arians at that time ejected, but
who are now in peaceful possession of their churches, cannot
be too highly admired. For when the emissaries of their
enemies were urgent to accomplish its destruction, an im-

mense multitude of Novatians, aided by numbers of others
who held similar sentiments, having assembled around this
devoted church, pulled it down, and conveyed the materials
of it to Sycæ, which stands opposite the city, and forms its
thirteenth ward. This removal was effected in a very short
time, from the extraordinary ardour of the numerous persons
engaged in it: one carried tiles, another stones, a third timber; some loading themselves with one thing, and some
another. Even women and children assisted in the work,
regarding it as the realization of their best wishes, and esteem-
ing it the greatest honour to be accounted the faithful guard-
ians of things consecrated to God. In this way was the
church of the Novatians transported to Sycæ: when however
Constantius was dead, the emperor Julian ordered its former
site to be restored, and permitted them to rebuild it there.
The people therefore, as before, having carried back the materials, reared the church in its former position; and from this
circumstance, and its great improvement in structure and
ornament, they not inappropriately called it *Anastasia.*[1] This
was done, as we before said, in the reign of Julian. But at
that time both the Catholics[2] and the Novatians were alike
subjected to persecution: for the former abominated offering
their devotions in those churches in which the Arians assembled, choosing rather to frequent the other three churches at
[91] Constantinople which belonged to the Novatians, and to engage
in Divine service with them. Indeed they would have been
wholly united, had not the Novatians opposed this from regard
to their ancient precepts. In other respects, however, they mutually maintained such a degree of cordiality and affection, as
to be ready to lay down their lives for one another: both parties
were therefore persecuted indiscriminately, not only at Constantinople, but also in other provinces and cities. At Cyzicum,
Eleusius the bishop of that place perpetrated the same kind of
enormities against the Christians there, as Macedonius had done
elsewhere, harassing and putting them to flight in all directions;
and among other things he completely demolished the church
of the Novatians at Cyzicum. But Macedonius consummated
his wickedness in the following manner. Hearing that there
was a great number of the Novatian sect in the province of

[1] i. e. the Church of the *Resurrection.*
[2] Οἵ τῆς ἐκκλησίας. The adherents of the Nicene Faith.

Paphlagonia, and especially at Mantinium, and perceiving that such a numerous body could not be driven from their homes by ecclesiastics alone, he caused by the emperor's permission four companies of soldiers to be sent into Paphlagonia, that through dread of the military they might receive the Arian opinion. But those who inhabited Mantinium, animated to desperation by zeal for their religion, armed themselves with long reap-hooks, hatchets, and whatever weapon came to hand, and went forth to meet the troops; on which a conflict ensuing, many indeed of the Paphlagonians were slain, but nearly all the soldiers were destroyed. I learnt these things from a countryman of Paphlagonia, who said that he was present at the engagement; and many others of that province corroborate this account. Such were the exploits of Macedonius on behalf of Christianity, consisting of murders, battles, incarcerations, and civil wars: proceedings which rendered him odious not only to the objects of his persecution, but even to his own party. He became obnoxious also to the emperor on these accounts, and particularly so from the circumstance I am about to relate. The church where the coffin lay that contained the relics of the emperor Constantine threatened to fall, so as to cause great alarm to those who had entered it, as well as to those who were accustomed to remain there for devotional purposes; and so Macedonius wished to remove the emperor's remains, lest the coffin should be injured by the ruins. The populace getting intelligence of this, endeavoured to prevent it, insisting that the emperor's bones should not be disturbed, as such a disinterment would be sacrilege: many however affirmed that its removal could not possibly injure the dead body, and thus two parties were formed on this question; such as held the doctrine of consubstantiality joining with those who opposed it on the ground of its impiety. Macedonius, in total disregard of these prejudices, caused the emperor's remains to be transported to the church where those of the martyr Acacius lay. Whereupon a vast multitude rushed toward that edifice in two hostile divisions, which attacked one another with such fury, that great numbers lost their lives; and not only was the church-yard covered with gore, but the well also which was in it overflowed with blood, which ran into the adjacent portico, and thence even into the very street. When the emperor was informed of this disastrous encounter, he was highly incensed against Macedonius, not only on account of the slaughter which he had occasioned, but especially because he had dared to remove his father's body without consulting him.   Having therefore left the Cæsar Julian to take care of the Western parts, he himself set out for the East.   How Macedonius was a short time afterwards deposed, and thus suffered a most inadequate punishment for his infamous crimes, I shall hereafter relate.

CHAP. XXXIX.—OF THE SYNOD AT SELEUCIA, A CITY OF ISAURIA.

BUT I must now give an account of the other synod, which the emperor's edict had convoked in the East, as a rival to that of Rimini.   It was at first determined that the bishops should assemble at Nicomedia in Bithynia; but a great earthquake having nearly destroyed that city, prevented their being convened there.   This happened in the consulate of Datian and Cerealis, on the 28th day of August.   They therefore resolved to transfer the council to the neighbouring city of Nice: but this plan was again altered, as it seemed more convenient to meet at Tarsus in Cilicia.   Being dissatisfied with this arrangement also, they at last assembled themselves at Seleucia, surnamed Aspera, a city of Isauria.   This took place in the same year in which the council of Rimini was held, under the consulate of Eusebius and Hypatius, the number of those convened amounting to 160.   There was present on this occasion Leonas, an officer of distinction attached to the imperial household, before whom the emperor's edict had enjoined that the discussion respecting the faith should be entered into.   Lauricius also, the commander-in-chief of the troops in Isauria, was ordered to be there, to supply the bishops with such things as they might require.   In the presence of these personages, therefore, the bishops were there convened on the 27th of the month of September, and immediately began a discussion respecting the public records, notaries being present to write down what each might say.   Those who desire to learn the particulars of the several speeches, will find copious details of them in the collection of Sabinus; but we shall only notice the more important heads. On the first day of their being convened, Leonas ordered each one to propose what he thought fit: but those present said that no question ought to be agitated in the absence of those prelates whose attendance there was expected; for Macedonius bishop of Constantinople, Basil of Ancyra, and some others who were apprehensive of an impeachment for their misconduct, had not made their appearance. Macedonius pleaded indisposition, as an excuse for non-attendance; Patrophilus pretended an ophthalmic affection, which made it needful that he should remain in the suburbs of Seleucia; and the rest offered various pretexts to account for their absence. When however Leonas declared that the subjects which they had met to consider must be entered on, notwithstanding the absence of these persons, the bishops replied that they could not proceed to the discussion of any question, until the life and conduct of the parties accused had been investigated: for Cyril of Jerusalem, Eustathius of Sebastia in Armenia, and some others, had been charged with misconduct on various grounds long before. A sharp contest arose in consequence of this demur; some affirming that cognizance ought first to be taken of all such accusations, and others denying that anything whatever should have precedence of matters of faith. The emperor's orders contributed not a little to augment this dispute, inasmuch as he had, in different parts of his letter, inadvertently given contrary directions as to the priority of consideration of these points. A schism was thus made which divided the Seleucian council into two factions, one of which was headed by Acacius of Cæsarea in Palestine, George of Alexandria, Uranius of Tyre, and Eudoxius of Antioch, who were supported by only about thirty-two other bishops. Of the opposite party, which was by far the more numerous, the principal were George of Laodicea in Syria, Sophronius of Pompeiopolis in Paphlagonia, and Eleusius of Cyzicum. It being determined by the majority to examine doctrinal matters first, the party of Acacius openly opposed the Nicene creed, and wished to introduce another instead of it. The other faction, which was considerably more numerous, concurred in all the decisions of the council of Nice, except its adoption of the term Consubstantial, to which it strongly objected. A keen debate on this point immediately ensued, which was continued until evening, when Silvanus, who presided over the Church at Tarsus, insisted with much vehemence of manner, that there was no need of a new exposition of the faith; but that it was their duty rather to confirm that which was published at Antioch,[1] at the consecration of the church in that place. On this declaration, Acacius and his partisans privately withdrew from the council ; while the others, producing the creed composed at Antioch, read it, and then separated for that day. Assembling in the church of Seleucia on the day following, after having closed the doors, they again read the same creed, and ratified it by their signatures, the readers and deacons present signing it on behalf of certain absent bishops, who had intimated their acquiescence in its form.

CHAP. XL.—ACACIUS BISHOP OF CÆSAREA DICTATES ANOTHER FORM OF THE CREED IN THE SYNOD AT SELEUCIA.

ACACIUS and his adherents loudly exclaimed against this act of covertly affixing their signatures when the church doors were closed ; declaring that all such secret transactions were justly to be suspected, and had no validity whatever. These objections were prompted by another motive, as he was anxious to bring forward an exposition of the faith drawn up by himself, which he had already submitted to the governors Leonas and Lauricius, and was now intent on getting confirmed and established, instead of that which had been subscribed. The second day was thus occupied with nothing else but exertions on his part to effect this object. Leonas, on the third day, endeavoured to produce an amicable meeting of both parties ; Macedonius of Constantinople and Basil of Ancyra having at length arrived. But when the Acacians found that both these persons had attached themselves to the opposite party, they refused to meet; saying that not only those who had before been deposed, but also such as were at present under any accusation, ought to be excluded from the assembly. After much cavilling on both sides,

[1] See above, chaps. viii. and x.

this opinion prevailed ; and accordingly those who lay under
any charge went out of the council, and the party of Acacius
entered.   Leonas then said that a document had been put into
his hand by Acacius, to which he desired to call their attention :
but he did not state that it was the draught of a creed, which
in some particulars covertly, and in others unequivocally, con-
tradicted the former.   Silence having been made, the bishops
anticipating anything rather than what it actually was, the
following creed composed by Acacius, together with its pre-
amble, was read :—

" We having yesterday assembled by the emperor's command
at Seleucia, a city of Isauria, on the 27th day of September,
exerted ourselves to the utmost, with all moderation, to preserve the peace of the Church, and to determine doctrinal
questions on prophetic and evangelical authority ; so as to sanction nothing in the ecclesiastical confession of faith at variance with the sacred Scriptures, as our emperor Constantius
most beloved of God has ordered.   But inasmuch as certain
individuals in the synod have acted injuriously toward several
of us, preventing some from expressing their sentiments, and
excluding others from the council against their wills ; and at
the same time have introduced such as have been deposed,
and persons who were ordained contrary to the ecclesiastical
canon, so that the synod has presented a scene of tumult
and disorder of which the most illustrious Count Leonas and
the most eminent Lauricius, governor of the province, have been
eye-witnesses, we are therefore under the necessity of making
this declaration.   Not that we repudiate the faith which was
ratified at the consecration of the church at Antioch ; for we
give it our decided preference, because it received the concurrence of our fathers who were assembled there to consider
some controverted points.   Since however the terms *consubstantial,* [ὁμοούσιον,] and *of like substance,* [ὁμοιούσιον,] have
in time past troubled the minds of many, and still continue to
disquiet them ; and moreover that a new term has recently
been coined by some who assert the *dissimilitude* [ἀνόμοιον]
of the Son to the Father ; we reject the first two, as expressions
which are not found in the Scriptures ; but we utterly anathematize the last, and regard such as countenance its use, as
alienated from the Church.   We distinctly acknowledge the

likeness [ὅμοιον] of the Son to the Father, in accordance with
what the apostle has declared concerning him, (Col. i. 15,)
'Who is the image of the invisible God.'

"We confess, then, and believe in one God the Father Almighty, the Maker of heaven and earth, and of things visible
and invisible. We believe also in his Son our Lord Jesus Christ,
who was begotten of him without passion before all ages,
God the Word, the only-begotten of God, the Light, the Life,
the Truth, the Wisdom ; by whom all things were made which
are in the heavens and upon the earth, whether visible or invisible. We believe that he took flesh of the holy Virgin
Mary, at the end of the ages,[1] in order to abolish sin ; that he
was made man, suffered for our sins, rose again, was taken up
into the heavens, and sits at the right hand of the Father,
whence he will come again in glory to judge the living and
the dead. We believe moreover in the Holy Spirit, whom our
Lord and Saviour has denominated the Comforter, and whom
he sent to his disciples after his departure, according to his
promise : by whom also he sanctifies all believers in the
Church, who are baptized in the name of the Father, and of
the Son, and of the Holy Ghost. Those who preach anything
contrary to this creed, we regard as alienated from the Catholic
Church."

Such was the declaration of faith proposed by Acacius, and
subscribed by himself and as many as adhered to his opinion,
the number of whom we have already given. When this had
been read, Sophronius bishop of Pompeiopolis in Paphlagonia,
thus expressed himself :—" If the explaining of our own private opinion day after day be received as the exposition of the
faith, we shall never arrive at any accurate understanding of
the truth." These were the words of Sophronius. And I
firmly believe, that if the predecessors of these prelates, as
well as their successors, had entertained similar sentiments in
reference to the Nicene creed, all polemical debates would
have been avoided, nor would the Church have been agitated
by such violent and irrational disturbances : nevertheless it is
for the prudent to determine for themselves respecting these
matters. After many remarks on all sides had been made,
both in reference to the doctrinal statement which had been

[1] ἐν τῇ συντελείᾳ τῶν αἰώνων. For the meaning of this phrase, see
Elsley on St. Matt. xiii. 39.

recited, and in relation to the parties accused, the assembly was dissolved for that time. On the fourth day they all again met in the same place, and resumed their proceedings in the same contentious spirit as before. On this occasion Acacius expressed himself in these terms:—"Since the Nicene creed has been altered not once only, but frequently, there is no hinderance to our publishing another at this time." To which Eleusius bishop of Cyzicum replied—"The synod is at present convened not to learn what it had a previous knowledge of, nor to receive a creed which it had not assented to before, but to confirm the faith of the fathers, from which it should never recede, either in life or death." Eleusius, in thus opposing Acacius, meant by the faith of the fathers, that creed which had been promulgated at Antioch. But surely he too might have been fairly answered in this way:—"How is it, O Eleusius, that you call those convened at Antioch *the fathers*, seeing that you do not recognise those who were their fathers? The framers of the Nicene creed, by whom the Homoousian faith was acknowledged, have a far higher claim to the title of *the fathers;* both as having the priority in point of time, and also because those assembled at Antioch were by them invested with the sacerdotal office. Now if those at Antioch have disowned their own fathers, those who follow them are unconsciously following parricides. Besides, how can they have received a legitimate ordination from those whose faith they pronounce unsound and impious? If those who constituted the Nicene synod had not the Holy Spirit which is imparted by the imposition of hands,[1] those at Antioch have not duly received the priesthood: for how could they have received it from those who had not the power of conferring it?" Such considerations as these might have been submitted to Eleusius in reply to his objections. They then proceeded to another question, connected with the assertion made by Acacius in his exposition of the faith, "that the Son was like the Father;" inquiring of one another in what this resemblance consisted. The Acacian party affirmed that the Son was like the Father as it respected his will only, and not

---

[1] Upon the belief of the early Church in the bestowal of the Holy Spirit in and through ordination, see St. Chrysostom, Homilies 9 and 27 upon the Acts of the Apostles, and also Homily 1 upon the 2nd Ep. to Timothy.

his *substance* or *essence;* but the rest maintained that the likeness extended to both essence and will. In altercations on this point the whole day was consumed; and Acacius, being confuted by his own published works, in which he had asserted that " the Son is *in all things* like the Father," his opponents asked him how he could consistently deny the likeness of the Son to the Father as to his *essence?* Acacius in reply said, that no author, ancient or modern, was ever condemned out of his own writings. After pursuing their debate on this matter to a most tedious extent, with much acrimonious feeling and subtilty of argument, but without any approach to unity of judgment, Leonas arose and dissolved the council. Indeed this was properly the conclusion of the synod at Seleucia: for Leonas on the following day was inflexible to their entreaties that he would again be present in their assembly. " I have been deputed by the emperor," said he, " to preside in a council where unanimity was expected to prevail; but since you can by no means come to a mutual understanding, I can no longer be present: go therefore to the church, if you please, and indulge in this vain babbling there." The Acacian faction, conceiving this decision to be advantageous to themselves, refused also to assemble with the others; although the adverse party had sent to request their attendance in the church, that cognizance might be taken of the case of Cyril bishop of Jerusalem: for that prelate had been accused long before, on what grounds however I am unable to state. He had even been deposed, because he had not made his appearance during two whole years, after having been repeatedly summoned in order that the charges against him might be investigated. Nevertheless when he was deposed he sent a written notification to those who had condemned him, that he should appeal to a higher jurisdiction: and this course of his received the sanction of the emperor Constantius. Cyril was thus the first and indeed only clergyman who ventured to break through ecclesiastical usage, by becoming an appellant, in the way commonly done in the secular courts of judicature.[1] Being now present at Seleucia, ready to be put upon his trial, the other bishops invited the Acacian party to take their

---

[1] Appeals from an ecclesiastical to a secular tribunal were forbidden under severe penalties by the council of Constantinople, (Canon vi.,) and that of Antioch (Canon xii.).

places in the assembly, that in a general council a definite judgment might be pronounced on the case of those who were arraigned : for others also charged with various misdemeanours had been cited to appear before them at the same time, who to protect themselves had sought refuge among the partisans of Acacius. When therefore that faction persisted in their refusal to meet, after being repeatedly summoned, the bishops deposed Acacius himself, together with George of Alexandria, Uranius of Tyre, Theodulus of Chæretapi in Phrygia, Theodosius of Philadelphia in Lydia, Evagrius of the island of Mytilene, Leontius of Tripolis in Lydia, and Eudoxius who had formerly been bishop of Germanicia, but had afterwards insinuated himself into the bishopric of Antioch in Syria. They also deposed Patrophilus for contumacy, in not having presented himself to answer a charge preferred against him by a presbyter named Dorotheus. Besides deposing those above mentioned, they excommunicated Asterius, Eusebius, Abgarus, Basilicus, Phœbus, Fidelis, Eutychius, Magnus, and Eustathius ; determining that they should not be restored to communion, until they made such a defence as would clear them from the imputations under which they lay. This being done, they address explanatory letters to each of the Churches whose bishops had been deposed. Anianus was then constituted bishop of Antioch instead of Eudoxius : but the Acacians having soon after apprehended him, he was delivered into the hands of Leonas and Lauricius, by whom he was sent into exile. The bishops who had ordained him being incensed on this account, lodged a protest against the Acacian party with Leonas and Lauricius, in which they openly charged them with having violated the decisions of the synod. Finding that no redress could be obtained by this means, they went to Constantinople to lay the whole matter before the emperor.

CHAP. XLI.—ON THE EMPEROR'S RETURN FROM THE WEST, THE ACACIANS ARE CONVENED AT CONSTANTINOPLE, AND CONFIRM THE CREED BROUGHT FORWARD AT RIMINI, AFTER MAKING SOME ADDITIONS TO IT.

THE emperor, after his return from the West, appointed Honoratus the first prefect[1] of Constantinople, having abolished

---

[1] ἔπαρχος. This title is generically used by Polybius and Diodorus

²³the office of pro-consul. But the Acacians being beforehand with the bishops, calumniated them to the emperor, informing him that the creed which they had proposed was not admitted. This so annoyed the emperor that he resolved to disperse them ; he therefore published an edict, commanding that such of them as were subject to fill certain public offices should be no longer exempted from the performance of the duties attached to them. For several of them were liable to be called on to occupy various official departments,¹ connected both with the city magistracy, and in subordination² to the pre- ²⁴sidents and governors of provinces. The partisans of Acacius having effected this dispersion, remained for a considerable time at Constantinople ; and at length sending for the bishops of Bithynia, they held another synod. About fifty were assembled on this occasion, among whom was Maris bishop of Chalcedon : these confirmed the creed which was read at Rimini, and to which the names of the consuls had been prefixed. It would have been unnecessary to repeat it here, had there not been some additions made to it ; but since that was done, it may be desirable to transcribe it in its new form.

"We believe in one God the Father Almighty, of whom are all things. And in the only-begotten Son of God, begotten of God before all ages, and before every beginning ; by whom all things visible and invisible were made : who is the only-begotten born of the Father, the only of the only, God of God, like to the Father who begat him, according to the Scriptures, and whose generation no one knows but the Father only that begat him. We know that this only-begotten Son of God, as sent of the Father, came down from the heavens, as it is written, for the destruction of sin and death : that he was born of the Holy Spirit, and of the Virgin Mary according to the flesh, as it is written, and conversed with his disciples ; and that after having fulfilled every dispensation according to his Father's will, he was crucified and died, was

Siculus to denote the dependent governors of any country, under whatever title they might chance to hold office.
¹ This mixing up of the clerical office with political and worldly matters was afterwards forbidden, under pain of anathema, by the council of Chalcedon, in A. D. 451. See seventh Canon of that council.
² Τῶν ἐν ταῖς ἐπαρχίαις τάξεων. The sodalities of officials, or apparitors who attended on the governors of provinces.

buried and descended into the lower parts of the earth, at whose presence hell itself trembled: that he arose from the dead on the third day, again conversed with his disciples, and after the completion of forty days was taken up into the heavens, and sits at the right hand of the Father, whence he will come in the last day, i. e. the day of the resurrection, in his Father's glory, to requite every one according to his works. We believe also in the Holy Spirit, whom he himself, the only-begotten of God, Christ our Lord and God, promised to send to mankind as the Comforter, according as it is written, the Spirit of truth; whom he sent to them after he was received into the heavens. But since the term οὐσία, *substance* or *essence*, which was used by the fathers in a very simple and intelligible sense, but not being understood by the people, has been a cause of offence, we have thought proper to reject it, as it is not contained in the sacred writings;[1] and we deprecate the least mention of it in future, inasmuch as the Holy Scriptures have nowhere mentioned the substance of the Father and of the Son. Nor ought the *subsistence* (ὑπόστασις) of the Father, and of the Son, and of the Holy Spirit to be even named. But we affirm that the Son is like (ὅμοιον) the Father, in such a manner as the sacred Scriptures declare and teach. Let therefore all heresies which have been already condemned, or may have arisen of late, which are opposed to this exposition of the faith, be anathema."

Such was the creed set forth at that time at Constantinople. And having at length wound our way through the labyrinth of all the various forms of faith, we will now reckon the number of them. After that which was promulgated at Nice, two others were proposed at Antioch at the dedication of the church there. A third was presented to the emperor Constans in the Gallias by Narcissus and those who accompanied him. The fourth was sent by Eudoxius into Italy. There were three forms of the creed published at Sirmium, one of which having the consuls' names prefixed was read at Rimini. The Acacian party produced an eighth at Seleucia. The last was that of Constantinople, containing the prohibitory clause respecting the mention of *substance* or *subsistence* in relation to

---

[1] This, of course, was a mere pretext; for the very term "Trinity," to say nothing of other theological terms of less importance, does not occur in Scripture.

God. To this creed Ulfilas bishop of the Goths gave his assent, although he had previously adhered to that of Nice; for he was a disciple of Theophilus bishop of the Goths, who was present at the Nicene council, and subscribed what was there determined.

CHAP. XLII.—ON THE DEPOSITION OF MACEDONIUS, EUDOXIUS OBTAINS THE BISHOPRIC OF CONSTANTINOPLE.

ACACIUS, Eudoxius, and those at Constantinople who took part with them, became exceedingly anxious that they also on their side might depose some of the opposite party. Now it should be observed that in all these cases of degradation, neither of the factions were influenced by religious considerations, but by motives of a far more questionable character: for although they did not agree respecting the faith, yet the ground of their reciprocal depositions was not error in doctrine. The Acacian party therefore, availing themselves of the emperor's long-cherished indignation against Macedonius, and at the same time endeavouring to direct it against others, in the first place depose Macedonius, both on account of his having occasioned so much slaughter, and also because he had admitted to communion a deacon who was guilty of fornication.[1] They then depose Eleusius bishop of Cyzicum, for having baptized, and afterwards invested with the diaconate, a priest of Hercules at Tyre named Heraclius, who was known to have practised magic arts.[2] A like sentence was pronounced against Basil, or Basilas, as he was also called, who had been constituted bishop of Ancyra instead of Marcellus: the causes assigned for this condemnation were, that he had unjustly imprisoned a certain individual, loaded him with chains, and put him to the torture; that he had traduced some persons; and that he had disturbed the Churches of Africa by his epistles. Dracontius was also deposed by them, because he had

[1] See Apost. Canon. xxv.
[2] Upon the punishments imposed by the Church upon the practice of all magical arts and enchantments, see Bingham's Eccl. Antiq. xvi. 5. Compare Tertullian de Idol. ch. ix., " Post evangelium nusquam invenies aut Sophistas, aut Chaldæos, aut Incantatores, aut Conjectores, aut Magos, nisi plane punitos."

left the Galatian Church for that of Pergamos. Moreover they ejected, on various pretences, Neonas bishop of Seleucia, the city in which the synod had been convened, Sophronius of Pompeiopolis in Paphlagonia, Elpidius of Satala in Macedonia, and Cyril of Jerusalem.

CHAP. XLIII.—OF EUSTATHIUS BISHOP OF SEBASTIA.

BUT Eustathius bishop of Sebastia in Armenia, was not even permitted to make his defence; because he had been long before deposed by Eulalius his own father, who was bishop of Cæsarea in Cappadocia, for dressing in a style unbecoming the sacerdotal office.[1] Meletius was appointed his successor, of whom we shall hereafter speak. Eustathius indeed was subsequently condemned by a synod convened on his account at Gangra in Paphlagonia; he having, after his deposition by the council at Cæsarea, done many things repugnant to the ecclesiastic canons. For he had forbidden marriage,[2] and maintained that meats were to be abstained from: he even separated many from their wives, and persuaded those who disliked to assemble in the churches[3] to communicate at home. Under the pretext of piety, he also seduced servants from their masters. He himself wore the habit of a philosopher, and induced his followers to adopt a new and extraordinary garb, directing that the hair of women should be cropped. He permitted the prescribed fasts to be neglected, but recommended fasting on Sundays. In short he forbad prayers to be offered in the houses of married persons; and declared that both the benediction and the com-

[1] Upon the question of the clerical habit and the penalty imposed on those who did not constantly adopt it, see Bingham's Eccl. Antiq. b. vi. ch. iv. 15.

[2] As to the opinion entertained by many ancient heretics upon marriage, as a thing unlawful and to be condemned, consult Bingham's Eccl. Antiq. b. xxii. ch. i. Such were Saturninus and Marcion, (see Irenæus, i. 30, and compare Euseb. iv. 29,) the Apostolici, the Encratites, and the Manichees, according to St. Austin, de Hæret. chaps. xxv. xl. and xlvi. See also Apostolical Canons, li.

[3] i. e. these *separated ones*, as claiming greater *purity* than other believers.

munion of a presbyter who continued to live with a wife
whom he might have lawfully married before entering into
holy orders, ought to be shunned as an abomination.[1] For
doing and teaching these things and many others of a similar
nature, a synod convened, as we have said, at Gangra in
Paphlagonia deposed him, and anathematized his opinions.
This however was done afterwards. But on Macedonius
being ejected from the see of Constantinople, Eudoxius, who
now despised that of Antioch, was promoted to the vacant
bishopric ; being consecrated by the Acacians, who in this instance cared not to consider that it was inconsistent with their
former proceedings. For they who had deposed Dracontius
because of his translation from Galatia to Pergamos, were
clearly acting in contrariety to their own principles and decisions, in ordaining Eudoxius, who then made a second remove. After this they sent their own exposition of the faith,
in its corrected and supplementary form, to Rimini, ordering
that all those who refused to sign it should be exiled, on the
authority of the emperor's edict. They also informed such
other prelates in the East as coincided with them in opinion
of what they had done ; and more especially, Patrophilus
bishop of Scythopolis, who on leaving Seleucia had proceeded
directly to his own city. Eudoxius having been constituted
bishop of the imperial city,[2] the great church named Sophia
was at that time[3] consecrated, in the tenth consulate of Constantius, and the third of Julian Cæsar, on the 15th day of
February. It was while Eudoxius occupied this see, that he
first uttered that sentence which is still everywhere current,
" The Father is impious, the Son is pious." When the people
seemed startled by this expression, and a disturbance began
to be made, "Be not troubled," said he, " on account of what
I have just said : for the Father is impious, because he worships no person ; but the Son is pious, because he worships
the Father." With this sort of badinage he appeased the tumult, and great laughter was excited in the church : and this
saying of his continues to be a jest, even in the present day.

[1] Compare the fourth canon of the council of Gangra. " If any one
asserts concerning a married presbyter that it is not lawful to partake
of the oblation when he performs the Divine service, let him be anathema."
[2] Constantinople.
[3] This was its second consecration, it having been ruined and rebuilt.
It was originally consecrated in A. D. 326 : see above, book i. chap. xvi.

[SOCRATES.]   M

The heresiarchs indeed frequently devised such subtle phras
as these, and by them rent the Church asunder. Thus w:
the synod at Constantinople terminated.

CHAP. XLIV.—OF MELETIUS[1] BISHOP OF ANTIOCH.

IT becomes us now to speak of Meletius, who, as we ha$
recently observed, was created bishop of Sebastia in Armeni
after the deposition of Eustathius ; but he was afterwar(
translated from Sebastia to Berœa, a city of Syria. Beir
present at the synod of Seleucia, he subscribed the creed $
forth there by Acacius, and immediately returned thence
Berœa. On the convention of the synod at Constantinopl
when the people of Antioch understood that Eudoxius, ca
tivated by the magnificence of the see of Constantinople, h$
contemned the presidency over their Church, they sent f
Meletius, and invested him with the bishopric of the Chur(
at Antioch. After this, he at first avoided all doctrinal que
tions, confining his discourses to moral subjects ; but subs
quently he expounded to his auditors the Nicene creed, a$
asserted the doctrine of consubstantiality. The empen
being informed of this, ordered that he should be sent in
exile ; and caused Euzoïus, who had before been deposed t
gether with Arius, to be installed bishop of Antioch in h
stead. Such however as were attached to Meletius, separat(
themselves from the Arian congregation, and held their a
semblies apart : nevertheless those who originally embrac(
the Homoousian opinion would not communicate with the
because Meletius had been ordained by the Arians, and h
adherents had been baptized by them. Thus was the Ant
ochian Church divided, even in regard to those whose viev
on matters of faith exactly corresponded. Meanwhile tl
emperor, getting intelligence that the Persians were preparir
to undertake another war against the Romans, repaired
great haste to Antioch.

[1] This name is sometimes written Melitius.

CHAP. XLV.—THE HERESY OF MACEDONIUS.

MACEDONIUS, after his ejection from Constantinople, could ll bear his condemnation; becoming restless, therefore, he associated himself with the other faction that had deposed Acacius and his party at Seleucia. He accordingly sent a deputation to Sophronius and Eleusius, to encourage them to adhere to that creed which was first promulgated at Antioch, and afterwards confirmed at Seleucia, proposing to give it the counterfeit[1] name of the *Homoiousian* creed.[2] By this means he drew around him a great number of adherents, who from him are still denominated Macedonians. And although such dissented from the Acacians at the Seleucian synod had not previously used the term *Homoiousios*, yet from that period they distinctly asserted it. It is however insisted by some that this term did not originate with Macedonius, but was the invention rather of Marathonius, who a little before had been set over the Church at Nicomedia; on which account the maintainers of this doctrine were also called Marathonians. To this party Eustathius joined himself, who for the reasons before stated had been ejected from the Church at Sebastia. But when Macedonius began to deny the Divinity of the Holy Spirit in the Trinity, Eustathius said; "I can neither admit that the Holy Spirit is God, nor can I dare affirm him to be a creature." For this reason those who hold the consubstantiality of the Son call these heretics *Pneumatomachi*.[3] What means these Macedonians became so numerous in the Hellespont, I shall state in its proper place. The Acacians meanwhile became extremely anxious that another synod should be convened at Antioch, in consequence of having changed their mind respecting their former assertion of the likeness *in all things* of the Son to the Father. A small number of them therefore assembled in the following year, in the consulate of Taurus and Florentius, at Antioch in

[1] Παράσημος (used metaphorically, from money which has a false stamp.) As to the term Homoiousios, ('Ομοιούσιος, of like substance or essence,) see above, note on book i. ch. viii.
[2] See Theodoret, b. ii. ch. vi.
[3] Πνευματομάχους, i. e. Adversaries of the Holy Spirit.

M 2

Syria, where the emperor was at that time residing, Euzoïus
being bishop. A discussion was then renewed on some of
those points which they had previously determined, in the
course of which they declared that the term *Homoios*, (ὅμοιος,
like the Father,) ought to be erased from the form of faith
which had been published both at Rimini and Constantinople.
Nay, so completely did they unmask themselves, as to openly
contend that the Son was altogether *unlike* (ἀνόμοιος) the
Father, not merely in relation to his *essence*, but even as it respected his *will:* asserting boldly also, as the Arians had
already done, that he was made *of that which was not.* Those
in that city who favoured the heresy of Aëtius, gave their
assent to this opinion ; from which circumstance, in addition to the general appellation of Arians they were also
termed Anomeans, and Exucontians, by those at Antioch who
embraced the orthodox faith, who nevertheless were at that
time divided among themselves on account of Meletius, as we
have before observed. The Homoousians therefore having
asked them, how they dared to affirm that the Son is unlike
the Father, and has his existence from nothing, after having
acknowledged him God of God in their former creed, they
endeavoured to elude this objection by such fallacious subter-
fuges as these. "The expression 'God of God,'" said they,
"is to be understood in the same sense as the words of the
apostle (1 Cor. xi. 12), 'but all things of God.' Wherefore
the Son is *of God*, as being one of these *all things:* and it is
for this reason the words *according to the Scriptures* are
added in the draught of the creed." The author of this sophism
was George, bishop of Laodicea, who being unskilled in such
phrases, was ignorant of the manner in which Origen had
formerly analysed and explained these peculiar expressions
of the apostle. But notwithstanding these evasive cavillings,
their inability to bear the reproach and contumely they had
drawn upon themselves induced them to fall back upon the
creed which they had before put forth at Constantinople ;
and so each one retired to his own district. George, returning to Alexandria, resumed his authority over the churches
there, Athanasius still not daring to appear. Those in that
city who were opposed to his sentiments he persecuted ; and
conducting himself with great severity and cruelty, he ren-

dered himself extremely odious to the people. At Jerusalem
Herrenius[1] was placed over the Church instead of Cyril: we
may also remark that Heraclius was ordained bishop there
after him, to whom Hilary succeeded. At length however
Cyril returned to Jerusalem, and was again invested with the
presidency over the Church there. But about the same time
another heresy sprang up, which arose from the following circumstance.

CHAP. XLVI.—OF THE APOLLINARISTÆ, AND THEIR HERESY.

THERE were at Laodicea in Syria a father and son each
named Apollinaris, the former of whom was a presbyter, and
the latter a reader in that Church. Both taught Greek literature, the father grammar, and the son rhetoric. The elder
was a native of Alexandria, and at first taught at Berytus,
but afterwards removed to Laodicea, where he married, and
the younger Apollinaris was born. Epiphanius the sophist
was their contemporary, with whom they formed an intimate
acquaintance; but Theodotus, bishop of Laodicea, interdicted
their intercourse with him, lest such communication should
pervert their principles, and lead them into Paganism: this
prohibition however they paid but little attention to, their
familiarity with Epiphanius being still continued. George,
the successor of Theodotus, also endeavoured to prevent their
conversing with Epiphanius; but finding them altogether
refractory on this point, he excommunicated them. The
younger Apollinaris regarding this severe procedure as an act
of injustice, and relying on the resources of his rhetorical so-
phistry, originated a new heresy, which was named after its
inventor, and still has many supporters. Nevertheless some
affirm that the reason above assigned was not the cause of
their dissent from George, but their perception of the unset-
tledness and inconsistency of his profession of faith; since he
sometimes maintained that the Son is like the Father, in accordance with what had been determined in the synod at
Seleucia, and at other times countenanced the Arian view.
They therefore made this a pretext for separation from him:

---

[1] The name is spelt Errenius in the Allatian MS.

but finding no one follow their example, they introduced a new form of doctrine, asserting that in the economy of the incarnation, God the Word assumed a human body without a soul. This however they afterward retracted, admitting that he took a soul indeed, but that it was an irrational one, God the Word himself being in the place of a mind. The followers of these heresies, who from them are termed Apollinaristæ, affirm that this is the only point of difference between themselves and the Catholics; for they recognise the consubstantiality of the persons in the Trinity. But further mention of the two Apollinares will be made in the proper place.[1]

CHAP. XLVII.—DEATH OF THE EMPEROR CONSTANTIUS.

WHILE the emperor Constantius continued his residence at Antioch, Julian Cæsar engaged with an immense army of barbarians in the Gallias, and obtained a distinguished victory over them: on which account having become extremely popular among the soldiery, he was proclaimed emperor by them. Intelligence of this affected the emperor Constantius with the most painful sensations; he was therefore baptized by Euzoïus, and immediately prepared to undertake an expedition against Julian. On arriving at the frontiers of Cappadocia and Cilicia, his excessive agitation of mind produced apoplexy, which terminated his existence at Mopsucrene, in the consulate of Taurus and Florentius, on the 3rd of November, in the first year of the 285th Olympiad. This prince was at the time of his death forty-five years old, having reigned thirty-eight years, for thirteen of which he was his father's colleague in the empire, and during the remaining twenty-five he had the sole administration, the history of which latter period is contained in this Book.

[1] See below, b. iii. ch. xvi.

BOOK III.

CHAP. I.—Of JULIAN; HIS LINEAGE AND EDUCATION: HIS APOSTASY TO PAGANISM AFTER HIS ELEVATION TO THE IMPERIAL DIGNITY.

THE emperor Constantius having died on the frontiers of Cilicia on the third of November, during the consulate of Taurus and Florentius, Julian left the western parts of the empire about the eleventh of December following, under the same consulate, and came to Constantinople, where he was proclaimed emperor. And as I must needs speak of the character of this prince, who was eminently distinguished for his eloquence, let not his admirers expect that I should attempt a pompous, rhetorical style, as if to make the delineation correspond with the dignity of the subject: for my object being to compile a history of the Christian religion, it is both proper, in order to the being better understood, and consistent with my original purpose, to maintain a simple and unaffected style.[1] Having to describe his person, birth, education, and the manner in which he became possessed of the sovereignty, to give a clear view of these matters it will be needful to enter into some antecedent details. Constantine, who gave Byzantium his own name, had two brothers, named Dalmatius and Constantius, the offspring of the same father, but by a different mother. Dalmatius had a son who bore his own name: Constantius had two sons, Gallus and Julian. When, after the death of Constantine who founded Constantinople, the soldiery had put the younger Dalmatius to death, then the other two children, bereft of the protection of their father, were within a little of sharing the fate of Dalmatius: but a disease which threatened to be fatal preserved Gallus from the violence of his father's murderers; while the tenderness of Julian's age, who was not then eight years old, protected him. The emperor's jealousy toward them having been gradually subdued, Gallus attended the schools at Ephesus in Ionia, in which country considerable

---

[1] Compare the remarks in b. i. chap. i.

hereditary possessions had been left them. And Julian, when he was grown up, pursued his studies at Constantinople, going constantly to the palace, where the schools then were, in plain clothes, under the superintendence of the eunuch Mardonius. Nicocles the Lacedemonian instructed him in grammar; and Ecebolius the sophist, who was at that time a Christian, taught him rhetoric; for the emperor was anxious that he should have no Pagan masters, lest he should be seduced from the Christian faith in which he had been educated, to the Pagan superstitions. His proficiency in literature soon became so remarkable, that it began to be said that he was capable of governing the Roman empire; and this popular rumour becoming generally diffused, greatly disquieted the emperor's mind, so that he had him removed from the Great City to Nicomedia, forbidding him at the same time to frequent the school of Libanius the Syrian sophist. This celebrated rhetorician having been driven from Constantinople, by a combination of the professors there against him, had retired to Nicomedia, where he opened a school;.and to revenge himself on his persecutors he composed an oration against them. Julian was however interdicted from being his auditor, because Libanius adhered to Paganism: nevertheless, he privately procured his orations, which he not only greatly admired, but also frequently and with close study perused, so as to become very expert in the rhetorical art. About this period, Maximus the philosopher arrived at Nicomedia, not he of Constantinople, Euclid's father, but he of Ephesus, whom the emperor Valentinian afterwards caused to be executed as a practiser of magic. The only thing that then attracted him to Nicomedia was the fame of Julian, to whom he imparted, in addition to the principles of philosophy, his own religious sentiments, and a desire to possess the empire. When the emperor was informed of these things, Julian, between hope and fear, became very anxious to lull the suspicions which had been awakened, and therefore began to assume the external semblance of what he once was in reality. He was shaved to the very skin,[1] and pretended to live a monastic life: and although in private he pursued his philosophical studies, in public he read the sacred writings of the Christians,

[1] On the ancient tonsure of Ecclesiastics, see Bingham's Antiq. b. vi. ch. iv. sub fin.

and moreover was constituted a reader in the Church of Nicomedia. But while by these specious pretexts, under the influence of fear, he succeeded in averting the emperor's displeasure, he by no means abandoned his hope ; telling his
friends that happier times were not far distant, when he
should possess the imperial sway. In this condition of things,
his brother Gallus, having been created Cæsar, on his way to
the East came to Nicomedia to see him. But when not long
after this Gallus was slain, the emperor becoming still more
suspicious of Julian, directed that a guard should be set over
him : he soon however found means of escaping from them,
and fled from place to place, until the empress Eusebia, having
discovered his retreat, persuaded the emperor to leave him
uninjured, and permit him to go to Athens to pursue his philosophical studies. From thence, to be brief, the emperor
recalled him, and after creating him Cæsar, united him in
marriage to his own sister Helen : and the barbarian mercenaries whom the emperor Constantius had engaged as auxiliary
forces against the tyrant Magnentius, beginning to pillage the
Roman cities, Julian was despatched into the Gallias against
them, with orders, on account of his youth, to undertake nothing without consulting the other military chiefs.

This restrictive power rendered these generals so lax in
their duties, that the barbarians were suffered to strengthen
themselves ; which Julian perceiving, allowed the commanders
to give themselves up to luxury and revelling, but exerted
himself to infuse courage into the soldiery, offering a stipu-
lated reward to any one who should kill a barbarian. By
these means he conciliated to himself the affections of the
army, while he effectually weakened the enemy. It is reported that as he was entering a town a civic crown, which
was suspended between two pillars, fell upon his head, which
it exactly fitted : upon which all present gave a shout of admiration, regarding it as a presage of his one day becoming
emperor. Some have affirmed that Constantius sent him
against the barbarians in the hope that he would perish in an
engagement with them. Whether he had such a design I
know not, let each form his own judgment of the matter ;
but it certainly is improbable that he should have first contracted so near an alliance with him, and then have sought
his destruction to the prejudice of his own interests. Be this

as it may, Julian's complaint to the emperor of the inertness
of his military officers, procured for him a coadjutor in the
command more consonant to his own ardour; and by their
combined efforts such an assault was made upon the barbarians, that they sent him an embassy, assuring him that they
had been ordered by the emperor's letters, which were produced, to march into the Roman territories. Instead of listening to these excuses, he cast the ambassador into prison, and
vigorously attacking the forces of the enemy, totally defeated
them; and having taken their king prisoner, he sent him
alive to Constantius. Immediately after this brilliant success
he was proclaimed emperor by the military; and inasmuch as
they had no imperial crown, one of his guards took the chain
which he wore about his own neck, and bound it around
Julian's head. Thus he obtained the object of his ambition:
but whether he subsequently conducted himself as became a
philosopher, let my readers determine. For he neither entered into communication with Constantius by an embassy,
nor paid him the least homage in acknowledgment of past
favours; but constituting other governors over the provinces,
he conducted everything just as it pleased him. Moreover he
sought to bring Constantius into contempt, by reciting publicly in every city the letters which he had written to the
barbarians; and thus having rendered the inhabitants of these
places disaffected, they were easily induced to revolt from
Constantius to himself. After this he no longer wore the
mask of Christianity, but everywhere opened the Pagan temples, offering sacrifice to the idols;[1] and designating himself
Pontifex Maximus, gave permission to such as would to celebrate their superstitious festivals. In this manner he managed to excite a civil war against Constantius; and thus
would have involved the empire in all the disastrous consequences of such a calamity; for this philosopher's aim could
not have been attained without much bloodshed: but God in
the sovereignty of his own councils checked the fury of these
antagonists without detriment to the state, by the removal of
one of them. For when Julian arrived among the Thracians,
intelligence was brought him that Constantius was dead; and
thus was the Roman empire at that time preserved from the

[1] Upon this act of idolatry, as a test and sign of apostasy from the
Christian faith, see Bingham's Eccl. Antiq. b. xvi. ch. iv. 5.

horrors that threatened it. Julian forthwith made his public
entry into Constantinople; and considering with himself how
he might best secure popular favour, he had recourse to the
following measures. He knew that Constantius had rendered
himself odious to the defenders of the Homoousian faith by
having driven them from the Churches, and proscribed their
bishops.[1] He was also aware that the Pagans were extremely
impatient of the prohibitions which prevented their sacrificing
to their gods, and were very anxious to get their temples
opened, with liberty to exercise their idolatrous rites. In
fact he was sensible that while both these classes secretly entertained rancorous feelings against his predecessor, the people
in general were exceedingly exasperated by the violence of
the eunuchs, and especially by the rapacity of Eusebius, the
chief officer of the imperial bed-chamber. Under these circumstances he treated all parties with a good deal of subtlety:
with some he dissimulated; others he attached to himself by
conferring obligations upon them, for he was fond of affecting
beneficence; but he unscrupulously manifested his own predilection for the idolatry of the heathens. And first, in order
to brand the memory of Constantius by making him appear
to have been cruel toward his subjects, he recalled the exiled
bishops, and restored to them their confiscated estates. He
next commanded his confidential agents to see that the Pagan
temples should be opened without delay. Then he directed
that such individuals as had been victims of the extortionate
conduct of the eunuchs should be repossessed of the property
of which they had been plundered. Eusebius, the chief of
the imperial bed-chamber, he punished with death, not only
on account of the injuries he had inflicted on others, but because he was assured that it was through his machinations
that his brother Gallus had been killed. Having taken care
that the body of Constantius should be honoured with an imperial funeral, he expelled the eunuchs, barbers, and cooks
from the palace. The eunuchs he dispensed with, because
they were unnecessary in consequence of his wife's decease,
as he had resolved not to marry again: the barbers, because
he said one was sufficient for a great many persons; and the
cooks, because he intended to maintain a very simple table.
The palace being cleared of these supernumeraries, he reduced

[1] See preceding Book of this history, chaps. vii. xiii. xvi. &c.

the majority of the secretaries to their former condition, and appointed those who were retained a salary befitting their office.   The mode of public travelling and conveyance of necessaries he also reformed, abolishing the use of mules, oxen, and asses for this purpose, and permitting horses only to be so employed.   These various retrenchments were highly lauded by some few, but strongly reprobated by all others, as tending to bring the imperial dignity into contempt, by stripping it of those appendages of pomp and magnificence which exercise so powerful an influence over the minds of the vulgar. At night he was accustomed to sit up composing orations which he afterwards delivered in the senate: though in fact he was the first and only emperor since the time of Julius Cæsar who made speeches in that assembly.   To those who were eminent for literary attainments he extended the most flattering patronage, and especially to the professors of philosophy; in consequence of which, abundance of pretenders to learning of this sort resorted to the palace from all quarters, wearing their palliums, being more conspicuous for their costume than their erudition.   These impostors, who invariably adopted the religious sentiments of their prince, were all inimical to the welfare of the Christians; and Julian himself, whose excessive vanity prompted him to deride his predecessors in a book which he wrote entitled "The Cæsars," was led by the same haughty disposition to compose treatises against the Christians also.[1]   In expelling the cooks and barbers he acted in a manner becoming a philosopher indeed, but not an emperor; but in condescending to vilify others he ceased to maintain the dignity of either, for such personages ought to be superior to the influence of jealousy and detraction. An emperor may be a philosopher in all that regards moderation and self-control; but should a philosopher attempt to imitate what might become an emperor, he would frequently depart from his own principles.   We have thus briefly spoken of the emperor Julian, tracing his extraction, education, temper of mind, and the way in which he became invested with the imperial power.

[1] For an account of his writings, see below, chap. xxiii.

CHAP. II.—OF THE SEDITION EXCITED AT ALEXANDRIA, AND
HOW GEORGE WAS SLAIN.

IT is now proper to mention what took place in the Churches
during this period. A great disturbance occurred at Alexandria in consequence of the following circumstance. There
was a place in that city which had long been abandoned to
neglect and filth, wherein the Pagans had formerly celebrated
their mysteries, and sacrificed human beings to Mithra.[1]
This being empty and otherwise useless, Constantius had
granted to the Church of the Alexandrians; and George,
wishing to erect a church[2] on the site of it, gave directions
that the place should be cleansed. In the process of clearing
it, an *adytum* of vast depth was discovered which unveiled the
nature of their heathenish rites: for there were found there
the skulls of many persons of all ages, who were said to have
been immolated for the purpose of divination by the inspection of entrails, when the Pagans were allowed to perform
these and such-like magic arts in order to enchant the souls
of men. The Christians, on discovering these abominations in
the adytum of the temple of Mithra, thought it their duty
to expose them to the view and execration of all; and therefore carried the skulls throughout the city, in a kind of triumphal procession, for the inspection of the people. When
the Pagans of Alexandria beheld this insult offered to their
religion, they became so exasperated, that they assailed the
Christians with whatever weapon chanced to come to hand, in
their fury destroying numbers of them in a variety of ways:
some they killed with the sword, others with clubs and
stones; some they strangled with ropes, others they crucified,
purposely inflicting this last kind of death in contempt of the
cross of Christ. Few indeed escaped being wounded; and as
it generally happens in such a case, neither friends nor relatives were spared, but friends, brothers, parents, and children
imbrued their hands in each other's blood. This outrageous
assault obliged the Christians to cease from cleansing the
temple of Mithra: the Pagans meanwhile having dragged
George out of the church, fastened him to a camel, and when

[1] Whom the Persians suppose to be the sun. See b. v. ch. xvi.
[2] Εὐκτήριον οἶκον, an oratory. See above, b. i. ch. xvii. and xviii.

they had torn him to pieces, they burnt him together with the camel.

CHAP. III. — THE EMPEROR, INDIGNANT AT THE MURDER OF
GEORGE, SEVERELY CENSURES THE ALEXANDRIANS BY LETTER.

THE emperor, highly resenting the assassination of George,
wrote to the citizens of Alexandria, rebuking their violence in
the strongest terms. It has been affirmed that those who
detested him because of Athanasius, were the perpetrators of
this outrage upon George; but although it is undoubtedly true
that such as cherish hostile feelings against particular individuals are often found identified with popular commotions,
yet the emperor in his letter evidently attaches the blame to
the populace, rather than to any among the Christians.
George however was at that time, and had for some time
previously been, exceedingly obnoxious to all classes, which is
sufficient to account for the indignation of the multitude against
him. The emperor's letter was expressed in the following
terms.

EMPEROR CÆSAR JULIAN MAXIMUS AUGUSTUS TO THE
CITIZENS OF ALEXANDRIA.

"Even if you have neither respect for Alexander the
founder of your city, nor, what is more, for that great and
most holy god Serapis; yet how is it you have forgotten not
only the universal claims of humanity and social order, but also
what is due to us, to whom all the gods, and especially the
mighty Serapis, have assigned the empire of the world, for
whose cognizance therefore it became you to reserve all
matters of public wrong? But you will probably plead the
impulse of rage and indignation, which, taking possession of
the mind, too often deceptively stimulate it to the most atrocious acts. It seems however that when your fury was in
some degree moderated, you aggravated your culpability by
adding a most heinous offence to that which had been committed under the excitement of the moment: nor were you of
the commonalty ashamed to perpetrate such acts as had deservedly drawn upon others the odium they deserved. By
Serapis I conjure you tell me, what enormities instigated you

to such unjustifiable violence toward George? You will perhaps answer, it was because he exasperated Constantius of
blessed memory against you : because he introduced an army
into the sacred city : because he induced the governor[1] of·
Egypt to despoil the god's most holy temple of its images,
votive offerings, and such other consecrated apparatus as
it contained ; who, when ye could not endure the sight of such
a foul desecration, but attempted to defend the god from sacrilegious hands, or rather to hinder the pillage of what had been
consecrated to his service, in contravention of all justice, law,
and piety, dared to send armed bands against you.   This he
probably did from his dreading George more than Constantius :
but he would have consulted better for his own safety had he
not been guilty of this tyrannical conduct, but persevered in
his former moderation toward you.   Being on all these accounts enraged against George as the adversary of the gods,
you have again polluted your sacred city ; whereas you ought
to have impeached him before the judges.   For had you thus
acted, neither murder, nor any other unlawful deed, would
have been committed ; but justice being equitably dispensed,
you would have been preserved from these disgraceful excesses,
while he would have suffered the punishment due to his impious
crimes.   Thus too, in short, the insolence of those would have
been curbed who contemn the gods, and respect neither cities
of such magnitude, nor so flourishing a population ; but make
the barbarities they practise against them the prelude, as it
were, of their exercise of power.   Compare therefore this our
present letter with that which we wrote you some time since.
With what high commendation did we then greet you !   But
now, by the immortal gods, with an equal disposition to praise
you, your heinous misdoings utterly oppose my wishes.   The
people have had the audacity to tear a man in pieces, like dogs ;
nor have they been subsequently ashamed of this inhuman
procedure, nor desirous of purifying their hands from such
pollution, that they may stretch them forth in the presence of
the gods undefiled by blood.   You will no doubt be ready to
say that George justly merited this chastisement ; and we
might be disposed perhaps to admit that he deserved still more
acute tortures.   Should you further affirm that on your account

---

[1] Artemius, whom Julian afterwards beheaded for this desecration of
the Pagan temple.

he was worthy of these sufferings, even this might also be granted. But should you add that it became *you* to inflict the vengeance due to his offences, that we could by no means acquiesce in ; for you have laws to which it is the duty of every one of you to be subject, and to evince your respect for both publicly as well as in private.   If any individual should transgress those wise and salutary regulations which were originally constituted for the well-being of the community, does that absolve the rest from obedience to them?   It is fortunate for you, ye Alexandrians, that such an atrocity has been perpetrated in our reign, who, by reason of our reverence for the gods, and on account of our grandfather and uncle whose name we bear, and who governed Egypt and your city, still retain a fraternal affection for you.   Assuredly that power which will not suffer itself to be disrespected, and such a government as is possessed of a vigorous and healthy constitution, could not connive at such unbridled licentiousness in its subjects ; but would unsparingly purge out the dangerous distemper by the application of remedies sufficiently potent.   We shall however in your case, for the reasons already assigned, restrict ourselves to the more mild and gentle medicine of remonstrance and exhortation ; to the which mode of treatment we are persuaded ye will the more readily submit, inasmuch as we understand ye are not only Greeks by original descent, but also still preserve in your memory and character the traces of the glory of your ancestors.   Let this be published to our citizens of Alexandria."

CHAP. IV.—ON THE DEATH OF GEORGE, ATHANASIUS RETURNS TO ALEXANDRIA, AND IS RE-ESTABLISHED IN HIS SEE.

SOON after this, Athanasius, returning from his exile, was received with great joy by the people of Alexandria, who expelled the Arians from the churches, and restored Athanasius to the possession of them.   The Arians meanwhile assembling themselves in low and obscure buildings, ordained Lucius to supply the place of George.   Such was the state of things at that time at Alexandria.

CHAP. V.—OF LUCIFER AND EUSEBIUS.

ABOUT the same time Lucifer and Eusebius were by an imperial order recalled from banishment out of the Upper Thebais; the former being bishop of Cagliari, a city of Sardinia, the latter of Verceil, a city of the Ligurians in Italy. These two prelates therefore consulted together on the most effectual means of preventing the neglected canons and discipline of the Church from being in future violated and despised.[1]

CHAP. VI.—LUCIFER GOES TO ANTIOCH AND ORDAINS
PAULINUS.

THEY decided therefore that Lucifer should go to Antioch in Syria, and Eusebius to Alexandria, that by assembling a synod in conjunction with Athanasius, they might confirm the doctrines of the Church.   Lucifer sent a deacon as his representative, by whom he pledged himself to assent to whatever the synod might decree; but he himself went to Antioch, where he found the Church in great disorder, the people not being agreed among themselves.   For not only did the Arian heresy, which had been introduced by Euzoïus, divide the Church, but, as we have before said, the followers of Meletius also, from attachment to their preceptor, separated themselves from those with whom they agreed in sentiment.   When therefore Lucifer had constituted Paulinus their bishop he again departed.

CHAP. VII.— BY THE CO-OPERATION OF EUSEBIUS AND ATHANASIUS A SYNOD IS CONVENED AT ALEXANDRIA, WHEREIN THE TRINITY IS DECLARED TO BE CONSUBSTANTIAL.

As soon as Eusebius reached Alexandria, he in concert with Athanasius immediately convoked a synod.   The bishops, assembled on this occasion out of various cities, took into consideration many subjects of the utmost importance.   They asserted the Divinity of the Holy Spirit,[2] and comprehended

[1] Reference here is made more especially to the Canons of the Council of Nice.
[2] It was not until the fourth century that any distinct denial was made

[SOCRATES.]   N

him in the consubstantial Trinity : they also declared that the
Word, in being made man, assumed not only flesh, but also a
soul, in accordance with the views of the early ecclesiastics.
For they avoided the introduction of any new doctrine of
their own devising into the Church, but contented themselves
with recording their sanction of those points which ecclesiastical tradition has insisted on from the beginning, and the
most profound Christian doctors have demonstratively taught.
Such sentiments the ancient fathers have uniformly maintained
in all their controversial writings.   Irenæus, Clemens, Apollinaris of Hierapolis, and Serapion who presided over the
Church at Antioch, assure us in their several works, that it
was the generally received opinion that Christ in his incarnation was endowed with a soul.   Moreover the synod convened
on account of Berillus bishop of Philadelphia in Arabia, re- 107
cognised the same doctrine in their letter to that prelate.   The
same thing is everywhere admitted by Origen, but he more
particularly explains this mystery in the ninth volume of his
"Comments upon Genesis," where he shows that Adam and
Eve were types of Christ and the Church.   That holy man
Pamphilus, and Eusebius who was surnamed after him, are authorities on this subject not to be contemned : both these witnesses in their joint Life of Origen, and admirable defence of
him in answer to such as were prejudiced against him, prove
that he was not the first who made this declaration, but that in
doing so he was the mere expositor of the mystical tradition
of the Church.   Those who assisted at the Alexandrine
council examined also with great minuteness the question
concerning *Essence* or *Substance*, and *Existence, Subsistence*, or
Personality.   For Hosius bishop of Cordova in Spain, who
has been before referred to as having been sent by the emperor Constantine to allay the excitement which Arius had
caused, originated the controversy about these terms in his
earnestness to overthrow the dogma of Sabellius the Libyan.
In the council of Nice however, which was held soon after,
this dispute was not agitated ; but in consequence of the contention about it which subsequently arose, the matter was

of the doctrine of the Divinity of the Holy Spirit, a denial which was first
started by Macedonius ; accordingly we find that even at the council of
Nice, the fathers there assembled contented themselves with simply declaring their belief in the Holy Ghost, without adding any definition.

freely discussed at Alexandria. It was there determined that
such expressions as *ousia* and *hypostasis* ought not to be used
in reference to God : for they argued that the word *ousia* is
nowhere employed in the sacred Scriptures ; and that the
apostle has misapplied the term *hypostasis*[1] in attempting to
describe that which is ineffable. They nevertheless decided
that in refutation of the Sabellian error these terms were ad-
missible, in default of more appropriate language, lest it should
be supposed that one thing was indicated by a threefold designation ; whereas we ought rather to believe that each of those
named in the Trinity is God in his own proper person. Such
were the decisions of this synod. If we may express our
own judgment on this matter, it appears to us that the
Greek philosophers have given us various definitions of *ousia*,
but have not taken the slightest notice of *hypostasis*.[2] Irenæus the grammarian indeed, in his Alphabetical Lexicon
entitled " Atticistes," declares it to be a barbarous term, which
is not to be found in any of the ancients, except occasionally
in a sense quite different from that which is attached to it in
the present day. Thus Sophocles, in his tragedy entitled
" Phœnix," uses it to signify *treachery :* in Menander it implies *sauces ;* and another calls the *sediment* at the bottom of
a hogshead of wine *hypostasis*. But although the ancient
philosophical writers scarcely noticed this word, the more
modern ones have frequently used it instead of *ousia*. This
term, as we before observed, has been variously defined : but
can that which is capable of being circumscribed by a definition be applicable to God who is incomprehensible ? Evagrius,[3] in his " Monachicus," cautions us against rash and
inconsiderate language in reference to God ; forbidding all
attempt to define the Divinity, inasmuch as it is wholly simple in its nature : " for," says he, " definition belongs only to

---

[1] He alludes to Heb. i. 3.

[2] ὑπόστασις, (from ὑπὸ and ἵσταμαι,) a standing under ; hence a suppression : that which supports another thing by standing beneath ; hence
a deposit, as lees of wine, &c.; thence, in a metaphorical sense, that which
lies at the bottom of anything : subsistence or reality, as opposed to shadow or pretence ; hence substance, essence, (so used in Lucian, Paras.
27,) and in the Greek theological writers, = the Latin " Persona," a
Person of the Godhead.

[3] This work is lost. The only work of Evagrius now extant is his
Eccles. History, in six books.

things which are compound." The same author further adds,
" Every proposition has either a *genus* which is predicated,
or a *species*, or a *differentia*, or a *proprium*, or an *accidens*,[1]
or that which is compounded of these: but none of these can
be supposed to exist in the sacred Trinity. Let then what
is inexplicable be adored in silence." Such is the reasoning
of Evagrius, of whom we shall again speak hereafter. We
have indeed made a digression here, but such as will tend to
illustrate the subject under consideration.

CHAP. VIII.—QUOTATIONS FROM ATHANASIUS'S APOLOGY FOR
HIS FLIGHT.

ON this occasion Athanasius recited to those present the
apology which he had composed some time before in justification of his flight; a few passages from which it may be of
service to introduce here, leaving the entire production, as
too long to be transcribed, to be sought out and perused by
the studious. " See," said he, " the daring enormities of these
impious persons! Such are their proceedings: and yet, instead of blushing at their former tyrannical conduct toward
us, they even now abuse us for having effected our escape out
of their murderous hands; nay, are grievously vexed that they
were unable to compass our destruction. In short, they overlook the fact that while they pretend to upbraid us with fear,
they are really criminating themselves: for if it be disgraceful to flee, it is still more so to pursue, since the one is only
endeavouring to avoid being murdered, while the other is
seeking to commit the deed. But Scripture itself directs us
to flee:[2] and those who persecute unto death, in attempting
to violate the law, constrain us to have recourse to flight.
They should rather therefore be ashamed of their persecution,
than reproach us for having sought to escape from it: let
them but cease to harass us, and we shall have no cause to
abscond. Nevertheless they set no bounds to their malevolence,
using every art to entrap us, in the consciousness that the
flight of the persecuted is the strongest condemnation of the

[1] See these dialectical terms explained in Whately's Logic, b. ii. ch. v.
[2] Matt. x. 23.

persecutor: for no one runs away from a mild and beneficent person, but from one who is of a barbarous and cruel disposition. Hence it was that 'Every one that was discontented and in debt' fled from Saul to David (1 Sam. xxii. 2). These foes of ours in like manner desire to kill such as conceal themselves, that no evidence may exist to convict them of their inhumanity. But in this also these misguided men most egregiously deceive themselves: for the more obvious the effort to elude their snares becomes, the more manifestly will their slaughters and exiles be exposed. If they act the part of assassins, the voice of the blood which is shed will cry against them; and if they condemn to banishment, they will raise so many living monuments of their own injustice and oppression. Surely, unless their intellects were unsound, they would perceive the dilemma in which their own counsels entangle them. It is infatuation of mind that incites them to become persecutors, and prevents their discovering their own impiety, even when they aim at the life of others. But if they reproach those who succeed in secreting themselves from the malice of their blood-thirsty adversaries, and revile such as flee from their persecutors, what will they say to Jacob's retreat from the rage of his brother Esau,[1] and to Moses[2] retiring into the land of Midian for fear of Pharaoh? And what apology will these babblers make for David's[3] flight from Saul, when he sent messengers from his own house to despatch him; and for his concealment in a cave, after contriving to extricate himself from the treacherous designs of Abimelech[4] by feigning madness? What will these reckless asserters of whatever suits their purpose answer, when they are reminded of the great prophet Elias,[5] who by calling upon God had recalled the dead to life, hiding himself from dread of Ahab, and fleeing on account of Jezebel's menaces? At which time the sons of the prophets also, being sought for in order to be slain, withdrew, and were concealed in caves by Obadiah (1 Kings xviii. 4). Are they unacquainted with these instances because of their antiquity? Have they forgotten also what is recorded in the Gospel, that the disciples retreated and hid themselves for fear of the Jews?[6]

---

[1] Gen. xxviii.   [2] Exod. ii. 15.   [3] 1 Sam. xix. 12.
[4] Or rather Achish, king of Gath. See 1 Sam. xxi. 10.
[5] Elijah. See 1 Kings xix. 3.   [6] Matt. xxvi. 56.

Paul,[1] when the governor of Damascus attempted to apprehend him, was let down from the wall in a basket, and thus
escaped the hands of him that sought him. Since then Scripture relates these circumstances concerning the saints, what
excuse can they fabricate for their temerity? If they charge
us with timidity, it is in utter insensibility to the condemnation it pronounces on themselves. If they asperse these holy
men by asserting that they acted contrary to the will of God,
they demonstrate their ignorance of Scripture. For it was
commanded in the law that cities of refuge should be constituted, (Num. xxxv. 11,) by which provision was made that
such as were pursued in order to be put to death might have
means afforded of preserving themselves. Again, in the consummation of the ages,[2] when the Word of the Father, who
had before spoken by Moses, came himself to the earth, he
gave this express injunction, ' When they persecute you in
one city, flee unto another:'[3] and shortly after, ' When therefore ye shall see the abomination of desolation, spoken of by
Daniel the prophet, stand in the holy place, (let whosoever
reads, understand,) then let those in Judea flee unto the
mountains : let him that is on the house-top not come down
to take anything out of his house; nor him that is in the
fields return to take his clothes.'[4] The saints therefore, knowing these precepts, acted in accordance with them : for what
the Lord then commanded, he had before his coming in the
flesh already spoken of by his servants. And this is a universal rule for man, leading to perfection, *to practise whatever
God has enjoined.* On this account the Word himself, becoming incarnate for our sake, deigned to conceal himself
when he was sought for;[5] and being again persecuted, con-
descended to withdraw to avoid the conspiracy against him.
For thus it became him, by hungering and thirsting and suffering other afflictions, to demonstrate that he was indeed
made man. Nay at the very commencement, as soon as he
was born, he gave this direction by an angel to Joseph:
' Arise and take the young child and his mother, and flee into
Egypt, for Herod will seek the infant's life.'[6] We see also
that after Herod's death, apprehension of his son Archelaüs

---

[1] 2 Cor. xi. 32, 33. [2] See above, note on b. ii. ch. xl.
[3] Matt. x. 23. [4] Matt. xxiv. 15—18. [5] John viii. 59.
[6] Matt. ii. 13.

induced him to retire to Nazareth.[1] Subsequently Jesus, having given unquestionable evidence of his Divine character by healing the withered hand, when the Jews took counsel how they might destroy him,[2] he knowing their wickedness withdrew himself thence. Moreover when he had raised Lazarus from the dead, and they had become still more intent on destroying him, we are told that Jesus walked no more openly among the Jews,[3] but retired into a region on the borders of the desert. Again, when the Saviour said, ' Before Abraham was, I am,'[4] and the Jews took up stones to cast at him; Jesus prevented their recognising him, and going through the midst of them out of the Temple, went away thence, and so escaped. Since then they see these things, or rather hear them, (for they will not see,) are they not deserving of being burnt with fire, according to what is written, for acting and speaking so plainly contrary to all that the Lord did and taught? Finally, when John had suffered martyrdom, and his disciples had buried his body, Jesus having heard what was done, departed thence by ship into a desert place apart.[5] Such were the precepts and example of our blessed Master. But would that these men of whom I speak had the modesty to confine their rashness to men only, without daring to be guilty of such madness as to accuse the Saviour himself of timidity; especially after having already uttered blasphemies against him. Is their impiety to be tolerated? or will not rather their ignorance of the gospels be detected by every one? There is then a rational and consistent cause for retreat and flight under such circumstances as these, of which the evangelists have afforded us precedents in the conduct of our Saviour himself: from which it may be inferred that the saints have always been justly influenced by the same principle, since whatever is recorded of him as man, is applicable to mankind in general. In taking our nature, he exhibited in himself the affections of our infirmity, which John has thus indicated: 'Then they sought to take him; but no man laid hands on him, because his hour was not yet come.'[6] Moreover, before that hour came, he himself said to his mother, 'Mine hour is not yet come:'[7] and to those who were denominated

---

[1] Matt. ii. 22, 23. [2] Matt. xii. 14, 15. [3] John xi. 53, 54.
[4] John x. 39, 40. [5] Matt. xiv. 13. [6] John vii. 30.
[7] John ii. 4.

his brethren, 'My time is not yet come.'[1]   Again, when the
time had arrived, he said to his disciples, 'Sleep on now, and
take your rest: for behold the hour is at hand, and the Son
of man shall be betrayed into the hands of sinners.'[2] So that
he neither permitted himself to be apprehended before the
time came ; nor when the time was come did he conceal himself, but voluntarily gave himself up to those who had conspired against him.   Thus also the blessed martyrs have
guarded themselves in times of persecution : being persecuted
they fled, and kept themselves concealed ; but being discovered
they suffered martyrdom."   Such is the reasoning of Athanasius in his apology for his own flight.

CHAP. IX.—AFTER THE SYNOD OF ALEXANDRIA, COMPOSED OF
THE SUPPORTERS OF THE DOCTRINE OF CONSUBSTANTIALITY,
EUSEBIUS PROCEEDING TO ANTIOCH FINDS THE CATHOLICS AT
VARIANCE ON ACCOUNT OF PAULINUS'S ORDINATION ; AND HAV-
ING EXERTED HIMSELF IN VAIN TO RECONCILE THEM, HE
DEPARTS.

As soon as the council of Alexandria was dissolved,
Eusebius bishop of Verceil went to Antioch ; where finding
that Paulinus had been ordained by Lucifer, and that the
people were disagreeing among themselves, (for the partisans
of Meletius held their assemblies apart,) he was exceedingly
grieved at their want of unanimity concerning this election,
and in his own mind disapproved of what had taken place.
His respect for Lucifer however induced him to be silent
about it, and on his departure he engaged that all things
should be set right by a council of bishops.   Subsequently he
laboured with great earnestness to unite the dissentients,
but without effect.   Meanwhile Meletius returned from exile ; and finding his followers holding their assemblies apart
from the others, he set himself at their head.   But Euzoïus,
a prelate of the Arian heresy, had possession of the churches :
Paulinus[3] only was permitted to retain a small one within the
city, from which Euzoïus had not ejected him, on account of
his personal respect for him.   But Meletius assembled his adherents without the gates of the city.   It was under these

[1] John vii. 6.   [2] Matt. xxvi. 45.   [3] See b. v. ch. v.

circumstances that Eusebius left Antioch at that time. When Lucifer understood that his ordination of Paul was not approved of by Eusebius, regarding it as an injury done him, he became highly incensed; and not only separated himself from communion with him, but also began, in a contentious spirit, to condemn what had been determined by the synod. These things occurring at a season of grievous disorder, created still further schism; for many attached themselves to Lucifer, and so became a distinct sect, and were called by his name.[1] Nevertheless he was unable to give full expression to his anger, inasmuch as he had pledged himself by his deacon to assent to whatever should be decided on by the synod. Wherefore he adhered to the tenets of the Church, and returned to Sardinia to his own see: but such as at first identified themselves with his quarrel, still continue separatists. Eusebius, on the other hand, travelling throughout the Eastern provinces, like a good physician, completely restored those who were weak in the faith, instructing and establishing them in ecclesiastical principles. After this he went to Illyricum, and thence to Italy, where he pursued a similar course.

CHAP. X.—OF HILARY BISHOP OF POICTIERS.

. THERE, however, Hilary bishop of Poictiers, a city of Aquitania Secunda, had anticipated him, having previously confirmed the bishops of Italy and Gaul in the doctrines of the orthodox faith; for he first had returned from exile to these countries. Both therefore nobly combined their energies in defence of the faith: and Hilary, being a very eloquent man, maintained with great power the consubstantiality of the Son of God, and unanswerably confuted the Arian tenets in the works which he wrote in Latin. These things took place shortly after the recall of those who had been banished. But it must be observed, that at the same time Macedonius, Eleusius, Eustathius, and Sophronius, with all their partisans, who had but the one common designation of Macedonians, held frequent synods in various places. Having called together those of Seleucia who embraced their views, they anathematized the

[1] The Luciferians. See Sozomen, iii. 15, and v. 12.

prelates of the other party, that is, the Acacian; and rejecting
the creed of Rimini, they confirmed that which had been read
at Seleucia; which, as I have stated in the preceding Book,
was the same as had been before promulgated at Antioch.
When they were asked by some one, "Why have ye who are
called Macedonians hitherto retained communion with the
Acacians, as though ye agreed in opinion, if ye really hold
different sentiments?" they replied thus, through Sophronius [112]
bishop of Pompeiopolis, a city of Paphlagonia:—"Those in
the West," said he, "were infected with the Homoousian
error as with a disease: Aëtius in the East adulterated the
purity of the faith by introducing the assertion of a dissimilitude of substance. Now both of these dogmas are impious:
for the former rashly blended into one the distinct persons of
the Father and the Son, binding them together by that cord
of iniquity the term *consubstantial;* while Aëtius wholly
separated that affinity of nature of the Son to the Father, by
the expression *unlike as to substance or essence.* Since then
both these opinions run into the very opposite extremes, the
middle course between them appeared to us to be more consistent with truth and piety: we accordingly assert that the
Son is like the Father *as to subsistence.*" Such was the answer the Macedonians made by Sophronius to that question,
as Sabinus assures us in his *Collection of the Acts of Synods.*
But in decrying Aëtius as the author of the Anomoian doctrine, and not Acacius, they flagrantly disguise the truth, in
order to seem as far removed from the Arians on the one side,
as from the Homoousians on the other: for their own words
convict them of having separated from them both, merely from
the love of innovation. With these remarks we close our notice of these persons.

CHAP. XI.—THE EMPEROR JULIAN EXACTS MONEY FROM THE CHRISTIANS.

ALTHOUGH at the beginning of his reign the emperor Julian
conducted himself mildly toward all men, he did not continue
to exhibit the same equanimity. He most readily indeed acceded to the requests of the Christians, when they tended in

·any way to cast odium on the memory of Constantius; but when no inducement of this kind influenced him, he make no .effort to conceal the rancorous feelings which he entertained ·towards Christians in general. Accordingly he soon issued a ·mandate that the Church of the Novatians at Cyzicum, which ·Euzoïus had totally demolished, should be rebuilt, imposing a very heavy penalty upon Eleusis bishop of that city, if he failed to complete that structure at his own expense within the space of two months. Moreover he favoured the Pagan superstitions with the whole weight of his authority : for he not only opened their idolatrous temples, as we have before stated ; but he himself also publicly offered sacrifices to the tutelar divinity [1] of the city of Constantinople in the cathedral,[2]
113 where its image was erected.

CHAP. XII.—Of MARIS BISHOP OF CHALCEDON.

ABOUT this time, Maris bishop of Chalcedon in Bithynia being led by the hand into the emperor's presence, because of his great age, and a disease which he had in his eyes termed *the pin and web*,[3] or *cataract*, severely rebuked his impiety, apostasy, and atheism. Julian answered his reproaches by loading him with contumelious epithets : " You blind old fool," said he, " this Galilæan God of yours will never cure you." For he was accustomed to term Christ *the Galilæan*, and Christians Galilæans.[4] Maris with still greater boldness replied, " I thank God for bereaving me of my sight, that I might not behold the face of one who has fallen into such awful impiety." The emperor suffered this to pass without further notice at that time ; but he afterwards had his revenge. Observing that those who suffered martyrdom under the reign of Diocletian were greatly honoured by the Christians, and knowing that many among them were eagerly desirous of becoming martyrs, he determined to wreak his

---

[1] Τύχη, the public Genius.   [2] Βασιλικῇ.   [3] Ὑπόχυσιν ὀφθαλμῶν.
[4] Such was the term of reproach as early as the day of Pentecost.
"Are not all these who speak Galilæans ? " Acts ii. 7. The meaning of the term as one of reproach is sufficiently explained by the question of Nathaniel, (John i. 46,) " Can any good thing come out of Nazareth ? "

vengeance upon them in some other way. Abstaining therefore from the excessive cruelties which had formerly been
practised, he nevertheless directed a persecution against them
of a less outrageous kind (for any measures adopted to disquiet and molest may justly be regarded as persecution).
This then was the plan he pursued: he enacted a law by
which Christians were excluded from the cultivation of literature; "Lest," said he, "when they have sharpened their
tongue, they should be able the more readily to meet the
arguments of the heathen."[1]

CHAP. XIII.—OF THE TUMULT EXCITED BY THE PAGANS
AGAINST THE CHRISTIANS.

HE moreover interdicted such as would not abjure Christianity, and offer sacrifice to idols, from holding any office at
court: nor would he allow Christians to be governors of provinces; "for," said he, "their law forbids them to use the
sword against offenders worthy of capital punishment."[2] He
also induced many to sacrifice, partly by flatteries, and partly
by gifts. Tried in this furnace as it were, it at once became
evident to all who were the real Christians, and who were
merely nominal ones. Such as were Christians in integrity
of heart, very readily resigned their commission,[3] choosing to
endure anything rather than deny Christ. Of this number
were Jovian, Valentinian, and Valens, each of whom was
afterwards invested with the imperial dignity. But others
of unsound principles, who preferred the riches and honour
of this world to the true felicity, sacrificed without hesitation.
Such was Ecebolius, a sophist[4] of Constantinople, who accom-
modating himself to the dispositions of the emperors, pretended
in the reign of Constantius to be a very zealous Christian;
while in Julian's time he appeared an equally ardent Pagan:

---

[1] See below, chap. xvi.
[2] The emperor probably alludes to such passages as Matt. xxvi. 52, and
John xviii. 11, which he throws in the teeth of Christians, as incapacitat-
ing them for civil office.
[3] Ζώνην ἀπετίθεντο, literally, "put off their girdle."
[4] Professor of rhetoric.

nay, after Julian's death, he again made a profession of Christianity, prostrating himself before the church doors, and calling out, " Trample on me, for I am as salt that has lost its savour." Of so fickle and inconstant a character was this person, throughout the whole period of his history. About this time the emperor became anxious to make reprisals on the Persians, for the frequent incursions they had made on the Roman territories in the reign of Constantius, and therefore marched with great expedition through Asia into the' East. But as he well knew what a train of calamities attend a war, and what immense resources are needful to carry it on successfully, he craftily devised a plan for replenishing his treasury by extorting money from the Christians. On all those who refused to sacrifice he imposed a heavy fine, which was exacted with great rigour from such as were true Christians, every one being compelled to pay in proportion to what he possessed. By these unjust means the emperor soon amassed immense wealth ; for this law was put in execution, not only where Julian was personally present, but also throughout all parts of the empire. The Pagans at the same time assailed the Christians ; and there was a great concourse of those who styled themselves philosophers. They then proceeded to institute certain abominable mysteries ;[1] and sacrificing children of both sexes, they not only inspected their entrails, but even tasted their flesh. These infamous rites were practised in other cities, but more particularly at Athens and Alexandria ; in which latter place, a calumnious accusation was made against Athanasius the bishop, the emperor being assured that he was intent on desolating not that city only, but all Egypt, and that nothing but his expulsion out of the country could save it. The governor of Alexandria was therefore instructed by an imperial edict to apprehend him.

---

[1] Thereby proving themselves guilty of the very crimes which, had they not been conscious of themselves, they would never have cast in the teeth of the Christians. See Tertullian, (Apology, chap. ix.,) who throws the accusation back upon the heathen, and substantiates his arguments by undeniable facts. " In the bosom of Africa, infants were publicly sacrificed to Saturn, even to the days of a proconsul under Tiberius," &c. &c.

CHAP. XIV.—FLIGHT OF ATHANASIUS.

BUT he fled again, saying to his friends, "Let us retire for a little while; it is but a small cloud which will soon pass away." He then immediately embarked, and crossing the Nile, hastened with all speed into Egypt, closely pursued by those who sought to take him. When he understood that his · pursuers were not far distant, and his attendants were urging him to retreat once more into the desert, he had recourse to an artifice that enabled him to effect his escape. He persuaded those who accompanied him to turn back and meet his adversaries, which they instantly did; and on approaching them they were simply asked whether they had seen Athanasius: to which they replied that he was not a great way off, and that if they hastened they would soon overtake him. Being thus deluded, they started afresh in pursuit with quickened speed, but to no purpose; for Athanasius making good his retreat, returned secretly to Alexandria, and remained there concealed until the persecution was at an end. Such were the perils to which the bishop of Alexandria was exposed, after having been before subjected to so many afflictions and calamities, arising partly from Christians, and partly from the heathen. In addition to these things, the governors of the provinces, taking advantage of the emperor's superstition to feed their own cupidity, committed more grievous outrages on the Christians than their sovereign had given them a warrant for; sometimes exacting larger sums of money than they ought to have done, and at others inflicting on them corporal punishments. The emperor was not ignorant of these excesses, but connived at them; and when the sufferers appealed to him against their oppressors, he tauntingly said, "It is your duty to bear these afflictions patiently; for this is the command of your God."

CHAP. XV.—MARTYRS AT MERUS IN PHRYGIA, UNDER THE REIGN OF JULIAN.

AMACHIUS governor of Phrygia ordered that the temple at Merus, a city of that province, should be opened, and cleared of the filth which had accumulated there by lapse of time: also that the statues it contained should be fresh polished. This revival of superstition was so obnoxious to the Christians, that three of their number, Macedonius, Theodulus, and Tatian, unable to endure the indignity thus put upon their religion, and impelled by a fervent zeal for virtue, rushed by night into the temple, and brake the images in pieces. The governor, infuriated at what had been done, would have destroyed many in that city who were altogether innocent, had not the authors of the deed voluntarily surrendered themselves, choosing rather to die themselves in defence of the truth, than to see others put to death in their stead. Being seized, they were ordered to expiate the crime they had committed by sacrificing: on their refusal to do this, their judge menaced them with tortures; but they despising his threats, being endowed with great courage, declared their readiness to undergo any sufferings, rather than pollute themselves by sacrificing. After being racked with a variety of torments, they were at last laid on gridirons, under which a fire was placed, and thus they were destroyed. But even in this last extremity they gave the most heroic proofs of fortitude, addressing the ruthless governor thus :—" If you wish to eat broiled flesh, Amachius, turn us on the other side also, lest we should appear but half-cooked to your taste."

CHAP. XVI.—On the emperor's prohibiting christians being instructed in greek literature, the two apollinares compose books in that language.

The imperial law which forbade Christians to study Grecian literature,[1] rendered the two Apollinares, of whom we have above spoken, much more distinguished than before. For both being skilled in polite learning, the father as a grammarian, and the son as a rhetorician, they each became exceedingly serviceable to the Christians at this crisis. For the former, according to his art, composed a grammar consistent with the Christian faith: he also translated the Books of Moses into heroic verse; and paraphrased all the historical

[1] See Sozomen, b. v. ch. xviii.

books of the Old Testament, putting them partly into dactylic
measure, and partly reducing them to the form of dramatic
tragedy.   He purposely employed all kinds of verse, that no
form of expression peculiar to the Greek language might
be unknown or unheard of amongst Christians.   The younger
Apollinaris, who was well trained in eloquence, expounded the
Gospels and apostolic doctrines in the way of dialogue, following
Plato among the Greeks as his model.   By this joint service
to the Christian cause, they baffled the emperor's subtlety.   But
Divine Providence was more potent than either of their labours,
or the craft they had to contend with : for death in carrying off
its framer, in the manner we shall hereafter explain,[2] rendered
the law wholly inoperative ; and the works of these men are
now of no greater importance, than if they had never been
written.   I can imagine an objector demurring here, and
making this inquiry :—" On what grounds do you affirm that
both these things were effected by the providence of God ?
That the emperor's sudden death was very advantageous to
Christianity is indeed evident : but surely the rejection of the
Christian compositions of the two Apollinares, and the Christians beginning afresh to imbue their minds with the philosophy of the heathens, in which there is the constant assertion
of Polytheism, instead of being conducive to the promotion of
true religion, is rather to be deprecated as subversive of it."
This objection I shall meet with such considerations as at present occur to me.   Greek literature certainly was never recognised either by Christ or his apostles as divinely inspired,
nor on the other hand was it wholly rejected as pernicious. And
thus they left it, I conceive, not inconsiderately.   For there
were many philosophers among the Greeks who were not far
from the knowledge of God ; and these, being disciplined by
logical science, strenuously opposed the Epicureans and other
contentious Sophists who denied Divine Providence, confuting
their ignorance.   The writings of such men have ever been
appreciated by all lovers of real piety : nevertheless they themselves were unacquainted with the Head of true religion, being
ignorant of the mystery of Christ which had been hidden from
generations and ages (Col. i. 26).   And that this was so, the
apostle in his Epistle to the Romans[2] thus declares :—" For
the wrath of God is revealed from heaven against all ungod-

---

[1] See below, ch. xxi.   [2] Rom. i. 18—21.

liness and unrighteousness of men, who hold the truth in unrighteousness.   Because that which may be known of God is
manifest in them ; for God has shown it unto them.   For the
invisible things of him from the creation of the world are
clearly seen, being understood by the things that are made,
even his eternal power and Godhead, that they may be without
excuse : because that when they knew God, they glorified him
not as God."   From these words it appears that they had
the knowledge of truth, which God had manifested to them ;
but were culpable on this account, that when they knew God,
they glorified him not as God.   Wherefore since it is not forbidden us to study the learned works of the Greeks, we are
left at liberty to do so if we please.   This is our first argument
in defence of the position we took : another may be thus put.
The divinely-inspired Scriptures undoubtedly inculcate doctrines that are both admirable in themselves, and heavenly in
their character : they also eminently tend to produce piety
and integrity of life in those who are guided by their precepts,
pointing out a walk of faith which is highly approved of God.
But they do not instruct us in the art of reasoning, by means
of which we may be enabled successfully to resist those who
oppose the truth.   Besides, adversaries are most easily foiled,
when we can turn their own weapons against them.   But this
power was not supplied to Christians by the writings of the
Apollinares.   Julian well knew when by law he prohibited Christians from being educated in Greek literature, that the fables
it contains would expose the whole Pagan system, of which
he had become the champion, to ridicule and contempt.
Even Socrates, the most celebrated of their philosophers, despised these absurdities, and was condemned to die on account
of it, as if he had attempted to violate the sanctity of their
deities.   Moreover both Christ and his apostle enjoin us " to
become discriminating money-changers,[1] so that we might
' prove all things, and hold fast that which is good :' "[2] directing us also to " beware lest any one should spoil us through
philosophy and vain deceit."[3]   But this we cannot do, unless
we possess ourselves of the weapons of our adversaries : taking

---

[1] Τραπεζῖται δόκιμοι.   This expression is not now found in Scripture,
though Origen and Jerome attest it ; and Usher supposes it to have been
recorded as a saying of our Lord in " the Gospel according to the Hebrews."   [2] 1 Thes. v. 21.   [3] Col. ii. 8.

care that in making this acquisition we do not adopt their
sentiments, but analyzing whatever is presented to us, reject
the evil, but retain what is good and true; for good, wherever
it is found, is a property of truth.   Should any one imagine
that in making these assertions we wrest the Scriptures from
their legitimate construction, let it be remembered that the
apostle not only does not forbid our being instructed in Greek
learning, but that he himself seems by no means to have neglected it, inasmuch as he often quotes from Greek authors.
Whence did he get the saying, "The Cretians are always
liars, evil beasts, slow-bellies,"[1] but from a perusal of "The
Oracles of Epimenides," the Cretan Initiator? · Or how would
he have known this, "For we are also his offspring,"[2] had he
not been acquainted with "The Phenomena of Aratus" the
astronomer?   Again, this sentence, "Evil communications
corrupt good manners,"[3] is a sufficient proof that he was conversant with "The Tragedies of Euripides."[4]   But what need
is there of enlarging on this point?   It is well known that
in ancient times the doctors of the Church by uninterrupted
usage were accustomed to exercise themselves in the learning
of the Greeks, until they had reached an advanced age: this
they did with a view to strengthen and polish the mind, as
well as to improve in eloquence; and at the same time to enable them to refute the errors of the heathen.   With these
remarks we close our allusion to the two Apollinares.

CHAP. XVII.—THE EMPEROR, PREPARING AN EXPEDITION
AGAINST THE PERSIANS, ARRIVES AT ANTIOCH, WHERE HAVING
PROVOKED THE RIDICULE OF THE INHABITANTS, HE RETORTS
ON THEM BY A SATIRICAL PUBLICATION ENTITLED "MISOPO-
GON, OR THE BEARD-HATER."

THE emperor, having extorted immense sums of money
from the Christians, accelerates his expedition against the
Persians, and proceeds to Antioch in Syria.   There, desiring
to show the citizens how much he affected glory, he unduly
depressed the prices of commodities; neither taking into ac-

---

[1] Titus i. 12.   [2] Acts xvii. 28.   [3] 1 Cor. xv. 33.
[4] Socrates is here under a mistake.   It is not from Euripides, but from
Menander, that this line is quoted by St. Paul.

count the circumstances of that time, nor reflecting how much
the presence of an army inconveniences the population of a
province, and lessens the supply of provisions to the cities.
¹¹⁵ The merchants and retailers therefore left off trading, being
unable to sustain the losses which the imperial edict entailed
upon them ; consequently the markets were unfurnished with
necessaries. This arbitrary conduct, together with its effect,
so exasperated the Antiochians, a people naturally predisposed
to insolence, that they instantly broke forth into invectives
against Julian ; caricaturing his beard also, which was a very
long one, and saying that it ought to be cut off and manufac-
tured into ropes. They added that the bull which was im-
pressed upon his coin, was a symbol of his having desolated
the world. For this emperor, in his excess of superstitious
devotion, was continually sacrificing bulls¹ on the altars of
his idols ; and had ordered the impression of a bull and altar
to be made on his coin. Irritated by these scoffs, he threatened to punish the city of Antioch, and to return to Tarsus
in Cilicia, giving orders that preparations should be made for
his speedy departure thence. Libanius the sophist made this
an occasion of composing two orations, one addressed to the
emperor in behalf of the Antiochians, the other to the inhabitants of Antioch on the emperor's displeasure. It is however
affirmed that these compositions were merely written, and
never recited in public. Julian, abandoning his former purpose of revenging himself on his satirists by injurious deeds,
expended his wrath in reciprocating their abusive taunts ; for
he wrote a pamphlet against them which he entitled " Anti-
ochicus or Misopogon," thus leaving an indelible stigma upon
that city and its inhabitants. But we must now speak of the
evils which he brought upon the Christians at Antioch.

CHAP. XVIII.—THE EMPEROR CONSULTING AN ORACLE, THE
DEMON GIVES NO RESPONSE, BEING AWED BY THE PROXIMITY
OF BABYLAS THE MARTYR.

HAVING ordered that the Pagan temples at Antioch should
be opened, he was very eager to obtain an oracle from *Apollo*

¹ Hence Gregory of·Nazianzen styles him καυσίταυρον, bull-burner.

Daphnæus. But the demon that inhabited the temple remained silent through fear of his neighbour Babylas the martyr; for the coffin which contained the body of that saint was
close by. When the emperor was informed of this circumstance, he commanded that the coffin should be immediately
removed: upon which the Christians of Antioch, including
women and children, transported the coffin from Daphne to
the city, with solemn rejoicings and chanting of psalms. The
psalms were such as cast reproach on the gods of the heathen,
and those who put confidence in them and their images.

CHAP. XIX.—WRATH OF THE EMPEROR, AND FIRMNESS OF
THEODORE THE CONFESSOR.

THE emperor's real temper and disposition, which he had
hitherto kept as much as possible from observation, now became fully manifested: for he who had boasted so much of
his philosophy, was no longer able to restrain himself; but
being goaded almost to madness by these reproachful hymns,
he was ready to inflict the same cruelties on the Christians,
with which Diocletian had formerly visited them. Nevertheless his solicitude about the Persian expedition afforded him
no leisure for personally executing his wishes; he therefore
commanded Sallust the Prætorian prefect to seize those who
had been most conspicuous for their zeal in psalm-singing, in
order to make examples of them. The prefect, though a
Pagan, was far from being pleased with his commission; but
since he durst not contravene it, he caused several of the
Christians to be apprehended, and some of them were imprisoned. On one young man named Theodore, whom the
heathens brought before him, he inflicted a variety of tortures,
causing his person to be so lacerated that he was released
from further punishment, under the supposition that he could
not possibly outlive the torments he had endured: yet God
preserved this sufferer, so that he long survived that confession. Rufinus, the author of an "Ecclesiastical History"
written in Latin, states that he himself conversed with the
same Theodore a considerable time afterwards: and on inquiring of him whether in the process of scourging and rack-

ing he had not felt the most agonizing pains, his answer was, that he was but little sensible of the tortures to which he was subjected; and that a young man stood by him who both wiped off the sweat which was produced by the acuteness of the ordeal through which he was passing, and at the same time strengthened his mind, so that he rendered this time of trial a season of rapture rather than of suffering. Such was the testimony of the excellent Theodore. About this time Persian ambassadors came to the emperor, requesting him to terminate the war on certain express conditions. But Julian abruptly dismissed them, saying, " You shall very shortly see us in person, so that there will be no need of an embassy."

CHAP. XX.—THE JEWS BEING INSTIGATED BY THE EMPEROR TO REBUILD THEIR TEMPLE, ARE FRUSTRATED IN THEIR ATTEMPT BY MIRACULOUS INTERPOSITION.

THE superstition of the emperor became still more apparent in his further attempts to molest the Christians. Being fond of sacrificing, he not only himself delighted in the blood of victims, but considered it an indignity offered to him, if others did not manifest a similar taste. And as he found but few persons of this stamp, he sent for the Jews and inquired of them why they abstained from sacrificing, since the law of Moses enjoined it? On their replying that it was not permitted them to do this in any other place than Jerusalem, he immediately ordered them to rebuild Solomon's temple. Meanwhile he himself proceeded on his expedition against the Persians. The Jews, who had been long desirous of obtaining a favourable opportunity for rearing their temple afresh, in order that they might therein offer sacrifice, applied themselves very vigorously to the work ; and conducting themselves with great insolence toward the Christians, threatened to do them as much mischief as they had themselves suffered from the Romans. The emperor having ordered that the expenses of this structure should be defrayed out of the public treasury, all things were soon provided ; so that they were furnished with timber and stone, burnt brick, clay, lime, and all other materials necessary for building. On this occasion Cyril bishop of

Jerusalem, calling to mind the prophecy of Daniel, which Christ also in the holy Gospels has confirmed, predicted in the presence of many persons that the time would very soon come in which one stone should not be left upon another in that temple, but that the Saviour's prophetic declaration should have its full accomplishment. Such were the bishop's words: and on the night following a mighty earthquake tore up the stones of the old foundations of the temple, and dispersed them all together with the adjacent edifices. This circumstance exceedingly terrified the Jews; and the report of it brought many to the spot who resided at a great distance: when therefore a vast multitude was assembled another prodigy took place. Fire came down from heaven and consumed all the builders' tools: so that for one entire day the flames were seen preying upon mallets, irons to smooth and polish stones, saws, hatchets, adzes, in short all the various implements which the workmen had procured as necessary for the undertaking. The Jews indeed were in the greatest possible alarm, and unwillingly confessed that Christ is God: yet they did not his will; but influenced by inveterate prepossessions they still clung to Judaism. Even a third miracle which afterwards happened failed to induce a belief of the truth. For the next night luminous impressions of a cross appeared imprinted on their garments, which at daybreak they in vain attempted to rub or wash out. They were therefore blinded as the apostle says,[1] and cast away the good which they had in their hands: and thus was the temple, instead of being rebuilt, at that time wholly overthrown.

CHAP. XXI.—THE EMPEROR'S IRRUPTION INTO PERSIA, AND DEATH.

JULIAN having learnt that the Persians were greatly enfeebled and totally spiritless in winter, and that from their inability to endure cold, and abstaining from military service at that season, it became a proverb that *a Mede will not then draw his hand from underneath his cloak,* marched his army into the Persian territories a little before spring; well know-

[1] Rom. xi. 25.

ing that the Romans were inured to brave all the rigours of
the atmosphere. After devastating a considerable tract of
country, including numerous villages and fortresses, they next
assailed the cities; and having invested the great city Ctesiphon, the king of the Persians was reduced to such straits
that he sent repeated embassies to the emperor, offering to surrender a portion of his dominions, on condition of his quitting
the country, and putting an end to the war. But Julian was
unaffected by these submissions, and showed no compassion
to a suppliant foe: forgetful of the adage, *To conquer is honourable, but to be more than conqueror*[1] *is odious.* Giving
credit to the divinations of the philosopher Maximus, with
whom he was in continual intercourse, he was deluded into
the belief that his exploits would not only equal, but exceed
those of Alexander of Macedon; so that he spurned with
contempt the entreaties of the Persian monarch. Nay, so
imposed on was he by the absurd notions of Pythagoras and
Plato on *the transmigration of souls,*[2] that he imagined himself to be possessed of Alexander's soul, or rather that he
himself was Alexander in another body. These ridiculous
fancies preventing his listening to any negotiations for peace,
the king of the Persians was constrained to prepare for conflict, and therefore on the next day after the rejection of his
embassy, he drew out in order of battle all the forces he had.
The Romans indeed censured their prince for not avoiding
an engagement when he might have done so with advantage:
nevertheless they attacked those who opposed them, and again
put the enemy to flight. The emperor was present on horse-
back, and encouraged his soldiers in battle; but confiding in
his hope of success, he wore no armour. In this defenceless
state, a dart cast by some one unknown pierced through his
arm and entered his side, making a wound that caused his
death. Some say that a certain Persian hurled the javelin,
and then fled; others assert that one of his own men was the
author of the deed, which indeed is the best corroborated and
most current report. But Callistus, one of his body-guards,
who celebrated this emperor's deeds in heroic verse, says, in
narrating the particulars of this war, that the wound of which

[1] Ὑπερνικᾷν, the same expression as is used in Rom. viii. 37, though
with a slight difference of meaning.
[2] Μετενσωμάτωσις, as nearly as possible equivalent to μετεμψύχωσις.

he died was inflicted by a demon.   This is possibly a mere
poetical fiction, or perhaps it was really the fact; for vengeful
furies have undoubtedly destroyed many persons.   Be the
case however as it may, this is certain, that the ardour of his
natural temperament rendered him incautious, his learning
made him vain, and his affectation of clemency exposed him
to contempt.   Thus Julian's existence was terminated in [III]
Persia, as we have said, in his fourth consulate, which he
bore with Sallust his colleague.   This event occurred on the
26th of June, in the third year of his reign, and the seventh
from his having been created Cæsar by Constantius, he being
at that time in the thirty-first year of his age.

CHAP. XXII.—JOVIAN IS PROCLAIMED EMPEROR.

THE soldiery, in extreme perplexity at an event so unexpected, on the following day proclaim Jovian emperor, a person alike distinguished by his courage and birth.   He was a
military tribune when Julian put forth an edict giving his
officers the option of either sacrificing or resigning their rank
in the army, and chose rather to lay down his commission,[1]
than to obey the mandate of an impious prince.   Julian however being pressed by the urgency of the war which was before him, would not accept his resignation, but continued him
among his generals.   On being saluted emperor, he positively
declined to accept the sovereign power: and when the soldiers
brought him forward by force, he declared that, being a Christian, he did not wish to reign over a people devoted to idolatrous superstitions.   They all then with one voice answered
that they also were Christians: upon which he allowed himself to be invested with the imperial dignity.   Perceiving
himself suddenly left in very difficult circumstances, in the
heart of a hostile country, where his army was in danger of
perishing for want of necessaries, he agreed to terminate the
war, even on terms by no means honourable to the glory of
the Roman name; although the exigencies of the present
crisis obliged him to accede to them.   Submitting therefore

---

[1] See above, chap. xiii.

L.

to the loss of the borders[1] of the empire, (i. e. the districts beyond the Tigris,) and giving up also Nisibis, a city of Mesopotamia, to the Persians, he withdrew from their territories. The announcement of these things gave fresh hope to the Christians; while the Pagans vehemently bewailed Julian's death. Nevertheless the whole army reprobated the intemperate heat of the latter, and ascribed to his rashness in listening to the wily reports of a Persian deserter the humiliating position in which they found themselves subsequently placed: for being imposed upon by the statements of this fugitive, he was induced to burn the ships which supplied them with provisions by water, by which means they were exposed to all the horrors of famine. Libanius composed a Funeral Oration on him, which he designated *the Julianian Epitaph*, wherein he not only celebrates with lofty encomiums almost all his actions; but in referring to the [118] books which Julian wrote against the Christians, says that he has therein clearly demonstrated the ridiculous and trifling character of their sacred books. Had this sophist contented himself with extolling the emperor's other acts, I should have quietly proceeded with the course of my history; but since this violent declaimer has thought proper to take occasion to inveigh against the Christian Religion, we shall pause a little to consider his words.

CHAP. XXIII.—REFUTATION OF THE STATEMENTS OF LIBA-
NIUS THE SOPHIST CONCERNING JULIAN.

" WHEN the winter," says he, " had lengthened the nights, the emperor undertook an examination of those books which make the man of Palestine both God, and the Son of God: and by a long series of arguments he has incontrovertibly proved that these writings, which are so much revered by Christians, abound with the most superstitious extravagances. In this matter therefore he has evinced himself wiser and more

---

[1] The original is τοὺς Σύρους τῆς ἀρχῆς, the government of Syria, which is confirmed by Epiphanius and Nicephorus: but Valerius denies the fact, and argues that the true reading should be τοὺς ὅρους τῆς ἀρχῆς, which seems to be afterwards established by Socrates himself.

skilful than the Tyrian[1] old man. But may this Tyrian sage be propitious to me, and mildly bear with what has been affirmed, seeing that he has been excelled by his son!" Such is the language of Libanius, who was unquestionably a man of great oratorical ability. But I am persuaded that, had he not coincided with the emperor in religious sentiment, he would not only have given expression to all that has been said against him by Christians, but would have magnified every ground of censure with all the elaborateness of his art. While Constantius was alive he wrote encomiums upon him; but after his death he brought the most insulting and reproachful charges against him. If Porphyry had been emperor, Libanius would certainly have preferred his books to Julian's: and had Julian been a mere sophist, he would have termed him a very indifferent one, as he does Ecebolius in his "Epitaph upon Julian." Since then he has spoken in the spirit of a Pagan, a sophist, and the friend of him whom he lauded, we shall endeavour to meet what he has advanced, as far as we are able. In the first place, he says that the emperor undertook to examine these books during the long winter nights; by which he means that he devoted that time in writing a confutation of them, as the sophists commonly do in teaching the rudiments of their art; for he had perused these books long before. But throughout the whole tedious contest into which he entered, instead of attempting to disprove anything by sound reasoning, as Libanius asserts, the conscious want of truth and solid argument obliged him to have recourse to sneers and contemptuous jests, of which he was excessively fond; and thus he sought to hold up to derision, what is too firmly established to be overthrown. Thus too we often see one who enters into controversy with another, sometimes trying to pervert the truth, and at others to conceal it, endeavouring by every possible means to obtain an unfair advantage over his antagonist. And an adversary is not satisfied with doing malignant acts against one with whom he is at variance, but will speak against him also, and charge upon the object of his dislike the very faults he is conscious of in himself. That both Julian and Porphyry, whom Libanius calls the Tyrian old man, took great delight in scoffing, is evident from their own works. For Porphyry

[1] Porphyry. See above, b. i. chap. ix.

in his " History of the Philosophers " has treated with ridicule the life of Socrates, the most eminent of them all, making such remarks on him as neither Melitus, nor Anytus, his accusers, would have dared to utter : a man admired by all the Greeks for his modesty, justice, and other virtues ; whom Plato,[1] the most admirable among them, Xenophon, and the rest of the philosophic band, not only honour as one beloved of God, but also account as having been endowed with superhuman intelligence.   And Julian, imitating his father,[2] displayed a like morbidness of mind in his book entitled " The Cæsars," wherein he traduces all his imperial predecessors, not sparing even Mark the philosopher.   Their own writings therefore show that they took pleasure in taunts and reviling : and that such was the natural propensity of Julian in particular, is thus attested by Gregory of Nazianzen, in his " Second Oration against the Pagans."

" These things were made evident to others by experience, after the possession of imperial authority had left him free to follow the bent of his inclinations : but I had foreseen it all, from the time I became acquainted with him at Athens. Thither he came, by permission of the emperor, soon after the change in his brother's fortune. His motive for this visit was twofold : one reason was honourable to him, viz. to see Greece, and attend the schools there ; the other was a clandestine one, which few knew anything about, for his impiety had not yet presumed to openly avow itself, viz. to have opportunity of consulting the sacrificers and other impostors respecting his own destiny. I well remember that even then I was no bad diviner concerning this person, although I by no means pretend to be one of those skilled in the art of divination : but the fickleness of his disposition, and the incredible extravagancy of his mind, rendered me prophetic ; if indeed he is the best prophet whose conjectures are verified by subsequent events. For it seemed to me that no good was portended by a neck seldom steady, the frequent shrugging of shoulders, an eye scowling and always in motion, together with a phrenzied aspect ; a gait irregular and tottering, a nose breathing only contempt and insult, with ridiculous contortions of countenance expres-

[1] See his character as given by Plato, especially in his Phædrus, and by Xenophon in his Memorabilia Socratis.
[2] i. e. his father in philosophy, Porphyry.

sive of the same thing; immoderate and very loud laughter, nods as it were of assent, and drawings-back of the head as if in denial, without any visible cause; speech with hesitancy and interrupted by his breathing; disorderly and senseless questions, with answers of a corresponding character, all jumbled together without the least consistency or method. Why need I enter into more minute particulars? Long before time had developed in action the sort of person he really was, I had foreseen what his conduct has made manifest. And if any of those who were then present and heard me, were now here, they would readily testify that when I observed these prognostics, I exclaimed, *Ah! how great a mischief to itself is the Roman empire fostering!* And that when I had uttered these words, I prayed God that I might be a false prophet. For it would have been far happier that I should have been convicted of having formed an erroneous judgment, than that the world should be filled with so many calamities, by the existence of a monster such as never before appeared; although many deluges and conflagrations are recorded, many earthquakes and chasms, and descriptions are given of many ferocious and inhuman men, as well as prodigies of the brute creation, compounded of different races, of which nature has produced unusual forms. His end has indeed been such as corresponds with the madness of his career."

This is the sketch which Gregory has given us of Julian. Moreover that in their various compilations they have endeavoured to subvert the truth, sometimes by the corruption of passages of sacred Scripture, at others by either adding or taking away from the express words, and putting such a construction upon them as suited their own purpose, many have demonstrated, who in answering their cavils have abundantly exposed their fallacies. Origen in particular, who lived long us before Julian's time, by himself raising objections to such passages of Holy Scripture as seemed to disturb some readers, and then fully meeting them, has repelled the invidious clamours of the ill-affected. And had Julian and Porphyry given his writings a candid and serious perusal, they would have discoursed on other topics, and not have lent their minds to the framing of blasphemous sophisms. It is also very obvious that the emperor in his discourses was intent on beguiling the ignorant, and did not address himself to those

who retain an impression of the truth as it is presented in
the sacred Scriptures. For having grouped together various
expressions in which God is spoken of dispensationally,[1] and
more according to the manner of men, he thus comments on
them. "Every one of these expressions is full of blasphemy
against God, unless the phrase contains some occult and
mysterious sense, which indeed I can suppose." This is the
language he uses in his third book *against the Christians.*
But in his treatise "On the Cynic Philosophy," where he
shows to what extent fables may be invented on religious
subjects, he says that in such matters the truth must be veiled:
"For," to quote his very words, "Nature loves concealment;
and the hidden substance of the gods cannot endure being cast
into polluted ears in naked words." From which it is manifest that the emperor entertained this notion concerning the
divine Scriptures, that they are mystical discourses, containing
in them some abstruse meaning. He is also very indignant
because all men do not form the same opinion of them; and
inveighs against those Christians who understand the sacred
oracles in a more literal sense. But it ill became him to rail
so vehemently against the simplicity of the vulgar, and on
their account to behave so arrogantly towards the sacred
Scriptures: nor was he warranted in turning with aversion
from those things which others rightly apprehended, because
they understood them otherwise than he desired they should.
A similar cause of disgust seems to have operated upon him
that affected Porphyry, who having been beaten by some
Christians at Cæsarea in Palestine, from the working of
unrestrained rage renounced the Christian religion: and his
hatred of those who had beaten him further urged him to
write blasphemous works against Christians, which have been
ably answered by Eusebius Pamphilus, who at the same time
exposes the motives by which he was influenced. So the
emperor having uttered disdainful expressions against the
Christians in the presence of an unthinking multitude, through
the same morbid condition of mind fell into Porphyry's blasphemies. Since therefore they both wilfully broke forth into
impiety, they are punished by the consciousness of their guilt.
But when Libanius the sophist says in derision, that the
Christians make a man of Palestine both God and the Son

[1] See above, note on b. ii. ch. xxi.

of God, he appears to have forgotten that he himself has
deified Julian at the close of his oration. "For they almost
killed," says he, "the first messenger of his death, as if he had
lied against a god." And a little afterwards he adds, "O
thou cherished one of the demons! thou disciple of the
demons! thou assessor with the demons!" Now although
Libanius may have meant otherwise, yet inasmuch as he did
not avoid the ambiguity of a word which is sometimes taken
in a bad sense, he seems to have said the same things as the
Christians had done reproachfully. If then it was his intention to praise him, he ought to have avoided equivocal terms; as
he did on another occasion, when he substituted a more definite
word for one which had been objected to. Moreover that
man in Christ was united to the Godhead, so that while he
was apparently but man, he was the invisible God, and that
both these things are most true, the divine books of Christians
distinctly teach. But the heathen before they believe cannot
understand: for it is the oracle of God that declares (Isa. vii.
9), "Unless ye believe, assuredly ye shall not understand."[1]
Wherefore they are not ashamed to place many men among
the number of their gods: and would that, as to their morals,
they had at least been good, just, and sober, instead of being
impure, unjust, and addicted to drunkenness, like the Hercules,
the Bacchus, and the Æsculapius, by whom Libanius does not
blush to swear frequently in his orations. It would lead me
into a tedious digression were I to attempt to describe the
unnatural debaucheries and infamous adulteries of these
objects of their worship: but those who desire to be informed
on the subject, will find abundant evidence in "Aristotle's
Peplum," "Dionysius's Corona," "Rheginus's Polymnemon,"
and the whole host of poets, that the Pagan theology is a tissue
of extravagant absurdities. We might indeed show by a variety of instances that the practice of deifying human beings [120]
was far from uncommon among the heathen, nay, that they did
so without the slightest hesitation: let a few examples suffice.
The Rhodians having consulted an oracle on some public
calamity, a response was given directing them to pay their
adoration to Atys, a Pagan priest who instituted frantic rites
in Phrygia. The oracle was thus expressed:—

[1] From LXX. Καὶ ἐὰν μὴ πιστεύσητε, οὐδὲ μὴ συνῆτε.

"Atys, the mighty god, propitiate,
Adonis chaste devoutly supplicate;
The fair-hair'd Bacchus claims your pious vows,
Who life's best gifts abundantly bestows."

Here Atys, who from an amatory mania had castrated himself, is by the oracle designated as Adonis and Bacchus.

Again, when Alexander king of the Macedonians passed
over into Asia, the Amphictyons courted his favour, and the
Pythoness uttered this oracle:—

"To Jove supreme who holds o'er gods his sway,
And Pallas Triton-born due homage pay;
The king divine in mortal form conceal'd,
His glorious lineage by his acts reveal'd:
Justice and Truth his heaven-born race proclaim,
And nations bow at Alexander's name."

These are the words of the demon at Delphi, who when he
wished to flatter potentates, did not scruple to assign them a
place among the gods. The motive here was plainly to con-
ciliate by adulation: but what adequate inducement was there
in the case of Cleomedes the pugilist, whom they ranked among
the gods in this oracle:—

"To Cleomedes, mortal now no more,
As last of heroes, full libations pour."

Diogenes the cynic, and Oenomaus the philosopher, strongly
condemned Apollo because of this oracle. The inhabitants of
Cyzicum declared Adrian to be the thirteenth god; and that
emperor himself deified his own catamite Antinoüs. Libanius
does not term these ridiculous and contemptible absurdities,
although he was familiar with these oracles, as well as with
Lucian's[1] Life of Alexander (the pseudo-prophet of Paphlagonia): nor does he himself hesitate to dignify Porphyry in a
similar manner, when, after having preferred Julian's books to
his, he says, "May the Syrian be propitious to me." This
digression will suffice to repel the scoffs of the sophist, without following him further, in what he has advanced; for to
enter into a complete refutation would require an express work.
We shall therefore proceed with our history.

[1] Adrias in the original, Andrias in Flor. MS., Adrian according to
Langus, and others write Arrian; Valesius, however, doubts the authenticity
of each of the above, believing that Socrates here alludes to the 'Αλέξανδρος
ἡ ψευδόμαντις of Lucian.

CHAP. XXIV.—ANXIETY OF THE BISHOPS TO INDUCE JOVIAN
TO FAVOUR THEIR OWN CREED.

AFTER Jovian's return from Persia, ecclesiastical commotions were again renewed : for those who presided over the Churches endeavoured to anticipate each other, in the hope of influencing the emperor to favour their own tenets.   He however had from the beginning adhered to the Homoousian faith, and openly declared that he preferred this to all others.   He wrote also by way of encouragement to Athanasius, who immediately after Julian's death had recovered the Alexandrine Church ; and recalled from exile all those prelates whom Constantius had banished, and who had not been re-established by Julian.   Moreover the Pagan temples were again shut up, and their priests secreted themelves wherever they were able.   The philosophers also laid aside their palliums, and clothed themselves in ordinary attire.   That public pollution by the blood of victims, which had been profusely lavished even to disgust in the preceding reign, was now likewise taken away.

CHAP. XXV.—THE MACEDONIANS AND ACACIANS CONVENE AT
ANTIOCH, AND DECLARE THEIR ASSENT TO THE NICENE CREED.

MEANWHILE the state of the Church was by no means tranquil ; for the heads of each party assiduously paid their court to the emperor, with a view of obtaining, not only protection for themselves, but also power against their opponents.   And first the Macedonians present a petition to him, in which they begged that all those who asserted the Son to be unlike the Father might be expelled from the Churches, and themselves allowed to take their place.   This supplication was presented by Basil bishop of Ancyra, Silvanus of Tarsus, Sophronius of Pompeiopolis, Pasinicus of Zelæ, Leontius of Comani, Callicrates of Claudiopolis, and Theophilus of Castabali.   The emperor, having perused it, dismissed them without any other answer than this : " I abominate contentiousness ; but I love and honour those who exert themselves to promote unanimity."   When this remark became generally known, it effected the emperor's purpose in making it, by subduing the violence of those who were desirous of altercation. At this time the real spirit of the Acacian sect, and their readiness to accommodate their opinions to those invested with supreme authority, became more conspicuous than ever. For assembling themselves at Antioch in Syria, they entered into a conference with Meletius, who had separated from them a little before, and embraced the Homoousian opinion. This they did because they saw Meletius was in high estimation with the emperor, who then resided at Antioch. Having therefore followed his example, and assented to the Nicene creed, they by common consent drew up a declaration of their sentiments, and presented it to Jovian. It was expressed in the following terms :—

"The synod of bishops convened at Antioch out of various provinces, to the most pious and dear to God, our lord Jovian Victor Augustus.

"That your piety has above all things aimed at establishing the peace and harmony of the Church, we ourselves, most devout emperor, are fully aware. Nor are we insensible that you have wisely judged an acknowledgment of the orthodox faith to be the fountain-head of this unity. Wherefore lest we should be included in the number of those who adulterate the doctrine of the truth, we hereby declare to your piety that we embrace and stedfastly hold the faith of the holy synod formerly convened at Nice. Especially since the term ὁμοούσιος, *consubstantial*, which to some seems novel and inappropriate, has been judiciously explained by the fathers to denote simply that the Son was begotten of the Father's substance, and that he is like the Father as to substance. Not indeed that any passion is to be understood in relation to that ineffable generation. Nor is the term (οὐσία) *substance* taken by the fathers in any usual signification of it among the Greeks; but it has been employed for the subversion of what Arius impiously dared to assert concerning Christ, viz.—that he was made of things not existing. Which heresy the Anomoians,[1] who have lately sprung up, still more audaciously maintain, to the utter destruction of ecclesiastical unity. We have therefore annexed to this our declaration, a copy of the faith

[1] Namely, those who rejected the Nicene faith, but at the same time refused assent to the doctrine propounded by Ursacius and Valens, at Rimini, that the Son was *not of like substance* to the Father.

[SOCRATES.]   P

set forth by the bishops assembled at Nice, which we also fully recognise. It is this:—'We believe in one God the Father Almighty,' and all the rest of the creed. We, the undersigned, in presenting this statement, most cordially assent to its contents. Meletius bishop of Antioch, Eusebius of Samosata, Evagrius of Sicily, Uranius of Apamæa, Zoilus of Larissa, Acacius of Cæsarea, Antipater of Rhosus, Abramius of Urimi, Aristonicus of Seleucia-upon-Belus, Barlamenus of Pergamus, Uranius of Melitina, Magnus of Chalcedon, Eutychius of Eleutheropolis, Isacoces of Armenia Major, Titus of Bostra, Peter of Sippi,[1] Pelagius of Laodicæa, Arabian of Antros, Piso of Adani, Lamydrion a presbyter, Sabinian bishop of Zeugma, Athanasius of Ancyra, Orphitus and Aëtius presbyters, Irenius bishop of Gaza, Piso of Augusta, Patricius of Paltus, Lamyrion a presbyter, Anatolius bishop of Berœa, Theotinus of the Arabs, and Lucian of Arce."

This declaration we found recorded in that work of Sabinus, entitled "A collection of the Acts of Synods." But the emperor had resolved to allay if possible the contentious spirit of the parties at variance, by bland manners and persuasive language toward them all; declaring that he would not molest any one on account of his religious sentiments, and that he should love and highly esteem such as would zealously promote the unity of the Church. The philosopher Themistius attests that such was his conduct, in the oration he composed on his consulate; in which he extols the emperor for his liberality in freely permitting every one to worship God according to the dictates of his conscience. And in allusion to the check which the sycophants received, he facetiously observes that experience has made it evident that such persons worship the purple and not the Deity; and resemble the changeful Euripus,[2] which sometimes rolls its waves in one direction, and at others the very opposite way.

[1] Σίππων, Valesius says it should be Hippi.
[2] Now known under the modern name of the Straits of Negropont.

CHAP. XXVI.—DEATH OF THE EMPEROR JOVIAN.

THUS did the emperor repress at that time the impetuosity of those who were disposed to cavil: and immediately departing from Antioch, he went to Tarsus in Cilicia, where after the due performance of the funeral obsequies of Julian, he was declared consul. Proceeding thence direct to Constantinople, he arrived at a place named Dadastana, situated on the frontiers of Galatia and Bithynia. There Themistius the philosopher, with others of the senatorian order, met him, and pronounced the consular oration before him, which he afterwards recited before the people at Constantinople. The Roman empire, blest with so excellent a sovereign, would doubtless have flourished exceedingly, as it is likely that both the civil and ecclesiastical departments would have been happily administered, had not his sudden death bereft the state of so eminent a personage. But disease, caused by some obstruction, having attacked him at the place above-mentioned during the winter season, he died there on the 17th day of February, in his own and his son Varronian's consulate, in the thirty-third year of his age, after having reigned but seven months.

This Book contains an account of the events which took place in the space of two years and five months.

BOOK IV.

CHAP. I.—AFTER JOVIAN'S DEATH, VALENTINIAN IS PROCLAIMED EMPEROR, WHO MAKES HIS BROTHER VALENS HIS COLLEAGUE IN THE EMPIRE; VALENTINIAN HOLDING THE ORTHODOX FAITH, BUT VALENS BEING AN ARIAN.

THE army leaving Galatia after the death of Jovian, arrived at Nice in Bithynia in seven days' march, and there unanimously proclaimed Valentinian emperor, on the 25th of

February, in the same consulate. He was born at Cibalis, a
city of Pannonia, and being intrusted with a military command, had displayed great skill in tactics. He was moreover
endowed with such greatness of mind, that he always appeared superior to any degree of honour he might have attained. After having been created emperor, he proceeded
forthwith to Constantinople; and thirty days after his own
possession of the imperial dignity, he makes his brother Valens his colleague in the empire. They both professed Christianity, but did not hold the same religious sentiments: for
Valentinian respected the Nicene creed; but Valens, having been baptized by Eudoxius bishop of Constantinople,
was prepossessed in favour of the Arian opinions. Each of
them was zealous for the views of his own party; but when
they had attained sovereign power, they manifested very different dispositions. In the reign of Julian, when Valentinian
was a military tribune, and Valens held a command in the
emperor's guards, they both proved their attachment to the
faith, by declaring themselves willing to relinquish their military rank, rather than renounce Christianity by sacrificing.[1]
Julian however, knowing their ability to serve the state, retained them in their respective places, as did also Jovian, his
successor in the empire. On their being invested with imperial authority, they exhibited equal diligence in the management of public affairs, but behaved themselves very differently
in relation to ecclesiastical matters: for Valentinian, while he
favoured those who agreed with him in sentiment, offered no
violence to the Arians; but Valens, in his anxiety to promote
the Arian cause, grievously disturbed those who differed from
them, as the course of our history will show. Liberius at
that time presided over the Roman Church. Athanasius was
bishop of the Homoousians at Alexandria, while Lucius had
been constituted George's successor by the Arians. At Antioch Euzoïus was at the head of the Arians, but the Homoousians were divided into two parties, of one of which
Paul was chief, and Meletius of the other. Cyril was re-
established in the Church at Jerusalem. The Churches at
Constantinople were under the government of Eudoxius, who
openly taught the dogmas of Arianism, the Homoousians
having but one small edifice in the city wherein to hold their

_____
[1] See above, b. iii. ch. xiii.

assemblies. Those of the Macedonian heresy who had dissented from the Acacians at Seleucia, then retained their churches in every city. Such was the state of ecclesiastical affairs at that time.[1]

CHAP. II.—VALENTINIAN GOES INTO THE WEST, LEAVING VALENS AT CONSTANTINOPLE, WHO ACCEDES TO THE REQUEST OF THE MACEDONIANS THAT A SYNOD MIGHT BE CONVENED, BUT PERSECUTES THE HOMOOUSIANS.

THE exigencies of the state requiring the presence of one of the emperors in the western parts of the empire, Valentinian goes thither: meanwhile Valens, residing at Constantinople, is addressed by most of the prelates of the Macedonian heresy, requesting that another synod might be convened for the reformation of the creed. The emperor, supposing they agreed in sentiment with Eudoxius and Acacius, gave them permission to do so: these persons therefore made preparations for assembling in the city of Lampsacus. But Valens proceeds with the utmost despatch toward Antioch in Syria, fearing lest the Persians should violate the treaty into which they had entered for thirty years in the reign of Jovian, and invade the Roman territories. They however remained quiet; and Valens employed this season of external tranquillity to prosecute a war of extermination against all who acknowledged the Homoousian doctrine. Paulinus their bishop, because of his eminent piety, alone remained unmolested. Meletius was sent into exile: and all who refused to communicate with Euzoïus, were driven from the churches in Antioch, and subjected to various losses and punishments. It is even affirmed that the emperor caused many to be drowned in the river Orontes, which flows by that city.

[1] See below, b. v. ch. iii.

CHAP. III.—WHILE VALENS PERSECUTES THE ORTHODOX CHRIS-
TIANS IN THE EAST, A TYRANT ARISES AT CONSTANTINOPLE
NAMED PROCOPIUS: AND AT THE SAME TIME AN EARTHQUAKE
AND INUNDATION TAKE PLACE.

WHILE Valens was thus occupied in Syria, there arose a
tyrant at Constantinople named Procopius; who having collected a large body of troops in a very short time, meditated
an expedition against the emperor.   This intelligence, by
creating solicitudes of another kind, checked for a while the
persecution he had commenced against all who dared to differ
from him in opinion.   And while the commotions of a civil
war were painfully anticipated, an earthquake occurred which
did much damage to many cities.   The sea also changed its
accustomed boundaries, and overflowed to such an extent in
some places, that vessels might sail where roads had previously existed; and it retired so much from other places,
that the ground became dry.   These events happened in the
first consulate of the two emperors.

CHAP. IV.—THE MACEDONIANS CONVENE A SYNOD AT LAMP-
SACUS, DURING A PERIOD OF BOTH SECULAR AND ECCLESI-
ASTICAL AGITATION; AND AFTER CONFIRMING THE ANTIOCHIAN
CREED, AND ANATHEMATIZING THAT PROMULGATED AT RIMINI,
THEY AGAIN RATIFY THE DEPOSITION OF ACACIUS AND EU-
DOXIUS.

IN this unsettled condition of things, in relation both to the
Church and State, those who had been empowered by the
emperor to hold a council, assembled at Lampsacus in the
consulate just mentioned, being seven years after the council
of Seleucia.[1]   There, after confirming the Antiochian creed,
to which they had subscribed at Seleucia, they anathematize
that which had been set forth at Rimini[2] by those prelates
with whom they had formerly agreed in opinion.   They moreover again condemn the party of Acacius and Eudoxius, and
declare their deposition to have been just.[3]   The civil war

[1] See above, b. ii. ch. xl.
[2] In the year 359. See b. ii. ch. xxxvii.
[3] See above, b. ii. ch. xl. sub fin.

which was then impending, prevented Eudoxius bishop of Constantinople from either gainsaying or revenging these determinations. Wherefore Eleusius bishop of Cyzicum and his adherents continued for a little while the stronger party; inasmuch as they supported the views of Macedonius, which, although before but obscurely known, acquired great publicity through the synod at Lampsacus. Hence it was, I suppose, that the Macedonians became so numerous in the Hellespont, Lampsacus being situated in one of its narrow bays. Such was the issue of this council.

CHAP. V.—Engagement between Valens and Procopius near Nacolia in Phrygia; after which the tyrant is betrayed by his chief officers, and with them put to death.

The war was commenced in the following year under the consulate of Gratian and Dagalaïfus. For as soon as the tyrant Procopius, leaving Constantinople, began his march at the head of his army toward the emperor, Valens, on receiving intelligence of it, hastens from Antioch, and comes to an engagement with him near Nacolia, a city of Phrygia. The tyrant had the advantage in the first encounter; but soon after he was taken alive, through the treachery of Agilo and Gomarius, two of his generals, who together with their leader were despatched by the most extraordinary punishments. Valens had indeed pledged himself to spare the traitors, but disregarding his oaths, he caused them to be executed by being sawn asunder. Two trees standing near each other being forcibly bowed down, one of the tyrant's legs was fastened to each of them, after which the trees being suddenly permitted to recover their erect position, by their rise rent the tyrant into two parts, and thus miserably destroyed him.

CHAP. VI.—AFTER THE TYRANT'S DEATH, VALENS CONSTRAINS THOSE WHO COMPOSED THE SYNOD, AND ALL CHRISTIANS, TO PROFESS ARIAN TENETS.

THE emperor having thus successfully terminated the conflict, immediately began to disquiet the Christians, with the design of inducing all persons to acknowledge Arian sentiments. But he was especially incensed against those who had composed the synod at Lampsacus, not only on account of their deposition of the Arian bishops, but because they had anathematized the creed published at Rimini. On arriving therefore at Nicomedia in Bithynia, he sent for Eleusius bishop of Cyzicum, who, as I have before said, closely adhered to the opinions of Macedonius; and having convened a council of Arian bishops, he commanded Eleusius to give his assent to their faith. At first he refused to do so, but on being terrified with threats of banishment and confiscation of property, he reluctantly submitted. Immediately afterwards he repented; and returning to Cyzicum, bitterly complained in presence of all the people of the violence which had been used to extort an insincere acquiescence. He then exhorted them to seek another bishop for themselves, since he had been compelled to renounce his own opinion. But the inhabitants of Cyzicum loved and venerated him too much to think of losing him; they therefore refused to be subject to any other bishop, nor would they permit him to retire from his own Church: and thus continuing under his oversight, they remained stedfast in their own heresy.

CHAP. VII.—EUNOMIUS SUPERSEDES ELEUSIUS IN THE SEE OF CYZICUM. HIS ORIGIN AND IMITATION OF AETIUS, WHOSE AMANUENSIS HE HAD BEEN.

THE bishop of Constantinople being informed of this circumstance, constitutes Eunomius bishop of Cyzicum, inasmuch as he was a person able by his eloquence to win over the minds of the multitude to his own way of thinking. On his arrival at Cyzicum an imperial edict was published in which it was ordered that Eleusius should be ejected, and Eunomius

installed in his place. This being carried into effect, those
who attached themselves to Eleusius, after erecting a sacred
edifice without the city, assembled there with him. But
enough has been said of Eleusius : let us now give some account of Eunomius. He had been secretary to Aëtius, surnamed Atheus, of whom we have before spoken,[1] and had
learnt from conversing with him, to imitate his *sophistical*
mode of reasoning ; being little aware that while exercising
himself in framing fallacious arguments, and in the use of
certain insignificant terms, he was really deceiving himself.
This habit however inflated him with pride, and falling into
blasphemous heresies, he became an advocate of the dogmas
of Arius, and in various ways an adversary to the doctrines
of truth. He had but a very slender knowledge of the letter
of Scripture, and was wholly unable to enter into the spirit
of it. Yet he abounded in words, and was accustomed to repeat the same thoughts in different terms, without ever arriving at a clear explanation of what he had proposed to himself.
Of this his seven books on the apostle's Epistle to the Romans, on which he bestowed a quantity of vain labour, is a
remarkable proof : for although he has employed an immense
number of words in the attempt to expound it, he has by no
means succeeded in apprehending the scope and object of that
Epistle. All other works of his extant are of a similar character, in which he that would take the trouble to examine
them, would find a great scarcity of sense, amidst a profusion
of verbiage. Such was the man promoted by Eudoxius to
the see of Cyzicum ; who being come thither, astonished his
auditors by the extraordinary display of his *dialectic* art, and
produced a great sensation : until at length the people, unable
to endure any longer the empty parade of his language, and
the empty assumption of his menaces, drove him out of their
city. He therefore withdrew to Constantinople, and taking
up his abode with Eudoxius, was regarded as a vacant[2] bishop.
But lest we should seem to have said these things for the
sake of detraction, let us hear what Eunomius himself has the
hardihood to utter in his sophistical discourses concerning the

[1] See book ii. ch. xxxv. sub fin.
[2] Σχολαῖος, titular. Upon the position of bishops without actual sees,
(called ἐπίσκοποι σχολαῖοι or σχολάζοντες,) see Bingham's Christ. Antiq.
b. iv. chap. ii. sect. 14.

Deity himself. "God," says he, "knows no more of his own substance, than we do; nor is this more known to him, and less to us: but whatever we know about the Divine substance, that precisely is known to God; and on the other hand, whatever he knows, the same also you will find without any difference in us." This is a fair specimen of the tedious and absurd fallacies which Eunomius, in utter insensibility to his own folly, delighted in stringing together. On what account he afterwards separated from the Arians, we shall state in its proper place.[1]

CHAP. VIII.—OF THE ORACLE FOUND INSCRIBED ON A STONE, WHEN THE WALLS OF CHALCEDON WERE DEMOLISHED BY ORDER OF THE EMPEROR VALENS.

AN order was issued by the emperor that the walls of Chalcedon, a city opposite to Byzantium, should be demolished: for he had sworn to do this, after he should have conquered the tyrant, because the Chalcedonians had not only sided with Procopius, but had used insulting language toward Valens, and shut their gates against him as he passed by their city. This decree therefore having been carried into execution, the stones were conveyed to Constantinople to serve for the formation of the public baths which are called Constantianæ. On one of these stones an oracle was found engraven, which had lain concealed for a long time, in which it was predicted that when the city should be supplied with abundance of water, then should the wall serve for a bath; and that innumerable hordes of barbarous nations having overrun the provinces of the Roman empire, and done a great deal of mischief, should themselves at length be destroyed. We shall here insert this oracle for the gratification of the studious :—

"When nymphs their mystic dance with wat'ry feet
  Shall tread through proud Byzantium's stately street;
  When rage the city walls shall overthrow,
  Whose stones to fence a bathing-place shall go:
  Then savage lands shall send forth myriad swarms,
  Adorn'd with golden locks and burnish'd arms,
  That having Ister's silver streams o'erpast,
  Shall Scythian fields and Mœsia's meadows waste.

[1] See b. v. chap. xxiv.

> But when with conquest flush'd they enter Thrace,
> Fate shall assign them there a burial-place."

.. Such was the prophecy. And indeed it afterwards happened, that when Valens by building an aqueduct supplied the city with abundance of water, the barbarous nations made various irruptions, as we shall hereafter see. But from the event, some have explained the prediction otherwise. For when that aqueduct was completed, Clearchus the governor of the city built a stately bath, to which the name of *the Plentiful Water*[1] was given, in that which is now called the Forum of Theodosius: on which account the people celebrated a festival with great rejoicings, whereby there was, say they, an accomplishment of those words of the oracle,—

> ————" their mystic dance with wat'ry feet
> Shall tread through proud Byzantium's stately street."

But the completion of the prophecy took place afterwards. When the walls were in the course of demolition, the Constantinopolitans besought the emperor to desist; and the inhabitants of Nicomedia and Nice sending from Bithynia to Constantinople, made the same request. Valens being exceedingly exasperated against the Chalcedonians, was with difficulty prevailed upon to listen to these petitions in their favour: but that he might perform his oath, he commanded that the walls should be pulled down, while at the same time the breaches should be repaired by being filled up with other small stones. Whence it is that in the present day one may see in certain parts of the wall, very inferior materials laid upon prodigiously large stones, forming those unsightly patches which were made on that occasion.

CHAP. IX.—VALENS PERSECUTES THE NOVATIANS, BECAUSE OF THEIR HOLDING THE ORTHODOX FAITH.

THE emperor now resumed his persecution of those who embraced the doctrine of consubstantiality, driving them away from Constantinople: and as the Novatians acknowledged the same faith, they also were subjected to similar treat-

---

[1] Δαψιλὲς ὕδωρ.

ment, their churches being ordered to be shut up. He commanded also that Agelius their bishop should be sent into exile; a person that had presided over their churches from the time of Constantine, and had led an apostolic life: for he always walked barefoot, and used but one coat, observing the injunction of the gospel. But the emperor's displeasure against this sect was moderated by the efforts of a pious and eloquent man named Marcian, who had formerly been in military service at the imperial palace, but was at that time a presbyter in the Novatian Church, and taught grammar to Anastasia and Carosa, the daughters of Valens; from the former of whom the public baths yet standing, which Valens erected at Constantinople, were named.[1] From respect for this person, therefore, the Novatian churches, which had been for some time closed, were again opened. The Arians however would not suffer this people to remain undisturbed, for they disliked them on account of the sympathy and love which the Novatians manifested toward the Homoousians, with whom they agreed in sentiment. Such was the state of affairs at that time. We may here remark that the war against the tyrant Procopius was terminated about the end of May, in the consulate of Gratian and Dagalaïfus.

CHAP. X.—THE EMPEROR VALENTINIAN BEGETS A SON, WHO IS NAMED AFTER HIS FATHER; GRATIAN HAVING BEEN BORN BEFORE HIS ACCESSION TO THE IMPERIAL DIGNITY.

SOON after the conclusion of this war, and under the same consulate, a son was born to Valentinian the emperor in the Western parts, to whom the same name as his father's was given. His other son, Gratian, had been born previously to his becoming emperor.

[1] Marcellinus affirms that the Anastasian baths were built by Constantine, and named after that emperor's sister.

CHAP. XI.—HAIL OF EXTRAORDINARY SIZE; AND EARTHQUAKES
IN BITHYNIA AND THE HELLESPONT.

ON the 2nd of July of the following year, in the consulate
of Lupicin and Jovian, there fell at Constantinople hail of
such a size as would fill a man's hand.   Many affirmed that
this was an intimation of the Divine displeasure, because of
the emperor's having banished several persons engaged in the
sacred ministry, on account of their refusal to communicate
with Eudoxius.[1]   During the same consulate, on the 24th of
August, the emperor Valentinian proclaimed his son Gratian
Augustus.   In the next year, when Valentinian and Valens
were a second time consuls, there happened on the 11th of
October an earthquake in Bithynia, which destroyed the city
of Nice.   This was about twelve years after Nicomedia had
been visited by a similar catastrophe.   Soon afterwards the
largest portion of Germa in the Hellespont was reduced to
ruins by another earthquake.   Nevertheless no impression
was made on the mind of either Eudoxius the Arian bishop,
or the emperor Valens, by these supernatural occurrences;
for they were not deterred thereby from their relentless persecution of those who dissented from them in matters of faith.
Meanwhile these convulsions of the earth were regarded as
typical of the disturbances which agitated the Churches: for
many of the clerical body were sent into exile, as we have
[127] stated; Basil and Gregory alone, by a special dispensation of
Divine Providence, being on account of their eminent piety
exempted from this punishment.   The former of these individuals was bishop of Cæsarea in Cappadocia ; while the latter
presided over Nazianzen, a little city in the vicinity of Cæsarea.   But we shall have occasion to mention both again in
the course of our history.[2]

[1] See above, b. ii. ch. xliii.
[2] He alludes to chap. xxvi. of the present book.

CHAP. XII.—THE MACEDONIANS PRESSED BY THE EMPEROR'S VIOLENCE TOWARD THEM, SEND A DEPUTATION TO LIBERIUS BISHOP OF ROME, AND SUBSCRIBE THE HOMOOUSIAN CREED.

WHEN the maintainers of the Homoousian doctrine had been thus severely dealt with, and put to flight, the persecutors began afresh to harass the Macedonians; who, impelled by fear rather than violence, send deputations to one another from city to city, declaring the necessity of appealing to Valentinian, the emperor's brother, and also to Liberius bishop [128] of Rome: and that it was far better for them to embrace their faith, than to communicate with the party of Eudoxius. They send[1] for this purpose Eustathius bishop of Sebastia, who had been several times deposed, Silvanus of Tarsus in Cilicia, and Theophilus of Castabali in the same province; charging them to dissent in nothing from Liberius[2] concerning the faith, but to enter into communion with the Roman Church, and confirm the Homoousian creed. These persons therefore proceeded to Old Rome, carrying with them the letters of those who had separated themselves from Acacius at Seleucia. To the emperor they could not have access; for he was occupied in the Gallias with a war against the Sarmatæ. They however presented their letters to Liberius, who at first refused to admit them; saying they were of the Arian faction, and could not possibly be received into communion by the Church, inasmuch as they had rejected the Nicene creed. To this they replied, that by change of sentiment they had acknowledged the truth, having long since renounced the Anomoian creed, and avowed the Son to be in every way like the Father: moreover that they considered the terms *like* and *consubstantial* to have precisely the same import. When they had made this statement, Liberius demanded of them a written confession of their faith; and they accordingly presented him a document in which the substance of the Nicene creed was inserted. I have not introduced here, because of their length, the letters

---

[1] Baronius accuses Socrates of an anachronism here: since the synod of Lampsacus was held in 365, and Damasus was bishop of Rome in 368, for Liberius died in September, 367. Valesius judges that the legates were sent in June, 367.   [2] Note on b. ii. ch. viii., as also two other passages in this chapter and ch. xxxvii.

from Smyrna, Asia, and from Pisidia, Isauria, Pamphylia, and Lycia, in all which places they had held synods : deeming it sufficient to transcribe the written profession which the deputies sent with Eustathius, delivered to Liberius.[1]

"To our Lord, Brother, and Fellow-Minister Liberius ; Eustathius, Theophilus, and Silvanus, salutations in the Lord.

"On account of the insane opinion of heretics, who cease not to give offence to the catholic Churches, we, being desirous of checking their career, come forward to express our approbation of the doctrines recognised by the synod of orthodox bishops which has been convened at Lampsacus, Smyrna, and various other places : from which synod we being constituted a deputation, bring a letter to your Excellence and all the Italian and Western bishops, by which we declare that we hold and maintain the catholic faith which was established in the holy council of Nice under the reign of Constantine of blessed memory, by three hundred and eighteen bishops, and has hitherto continued entire and unshaken ; in which creed the term *consubstantial* is holily and devoutly employed in opposition to the pernicious doctrine of Arius. We therefore, together with the aforesaid persons whom we represent, profess under our own hand, that we have held, do hold, and will maintain the same faith even unto the end. We condemn Arius, and his impious doctrine, with his disciples, and the abettors of his sentiments ; as also the whole heresy of Sabellius, the Patropassians,[2] the Marcionistæ, the Photinians, the Marcelliani, that of Paul of Samosata, and those who countenance such tenets ; in short, all the heresies which are opposed to the aforesaid sacred creed, which was piously and catholicly set forth by the holy fathers at Nice. But we especially anathematize that form of the creed which was recited at the synod of Rimini,[3] as altogether contrary to the before-mentioned creed of the holy synod of Nice, to which the bishops at Constantinople affixed their signatures, being deceived by artifice

---

[1] Liberius was deceived by this counterfeit subscription, as is clear from b. v. ch. iv.

[2] Those heretics who said that the Father, Son, and Holy Spirit were the same person, were so called by their adversaries of the orthodox party, because their principles, if pushed to their legitimate conclusion, in reality asserted that the Father, as much as the Son, died upon the cross. See above, b. ii. ch. xix.

[3] See b. ii. ch. xxxvii.

and perjury, by reason of its having been brought from Nice,¹ a town of Thrace. Our own creed, and that of those whose delegates we are, is this :—

" ' We believe in one God the Father Almighty, the Maker of all things visible and invisible : and in one only-begotten God, the Lord Jesus Christ, the Son of God ; begotten of the Father, that is, of the substance of the Father ; God of God, Light of Light, very God of very God ; begotten not made, of the same substance with the Father, by whom all things were made which are in heaven, and which are upon the earth : who for us men, and for our salvation, descended, became incarnate, and was made man ; suffered, and rose again the third day ; ascended into the heavens, and will come to judge the living and the dead. We believe also in the Holy Spirit. But the Catholic and Apostolic Church of God anathematizes those who assert that there was a time when he was not, and that he was not before he was begotten, and that he was made of things which are not ; or those that say the Son of God is of another hypostasis or substance than the Father, or that he is mutable or susceptible of change.'

" I Eustathius, bishop of the city of Sebastia, with Theophilus and Silvanus, legates of the synod of Lampsacus, Smyrna, and other places, have voluntarily subscribed this confession of faith with our own hands. And if, after the publication of this creed, any one shall presume to calumniate either us, or those who sent us, let him come with the letters of your Holiness before such orthodox bishops as your sanctity shall approve of, and bring the matter to an issue with us before them ; and if any charge shall be substantiated, let the guilty be punished."

Liberius having securely pledged the legates by this document, received them into communion, and afterwards dismissed them with this letter.

THE LETTER OF LIBERIUS BISHOP OF ROME, TO THE
BISHOPS OF THE MACEDONIANS.

" To our beloved brethren and fellow-ministers, Evethius,

---

¹ " In this way they attempted to deceive the more simple by the similarity of names, and to impose upon them as the creed promulgated at Nice in Bithynia, that which they had prepared at Nice in Thrace." B. ii. ch. xxxvii.

Cyril, Hyperechius, Uranius, Heron, Elipidius, Maximus, Eusebius, Eucarpius, Heortasius, Neon, Eumathius, Faustinus, Procleus, Pasinicus, Arsenius, Severus, Didymion, Brittanius, Callicrates, Dalmatius, Ædesius, Eustochius, Ambrosa, Gelon, Pardalius, Macedonius, Paul, Marcellus, Heraclius, Alexander, Adolius, Marcian, Stenelus, John, Macer, Charisius, Silvanus, Photinus, Antony, Anytho, Celsus, Euphranor, Milesius, Patricius, Severean, Eusebius,, Eumolpius, Athanasius, Diophantus, Menodores, Diocles, Chrysampelus, Neon, Eugenius, Eustathius, Callicrates, Arsenius, Martyrius, Heiracius, Leontius, Philagrius, Lucius, and to all the orthodox bishops in the East; Liberius bishop of Italy, and the bishops throughout the West, salutations always in the Lord.

"Your letters, beloved brethren, resplendent with the light of faith, delivered to us by our highly esteemed brethren, the bishops Eustathius, Silvanus, and Theophilus, brought to us the much longed for joy of peace and concord : and this chiefly because they have assured us that your opinion and sentiments are in perfect harmony with those both of our insignificance,[1] and also with those of all the bishops in Italy and the Western parts. We acknowledge this to be the Catholic and Apostolic faith, which from the Nicene synod hitherto has continued unadulterated and unshaken. This creed your legates have professed that they themselves hold, and to our great joy have obliterated every vestige and impression of an injurious suspicion, by attesting it not only in word, but also in writing. We have deemed it proper to subjoin to these letters a copy of this their declaration, lest we should leave any pretext to the heretics for entering into a fresh conspiracy, by which they might stir up the incentives of their own malice, and according to their custom, rekindle the flames of discord. Moreover our most esteemed brethren, Eustathius, Silvanus, and Theophilus, have professed this also, both that they themselves, and also your love, have always held, and will maintain unto the last, the creed approved of at Nice by 318 orthodox bishops : which contains the perfect

---

[1] τὴν ἐμὴν ἐλαχιστότητα. This cannot fairly be adduced in order to prove the equality of the bishop of Rome with other bishops; for if the word proves anything, it proves too much; viz. that the bishop of Rome held a rank inferior to the rest of his episcopal brethren, which has never been asserted, and is clearly absurd.

[SOCRATES.]   Q

truth, and both confutes and overthrows the whole swarm of
heretics. For it was not of their own will, but by Divine appointment, that so great a number of bishops was collected
against the madness of Arius, as equalled that of those by whose
assistance blessed Abraham through faith destroyed so many
thousand of his enemies.[1] This faith being comprehended
in the terms *Hypostasis* and *Homoousios*, is a strong and im-
pregnable fortress to check and repel all the assaults and vain
machinations of Arian perverseness. Wherefore when all the
Western bishops were assembled at Rimini, whither the craft
of the Arians had drawn them, in order that either by deceptive
persuasions, or, to tell the truth, by the coercion of the secular
power, they might erase, or indirectly revoke, what had been
introduced into the creed with so much prudence, their subtlety
was not of the least avail. For almost all those who at Rimini
were either allured into error, or at that time deceived, have
since taken a right view of the matter; and after anathematizing the exposition of faith set forth by those who were
convened at Rimini, have subscribed the Catholic and Apostolic Creed which was promulgated at Nice. These persons
having entered into communion with us, regard both the
dogma of Arius and his disciples with increased aversion.
Of which fact when the legates of your love saw the indu-
bitable evidences, they annexed yourselves to their own subscription; anathematizing Arius, and what was transacted at
Rimini against the creed ratified at Nice, to which even you
yourselves, beguiled by perjury, were induced to subscribe.
Whence it appeared suitable to us to write to your love, and
to accede to your just request, especially since we are assured
by the profession of your legates that the Eastern bishops
have recovered their senses, and now concur in opinion with
the orthodox prelates of the West. We further give you to
understand, lest ye should be ignorant of it, that the blasphemies of the Rimini synod have been anathematized by those
who seem *to have been at that time* deceived by fraud, and that
all have acknowledged the Nicene creed. It is fit therefore
that you should make it generally known, that such as have
had their faith vitiated by violence or guile, may now emerge
from heretical darkness into the divine light of catholic liberty.
But that whosoever of them, after this council, shall not dis-

[1] See Gen. xiv. 14.

gorge the poison of corrupt doctrine, by abjuring all the blasphemies of Arius, and anathematizing them, are themselves, together with Arius and his disciples and the rest of the serpents, whether Sabellians, Patropassians, or the followers of any other heresy, dissevered and excommunicated from the assemblies of the Church, which does not admit of illegitimate children. May God preserve you stedfast, beloved brethren."

After Eustathius and those who accompanied him had received this letter, they proceeded to Sicily, where they caused a synod of Sicilian bishops to be convened, and in their presence avowed the Homoousian faith, and professed their adherence to the Nicene creed : then having received from those also a letter to the same effect as the preceding, they returned to those who had sent them. On the receipt of these letters, they sent legates from city to city to the prominent supporters of the doctrine of Consubstantiality, exhorting them to assemble simultaneously at Tarsus in Cilicia, in order to confirm the Nicene creed, and terminate all the contentions which had subsequently arisen. And this would probably have been accomplished, had not the Arian bishop, Eudoxius, who at that time possessed great influence with the emperor, thwarted their purpose; for on learning that a synod had been summoned to meet at Tarsus, he became so exasperated, that he redoubled his persecution against them. That the Macedonians by sending legates to Liberius were admitted to communion with him, and professed the Nicene creed, is attested by Sabinus himself, in his *Collection of Synodic Transactions*.

CHAP. XIII.—EUNOMIUS SEPARATES FROM EUDOXIUS; THROUGH WHOM A DISTURBANCE BEING RAISED AT ALEXANDRIA, ATHANASIUS SECRETES HIMSELF AGAIN, UNTIL BY VIRTUE OF THE EMPEROR'S LETTERS HE IS RE-ESTABLISHED.

ABOUT the same time Eunomius separated himself from Eudoxius, and held assemblies apart, because after he had repeatedly entreated that his preceptor Aëtius might be received into communion, Eudoxius continued to oppose it. Yet Eudoxius in this did violence to his own inclination, for he entirely coincided in opinion with Aëtius ; but he yielded to the prevailing sentiment of his own party, who objected to Aëtius as heterodox. This was the cause of the division referred to, and such was the state of things at Constantinople. But the Church at Alexandria was disturbed by an edict of the Prætorian prefects, sent thither by means of Eudoxius. Whereupon Athanasius, dreading the irrational impetuosity of the multitude, and fearing lest he should be regarded as the author of any excesses that might be committed, concealed himself for four months in his father's tomb. When however the people, on account of their affection for him, became seditious in impatience of his absence, the emperor, on ascertaining the reason why such agitation prevailed at Alexandria, ordered by his letters that Athanasius should be suffered to preside over the Churches without molestation; in consequence of which the Alexandrian Church enjoyed tranquillity until the death of Athanasius. How the Arian faction became possessed of the Churches after his decease, we shall unfold in the course of our history.[1]

CHAP. XIV.—THE ARIANS ORDAIN DEMOPHILUS AFTER THE DECEASE OF EUDOXIUS AT CONSTANTINOPLE; BUT THE ORTHODOX PARTY CONSTITUTE EVAGRIUS HIS SUCCESSOR.

THE emperor Valens, leaving Constantinople again, set out towards Antioch; but on his arrival at Nicomedia his progress was arrested by the following circumstances. Eudoxius the Arian bishop, who had been in possession of the seat of the Constantinopolitan Church for nineteen[2] years, died soon after the emperor's departure from that city, in the third consulate of Valentinian and Valens. The Arians therefore appointed Demophilus to succeed him; but the Homoousians considering that an opportunity was afforded them, elected Evagrius, a person who maintained their own principles, and caused him to be ordained by Eustathius, who after having been ejected from the see of Antioch, had been recalled from exile by Jovian. This prelate had privately come to Constantinople, for the purpose of confirming the adherents to the doctrine of Consubstantiality.

[1] See below, chap. xxi.
[2] Epiphanius says not δεκαεννία, but δεκαένα, eleven.

CHAP. XV.—The homoousians are persecuted by the ARIANS, AFTER THE BANISHMENT OF EVAGRIUS AND EUSTA-THIUS.

THE Arians, exasperated by this election, renewed their persecution of the Homoousians: and the emperor, on being informed of what had taken place, apprehending the subversion of the city in consequence of the popular tumult, immediately sent troops from Nicomedia to Constantinople; ordering that both he who had been ordained, and the one who had ordained him, should be apprehended and sent into exile. Eustathius therefore was banished to Bizya, a city of Thrace; and Evagrius was conveyed to another place. After this the Arians, becoming more confident, grievously harassed the orthodox party, frequently beating and reviling them, causing some to be imprisoned, and others to be fined; in short, they practised such distressing and intolerable annoyances, that the sufferers were induced to appeal to the emperor for protection against their adversaries. But whatever hope of redress they might have cherished from this quarter, was altogether frustrated, inasmuch as they thus merely spread their grievances before him who was the very author of them.

CHAP. XVI.—Ecclesiastics burnt in a ship by order of VALENS. FAMINE IN PHRYGIA.

EIGHTY pious individuals of the clerical order, among whom Urbanus, Theodore, and Mendemus were the principal, proceeded to Nicomedia, and there presented to the emperor a supplicatory petition, complaining of the ill-usage to which they had been subjected. Valens, dissembling his displeasure in their presence, gave Modestus the prefect a secret order to apprehend these persons, and put them to death. The manner in which they were destroyed being unusual, deserves to be recorded. The prefect, fearing that he should excite the populace to a seditious movement against himself, if he attempted the public execution of so many, pretended to send them away into exile. Accordingly these men, who received the intelligence of their destiny with great firmness of mind, were embarked as if to be conveyed to their several places of banishment: but the sailors were commanded to set the vessel on fire, as soon as they reached the mid sea, that their victims, being so destroyed, might even be deprived of burial. This injunction was obeyed; for when they arrived at the middle of the Astacian Gulf, the crew set fire to the ship, and then took refuge in a small barque which followed them, and so escaped. Meanwhile the burning ship was fiercely driven by a strong easterly wind which then blew, until it reached a port named Decidizus, where it was utterly consumed together with the men who were shut up in it. Many have asserted that this impious deed was not suffered to go unpunished; for there immediately after arose so great a famine throughout all Phrygia, that a large proportion of the inhabitants were obliged to abandon their country for a time, and betake themselves some to Constantinople and some to other provinces. For the former place, notwithstanding the vast population it supplies, yet always abounds with the necessaries of life, all manner of provisions being imported into it by sea from various regions; and the Euxine, which lies near it, furnishes it with bread-corn to any extent it may require.[1]

CHAP. XVII.—THE EMPEROR VALENS, WHILE AT ANTIOCH, AGAIN PERSECUTES THE HOMOOUSIANS.

THE emperor Valens, little affected by the calamities produced by the famine, went to Antioch in Syria, and during his residence there cruelly persecuted such as would not embrace Arianism. For not content with ejecting out of almost all the Churches of the East those who maintained the Homoousian opinion, he inflicted on them various punishments besides. A greater number even than before were bereft of their lives by many different kinds of death, but especially by being drowned in the river.

[1] See Herod. vii. 147, where σιταγωγὰ πλοῖα ἐκ τοῦ Πόντου are mentioned as sailing to Ægina and the Peloponnese.

CHAP. XVIII.—TRANSACTIONS AT EDESSA: CONSTANCY OF
THE DEVOUT CITIZENS, AND COURAGE OF A PIOUS FEMALE.

BUT I must here mention a circumstance that occurred at
Edessa in Mesopotamia. There is in that city a magnificent
church[1] dedicated to St. Thomas the Apostle, wherein, on
account of the sanctity of the place, religious assemblies are
incessantly held. The emperor Valens wished to inspect this
edifice; when having learnt that all who usually congregated
there were opposed to the heresy which he favoured, he is
said to have struck the prefect with his own hand, because
he had neglected to expel them thence. The prefect, after
submitting to this ignominy, was most unwillingly constrained
to subserve the emperor's indignation against them; nevertheless, to prevent the slaughter of so great a number of persons, he privately warned them against resorting thither. But
his admonitions and menaces were alike unheeded; for on
the following day they all crowded to the church. And when
the prefect was going towards it with a large military force
in order to satisfy the emperor's rage, a poor woman leading
her own little child by the hand hurried hastily by on her
way to the church, breaking through the ranks of the soldiery.
The prefect, irritated at this, ordered her to be brought to
him, and thus addressed her: "Wretched woman! whither
are you running in so disorderly a manner?" She replied,
"To the same place that others are hastening." "Have you
not heard," said he, "that the prefect is about to put to death
all that shall be found there?" "Yes," said the woman,
"and therefore I hasten that I may be found there." "And
whither are you dragging that little child?" said the prefect:
the woman answered, "That he also may be vouchsafed the
honour of martyrdom."[2] The prefect, on hearing these things,

---

[1] Μαρτύριον. This was the term generally applied to churches where
the relics of some martyr were deposited. In respect of its use, the same
sacred building is called a little below, Εὐκτήριον τόπον, or an oratory.
See Bingham's Christ. Antiq. b. viii. 1.

[2] Upon the honour with which martyrdom was esteemed in the early
Churches, and the eagerness with which it was sought, see the passages
quoted by Gibbon in his Decline and Fall, (notes on chap. xvi.,) from
Sulpitius Severus, St. Ignatius, and Pearson's Vindiciæ Ignatianæ. So
strong was the desire to gain the crown of martyrdom that the council of

conjecturing that a similar resolution actuated the others who
were assembled there, immediately went back to the emperor,
and informed him that all were ready to die in behalf of their
own faith. He added that it would be preposterous to destroy
so many persons at one time, and thus succeeded in restrain-
ing the emperor's wrath. In this way were the people of
Edessa preserved from being massacred by order of their
sovereign.

CHAP. XIX.—SLAUGHTER OF MANY PERSONS BY VALENS ON
ACCOUNT OF THEIR NAMES, BY REASON OF A HEATHEN PRE-
DICTION.

THE cruel disposition of the emperor was at this time
abused by an execrable demon, who induced certain persons
to institute an inquiry by means of necromancy respecting
the successor of Valens. To their magical incantations the
demon gave responses not distinct and unequivocal, but, as [13]
the general practice is, full of ambiguity; for displaying the
four letters θ, ϵ, o, and δ, he declared that the compounded
name of the emperor's successor began with these. When
Valens was apprized of this oracle, instead of committing to
God, who alone can penetrate futurity, the decision of this
matter, in contravention of those Christian principles to which
he pretended the most zealous adherence, he put to death all
of whom he had the slightest suspicion that they aimed at
the sovereign power: thus such as were named Theodore,
Theodotus, Theodosius, Theodulus, and the like, were sacrificed to the emperor's fears; and among the rest was Theo-
dosiolus, a very brave man, descended from a noble family in
Spain. Many persons therefore, to avoid the danger to which
they were exposed, changed the names which they had received from their parents in infancy.

Illiberis was obliged to pass a canon, refusing the title of martyrs to such
as voluntarily exposed themselves to death by open assaults on heathen
images.

CHAP. XX.—DEATH OF ATHANASIUS, AND ELEVATION OF PETER TO HIS SEE.[1]

WHILE Athanasius bishop of Alexandria was alive, the emperor, restrained by the providence of God, abstained from molesting Alexandria and Egypt: indeed he knew very well that Athanasius was generally beloved there, and on that account he was careful lest the public affairs should be hazarded by the Alexandrians, who are an irritable race, being excited to sedition. But that eminent prelate, after being engaged in so many and such severe conflicts on behalf of the Church, departed this life in the second consulate of Gratian[2] and Probus, having governed that Church amidst the greatest perils forty-six years. He left as his successor Peter, a devout and eloquent man.

CHAP. XXI.—THE ARIANS INDUCE THE EMPEROR TO SET LUCIUS OVER THE SEE OF ALEXANDRIA, AND PETER IS IMPRISONED.

UPON this the Arians, emboldened by their knowledge of the emperor's religious sentiments, again take courage, and immediately inform him of the circumstance. He was then residing at Antioch, and Euzoïus, who presided over the Arians of that city, eagerly embracing the favourable opportunity thus presented, begs permission to go to Alexandria, for the purpose of putting Lucius the Arian in possession of the churches there. The emperor acceding to this request, Euzoïus proceeds forthwith to Alexandria, attended by the imperial troops, and Magnus the emperor's treasurer:[3] they were also the bearers of an imperial mandate to Palladius the governor of Egypt, enjoining him to aid them with a military

---

[1] With this chap. compare the parallel account given by Sozomen, b. vi. ch. xix., and Theodoret, b. iv. ch. xx.

[2] This would make it the year A. D. 371; but Jerome and others state that his demise took place in the year A. D. 373.

[3] Ὁ ἐπὶ τῶν βασιλικῶν θησαυρῶν. The person who presided over the royal treasures.

force. Wherefore having apprehended Peter, they cast him into prison; and after dispersing the rest of the clergy, they place Lucius in the episcopal chair.

CHAP. XXII.—FLIGHT OF PETER TO ROME. MASSACRE OF THE SOLITARIES AT THE INSTIGATION OF THE ARIANS.

OF the outrages perpetrated upon the instalment of Lucius, and the treatment of those who were ejected, both by judicial authority and otherwise, some being subjected to a variety of tortures, and others sent into exile even after this excruciating process, Sabinus[1] takes not the slightest notice. In fact, being half disposed to Arianism himself, he purposely veils the atrocities of his friends. Peter however has exposed them, in the letters he addressed to all the Churches, when he had escaped from prison, and fled to Damasus bishop of Rome.[2] The Arians, though not very numerous, becoming thus possessed of the Alexandrian Churches, soon after obtained an imperial edict directing the governor of Egypt to expel not only from Alexandria, but even out of the country, the favourers of the Homoousian doctrine, and all such as were obnoxious to Lucius. After this they assailed the monastic institutions in the desert; armed men rushing in the most ferocious manner upon those who were utterly defenceless, and who would not lift an arm to repel their violence: so that numbers of unresisting victims were in this manner slaughtered with a degree of wanton cruelty beyond description.

CHAP. XXIII.—A LIST OF HOLY MONKS WHO DEVOTED THEMSELVES TO A SOLITARY LIFE.[3]

SINCE I have referred to the monasteries of Egypt, it may be proper here to give a brief account of them. They were

---

[1] See above, note on ch. xii. sub fin.   [2] See above, ch. xii.
[3] On the gradual rise of the ascetic life and the monastic system, the reader will do well to consult the account given by Bingham in the seventh book of his Christian Antiquities.

founded probably at a very early period, but were greatly
enlarged and augmented by a devout man whose name was
Ammon. In his youth he had an aversion to matrimony;
but when some of his relatives urged him not to contemn this
ordinance, he was prevailed upon to marry. On leading the
bride with the customary ceremonies from the banquet-room
¹³² to the nuptial couch, after their mutual friends had withdrawn,
he read to his wife Paul's Epistle to the Corinthians, and
explained to her the apostle's admonitions to married persons.
Adducing many considerations besides, he descanted on the
inconveniencies and discomforts attending matrimonial intercourse, the pangs of child-bearing, and the trouble and anxiety
connected with rearing a family. He contrasted with all this
the advantages of chastity; described the liberty and im-
maculate purity of a life of continence; and affirmed that
virginity places persons in the nearest relation to the Deity.
By these and other arguments of a similar kind, he persuaded
his virgin bride to renounce with him a secular life, prior to
their having any conjugal knowledge of each other. Having
taken this resolution, they retired together to the mountain of
Nitria, and in a hut there inhabited for a short time one
common ascetic apartment, without regarding their difference
of sex, being, according to the apostle, "one in Christ." But
not long after, the recent and unpolluted bride thus addressed
Ammon: "It is unsuitable," said she, "for you who practise
chastity, to look upon a woman in so confined a dwelling;
let us therefore, if it is agreeable to you, perform our exercise
apart." Both parties being satisfied with this arrangement,
they separated, and spent the rest of their lives in abstinence
from wine and oil, eating dry bread alone, sometimes passing
over one day, at others fasting two, and sometimes more.
Athanasius bishop of Alexandria asserts in his "Life of
Antony," that the subject of his memoir, who was contemporary with this Ammon, saw his soul taken up by angels
after his decease. Ammon's mode of life was adopted by a
great number of persons, so that by degrees the mountains of
Nitria and Scetis were filled with monks, an account of whose
lives would require an express work. As however there
were among them persons of eminent piety, distinguished for
their strict discipline and apostolic lives, who said and did
many things worthy of being recorded, I shall introduce a

few particulars for the information of my readers. It is
said that Ammon never saw himself naked, being accustomed
to say that "it became not a monk to see his own person
exposed." And when once he wanted to pass a river, but
was unwilling to undress, he besought God to enable him to
cross without his being obliged to break his resolution; and
immediately an angel transported him to the other side of the
river. Another monk, named Didymus,[1] lived entirely alone
to the day of his death, although he had reached the age of
ninety years. Arsenius, another of them, would not separate
young delinquents from communion, but only those that were
advanced in age: "for," said he, "when a young person is
excommunicated he becomes hardened; but an elderly one is
soon sensible of the misery of excommunication." Pior was
accustomed to take his food as he walked along, assigning
this as a reason to one who asked him why he did so: "That
I may not seem," said he, "to make eating a serious business,
but rather a thing done by the way." To another putting
the same question he replied, "Lest in eating my mind should
be sensible of corporeal enjoyment." Isidore affirmed that he
had not been conscious of sin even in thought for forty years;
and that he had never consented either to lust or anger.
Pambos, being an illiterate man, went to some one for the
purpose of being taught a psalm; and having heard the first
verse of the thirty-eighth, "I said I will take heed to my ways
that I offend not with my tongue," he departed without staying to hear the second verse, saying, this one would suffice, if
he could practically acquire it. And when the person who
had given him the verse, reproved him because he had not
seen him for the space of six months, he answered that he had
not yet learnt to practise the verse of the psalm. After a
considerable lapse of time, being asked by one of his friends
whether he had made himself master of the verse, his answer
was, "I have scarcely succeeded in accomplishing it during
nineteen years." A certain individual having placed gold in
his hands for distribution to the poor, requested him to reckon
what he had given him. "There is no need of counting,"
said he, "but of integrity of mind." The same Pambos, at
the desire of Athanasius the bishop, came out of the desert to
Alexandria; and on beholding an actress there, he wept.

[1] Comp. chap. xxv.

When those present asked him the reason of his doing so, he replied, "Two causes have affected me: one is, the destruction of this woman; the other is, that I exert myself less to please my God, than she does to please wanton characters." Another said that a monk who did not work, ought to be regarded as a covetous man. Petirus was well-informed in many branches of natural philosophy, and was accustomed to enter into an exposition of the principles sometimes of one department of science, and sometimes of another, but he always commenced his lectures with prayer. There were also among the monks of that period, two of the same name, of great sanctity, each being called Macarius; one of whom was from Upper Egypt, the other from the city of Alexandria. Both were celebrated for their ascetic discipline, the purity of their life and conversation, and the miracles which were wrought by their hands. The Egyptian Macarius performed so many cures, and cast out so many devils, that it would require a distinct treatise to record all that the grace of God enabled him to do. His manner toward those who resorted to him was austere, yet at the same time calculated to inspire veneration. The Alexandrian Macarius, while in many respects resembling his Egyptian namesake, differed from him in this, that he was always cheerful to his visitors; and the affability of his manners attracted many young men to enter upon a 133 similar mode of life. Evagrius, becoming a disciple of these men, acquired from them the philosophy of deeds, whereas he had previously known that which consisted in words only. He had been ordained deacon at Constantinople by Gregory of Nazianzen, and afterwards went with him into Egypt, where he became acquainted with these eminent persons, and emulated their course of conduct: nor were the miracles done by his hands less numerous or important than those of his preceptors. He also composed some valuable works, one of which is entitled "The Monk, or, On Active Virtue;" another, "The Gnostic, or, To him who is deemed worthy of Knowledge:" this book is divided into fifty chapters. A third is designated "The Refutation," which contains selections from the Holy Scriptures against tempting spirits, distributed into eight parts, according to the number of the arguments. He wrote moreover "Six Hundred Prognostic Problems," and also two compositions in verse, one addressed "To the

Monks living in Communities," and the other " To the Virgin."
Whoever shall read these productions, will be convinced of
their excellence.[1]   It will not be out of place here, I conceive,
to subjoin to what has been before stated, a few things mentioned by him respecting the monks.   He thus speaks :—

"It becomes us to inquire into the habits of the pious
monks who have preceded us, in order that we may correct
ourselves by their example : for undoubtedly very many excellent things have been said and done by them.   One of them
was accustomed to say, that 'a dry and not irregular diet
combined with love, would quickly conduct a monk into the
haven of tranquillity.'   The same individual freed one of his
brethren from being troubled by apparitions at night, by enjoining him to minister while fasting to the sick.   And being
asked why he prescribed this : ' Such affections,' said he, ' are
dissipated by nothing so effectually as by the exercise of compassion.'   A certain philosopher of those times, coming to
Antony the Just, said to him, ' How can you endure, father,
being deprived of the comfort of books ?'   ' My book, O philosopher,' replied Antony, ' is the nature of things that are
made, and it is present whenever I wish to read the words of
of God.'   That chosen vessel, the aged Egyptian Macarius,
asked me, why we impair the strength of the retentive faculty
of the soul by cherishing the remembrance of injury received
from men ; while by remembering those done us by devils we
remain uninjured ?   And when I hesitated, scarcely knowing
what answer to make, and begged him to account for it :
' Because,' said he, ' the former is an affection contrary to nature, and the latter is conformable to the nature of the mind.'
Going on one occasion to the holy father Macarius about mid-
day, and being overcome with the heat and thirst, I begged
some water to drink : ' Content yourself with the shade,' was
his reply, ' for many who are now journeying by land, or
sailing on the deep, are deprived even of this.'   Discussing
with him afterwards the subject of abstinence, ' Take courage,
my son,' said he : ' for twenty years I have neither eaten,
drunk, nor slept to satiety ; my bread has always been
weighed, my water measured, and what little sleep I have had
has been stolen by reclining myself against a wall.'   The

---

[1] The treatises written by Evagrius are now all unfortunately lost, with
the exception of his Ecclesiastical History in six books.

death of his father was announced to one of the monks: 'Cease your blasphemy,' said he to the person that told him; 'my father is immortal.' One of the brethren who possessed nothing but a copy of the Gospels, sold it, and distributed the price in food to the hungry, uttering this memorable saying— 'I have sold the book which says, *Sell that thou hast and give to the poor.*' There is an island about the northern part of the city of Alexandria, beyond the lake Mareotis, where a monk from Parembole dwells, in high repute among the Gnostics. This person was accustomed to say, that the monks did nothing but for one of these five reasons;—on account of God, nature, custom, necessity, or manual labour. He moreover said that there was only one virtue in nature, but that it assumes various characteristics according to the dispositions of the soul: just as the light of the sun is itself without form, but accommodates itself to the figure of that which receives it. Another of the monks said, 'I withdraw myself from pleasures, in order to cut off the occasions of anger: for I know that it always contends for pleasures, disturbing my tranquillity of mind, and unfitting me for the attainment of knowledge.' One of the aged monks said that charity knows not how to keep a deposit either of provisions or money. He added, 'I never remember to have been twice deceived by the devil in the same thing." Thus wrote Evagrius in his book entitled "Practice."[1] And in that which he called "The Gnostic,". he says, "We learn from Gregory the Just, that there are four virtues, having distinct characteristics:—prudence, fortitude, temperance, and justice. That it is the province of prudence to contemplate abstractedly those sacred and intelligent powers, which are unfolded by wisdom: of fortitude, to adhere to truth against all opposition, and never to turn aside to that which is unreal: of temperance, to receive seed from the chief Husbandman,[2] but to repel him who would sow over it seed of another kind: and finally, of justice, to adapt discourse to every one, according to their condition and capacity; stating some things obscurely, and others in a figurative manner, while for the instruction of the less intelligent the clearest explanations are given. That pillar of truth, Basil of Cappadocia, used to say that the knowledge which men teach is perfected by constant study and exercise; but

---

[1] See above, note on b. iii. ch. vii.   [2] Matt. xiii. 24.

that which the grace of God communicates, by the practice of justice, patience, and mercy. That the former indeed is often developed in persons who are still subject to the passions; whereas the latter is the portion of those only who are superior to their influence, and who during the season of devotion, contemplate that peculiar light of the mind which illumines them. That luminary of the Egyptians, the holy Athanasius, assures us that Moses was commanded to place the table on the north[1] side. Let the Gnostics therefore understand what wind is contrary to them, and so nobly endure every temptation, and minister nourishment with a willing mind to those who apply to them. Sarapion, the angel of the Church of the Thmuïtæ, declared that the mind is completely purified by drinking in spiritual knowledge; that charity cures the inflammatory tendencies of the soul; and that the depraved lusts which spring up in it are restrained by abstinence. Exercise thyself continually, said the great and enlightened teacher Didymus, in reflecting on providence and judgment; and endeavour to bear in memory whatever discourses thou mayest have heard on these topics, for almost all fail in this respect. Thou wilt find reasonings concerning judgment in the difference of created forms, and the constitution of the universe; sermons on providence comprehended in those means by which we are led from vice and ignorance to virtue and knowledge."

These are a few extracts from Evagrius which I thought it would be appropriate to insert here. There was another excellent man among the monks, named Ammonius, who had so little interest in secular matters, that when he went to Rome with Athanasius, he paid no attention to any of the magnificent works of that city, contenting himself with examining the cathedral[2] of Peter and Paul only. And when they were about to compel this same Ammonius to enter upon the episcopal office, he cut off his own right ear, that by mutilation of his person he might disqualify himself for ordination. Evagrius, upon whom Theophilus bishop of Alexandria wished to force the prelacy, having effected his escape without maiming himself in any way, afterwards happened to meet Ammo-

---

[1] Exod. xxvi. 35.
[2] Μαρτύριον, so called because the church was erected over the tombs of those apostles. See above, note on ch. xviii.

nius, and told him jocosely, that he had done wrong in cutting off his own ear, as he had by that means rendered himself criminal in the sight of God.   To which Ammonius replied, "And do you think, Evagrius, that you will not be punished, who from self-love have cut out your own tongue, to avoid the exercise of that gift of utterance which has been committed to you?" There were at the same time in the monasteries very many other admirable and devout characters, whom it would be too tedious to enumerate in this place; and besides, if we should attempt to describe the life of each, and the miracles they did by means of that sanctity with which they were endued, we should necessarily digress too far from the object we have in view.   Should any one desire to become acquainted with their history, in reference both to their deeds and discourses for the edification of their auditors, as well as their subduing wild beasts to their authority, there is a specific treatise on the subject, composed by the monk Palladius, who was a disciple of Evagrius, in which all these particulars are minutely detailed.   In that work he also mentions several women, who practised the same kind of austerities as the men that have been referred to.   Both Evagrius and Palladius flourished a short time after the death of Valens.   We must now return to the point whence we diverged.

CHAP. XXIV.—ASSAULT UPON THE MONKS, AND BANISHMENT OF THEIR SUPERIORS, WHO EXHIBIT MIRACULOUS POWER.

THE emperor Valens having issued an edict commanding that the orthodox should be expelled both from Alexandria and the rest of Egypt, depopulation and ruin to an immense extent immediately followed: some were dragged before the tribunals, others cast into prison, and many tortured in various ways, all sorts of punishments being inflicted upon persons who aimed only at peace and quiet.   When these outrages had been perpetrated at Alexandria just as Lucius thought proper, and Euzoïus had returned to Antioch, Lucius the Arian, attended by the commander-in-chief of the army with a considerable body of troops, immediately proceeded to the monasteries of Egypt, where he in person assailed the

[SOCRATES.]   R

assemblage of holy men with greater fury even than the ruthless soldiery. On reaching these solitudes, they found the
monks engaged in their customary exercises, praying, healing
diseases, and casting out devils:[1] yet regardless of these extraordinary evidences of Divine power, they suffered them
not to continue their solemn devotions, but drove them out of
the oratories by force. Rufinus declares that he was not only
a witness of these cruelties, but also one of the sufferers.
Thus in them were renewed those things which are spoken of
by the apostle:[2] for "they were mocked, and had trial of
scourgings, were stripped naked, put in bonds, stoned, slain
with the sword, became tenants of the wilderness clad in
sheep-skins and goat-skins, being destitute, afflicted, tor-
mented, of whom the world was not worthy, wandering in
deserts, in mountains, in dens and caves of the earth." In all
these things the testimony of their faith was confirmed by
their works, and the cures which the grace of Christ wrought
by their hands. But it is probable that Divine Providence
permitted them to endure these evils, having for them provided something better, that through their sufferings others
might obtain the salvation of God, as subsequent events seem
to prove. When therefore these excellent persons remained
unmoved by all the violence which was exercised toward them,
Lucius in despair advised the military chief to send the fathers
of the monks into exile. These were the Egyptian Macarius,
and his namesake of Alexandria; both of whom were accordingly banished to an island where there was not a single
Christian, and in which there was an idolatrous temple, and
a priest whom the inhabitants worshipped as a god. The
arrival of these holy men at the island filled the demons of
that place with fear and trepidation. Now it happened at the
same time that the priest's daughter became suddenly possessed by a demon, and began to act with great fury, and to
overturn everything that came in her way; nor was any force
sufficient to restrain her, but she cried with a loud voice to
these saints of God, saying:—"Why are ye come here to cast
us out?"[3] Then did they there also display the greatness of
the power which they had received through Divine grace: for
having cast out the demon from the maid, and presented her
cured to her father, they converted not only the priest him-

---

[1] See Mark xvi. 17, 18.   [2] Heb. xi.   [3] See Matt. viii. 29.

self, but also all the inhabitants of the island, to the Christian faith. Whereupon they brake their images in pieces, and changed the form of their temple into that of a church; and having been baptized, they joyfully received instruction in the doctrines of Christianity. Thus these distinguished individuals, after enduring persecution on account of the Homoousian faith, were themselves more approved, became the means of salvation to others, and confirmed the truth of that for which they had suffered.

CHAP. XXV.—OF DIDYMUS THE BLIND MAN.

ABOUT the same period God brought into observation another faithful person, that by his testimony also the truth might be established: this was Didymus,[1] a most admirable and eloquent man, instructed in all the learning of the age in which he lived. At a very early age, when he had scarcely acquired the first elements of literature, he was attacked by disease in the eyes which deprived him of sight. But God compensated to him the loss of corporeal vision, by bestowing increased intellectual acumen, enabling him to attain by means of his hearing, what he could not learn by seeing; so that being from his childhood endowed with excellent abilities, he soon far surpassed his youthful companions who possessed the keenest sight. He made himself master of the principles of grammar and rhetoric with astonishing facility; and proceeding thence to the study of philosophy, logic, arithmetic, music, and the various other departments of knowledge to which his attention was directed, he so treasured up in his mind these branches of science, that he was prepared with the utmost readiness to enter into a discussion of these subjects with those who had become conversant therewith by the aid of books. His acquaintance with the Divine oracles contained in the Old and New Testament was so perfect, that he composed several treatises in exposition of them, besides three books on the Trinity. He published also commentaries on Origen's book "Of Principles," in which he shows the excel-

[1] This Didymus was probably not the same individual with that mentioned above, ch. xxiii.

lence of these writings, and the insignificance of those w
calumniate their author, and speak slightingly of his work
proving that his objectors were destitute of sufficient penetra
tion to comprehend the profound wisdom of that extraordina
man.   Those who may desire to form a just idea of the e
tensive erudition of Didymus, and the intense ardour of 1
mind, must peruse with attention his diversified and el
borate works.   It is said that after Antony had convers
for some time with Didymus, long before the reign of Vale
when he came from the desert to Alexandria on account
the Arians, perceiving the learning and intelligence of t
man, he said to him, " Didymus, let not the loss of yo
bodily eyes distress you; for although you are deprived
such organs as confer a faculty of perception common to gne
and flies, you should rather rejoice that you have eyes such
angels see with, by which the Deity himself is discerned, a
his light comprehended."   This address of the pious Anto
to Didymus was made long before the times we are describin
in fact Didymus was then regarded as the great bulwark
the true faith, and the most powerful antagonist of the Arin
whose sophistic cavillings he fully exposed, triumphantly 1
futing all their vain subtilties and deceptive reasonings.

CHAP. XXVI.—Of Basil bishop of Cæsarea, and Gregory of Nazianzen.

THE same Providence that opposed Didymus to the Aria
at Alexandria, raised up Basil of Cæsarea and Gregory
Nazianzen to confute them in other cities.   The merits of the
two eminent characters, of whom it will be seasonable to gi
a brief account in this place, are recorded in the memories
all men; and the extent of their knowledge is sufficien
perceptible in their writings to render any eulogy superfluo
Since however the exercise of their talents was of great si
vice to the Church, tending in a high degree to the maintenar
of the catholic faith, the nature of my history obliges me
take particular notice of these two persons.   Whoever co
pares Basil and Gregory with one another, and considers 1
life, morals, and virtues of each, will find it difficult to deci

to which of them he ought to assign the pre-eminence : so
equally did they both appear to excel, whether you regard the
rectitude of their conduct, or their deep acquaintance with
Greek literature and the sacred Scriptures. In their youth
[135] they were pupils[1] at Athens of Himerius and Prohæresius,
the most celebrated sophists of that age: subsequently they
frequented the school of Libanius at Antioch in Syria, where
they became highly accomplished in rhetoric.   Their proficiency induced many of their friends to recommend them to
teach eloquence as a profession ; others persuaded them to
practise the law ; but despising both these pursuits, they
abandoned their former studies, and embraced the monastic
life.   Having had some slight taste of philosophical science
from him who then taught it at Antioch, they procured Origen's works, and drew from them the right interpretation of
the sacred Scriptures ; and after a careful perusal of the
writings of that great man, whose fame was at that time celebrated throughout the world, they contended against the
Arians with manifest advantage.   And when the defenders
of Arianism quoted the same author in confirmation, as they
imagined, of their own views, these two confuted them, and
clearly proved that their opponents did not at all understand
his reasoning.   Indeed although Eunomius,[2] who was then
their champion, and many others on their side, were considered men of great eloquence, yet whenever they attempted
to enter into controversy with Gregory and Basil, they appeared in comparison with them mere ignorant and illiterate
cavillers.   Meletius bishop of Antioch first promoted Basil to
the office of deacon ; and from that rank he was elevated to
the bishopric of Cæsarea in Cappadocia, which was his native
country.   Thither he therefore hastened, fearing lest these
Arian dogmas should have infected the provinces of Pontus ;
and in order to counteract them, he founded several monasteries, diligently instructed the people in his own doctrines,
and confirmed the faith of those whose minds were wavering.
Gregory being constituted bishop of Nazianzen, a small city
of Cappadocia, over which his own father had before presided,

---

[1] 'Ακροαταὶ, literally " hearers."   This was the technical phrase.   So
in Latin " audire."   Thus Cicero, de Officiis i. 1, " annum jam audientem
Cratippum, idque Athenis."
[2] See above, chap. vii. of this book.

pursued a course similar to that which Basil took; for he
went throngh the various cities, strengthening the weak, and
establishing the feeble-minded. To Constantinople in parti- [137]
cular he paid frequent visits, and by his ministrations there,
so comforted and assured the orthodox believers, that a short
time after, by the suffrage of many bishops, he was invested
with the prelacy of that city. When intelligence of the proceedings of these two zealous and devoted men reached the
ears of the emperor Valens, he immediately ordered Basil to
be brought from Cæsarea to Antioch; where being arraigned
before the tribunal of the prefect, that functionary asked him [138]
why he would not embrace the emperor's faith? Basil with
much boldness condemned the errors of that creed which his
sovereign countenanced, and vindicated the doctrine of consubstantiality: and when the prefect threatened him with
death, "Would," said he, "that I might be released from the
bonds of the body for the truth's sake." The prefect having
exhorted him to re-consider the matter more seriously, Basil
is reported to have said, "I am the same to-day that I shall
be to-morrow: but I wish that you had not changed yourself."
Basil therefore remained in custody. It happened however
not long after that Galates, the emperor's infant son, was attacked with a dangerous malady, so that the physicians despaired of his recovery; when the empress Dominica his
mother assured the emperor that she had been greatly disquieted at night by terrific visions, which led her to believe
that the child's illness was a chastisement on account of the
ill treatment of the bishop. The emperor after a little reflection sent for Basil, and in order to prove his faith said to
him, "If the doctrine you maintain is the truth, pray that my
son may not die." "If your Majesty will believe as I do,"
replied Basil, "and will cause dissension and disunion to
cease in the Church, the child shall live." To these conditions
the emperor would not agree; "Let God's will concerning
the child be done then," said Basil; upon which the emperor
ordered him to be dismissed, and the child died shortly after.
Such is an epitome of the history of these distinguished ecclesiastics, both of whom have left us many admirable works,
some of which were translated into Latin by Rufinus, as he
himself testifies. Basil had two brothers, Peter and Gregory;
the former of whom adopted Basil's monastic mode of life;

while the latter emulated his eloquence in teaching, and completed after his death "Basil's Treatise on the Six Days' Work," which had been left unfinished. He also pronounced at Constantinople the funeral oration of Meletius bishop of Antioch; and many other orations of his are still extant.

CHAP. XXVII.—Of GREGORY THAUMATURGUS.

BUT since from the likeness of the name, and the title of the books attributed to Gregory, persons are liable to confound very different parties, it is important to observe that there was another Gregory, a native of Neocæsarea in Pontus, who was of greater antiquity than the one above referred to, inasmuch as he was a disciple of Origen.[1] This Gregory's fame was celebrated at Athens, at Berytus, throughout the entire diocese of Pontus, and I might almost add the whole world. When he had finished his education in the schools of Athens, he went to Berytus to study civil law; and there hearing that Origen expounded the Holy Scriptures at Cæsarea he quickly proceeded thither; and after his understanding had been opened to perceive the grandeur of these divine books, bidding adieu to all further cultivation of the Roman laws, he devoted himself wholly to the instructions of Origen, from whom he acquired a knowledge of the true philosophy. Being recalled soon after by his parents, he returned to his own country; and there, while still a layman, he performed many miracles, healing the sick, and casting out devils even by his letters, insomuch that the Pagans were no less attracted to the faith by his acts, than by his discourses. Pamphilus Martyr mentions this person in the books which he wrote in defence of Origen; to which there is added an oration of Gregory, composed in praise of Origen, when he was under the necessity of leaving him. There were then, to be brief, several Gregories: the first and most ancient was the disciple of Origen; the second was the bishop of Nazianzen; the third was Basil's brother; and there was another Gregory, whom the Arians constituted bishop during the exile of Athanasius. But enough has been said respecting them.

[1] See Euseb. Eccl. Hist. b. vi. ch. xxx.

CHAP. XXVIII. — OF NOVATUS AND HIS FOLLOWERS. THE NOVATIANS OF PHRYGIA ALTER THE TIME OF KEEPING EASTER.

ABOUT this time the Novatians[1] inhabiting Phrygia changed the day for celebrating the Feast of Easter. How this happened I shall state, after first explaining the reason of the strict discipline which is maintained in their Church, even to the present day, in the provinces of Phrygia and Paphlagonia. Novatus[2] a presbyter of the Roman Church, separated from it, because Cornelius the bishop received into communion believers who had sacrificed during the persecution which the emperor Decius had raised against the Church. Having seceded on this account, on being afterwards elevated to the episcopacy by such prelates as entertained similar sentiments, he wrote to all the Churches insisting that they should not admit to .the sacred mysteries those who had sacrificed ; but, exhorting them to repentance, leave the pardoning of their offence to God, who has the power to forgive all sin. These letters made different impressions on the parties in the various provinces to whom they were addressed, according to their several dispositions and judgments. The exclusion of those who after baptism had committed any deadly sin[3] from participation in the mysteries appeared to some a cruel and merciless course: but others thought it just and necessary for the maintenance of discipline, and the promotion of greater devotedness of life. In the midst of the agitation of this important question, letters arrived from Cornelius the bishop, promising indulgence to delinquents after baptism. On these two persons writing thus contrary to one another, and each confirming his own procedure by the testimony of the divine word, as it usually happens, every one identified himself with that view which favoured his previous habits and inclinations. Those who had pleasure in sin, encouraged by the licence thus granted them, took occasion from it to revel in every species of criminality. The Phrygians however appear to be

[1] Upon the Novatian heresy, see some remarks in the biography prefixed to this volume, and also compare h. i. ch. x.; Euseb. Eccl. Hist. b. vi. ch. xliii.

[2] The Greeks usually term him Novatus, but his right name was Novatian.

[3] Εἰς θάνατον ἁμαρτίαν, " a sin unto death." See 1 John v. 16, 17.

more temperate than other nations, and are seldom guilty of swearing. The Scythians and Thracians are naturally of a very irritable disposition : while the inhabitants of the East are addicted to sensual pleasures. But the Paphlagonians and Phrygians are prone to neither of these vices; nor are the sports of the circus nor theatrical exhibitions in much estimation among them even to the present day. And this will account, as I conceive, for these people, as well as others of a similar temperament and habit in the West, so readily assenting to the letters then written by Novatus. Fornication and adultery are regarded among the Paphlagonians and Phrygians as the grossest enormities; and it is well known that there is no race of men on the face of the earth who more rigidly govern their passions in this respect. Yet, although for the sake of stricter discipline Novatus became a separatist, he made no change in the time of keeping Easter, but invariably observed the practice that obtained in the Western Churches, of celebrating this feast after the equinox, according to the usage which had of old been delivered to them when first they embraced Christianity.[1] He himself indeed afterwards suffered martyrdom in the reign of Valerian, during the persecution which was then raised against the Christians. But those in Phrygia who from his name are termed Novatians, about this period changed the day of celebrating Easter, being averse to communion with other Christians even on this occasion. This was effected by means of a few obscure bishops of that sect convening a synod at the village of Pazum, which is situated near the sources of the river Sangarius; for there they framed a canon appointing its observance on the same day as that on which the Jews annually keep the feast of Unleavened Bread.[2] I obtained my information on this point from an aged man who was the son of a presbyter, and had been present with his father at this synod. But both Agelius bishop of the Novatians at Constantinople, and Maximus of Nice, were absent, as also the bishops of Nicomedia and Cotuœum, although the ecclesiastical affairs of that sect were for the most part under the control of these prelates. How their Church soon after was divided into two parties in conse-

[1] See above, note on b. i. chap. viii., for further remarks on the early disputes about the keeping of Easter.
[2] See the same note.

quence of this synod, shall be related in its proper course:[1]
but we must now notice what took place about the same time
in the Western parts.

CHAP. XXIX.—DAMASUS ORDAINED BISHOP OF ROME.[2] SEDI-
TION AND LOSS OF LIFE CAUSED BY THE RIVALRY OF URSINUS.

WHILE the emperor Valentinian enjoyed the utmost tranquillity, and interfered with no sect, Damasus after Liberius
undertook the administration[3] of the episcopate at Rome; 140
whereupon a great disturbance was caused on the following
account. Ursinus, a deacon of that Church, had been nominated among others when the election of a bishop took place;
and being unable to bear the frustration of his hope by Damasus being preferred, he held schismatic assemblies apart
from the Church, and even induced certain bishops of little
distinction to ordain him in secret. This ordination, which
was made not in a church,[4] but in a retired place called the
Palace of Sicinius, excited much dissension among the people;
their disagreement being not about any article of faith or
heresy, but simply this, who ought to obtain the episcopal
chair. Hence frequent conflicts arose, insomuch that many
lives were sacrificed in this contention; and many of the
clergy as well as laity were punished on that account by Maximin the governor of the city. Thus was Ursinus obliged to
desist from his pretensions at that time, and those who
espoused his cause were reduced to order.

---

[1] See b. v. ch. xxi.
[2] Jerome says this occurred in the year A. D. 367.
[3] Ἱερωσύνην τῆς ἐπισκοπῆς. Literally, "the *Priesthood* of the Episcopate."
[4] "Out of the church no ordination could be regularly performed."
Bingham's Christ. Antiq. b. iv. chap. vi. sect. 8. Compare Gregory Na-
zianz., (Carm. de Vitâ, p. 15,) who upbraids Maximus, a bishop intruded
into the see of Constantinople, that, "being excluded from the church, he
was ordained in the house of a minstrel."

CHAP. XXX.—Dissension about a successor to Auxentius
 bishop of Milan. Ambrose, governor of the province,
 going to appease the tumult, is by general consent,
 the emperor Valentinian also sanctioning it, elected
 to preside over that see.

About the same time[1] another event happened at Milan
well worthy of being recorded. On the death of Auxentius,
who had been ordained bishop of that Church by the Arians,
the people again became tumultuous respecting the election
of a successor; for as some proposed one person, and others
favoured another, the city was full of contention and uproar.
In this state of things, Ambrose, the governor of the province,
who was also of consular dignity, dreading some catastrophe
from the popular excitement, ran into the church in order to
quell the disturbance. When his presence had checked the
confusion that prevailed, and the irrational fury of the multitude was repressed by a long and appropriate hortatory address, all present suddenly came to an unanimous agreement,
crying out that Ambrose was worthy of the bishopric, and
demanding his ordination: for by that means only, it was
alleged, would the peace of the Church be secured, and all be
reunited in the same faith and judgment. The bishops then
present, believing that such unanimity among the people proceeded from some Divine appointment, immediately laid hands
on Ambrose; and having baptized him, he being then but a
catechumen, they were about to invest him with the episcopal
office. But although Ambrose willingly received baptism, he
with great earnestness refused to be ordained: upon which
the bishops referred the matter to the emperor Valentinian.
This prince, regarding the universal consent of the people as
the work of God,[2] authorized the bishops to ordain him; declaring that he was manifestly chosen of God to preside over
the Church, rather than elected by the people. Ambrose was
therefore ordained; and thus the Milanese, who were before
divided among themselves, were once more restored to unity.

[1] The date of this is rightly assigned, but it was seven years after the
promotion of Damasus to the Roman see.
[2] An instance of the well-known proverb, "Vox populi, vox Dei."

CHAP. XXXI.—DEATH OF VALENTINIAN.

THE Sarmatians after this having made incursions into the
Roman territories, the emperor marched against them with a
numerous army: but when the barbarians understood the
formidable nature of this expedition, they sent an embassy to
him to sue for peace on certain conditions.   On the ambassadors being introduced to the emperor's presence, and appearing to him to be a very contemptible set of fellows, he
inquired whether all the Sarmatians were such as they were?
They replied that the noblest personages of their whole nation
had come to him.   At this answer Valentinian became excessively enraged, and exclaimed with great vehemence, that
the Roman empire was indeed most wretched in devolving
upon him at a time when a nation of such despicable barbarians, not content with being permitted to exist in safety
within their own limits, dared to take up arms, invade the
Roman territories, and break forth into open war.   The violence of his manner and utterance of these words was so great,
that his veins were opened by the effort, and the arteries rup-
tured; and from the vast quantity of blood which thereupon
gushed forth he died.   This occurred at the Castle of Bergi-
tion, after Gratian's third consulate in conjunction with Equi-
tius, on the seventeenth day of November, in the fifty-fourth
year of his age, and the thirteenth of his reign.   Six days
after his death the soldiery proclaimed his son Valentinian,
then a young child, emperor, at Acincum, a city of Italy.[1]
This premature act greatly displeased the other two emperors,
one of whom (Gratian) was the brother, and the other (Valens)
the uncle of young Valentinian; not indeed because of his
having been declared emperor, but on account of the military
presuming to proclaim him without consulting them, when
they themselves wished to have done so.   They both however
ratified the transaction, and thus was Valentinian junior seated
on his father's throne.   Now this Valentinian was born of
Justina, whom Valentinian the elder married while Severa,
his former wife, was alive, under the following circumstances.
Justus, the father of Justina, who had been governor of Pice-
num under the reign of Constantius, had a dream in which he

---

[1] Or rather, of Pannonia.

seemed to himself to bring forth the imperial purple out of his right side. When this dream had been told to many persons, it at length came to the knowledge of Constantius, who conjecturing it to be a presage that a descendant of Justus would become emperor, caused him to be assassinated. Justina being thus bereft of her father, still continued a virgin. Some time after she became known to Severa, wife of the emperor Valentinian, and had frequent intercourse with the empress, until their intimacy at length grew to such an extent that they were accustomed to bathe together. Severa on seeing Justina in the bath was greatly struck with her virgin beauty, and spoke of her to the emperor; saying that the daughter of Justus was so lovely a creature, and possessed of such symmetry of form, that she herself, though a woman, was altogether charmed with her. This discourse having made a strong impression on the emperor's mind, he considered with himself how he could espouse Justina, without repudiating Severa, who had borne him Gratian, whom he had created Augustus a little while before. He accordingly framed a law, and caused it to be published throughout the cities, by which any man was permitted to have two lawful wives.[1] Having promulgated this law, he married Justina, by whom he had Valentinian junior, and three daughters, Justa, Grata, and Galla; the two former of whom persisted in their resolution of continuing virgins: but Galla was afterwards married to the emperor Theodosius the Great, who had by her a daughter named Placidia. For that prince had Arcadius and

[1] Upon the severity with which the ancient Church treated bigamy and polygamy, see the very complete account given in Bingham's Christ. Antiq. b. xvi. chap. xi., and St. Basil's Rules, Canon 80. The story here given by Socrates against Valentinian, however, is probably a fiction, which our author took up too readily from a chance informer: for even the heathen historians Zosimus and Ammian. Marcellinus never allege any such accusation against him. The latter, indeed, goes so far as to say that he was remarkable for his chastity both at home and abroad, (Hist. b. xxx. p. 462,) and the former states (Hist. b. iv.) that he did not marry his second wife until after the death of the first. Hence Baronius (An. 370, T. iv. p. 272) and Valesius (In Socratem, b. iv. c. 31) conclude that this story is after all a groundless fable, and that there never was any law in the Roman empire to sanction polygamy. Certain it is, says Bingham, (loc. cit.) that "there is no footstep of any such law in either of the Codes, but much to forbid it." It is to be observed that Socrates (Pref. to b. v.) professes to gather much of his information "from the narration of living witnesses." This perhaps will account for his occasional mistakes.

Honorius by Flaccilla his former wife: we shall however enter into particulars respecting Theodosius and his sons in the proper place.

CHAP. XXXII.—THE EMPEROR VALENS, APPEASED BY THE ORATION OF THEMISTIUS THE PHILOSOPHER, MITIGATES HIS PERSECUTION OF THE CHRISTIANS.

IN the mean while Valens, making his residence at Antioch, was wholly undisturbed by foreign wars; for the barbarians on every side restrained themselves within their own boundaries. Nevertheless he himself waged a most cruel war against those who maintained the Homoousian doctrine, inflicting on them more grievous punishments every day; until his severity was a little moderated by an oration addressed 141 to him by the philosopher Themistius. In this speech he tells the emperor, "That he ought not to be surprised at the difference of judgment on religious questions existing among Christians; inasmuch as that discrepancy was trifling when compared with the multitude of conflicting opinions current among the heathen,[1] amounting to above three hundred. That dissension indeed was an inevitable consequence of this disagreement; but that God would be the more glorified by a diversity of sentiment, and the greatness of his majesty be more venerated, from its being thus made manifest how difficult it is to know him." This discourse softened the rigour of the emperor's persecution, but did not effect an abolition of it; for although he ceased to put ecclesiastics to death, he continued to send them into exile, until this fury of his was repressed by other causes.

CHAP. XXXIII.—THE GOTHS, UNDER THE REIGN OF VALENS, EMBRACE CHRISTIANITY.

THE barbarians termed Goths, dwelling beyond the Danube, having engaged in a civil war among themselves, were divided into two parties, one of which was headed by Fritigernes, the

---

[1] Ἕλλησι. See above, note on b. i. chap. xvi.

other by Athanaric. When the latter had obtained an evident advantage over his rival, Fritigernes had recourse to the
Romans, and implored their assistance against his adversary.
This being reported to the emperor Valens, he ordered the
troops which were engarrisoned in Thrace, to assist those
barbarians who had appealed to him against their more powerful countrymen; and by means of this subsidy a complete
victory was obtained over Athanaric beyond the Danube, his
forces being totally routed.   Because of this, many of the
barbarians professed the Christian religion : for Fritigernes,
to express his sense of the obligation the emperor had conferred upon him, embraced the religion of his benefactor, and
persuaded those who were under his authority to do the same.
Therefore it is that so many of the Goths are even to the
present time infected with the errors of Arianism, they having on the occasion referred to become adherents to that
heresy on the emperor's account.   Ulfila, their bishop at that
time, after inventing the Gothic letters, translated the sacred
Scriptures into their own language, and undertook to instruct
these barbarians in the Divine oracles.   And as Ulfila did
not restrict his labours to the subjects of Fritigernes, but extended them to those who acknowledged the sway of Athanaric also, that chief regarding this innovation as an insult
offered to the religion of his ancestors, treated those who professed Christianity with great severity, so that many of the
Arian Goths of that period became martyrs.   Arius indeed,
failing in his attempt to refute the opinion of Sabellius the
Libyan, fell from the true faith, and asserted the Son of God
to be a new God : but the barbarians, embracing Christianity
with greater simplicity of mind, despised the present life for
the faith of Christ.   With these remarks we shall close our
notice of the Christianized Goths.

CHAP. XXXIV.—ADMISSION OF THE FUGITIVE GOTHS INTO
THE ROMAN TERRITORIES, WHICH CAUSED THE EMPEROR'S
OVERTHROW, AND EVENTUALLY THE SUBVERSION OF THE RO-
MAN EMPIRE.

NOT long after the barbarians had entered into a friendly
alliance with one another, they were again vanquished by

other barbarians their neighbours, called the Huns; and being driven out of their own country, they flee into the territory of the Romans, offering to be subject to the emperor, and to execute whatever he should command them. When Valens was made acquainted with this, not having the least presentiment of the consequences of his clemency, he ordered that the suppliants should be received with kindness and consideration; in this one instance alone showing himself compassionate. He therefore assigned them certain parts of Thrace for their habitation, deeming himself peculiarly fortunate in this matter: for he calculated that in future he should possess a ready and well-equipped army against all assailants; and hoped that the barbarians would be a more formidable guard to the frontiers of the empire even than the Romans themselves. For this reason he in future neglected to recruit his army by Roman levies; and despising those veterans by whose bravery he had subdued his enemies in former wars, he put a pecuniary value on that militia which the inhabitants of the provinces, village by village, had been accustomed to furnish, ordering the collectors of his tribute to demand eighty pieces of gold[1] for every soldier, although he had never before lightened the public burdens. This change was the origin of many disasters to the Roman empire subsequently.

CHAP. XXXV.—REMISSION OF PERSECUTION AGAINST THE CHRISTIANS BECAUSE OF THE WAR WITH THE GOTHS.

THE barbarians having been put into possession of Thrace, and securely enjoying that Roman province, were unable to bear their good fortune with moderation; but committing hostile aggressions upon their benefactors, devastated all Thrace and the adjacent countries. When these proceedings came to the knowledge of Valens, he desisted from sending the Homoousians into banishment; and in great alarm left Antioch, and came to Constantinople, where also the persecution of the orthodox Christians was for the same reason put an end to. At the same time Euzoïus,[2] bishop of the Arians at

---

[1] Each about the value of a crown sterling.
[2] See above, b. ii. chap. xliv.

Antioch, departed this life, in the fifth consulate of Valens, and the first of Valentinian junior ; and Dorotheus was appointed in his place.

CHAP. XXXVI.—The saracens, under mavia their queen, embrace christianity ; and moses, a pious monk, is ordained their bishop.

No sooner had the emperor departed from Antioch, than the Saracens,[1] who had before been in alliance with the Romans, revolted from them, being led by Mavia their queen, whose husband was then dead. All the regions of the East therefore were at that time ravaged by the Saracens : but their fury was repressed by the interference of Divine Providence in the manner I am about to describe. A person named Moses, a Saracen by birth, who led a monastic life in the desert, became exceedingly eminent for his piety, faith, and miracles. Mavia the queen of the Saracens was therefore desirous that this person should be constituted bishop over her nation, and promised on this condition to terminate the war. The Roman generals, considering that a peace founded on such terms would be extremely advantageous, gave immediate directions for its ratification. Moses was accordingly seized, and brought from the desert to Alexandria in order to his being initiated in the sacerdotal functions : but on his presentation for that purpose to Lucius, who at that time presided over the Churches in that city, he refused to be ordained by him, protesting against it in these words : " I account myself indeed unworthy of the sacred office ; but if the exigences of the state require my bearing it, it shall not be by Lucius laying his hand on me, for it has been filled with blood." When Lucius told him that it was his duty to learn from him the principles of religion, and not to utter reproachful language ; Moses replied, "Matters of faith are not

---

[1] For an account of the Saracens, their origin, &c., see Gibbon's Decl. and Fall, chap. l. He remarks, that " From Mecca to the Euphrates the Arabian tribes were confounded by the Greeks and Latins under the general appellation of Saracens." In a foot note on the same chap. he enters into an interesting question as to the origin of the name.

now in question: but your infamous practices against
the brethren sufficiently prove the inconsistency of your
doctrines with Christian truth. A Christian is no striker,
reviles not, does not fight; for it becomes not a servant of the
Lord to fight.[1] But your deeds cry out against you by those
who have been sent into exile, who have been exposed to the
wild beasts, and who have been delivered up to the flames.
Those things which our own eyes have beheld, are far more
convincing than what we receive from the report of another."
Moses having expressed himself in this manner, was taken
by his friends to the mountains, that he might receive ordination from those bishops who lived in exile there. His
consecration terminated the Saracen war: and so scrupulously
did Mavia observe the peace thus entered into with the Romans, that she gave her daughter in marriage to Victor, the
commander-in-chief of the Roman army. Such were the
transactions in relation to the Saracens.

CHAP. XXXVII.—After the departure of Valens from
Antioch, the Alexandrians eject Lucius, and restore
Peter.

As soon as the emperor Valens left Antioch, all those who
had anywhere been suffering persecution, began again to take
courage, and especially the Alexandrians. Peter returned to
that city from Rome, with letters from Damasus the Roman
bishop,[1] in which he confirmed the Homoousian faith, and
sanctioned Peter's ordination. The people therefore, resuming
confidence, expel Lucius,[3] who immediately embarked for
Constantinople: but Peter survived his re-establishment a
very short time, and at his death appointed his brother Timothy to succeed him.

[1] Titus i. 7.   [2] See above, ch. xii.
[3] See below, b. v. ch. vii.

CHAP. XXXVIII.—The emperor Valens is slain in an engagement with the Goths near Adrianople.

On the arrival of the emperor Valens at Constantinople, on the 30th of May, in the sixth year of his own consulate and the second of Valentinian junior's, he finds the people in a very dejected state of mind: for the barbarians, who had already desolated Thrace, were now laying waste the very suburbs of Constantinople, there being no adequate force at hand to resist them. But when they presumed to make near approaches, even to the walls of the city, the people became exceedingly troubled, and began to murmur against the emperor; accusing him of having been the cause of bringing the enemy thither, and then indolently wasting his time there, instead of at once marching out against the barbarians. Moreover at the exhibition of the sports of the Hippodrome, all with one voice exclaimed against the emperor's negligence of the public affairs, crying out with great earnestness, "Give us arms, and we ourselves will fight." The emperor, provoked at these seditious clamours, marches out of the city, on the 11th of June; threatening that, if he returned, he would punish the citizens not only for their insolent reproaches, but for having heretofore favoured the pretensions of the tyrant Procopius. After declaring therefore that he would utterly demolish their city, and cause the plough to pass over its ruins, he advanced against the barbarians, whom he routed with great slaughter, and pursued as far as Adrianople, a city of Thrace, situated on the frontiers of Macedonia. Having at that place again engaged the enemy, who had by this time rallied, he lost his life on the 9th of August, under the consulate just mentioned, and in the fourth year of the 289th Olympiad. Some have asserted that he was burnt to death in a village whither he had retired, which the Goths assaulted and set on fire. But others affirm, that having put off his imperial robe, he ran into the midst of the main body of infantry; and that when the cavalry revolted and refused to engage, the foot were surrounded by the barbarians, and completely destroyed. Among these it is said the emperor fell, but could not be distinguished, in consequence of his having laid aside his imperial habit. He died in the fiftieth year of his age,

s 2

having reigned in conjunction with his brother thirteen years, and three years after his death. This Book therefore contains the course of events during the space of sixteen years.

BOOK V.

THE PREFACE.

BEFORE we commence the fifth Book of our history, we must beg those who may peruse this work, not to censure us too hastily for intermingling with ecclesiastical matters such an account of the wars coeval with the period under consideration, as could be duly authenticated. For this plan of ours has been deliberately pursued for several reasons: first, in order to lay before our readers an exact statement of facts; secondly, to relieve their minds from a wearisome repetition of the contentious disputes of bishops, and their insidious designs against one another; but more especially that it might be made apparent, that whenever the affairs of the State were disturbed, those of the Church, as if by some vital sympathy, became disordered also. Indeed whoever shall attentively examine the subject will find, that the mischiefs of the State and the troubles of the Church have been inseparably connected; for he will perceive that they have either arisen together, or immediately succeeded one another. Sometimes the calamities of the Church take precedence; then commotions in the State follow: so that I cannot believe this invariable interchange is merely fortuitous, but am persuaded that it proceeds from our iniquities, of which these reciprocal convulsions are the merited chastisements. The apostle truly says, "Some men's sins are open beforehand, going before to judgment; and some men they follow after."[1] Hence it is that we have interwoven many affairs of the State with our ecclesiastical history. Of the wars carried on during the reign of Constantine we have made no mention, having found

[1] 1 Tim. v. 24.

no account of them that could be depended upon because of
their antiquity: but we have given a cursory sketch of subsequent events, in the order of their. occurrence, from the
narration of living witnesses.[1]   We have never failed to include the emperors in these historical details; because from
the time they began to profess the Christian religion, they
have exercised a powerful influence over the affairs of the
Church, to such an extent indeed, that the greatest synods
have been, and still are, convened by their appointment. Finally, we have particularly noticed the Arian heresy, from its
having so greatly disquieted the Churches. Having made
these prefatory remarks, we shall now proceed with our history.

CHAP. I.—THE GOTHS AGAIN ATTACK CONSTANTINOPLE, AND
ARE REPULSED BY THE CITIZENS, AIDED BY SOME SARACEN
AUXILIARIES.

AFTER the emperor Valens had thus lost his life,[2] in a manner which has never been satisfactorily ascertained, the barbarians again approached the very walls of Constantinople,
and laid waste the suburbs on every side of it. The people,
unable to endure this distressing spectacle, armed themselves
with whatever weapons they could severally lay hands on,
and sallied forth of their own accord against the enemy. The
empress Dominica caused the same pay to be distributed out
of the imperial treasury to such as volunteered to go out on
this service, as was usually allowed to soldiers.   On this occasion the citizens were assisted by a few of the Saracen confederates, who had been sent by Mavia their queen, to whom
allusion has been already made; and by this united resistance,
they obliged the barbarians to retire to a greater distance
from the city.

[1] See some observations in a note on b. iv. ch. xxxi.
[2] See Gibbon's Decline and Fall, chap. xxvi.

CHAP. II.—THE EMPEROR GRATIAN RECALLS THE ORTHODOX BISHOPS, AND EXPELS THE HERETICS FROM THE CHURCHES. HE TAKES THEODOSIUS AS HIS IMPERIAL COLLEAGUE.

GRATIAN being now in possession of the empire, together with Valentinian junior, and condemning the cruel policy of his uncle Valens towards the orthodox Christians, recalled those whom he had sent into exile. He moreover enacted that persons of all sects, without distinction, might securely assemble together in their oratories; the Eunomians,[1] Photinians,[2] and Manichæans[3] only were excluded from the Churches. Being also sensible of the languishing condition of the Roman empire, and of the growing power of the barbarians; perceiving too that the state was in need of a brave and prudent man, he created Theodosius his colleague in the sovereign power. This person was descended from a noble family in Spain, and had acquired so distinguished a celebrity for his prowess in the wars, that he was universally considered worthy of that honour, even before Gratian's election of him. Having therefore proclaimed him emperor, at Sirmium a city of Illyricum, in the consulate of Ausonius and Olybrius, on the 16th of January, he divides with him the care of managing the war against the barbarians.

CHAP. III.—THE PRINCIPAL BISHOPS WHO FLOURISHED AT THAT TIME.

DAMASUS, who had succeeded Liberius, then presided over the Church at Rome. Cyril was still in possession of that at Jerusalem. The Antiochian Church, as we have stated, was divided into three parts: for the Arians had chosen Dorotheus as the successor of their bishop Euzoïus; while one portion of the rest was under the government of Paulinus, and the other yielded obedience to Meletius, who had been recalled from exile. Lucius, although absent, having been compelled to leave Alexandria, yet maintained the episcopal authority among the Arians of that city; the Homoousians there being headed by Timothy, who succeeded Peter. At Constanti-

[1] See b. iv. ch. vii.　　[2] See b. ii. ch. xviii.　　[3] See b. i. ch. xxii.

nople Demophilus, the successor of Eudoxius, presided over
the Arian faction, and was in possession of the Churches;
but those who were averse to communion with him, held
their assemblies apart.[1]

CHAP. IV.—THE MACEDONIANS WHO HAD SUBSCRIBED THE
HOMOOUSIAN DOCTRINE, RETURN TO THEIR FORMER ERROR.

AFTER the deputation from the Macedonians to Liberius,[2]
that sect was admitted to entire communion with the Churches
in every city, intermixing themselves indiscriminately with
those who from the beginning had embraced the form of faith
published at Nice. But when the emperor Gratian had passed
the law which permitted the several sects to reunite in the
public services of religion, they again resolved to separate
themselves; and having met at Antioch in Syria, they came
to the decision afresh that the word *consubstantial* ought to
be rejected, and that communion was by no means to be held
with the supporters of the Nicene creed. They however derived no advantage from this attempt; for the majority of
their own party, being disgusted at the fickleness with which
they sometimes maintained one opinion, and then another,
withdrew from them, and thenceforward became firm adherents to those who professed the doctrine of consubstantiality.

CHAP. V.—TRANSACTIONS AT ANTIOCH IN CONNEXION WITH
PAULINUS AND MELETIUS.

ABOUT this time a serious contest was excited at Antioch
in Syria, on account of Meletius. It has been already observed[3] that Paulinus bishop of that city, because of his eminent piety, was not sent into exile: and that Meletius, after

[1] See above, b. iv. ch. i.
[2] An account of their mission to Liberius and their counterfeited subscription to the Nicene faith, both by word of mouth and by writing,
through which they induced him to readmit them to communion, is given
above in b. iv. ch. xii.
[3] See b. iii. ch. ix.

being restored by Julian, was again banished by Valens, and at length recalled in Gratian's reign.[1] On his return to Antioch, he found Paulinus greatly enfeebled by old age; his partisans therefore used their utmost endeavours to get him associated with that prelate in the episcopal office. And when Paulinus declared that it was contrary to the canons[2] to admit a coadjutor who had been ordained by the Arians, the people had recourse to violence, and caused him to be consecrated in one of the Churches without the city. A great disturbance arose from this transaction; but the popular ferment was afterwards allayed by the following stipulations being agreed to. Having assembled such of the clergy as were considered worthy of being intrusted with the bishopric, they find them six in number, of whom Flavian was one. All these they bound by an oath, not to use any effort to get themselves ordained, when either of the two prelates should die, but to permit the survivor to retain undisturbed possession of the see of the deceased. This arrangement appeased the jealousy of the contending parties: the Luciferians however separated themselves from the rest, because Meletius, who had been ordained by the Arians, was admitted to the episcopate. In this state of the Antiochian Church, Meletius was under the necessity of going to Constantinople.

CHAP. VI.—GREGORY OF NAZIANZEN IS TRANSLATED TO THE SEE OF CONSTANTINOPLE. THE EMPEROR THEODOSIUS FALLING SICK AT THESSALONICA, IS THERE BAPTIZED BY ASCHOLIUS THE BISHOP.

BY the common suffrage of many prelates, Gregory was at this time translated from the see of Nazianzen to that of Constantinople in the manner before described. And about the same time the emperors Gratian and Theodosius each obtained a victory over the barbarians. Immediately after this Gratian

[1] See above, ch. iii.
[2] Especially the 8th Canon of the Council of Nice, where the principle is laid down as one already established, that there should be only one bishop in each city. See Bingham, Christ. Antiq. b. ii. ch. xiii. sect. 1 and 2. Theodoret (b. v. ch. iii.) gives a somewhat different version of the story of the compromise entered into between Paulinus and Meletius.

set out for the Gallias, because the Alemanni were ravaging those provinces : but Theodosius, after erecting a trophy, hastened towards Constantinople, and arrived at Thessalonïca, where he was taken dangerously ill, and expressed a desire to receive Christian baptism.[1] Now he had been instructed in Christian principles by his ancestors, and professed the Homoousian faith. Becoming increasingly anxious to be baptized therefore, as his malady grew worse, he sent for the bishop of Thessalonica, and first asked him what doctrinal views he held ? The bishop replied, that the opinion of Arius had not yet invaded the provinces of Illyricum, nor had the novelty to which that heretic had given birth begun to prey upon the Churches in those countries ; but they continued to preserve unshaken that faith which from the beginning was delivered by the apostles, and had been confirmed in the Nicene synod. On hearing this, the emperor was most gladly baptized by the bishop Ascholius ; and having recovered from his disease not many days after, he came to Constantinople on the twenty-fourth of November, in the fifth consulate of Gratian and the first of his own.

CHAP. VII.—GREGORY ABDICATES THE EPISCOPATE OF CONSTANTINOPLE. THE EMPEROR ORDERS DEMOPHILUS THE ARIAN BISHOP EITHER TO ASSENT TO THE HOMOOUSIAN FAITH, OR LEAVE THE CITY.

GREGORY of Nazianzen, after his translation to Constantinople, held his assemblies within the city in a small oratory, adjoining to which the emperor afterwards built a magnificent church, and named it *Anastasia.* But Gregory, who far excelled in eloquence and piety all those of the age in which he lived, understanding that some murmured at his preferment because he was a stranger, after expressing his joy at the emperor's arrival, refused to remain at Constantinople. When the

---

[1] See above, note upon "*Clinical* Baptism," in b. i. ch. xxxix. It should be remarked that persons were called Christians *in a certain sense,* even before baptism : so here Theodosius is said to have "professed the Homoousian faith," as did also Constantine ; and yet each of the two emperors postponed his baptism to the latest moment of his life, or at least to that which he thought to be so.

emperor found the Church in this state, he began to consider
by what means he could make peace, effect a union, and enlarge
the Churches. Immediately therefore he intimated his desire
to Demophilus, who presided over the Arian party, and inquired whether he was willing to assent to the Nicene creed,
and thus reunite the people, and establish concord. Upon
Demophilus's declining to accede to this proposal, the emperor
said to him, "Since you reject peace and unanimity, I order
you to quit the churches." Which when Demophilus heard,
weighing with himself the difficulty of contending against superior power, he convoked his followers in the church, and,
standing in the midst of them, thus spoke: "Brethren, it is
written in the Gospel, 'If they persecute you in one city, flee
ye into another.'[1] Since therefore the emperor excludes us
from the churches, take notice that we will henceforth hold
our assemblies without the city." Having said this, he departed ; not however as rightly apprehending the meaning of
that expression in the Evangelist, for the real import of the
sacred oracle is, *that such as would avoid the course of this
world, must seek the heavenly Jerusalem.* He therefore, mis-
applying the passage, went outside the city gates, and there
in future held his assemblies. With him also Lucius went out,
who being ejected from Alexandria, as we have before related,[2]
had made his escape to Constantinople, and there abode. Thus
the Arians, after having been in possession of the churches
for forty years, in consequence of their opposition to the conciliatory measures of the emperor Theodosius, were driven
out of the city, in Gratian's fifth consulate and the first of
Theodosius Augustus, on the 26th of November. The professors of the Homoousian faith in this manner regained possession of the churches.

CHAP. VIII.[3]—A SYNOD[4] CONVENED AT CONSTANTINOPLE.
ORDINATION OF NECTARIUS.

AFTER this the emperor without delay summoned a synod
of the prelates of his own faith, in order that the Nicene

[1] Matt. x. 23.   [2] See ch. xxxvii. of the preceding book.
[3] With this chap. compare the parallel account as given by Sozomen,
b. vii. ch. vii.—ix.
[4] This was the second Œcumenical Council.

creed might be established, and a bishop of Constantinople ordained : and inasmuch as he was not without hope that the Macedonians might be won over to his own views, he invited those who presided over that sect to be present also.   There met therefore on this occasion, of the Homoousian party, Timothy from Alexandria, Cyril from Jerusalem, who at that time recognised the doctrine of consubstantiality, having retracted his former opinion ; Meletius from Antioch, who had arrived there previously to assist at the installation of Gregory ; Ascholius also from Thessalonica, and many others, amounting in all to one hundred and fifty.   Of the Macedonians, the principal persons were Eleusius of Cyzicum, and Marcian of Lampsacus ; these with the rest, most of whom came from the cities of the Hellespont, were thirty-six in number.   All being assembled in the month of May, under the consulate of Eucharius and Evagrius, the emperor used his utmost exertions, in conjunction with the bishops who entertained similar sentiments to his own, to bring over Eleusius and his adherents to his own side.   They were reminded of the deputation they had sent by Eustathius to Liberius then bishop of Rome ; that they had of their own accord not long since entered into promiscuous communion with the orthodox ; and the inconsistency and fickleness of their conduct was represented to them, in now attempting to subvert the faith which they once acknowledged, and professed agreement with the catholics in.   But the Macedonians, regardless alike of admonitions and reproofs, chose rather to maintain the Arian dogma, than to assent to the Homoousian doctrine.   Having made this declaration, they departed from Constantinople ; and writing to their partisans in every city, they charged them by all means to repudiate the creed of the Nicene synod.   The bishops of the other party remaining at Constantinople, entered into a consultation about the ordination of a bishop ; for Gregory, as we have before said,[1] had renounced that see, and was preparing to return to Nazianzen.   Now there was a person named Nectarius, of a senatorial family, mild and gentle in his manners, and admirable in his whole course of life, although he at that time bore the office of prætor.   This man the people seized upon, and elected to the episcopate, and he was ordained ac-

---

[1] See above, ch. vii.

cordingly by the huhdred and fifty bishops then present.[1] The same prelates moreover published a decree assigning the next prerogative of honour after the bishop of Rome, to the bishop of Constantinople, because that city was New Rome.[2] They also again confirmed the Nicene creed. Then too patriarchs were constituted, and the provinces distributed, so that no bishop might exercise any jurisdiction over other Churches out of his own diocese: for this had been often indiscriminately done before, in consequence of the persecutions. To Nectarius therefore was allotted the great city[3] and Thrace. Helladius, the successor of Basil in the bishopric of Cæsarea in Cappadocia, obtained the patriarchate of the Pontic diocese, in conjunction with Gregory, Basil's brother, bishop of Nyssa in Cappadocia, and Otreïus bishop of Meletina in Armenia. To Amphilochius of Iconium and Optimus of Antioch in Pisidia, was the Asian diocese assigned. The superintendence of the Churches throughout Egypt was committed to Timothy of Alexandria. On Pelagius of Laodicea, and Diodorus of Tarsus, devolved the administration of the Churches of the East ; without infringement however on the prerogatives of honour reserved to the Antiochian Church, and conferred on Meletius then present. They further decreed that, if necessity required it, a provincial synod should determine the ecclesiastic affairs of each province. These arrangements were confirmed by the emperor's approbation. Such was the result of this synod.

[1] Upon this method of election to the episcopal office, see other examples given by Bingham, Christ. Antiq. b. iv. ch. ii. sect. 8.
[2] See Council of Chalcedon, Canon xxviii. " We, following in all things the decision of the holy Fathers, and acknowledging the Canon of the 150 bishops . . . . do also determine and decree the same things respecting the privileges of the most holy city of Constantinople, New Rome. For the Fathers properly gave the primacy to the throne of the elder Rome." See also Canon vi. of Nice: " The Church of Rome has always had the primacy."
[3] Constantinople.

CHAP. IX.—The body of Paul bishop of Constantinople is honourably transferred from his place of exile. Death of Meletius.

A short time afterwards, the emperor caused to be removed from the city of Ancyra, the body of the bishop Paul, whom Philip the prefect of the Prætorium had banished at the instigation of Macedonius, and ordered to be strangled at Cucusus, a town of Armenia, as I have already mentioned.[1] His remains were therefore received by Theodosius with great reverence and honour, and deposited in the church which now takes its name from him; which the Macedonian party were formerly in possession of while they remained separate from the Arians, but were expelled from by the emperor, on their refusal to adopt his sentiments. About this period Meletius bishop of Antioch fell sick and died: in whose praise Gregory, the brother of Basil, pronounced a funeral oration. The body of the deceased prelate was by his friends conveyed to Antioch; where those who had identified themselves with his interests, again refused subjection to Paulinus, but caused Flavian to be substituted in the place of Meletius. Thus a fresh division arose among the people, rending the Antiochian Church into rival factions, not grounded on any difference of faith, but simply on a preference of bishops.

CHAP. X.—The emperor causes a synod to be convened composed of all the various sects. Arcadius is proclaimed Augustus. The Novatians permitted to hold their assemblies in the city of Constantinople.

Great disturbances occurred in other cities also when the Arians were ejected from the Churches. But I cannot sufficiently admire the emperor's prudence in this contingency, and the judicious course he pursued in order to arrest the disorders which prevailed: for conceiving that by a general conference of the bishops, their mutual differences would be likely to be adjusted, and unanimity established, he again

[1] Book ii. ch. xxvi.

ordered a synod to be convened in which the leaders of all the schismatics were included. And I am persuaded that it was to recompense this anxiety of the emperor's to promote peace in the Church, that his affairs were so prosperous at that time. In fact, by a special dispensation of Divine Providence the barbarous nations were reduced to subjection: and among others, Athanaric king of the Goths made a voluntary surrender of himself to him, with all his people, and died soon after at Constantinople. At this juncture the emperor proclaimed his son Arcadius Augustus, on the sixteenth of January, in the second consulate of Merobaudes and Saturninus. In the month of June, under the same consulate, the bishops of every sect arrived from all places: the emperor therefore sent for Nectarius the bishop, and consulted with him on the best means of freeing the Christian religion from dissensions, and reducing the Church to a state of unity. "The subjects of controversy," said he, "ought to be fairly discussed, that by the detection and removal of the sources of discord, an universal agreement may be effected." As this proposition gave Nectarius the greatest uneasiness, he communicated it to Agelius bishop of the Novatians, inasmuch as he entertained the same sentiments as himself in matters of faith. This man, though eminently pious, was by no means competent to maintain a dispute on doctrinal points; he therefore proposed to refer the subject to Sisinnius his reader, as a fit person to manage a conference. Sisinnius, who was not only eloquent, but possessed of great experience, and wellinformed both in the expositions of the sacred Scriptures and the principles of philosophy, knowing that disputations, far from healing divisions, usually create heresies of a more inveterate character, thought it highly desirable to avoid them. His advice to Nectarius therefore was, that since the ancients have nowhere attributed a beginning of existence to the Son of God, conceiving him to be co-eternal with the Father, it would be better to bring forward as evidences of the truth the testimonies of the ancients, instead of entering into logical debates. "Let the emperor," said he, "demand of the heads of each sect, whether they would pay any deference to the ancients who flourished before schism distracted the Church; or whether they would repudiate them, as alienated from the Christian faith? If they reject their authority, then let them

also anathematize them: and should they presume to take
such a step, they would themselves be instantly thrust out by
the people, and so the truth will be manifestly victorious.
But if, on the other hand, they are willing to admit the fathers,
it will then be our business to produce their books, by which
our views will be fully attested." Nectarius, approving of the
counsel of Sisinnius, hastened to the palace, and acquainted the
emperor with the plan which had been suggested to him;
who at once perceiving its wisdom and propriety, carried it
into execution with consummate prudence. For without discovering his object, he simply asked the chiefs of the heretics
whether they had any respect for and would recognise those
doctors of the Church who lived previous to the dissension?·
When they unhesitatingly replied that they highly revered
them as their masters; the emperor inquired of them again
whether they would defer to them as accredited witnesses of
Christian doctrine? At this question, the leaders of the several
parties, with their logical champions who had come prepared
for sophistical debate, found themselves extremely embarrassed.
Some acquiesced in the reasonableness of the emperor's
proposition; but others shrunk from it, conscious that it was
by no means favourable to their interests: so that all being
variously affected towards the writings of the ancients, they
could no longer agree among themselves, dissenting not only
from other sects, but those of the same sect differing from one
another. Accordant malice therefore, like the tongue of the
giants of old, was confounded, and their tower of mischief
overturned.[1] The emperor, perceiving by their confusion that
their sole confidence was in subtil arguments, and that they
feared to appeal to the expositions of the fathers, had recourse to another method: he commanded every sect to set
forth in writing their own peculiar tenets. Accordingly
those who were accounted the most skilful among them, drew
up a statement of their respective creeds, couched in terms the
most circumspect they could devise; and on the day appointed
them, the bishops selected for this purpose presented themselves at the palace. Nectarius and Agelius appeared as the
defenders of the Homoousian faith; Demophilus supported the
Arian dogma; Eunomius himself undertook the cause of the

[1] Alluding to the tower of Babel, and the dispersion of its builders,
Gen. xi.

Eunomians; and Eleusius bishop of Cyzicum represented the opinions of those who were denominated Macedonians. The emperor gave them all a courteous reception; and receiving from each their written avowal of faith, he shut himself up alone, and prayed very earnestly that God would assist him in his endeavours to ascertain the truth. Then perusing with great care the statement which each had submitted to him, he condemned all the rest, inasmuch as they introduced a separation of the Trinity, and approved of that only which contained the doctrine of consubstantiality. This decision caused the Novatians to flourish again: for the emperor, delighted with the consonance of their profession with that which he embraced, permitted them to hold their assemblies within the city; and having promulgated a law securing to them the peaceful possession of their own oratories, he assigned to their Churches equal privileges with those to which he gave his more especial sanction. But the prelates of the other sects, on account of their disagreement among themselves, were despised and censured even by their own followers: so that, overwhelmed with perplexity and vexation, they departed, addressing consolatory letters to their adherents, whom they exhorted not to be troubled because many had deserted them and gone over to the Homoousian party; for, said they, "Many are called, but few are chosen"—an expression which they never thought of using, when by force and terror they succeeded in rendering the majority of the people their disciples. Nevertheless the orthodox believers were not wholly exempt from inquietude; for the affairs of the Antiochian Church caused divisions among those who were present at the synod. The bishops of Egypt, Arabia, and Cyprus combined against Flavian, and insisted on his expulsion from Antioch: but those of Palestine, Phœnice, and Syria contended with equal zeal in his favour. The issue of this contest will be spoken of in its proper place.[1]

---

[1] See below, ch. xv.

CHAP. XI.—THE EMPEROR GRATIAN IS SLAIN BY THE TREA-
CHERY OF THE TYRANT MAXIMUS.   JUSTINA CEASES FROM
PERSECUTING AMBROSE.

. NEARLY at the same time with the holding of these synods
at Constantinople, the following events occurred in the Western
parts. Maximus coming from the island of Britain, invaded
the Roman empire, and took arms against Gratian, who was
then engaged in a war with the Alemanni. In Italy, Valentinian being still a' minor, Probus, a man of consular dignity,
had the chief administration of affairs, and was at that time
prefect of the Prætorium.   Justina, the mother of the young
prince, who entertained Arian sentiments, had been unable to
molest the Homoousians during her husband's life; but going
to Milan after the emperor's decease, she manifested great hostility to Ambrose the bishop, and commanded that he should
be banished.[1] While the people, from their excessive attachment to Ambrose, were offering resistance to those who were
charged with the execution of this order, intelligence was
brought that Gratian had been assassinated by the treachery
of the tyrant Maximus.   Andragathius, a general under Maximus, having concealed himself in a litter resembling a couch,
which was carried by mules, ordered his guards to spread a
report before him that the litter contained the emperor Gratian's
wife.   They met the emperor near the city of Lyons in
France just as he had crossed the river; and the latter, believing it to be his wife, and not expecting any treachery,
fell into the hands of his enemy as a blind man into the
ditch; for Andragathius, suddenly springing forth from the
litter, slew him.   Gratian thus perished in the consulate of
Merobaudes and Saturninus, in the twenty-fourth year of his
age, and the fifteenth of his reign.   This incident repressed
the empress Justina's indignation against Ambrose.   Afterwards Valentinian most unwillingly, but constrained by the
necessity of the time, admitted Maximus as his colleague in
the empire.   Probus, alarmed at the power of Maximus, resolved to retreat into the regions of the East: leaving Italy
therefore, he proceeded to Illyricum, and fixed his residence
at Thessalonica, a city of Macedonia.

[1] See above, b. iv. ch. xxx.

[SOCRATES.]   T

CHAP. XII.—WHILE THE EMPEROR THEODOSIUS IS ENGAGED
IN MILITARY PREPARATIONS AGAINST THE TYRANT, HIS SON
HONORIUS IS BORN.   HE THEN PROCEEDS TO MILAN IN OR-
DER TO ENCOUNTER MAXIMUS.

BUT the emperor Theodosius, filled with the utmost solicitude, levied a powerful army against the tyrant, fearing lest
he should meditate the destruction of the young Valentinian
also.   While engaged in this preparation, an embassy arrived
from the Persians, requesting peace from the emperor.   Then
also the empress Flaccilla bore him a son named Honorius, on
the 9th of September, in the consulate of Richomeres and
Clearchus.   Under the same consulate, and a little before the
birth of this prince, Agelius bishop of the Novatians died.   In
the year following, wherein Arcadius Augustus bore his first
consulate in conjunction with Bauton, Timothy bishop of
Alexandria died, and was succeeded in the episcopate by Theophilus.   About a year after this, Demophilus the Arian prelate having departed this life, the Arians sent for Marinus, a
leader of their own heresy, out of Thrace, to whom they intrusted the bishopric: but he did not long occupy that position, for under him that sect was divided into two parties, as
we shall hereafter explain; they therefore invited Dorotheus
to come to them from Antioch in Syria, and constituted him
their bishop.   Meanwhile the emperor Theodosius proceeded
to the war against Maximus, leaving his son Arcadius with
imperial authority at Constantinople.   On his arrival at Thessalonica he finds Valentinian and those about him in great
anxiety, because through compulsion they acknowledged the
tyrant as emperor.   Without however giving expression to
his sentiments, he neither rejected nor admitted the embassy
of Maximus: but unable to endure tyrannical domination over
the Roman empire, under the assumption of an imperial name,
he hastily mustered his forces and advanced to Milan, whither
the usurper had already come.

CHAP. XIII.—THE ARIANS EXCITE A TUMULT AT
CONSTANTINOPLE.

WHILE the emperor was thus occupied on his military expedition, the Arians excited a great tumult at Constantinople by such devices as these. Men are fond of fabricating statements respecting matters about which they are kept in ignorance; and the tendency to do this is greatly stimulated, when, in addition to the general love of change, circumstances render them peculiarly desirous of promoting it, as they are then tempted to spread reports favourable to their own wishes. This was strongly exemplified at Constantinople on the present occasion: for each invented news concerning the war which was carrying on at a distance, according to his own caprice, always presuming upon the most disastrous results; and before the contest had yet commenced, they spoke of transactions in reference to it, of which they knew nothing, with as much assurance as if they had been spectators on the very scene of action. Thus it was confidently affirmed that the tyrant had defeated the emperor's army, even the number of men slain on both sides being specified; and that the emperor himself had nearly fallen into the tyrant's hands. Then the Arians, who had been excessively exasperated by those being put in possession of the Churches within the city who had previously been the objects of their persecution, began to augment these rumours by additions of their own. The currency of such stories with increasing exaggeration, in time imposed upon even the framers themselves; until they were induced to believe that they were not really fictions of their own imagination, but literal and positive facts. For those who had circulated them from hearsay, affirmed to the authors of these falsehoods, that the accounts they had received from them had been fully corroborated elsewhere. Thus deluded, the Arians were emboldened to commit acts of violence, and among other outrages, to set fire to the house of Nectarius the bishop. This was done in the second consulate[1] of Theodosius Augustus, which he bore with Cynegius.

[1] In this year the works of Porphyry were burnt by order of Theodosius.

CHAP. XIV.—Overthrow and Death of the Tyrant Maximus.

THE intelligence of the formidable preparations made by the emperor against the tyrant, so alarmed the troops under Maximus, that instead of fighting for him, they delivered him bound to the emperor, who caused him to be put to death, on the twenty-seventh of August, under the same consulate. Andragathius, who with his own hand had slain Gratian, understanding the fate of Maximus, precipitated himself into an adjacent river, and was drowned. Both the victorious emperors then made their public entry into Rome, accompanied by Honorius the son of Theodosius, still a mere boy, whom his father had sent for from Constantinople immediately after Maximus had been vanquished. They continued therefore at Rome celebrating their triumphal festivals: during which time the emperor Theodosius exhibited a remarkable instance of clemency toward Symmachus, a man who had borne the consular office, and was at the head of the senate at Rome. This person was distinguished for his eloquence, and many of his orations are still extant composed in the Latin tongue: but inasmuch as he had written a panegyric on Maximus, and pronounced it before him publicly, he was afterwards impeached for high treason; wherefore to escape capital punishment he took sanctuary in a church.[1] The emperor's veneration for religion led him not only to honour the prelates of his own communion, but to treat with consideration those of the Novatians also, who embraced the Homoousian creed: to gratify therefore Leontius the bishop of the Novatian Church at Rome, who interceded in behalf of Symmachus, he graciously pardoned that criminal. Symmachus, after he had obtained his pardon, wrote an apologetic address to the emperor Theodosius. Thus was the war, which at its com-

[1] Upon the ancient, churches, as recognised places of asylum and refuge, see Bingham's Christ. Antiq. b. viii. end of ch. x. and ch. xi. Thus, in b. i. ch. xviii., we read that the cubit of Serapis was laid up in a Christian church. Compare the expressions of Augustine de Civ. Dei, (b. i. ch. i.) where, speaking of the heathen and of Christian churches, he says, "They would not open their lips against them, did they not, in flying from the darts of the enemy, find life in our sanctuaries." Thus, even Alaric the Goth, when he sacked Rome, spared the churches of the city.

mencement appeared so terrible, brought to a speedy termination.

CHAP. XV.—Of FLAVIAN BISHOP OF ANTIOCH.

ABOUT the same period, the following events took place at Antioch in Syria. After the death of Paulinus, the people who had been under his superintendence refused to submit to the authority of Flavian, but caused Evagrius to be ordained bishop of their own party. He not having long survived his ordination, Flavian had the address to prevent any other being constituted in his place: nevertheless those who disliked Flavian on account of his having violated his oath, held their assemblies apart.[1] Meanwhile Flavian left no stone unturned, as the phrase is, to bring these also under his control; and this he soon after effected, when he had appeased the anger of Theophilus, then bishop of Alexandria, by whose mediation he conciliated Damasus bishop of Rome also. For both these prelates had been greatly displeased with Flavian, as well for the perjury of which he had been guilty, as for the schism he had occasioned among the people who had been previously united. Theophilus therefore being pacified, sent Isidore a presbyter to Rome, and thus reconciled Damasus who was still offended; representing to him the propriety of overlooking Flavian's misconduct, for the sake of producing concord among the people. Communion being in this way restored to Flavian, the people of Antioch were in the course of a little while induced to lay aside their opposition to him. Such was the conclusion of this affair at Antioch. But the Arians of that city being ejected from the churches, were accustomed to hold their meetings in the suburbs. Moreover Cyril bishop of Jerusalem, having died about this time, was succeeded by John.

CHAP. XVI.—DEMOLITION OF THE IDOLATROUS TEMPLES AT ALEXANDRIA; AND CONFLICT BETWEEN THE PAGANS AND CHRISTIANS.

AT the solicitation of Theophilus bishop of Alexandria, the emperor issued an order at this time for the demolition of the

[1] See b. vi. ch. ix.

heathen temples in that city; commanding also that it should
be put in execution under the direction of Theophilus,
which occasioned a great commotion. For thus authorized,
Theophilus exerted himself to the utmost to expose the
Pagan mysteries to contempt. The temple of Mithra[1] he
caused to be cleared-out, and exhibited to public view the
tokens of its bloody mysteries. The temple of Serapis he
destroyed: and to show how full of extravagance the superstitions connected with that idol and the other false gods were,
he had the phalli of Priapus carried through the midst of the
forum. The Pagans of Alexandria, and especially the professors of philosophy, unable to repress their rage at this
exposure, exceeded in revengeful ferocity their outrages on a
former occasion: for with one accord, at a pre-concerted
signal, they rushed impetuously upon the Christians, and
murdered every one they could lay hands on; and as an attempt
was made to resist the assailants, the mischief was the more
augmented. This desperate affray was prolonged until both
parties were exhausted, when it was discovered that very·few
of the heathens had been killed, but a great number of Christians; while the amount of wounded on each side was almost
incredible. The Pagans thus sated with blood and slaughter
absconded, being apprehensive of the emperor's displeasure:
some fled in one direction, some in another, and many, quitting
Alexandria, dispersed themselves in various cities. Among
these were the two grammarians Helladius and Ammonius,
whose pupil I was in my youth at Constantinople. The former
was said to be the priest of Jupiter, the latter of Simius.
After this disturbance had been thus terminated, the governor
of Alexandria, and the commander-in-chief of the troops in
Egypt, assisted Theophilus in demolishing the heathen temples. These were therefore razed to the ground, and the
images of their gods molten into pots and other convenient
utensils for the use of the Alexandrian church; for the
emperor had instructed Theophilus to so distribute them for
the relief of the poor. All the images were accordingly
broken to pieces, except one statue of the god before mentioned, which Theophilus preserved and set up in a public
place; "Lest," said he, "at a future time the heathens should
deny that they had ever worshipped such gods." This action

[1] See above, b. iii. ch. ii.

gave great umbrage to Ammonius the grammarian in particular, who to my knowledge was accustomed to say, that the religion of the Gentiles was grossly abused and misrepresented by the reservation of this one image only, in order to render that religion ridiculous.   Helladius however did not scruple to boast, that he had the satisfaction in that desperate onset of sacrificing nine victims with his own hand at the shrine of the insulted deities.   Such were the doings in Alexandria at that time.

CHAP. XVII.—OF THE HIEROGLYPHICS FOUND IN THE
TEMPLE OF SERAPIS.

WHEN the temple of Serapis was torn down and laid bare, there were found in it, engraven on stones, certain characters which they called hieroglyphics, having the forms of crosses. Both the Christians and Pagans, on seeing them, thought they had reference to their respective religions: for the Christians, who affirm that the cross is the sign of Christ's saving passion, claimed this character as peculiarly theirs; but the Pagans alleged that it might appertain to Christ and Serapis in common; " for," said they, " it symbolizes one thing to Christians and another to Heathens."   Whilst this point was controverted amongst them, some of the heathen converts to Christianity, who were conversant with these .hieroglyphic characters, interpreted that in the form of a cross to signify *the Life to come*. This the Christians exultingly laid hold of, as decidedly favourable to their religion.   But after other hieroglyphics had been deciphered containing a prediction that *When* (the character in the form of a cross, representing) *the Life to come*
147 *should appear, the Temple of Serapis would be destroyed*, a very great number of the Pagans embraced Christianity, and confessing their sins, were baptized.   Such are the reports I have heard respecting the discovery of this symbol in form of a cross.   But I cannot imagine that the Egyptian priests foreknew the things concerning Christ, when they engraved the figure of a cross.   For if *the mystery* of our Saviour's advent *was hid from ages and from generations*, as the apostle declares;[1] and if the devil himself, the prince of wickedness,

[1] 1 Cor. ii. 7, 8; Eph. iii. 5, 6.

knew nothing of it, his ministers the Egyptian priests are
likely to have been still more ignorant of the matter. Providence doubtless purposed that in the inquiry concerning this
character, there should something take place analogous to what
happened heretofore at the preaching of Paul. For he, made
wise by the Divine Spirit, employed a similar method in relation to the Athenians, many of whom he brought over to
the faith, when on reading the inscription on one of their
altars[1] he accommodated it to his own discourse. Unless indeed any one should say, that the Word of God wrought in
the Egyptian priests, as it did on Balaam[2] and Caiaphas,[3]
causing them to utter prophecies of good things in spite of
themselves.

CHAP. XVIII.—REFORMATION OF ABUSES AT ROME BY THE
EMPEROR THEODOSIUS.

DURING the short stay of the emperor Theodosius in Italy,
he conferred the greatest benefit on the city of Rome, by
grants on the one hand, and abrogations on the other. His
largesses were very munificent ; and he removed two most
infamous abuses which existed in that mighty city. There
were buildings of immense magnitude erected in former times,
in which bread was made for distribution among the people.
Those who had the charge of these edifices, whom the Romans
in their language term Mancipes, in process of time converted them into receptacles for thieves. Now the bake-houses in
these structures being placed underneath, they built taverns
at the side of each, where prostitutes were kept; by which
means they entrapped many of those who went thither either
for the sake of refreshment, or to gratify their lusts, for by a
certain mechanical contrivance they precipitated them from
the tavern into the bake-house below. This was practised
chiefly upon strangers; and such as were in this way tre-
panned, were compelled to work in the bake-houses, where
they were immured until old age, their friends concluding that
they were dead. It happened that one of the soldiers of the
emperor Theodosius fell into this snare ; who being shut up

---

[1] Acts xvii. 23.   [2] Num. xxiv.   [3] John xi. 51.

in the bake-house, and hindered from going out, drew a dagger which he wore and killed those who stood in his way: the rest being terrified, suffered him to escape.   When the emperor was made acquainted with the circumstance he punished [148] the Mancipes, and ordered these haunts of lawless and abandoned characters to be pulled down.   This was one of the disgraceful nuisances of which the emperor purged the imperial city: the other was of this nature.   When a woman was detected in adultery, they punished the delinquent in a way that rather aggravated her offence than tended to reform her. For shutting her up in a narrow brothel, they obliged her to prostitute herself in a most disgusting manner; causing little bells to be rung at the time, that those who passed by might not be ignorant of what was doing within.   This was doubtless intended to brand the crime with greater ignominy in public opinion.   As soon as the emperor was apprized of this indecent usage, he would by no means tolerate it; but having ordered the *Sistra* (for so these places of penal prostitution were denominated) to be pulled down, he appointed other laws for the punishment of adulteresses.   Thus did the emperor Theodosius free the city from two of its most discreditable abuses: and when he had arranged all other affairs to his satisfaction, leaving the young emperor Valentinian at Rome, he returned with his son Honorius to Constantinople, and entered that city on the 10th of November, in the consulate of Tatian and Symmachus.

CHAP. XIX.—THE OFFICE OF PENITENTIARY PRESBYTER
ABOLISHED.

IT was deemed requisite at this time to abolish the office of those presbyters in the churches who superintended the [149] confessional:[1] this was done on the following account. When the Novatians separated themselves from the Church because they would not communicate with those who had lapsed during the persecution under Decius, the bishops added to the ecclesiastical canon a presbyter whose duty it should be

---

[1] This officer was called the Penitentiary. See Bingham's Chr. Antiq. b. xviii. ch. iii.

to receive the confession of penitents who had sinned after baptism. And this mode of discipline is still maintained among other heretical institutions by all the rest of the sects; the Homoousians only, together with the Novatians, who hold the same doctrinal views, having rejected it. The latter indeed would never admit of its establishment: and the Homoousians, who are now in possession of the Churches, after retaining this function for a considerable period, abrogated it in the time of Nectarius, in consequence of what occurred in the Constantinopolitan Church. A woman of noble family coming to the penitentiary, made a general confession of those sins she had committed since her baptism; and the presbyter enjoined fasting and prayer continually, that together with the acknowledgment of error, she might have to show works also meet for repentance. Some time after this, the same lady again presented herself, and confessed that she had been guilty of another crime, a deacon of that Church having lain with her. On this information the deacon was ejected from the Church:[1] but the people were very indignant, being not only offended at what had taken place, but also because the exposure of the fact had brought scandal and degradation upon the Church. When, in consequence of this, ecclesiastics were subjected to taunting and reproach, Eudæmon, a presbyter of that Church, by birth an Alexandrian, persuaded Nectarius the bishop to abolish the office of penitentiary presbyter, and to leave every one to his own conscience with regard to the participation of the sacred mysteries:[2] for thus only, in his judgment, could the Church be preserved from obloquy. I have not hesitated to insert this in my history, since I myself heard the explanation of the matter from Eudæmon: for, as I have often remarked, I have spared no pains to procure an authentic account of affairs from those who were best acquainted with them, and to scrutinize every report, lest I should advance what might be untrue. My observation to Eudæmon, when he first related the circumstance, was this: " Whether,

---

[1] " If a Bishop, Presbyter, or Deacon, be found guilty of fornication . . . . let him be deposed." Apostol. Canon xxv.

[2] i. e. partaking of the Eucharist, so called κατ' ἐξοχήν, and through a reserve, occasioned by fear of allowing the heathen any knowledge of the sacramental acts and worship of the Church. This is generally known as the " Disciplina arcani." See Bingham's Christian Antiq. b. x. ch. v.

O presbyter, your counsel has been profitable for the Church
or otherwise, God knows; but I see that it takes away the
means of rebuking one another's faults, and prevents our
acting upon that precept of the apostle, *Have no fellowship*
[150] *with the unfruitful works of darkness, but rather reprove them.*"

CHAP. XX.—DIVISIONS AMONG THE ARIANS AND OTHER
HERETICS.

I CONCEIVE it right moreover to notice the proceedings of
the other religious bodies, viz. the Arians,[1] Novatians, and
those who received their denominations from Macedonius and
Eunomius.   For the Church once being divided, rested not in
that schism, but the separatists, taking occasion from the most
frivolous pretences, disagreed among themselves.   The manner
and time, as well as the causes for which they raised mutual
dissensions, will be stated as we proceed.   But let it be
observed here, that the emperor Theodosius persecuted none
of them except Eunomius, whom he banished; because by
holding meetings in private houses at Constantinople, where
he read the works he had composed, he corrupted many with
his doctrines.   The other heretics were not interfered with by
the emperor, nor did he constrain them to hold communion
with himself; but he allowed them all to assemble in their own
conventicles, and to entertain their own opinions on points of
Christian faith.   Permission to build themselves oratories
without the cities was granted to the rest: but inasmuch as
the Novatians held sentiments precisely identical with his own
as to faith, he ordered that they should be suffered to continue
unmolested in their churches within the cities, as I have before
noticed.   I think it opportune however to give in this place
some further account of them, and shall therefore retrace a few
circumstances in their history.[2]

[1] See below, ch. xxiii.
[2] It is from his peculiarly detailed account of the Novatian heresy, and
from the way in which he represents it as very nearly approaching to the
orthodox doctrine, that Socrates has been charged with being a Novatian.
See Life, prefixed to this volume, and note on b. ii. ch. xxxviii.

CHAP. XXI.—PECULIAR SCHISM AMONG THE NOVATIANS.[1]

THE Novatian Church at Constantinople was presided over
by Agelius for the space of forty years, viz. from the reign of
Constantine until the sixth year of that of the emperor Theodosius, as I remember to have stated elsewhere. He perceiving his end approaching, ordains Sisinnius[2] to succeed him in
the bishopric. This person was a presbyter of the Church
over which Agelius presided, remarkably eloquent, and had
been instructed in philosophy by Maximus, at the same
time as the emperor Julian. The Novatian laity were
dissatisfied with this election, and wished rather that he had
ordained Marcian, a man of eminent piety, by whose influence
their sect had been left unmolested during the reign of Valens;
Agelius therefore, to allay his people's discontent, laid his hands
on Marcian also. Having recovered a little from his illness,
on again entering the church he thus of his own accord addressed the congregation: "After my decease let Marcian be
your bishop; and after Marcian, Sisinnius." He survived
these words but a short time, and Marcian was constituted his
immediate successor; during whose episcopate a division
arose in their Church also, from this cause. Marcian had promoted to the rank of presbyter a converted Jew named Sabbatius, who nevertheless continued to retain many of his
Jewish prejudices; and moreover he was very ambitious of
being made a bishop. Having therefore attached to his interest two presbyters, Theoctistus and Macarius, who were
cognizant of his designs, he resolved to defend that innovation
made by the Novatians in the time of Valens, at Pazum a
village of Phrygia, concerning the festival of Easter, to which
I have already adverted. And in the first place, under pretext of more ascetic austerity, he privately withdrew from the
Church, saying that he was grieved on account of certain
persons whom he suspected of being unworthy of communicating in the mysteries. It was however soon discovered that
his object was to hold assemblies apart: which when Marcian
understood, he bitterly complained of his own error, in ordaining to the presbyterate persons so intent on vain-glory; and
frequently said, "That it had been better for him to have laid

[1] See above, b. iv. ch. xxviii.   [2] See b. vi. ch. i.

his hands on thorns, than to have imposed them on Sabbatius."
To check his proceedings, he procured a synod of Novatian
bishops to be convened at Sangarum, a commercial town near
Helenopolis, where Sabbatius was summoned, and desired to
explain the cause of his discontent.   Upon his affirming that
he was troubled about the disagreement that existed respecting
the Feast of Easter,[1] and that it ought to be kept according to
the custom of the Jews, and agreeable to that sanction which
those convened at Pazum had appointed ; the bishops present
at the synod, imagining this assertion to be a mere subterfuge
to disguise his desire after the episcopal chair, obliged him to
pledge himself on oath that he would never accept a bishopric.
When he had so sworn, they passed a canon respecting this
feast, which they entitled Indifferent, declaring that a disagreement on such a point was not a sufficient reason for
separation from the Church; and that the council of Pazum
had done nothing prejudicial to the catholic canon.   That although the ancients who lived nearest to the apostolic times
differed about the observance of this festival, it did not prevent
their communion with one another, nor create any dissension.
That the Novatians at imperial Rome had never followed the
Jewish usage, but always kept Easter after the equinox ;[2] and
yet they did not separate from those of their own faith, who
celebrated it on a different day.   From these and many such
considerations, they made the *Indifferent* Canon, above-mentioned, concerning Easter, whereby every one was left at liberty
to do as his own predilection led him in this matter, without
violating the unity of the Church.   After this rule had been
thus established, Sabbatius, being bound by his oath, anticipated the fast by keeping it in private, whenever any discrepancy existed in the time of the Paschal solemnity, and
having watched all night, he celebrated the sabbath of the
passover ;   then on the next day he went to church, and with
the rest of the congregation partook of the mysteries.   He
pursued this course for many years, so that it could not be
concealed from the people ; in imitation of which some of
the more ignorant, and chiefly the Phrygians and Galatians,
supposing this precedent a sufficient justification for them,
also kept the Passover in secret.   But Sabbatius afterwards
disregarding the oath by which he had renounced the episcopal

---

[1] See b. i. note on ch. viii.   [2] Ἰσημερίαν.

dignity, held schismatic meetings, and was constituted bishop of his followers, as we shall show hereafter.[1]

CHAP. XXII.—THE AUTHOR'S VIEWS RESPECTING THE CELE-BRATION OF EASTER ; WITH OBSERVATIONS ON BAPTISM, FASTING, MARRIAGE, THE EUCHARIST, AND OTHER ECCLESIAS-TICAL RITES.

I MAY perhaps be permitted here to make a few reflections on Easter. It appears to me that neither the ancients nor moderns who have affected to follow the Jews, have had any rational foundation for contending so obstinately about it. For they have altogether lost sight of the fact, that when our religion superseded the Jewish economy, the obligation to observe the Mosaic law and the ceremonial types ceased. That it is incompatible with Christian faith to practise Jewish rites, is manifest from the apostle's expressly forbidding it ; and not only rejecting circumcision, but also deprecating contention about festival days. In his Epistle to the Galatians[2] he writes, " Tell me, ye that desire to be under the law, do ye not hear the law ? " And continuing his train of argument, he demonstrates that the Jews were in bondage as servants, but that Christians are called into the liberty of sons. Moreover he exhorts them to disregard days, and months, and years.[3] Again, in his Epistle to the Colossians[4] he distinctly declares that such observances are merely shadows : wherefore he says, " Let no man judge you in meat, or in drink, or in respect of any holy-day, or of the new moon, or of the sabbath days ; which are a shadow of things to come." The same truths are also confirmed by him in the Epistle to the Hebrews,[5] in these words : " For the priesthood being changed, there is made of necessity a change also of the law." Neither the apostle therefore, nor the evangelists, have anywhere imposed the yoke of servitude on those who have embraced the gospel ; but have left Easter and every other feast to be

---

[1] See b. vii. ch. v. and xii.   [2] Gal. iv. 21.
[3] Gal. iv. 10, 11, where the observance of Jewish ordinances is mentioned in a tone of reproof.
[4] Col. ii. 16, 17.   [5] Heb. vii. 12.

honoured by the gratitude of the recipients of grace. Men
love festivals, because they afford them cessation from labour ;
and therefore it is that each individual in every place, according to his own pleasure, has by a prevalent custom celebrated
the memory of the saving passion.   The Saviour and his
apostles have enjoined us by no law to keep this feast ; nor in
the New Testament are we threatened with any penalty,
punishment, or curse for the neglect of it, as the Mosaic law
does the Jews.   It is merely for the sake of historical accuracy, and for the reproach of the Jews, because they polluted
themselves with blood on their very feasts, that it is recorded
in the Gospels that our Saviour suffered "in the days of unleavened bread."   The apostles had no thought of appointing
festival days, but of promoting a life of blamelessness and
piety.   And it seems to me that the feast of Easter has been
introduced into the Church from some old usage, just as many
other customs have been established.   In Asia Minor most
people kept the fourteenth day of the moon, disregarding the
sabbath : yet they never separated from those who did otherwise, until Victor bishop of Rome, influenced by too ardent a
zeal, fulminated a sentence of excommunication against the
Quartodecimans¹ in Asia.   But Irenæus bishop of Lyons in
France, severely censured Victor by letter for his immoderate
heat ; telling him that although the ancients differed in their
celebration of Easter, they did not depart from intercom-
munion.   Also that Polycarp bishop of Smyrna, who after-
151 wards suffered martyrdom under Gordian, continued to communicate with Anicetus bishop of Rome, although he himself,
according to the usage of his country, kept Easter on the
fourteenth day of the moon, as Eusebius attests in the fifth
Book of his "Ecclesiastical History."²   While therefore some
in Asia Minor observed the day above-mentioned, others in
the East kept that feast on the sabbath indeed, but not in the
same month: The former thought the Jews should be followed, though they were not exact: the latter kept Easter
after the equinox, refusing to be guided by the Jews ; "for,"
said they, "it ought to be celebrated when the sun is in Aries,
in the month which the Antiochians term Xanthicus, and the
Romans April."   In this practice, they averred, they con-

---

¹ Those who observed Easter on the fourteenth day of the new moon.
² Euseb. b. v. chap. xxiv.

formed not to the modern Jews, who are mistaken in almost everything, but to the ancients of that nation, and what Josephus has written in the third Book of his "Jewish Antiquities."[1]   Thus these people were at issue.   But all other Christians in the Western parts, as far as the ocean itself, are found to have celebrated Easter after the equinox, from a very ancient tradition, and have never disagreed on this subject.   It is not true, as some have pretended, that the synod under Constantine altered this festival: for that emperor himself, writing to those who differed respecting it, recommended them, as few in number, to agree with the majority of their brethren.   His letter is given at length by Eusebius in his third Book of the Life of that sovereign ;[2] but the part relative to Easter runs thus :—"It is a becoming order, which all the Churches in the Western, Southern, and Northern parts of the world observe, and some places in the East also.   Wherefore all on the present occasion have judged it right, and I have pledged myself that it will have the acquiescence of your prudence, that what is unanimously observed in the city of Rome, throughout Italy, Africa, and Egypt, in Spain, France, Britain, Libya, and all Greece, the Asian and Pontic diocese, and Cilicia, your wisdom also will readily embrace ; considering not only that the number of Churches in the aforesaid places is greater, but also that while there should be a universal concurrence in what is most reasonable, it becomes us to have nothing in common with the perfidious Jews."   Such is the tenor of the emperor's letter.   Moreover the Quartodecimans affirm that the observance which they maintain was delivered to them by the apostle John ; while the Romans and those in the Western parts assure us that their usage originated with the apostles Peter and Paul.   Neither of these parties however can produce any written testimony in confirmation of what they assert.   But that the time of keeping Easter in various places is dependent on usage, I infer from this, that those who agree in faith, differ among themselves on this question.   And it will not perhaps be unseasonable to notice here the diversity of customs in the Churches.[3]   The fasts before Easter are differently observed.   Those at Rome fast

---

[1] See Josephus, b. iii. chap. x.   [2] See chap. xix. of that book.
[3] See the whole question fully discussed by Bingham, Christian Antiq. b. xx. ch. v.

152 three successive weeks before Easter, excepting Saturdays and
Sundays. The Illyrians, Achaians, and Alexandrians observe
a fast of six weeks, which they term "the forty days' fast."
Others commencing their fast from the seventh week before
Easter, and fasting three five days only, and that at intervals,
yet call that time "the forty days' fast." It is indeed surprising that, thus differing in the number of days, they should
both give it one common appellation; but some assign one
reason for it, and others another, according to their several
fancies. There is also a disagreement about abstinence from
food, as well as the number of days. Some wholly abstain
from things that have life: others feed on fish only of all
living creatures: many, together with fish, eat fowl also,
saying that, according to Moses, these were likewise made out
of the waters. Some abstain from eggs, and all kinds of
fruits; others feed on dry bread only; and others eat not
even this; while others, having fasted till the ninth hour,
afterwards feed on any sort of food without distinction.
And among various nations there are other usages, for which
innumerable reasons are assigned. Since however no one
can produce a written command as an authority, it is evident
that the apostles left each one to his own free-will in the
matter, to the end that the performance of what is good might
not be the result of constraint and necessity. Nor is there
153 less variation in the services performed in their religious
assemblies, than there is about fastings. For although almost
all Churches throughout the world celebrate the sacred mysteries on the sabbath of every week,[1] yet the Christians of
Alexandria and at Rome, on account of some ancient tradition,
refuse to do this. The Egyptians in the neighbourhood of
Alexandria, and the inhabitants of Thebaïs, hold their religious
meetings on the sabbath, but do not participate of the mys-

---

[1] That is, upon the Saturday. It should be observed, that Sunday is
never called "the sabbath" (τὸ σάββατον) by the ancient Fathers and
historians, but "the Lord's day" (ἡ κυριακή). Many of the early Christians, from their Jewish education and prejudices, continued, even as
Christians, to observe the sabbath, as well as the first day of the week.
Upon the whole question, see Bingham's Christ. Antiq. b. xx. ch. iii. The
Latins kept the sabbath as a fast, the Greeks as a feast; and the 64th of
the Apostolical Canons forbids any of the clergy to fast on the sabbath
(Saturday) under pain of being deposed, and likewise a layman under
the penalty of excommunication.

[SOCRATES.]   U

teries in the manner usual among Christians in general : for after having eaten and satisfied themselves with food of all kinds, in the evening, making their oblations,[1] they partake of the mysteries. At Alexandria again, on *the 4th Feria*, (i. e. the Wednesday in Passion week,) and on that termed the *Preparation day*,[2] the Scriptures are read, and the doctors expound them; and all the usual services are performed in their assemblies, except the celebration of the mysteries. This practice in the city is of great antiquity, for it is well known that Origen most commonly taught in the church on these days. He being very learned in the sacred books, and perceiving that the impotency[3] of the Mosaic Law could not be explained literally, gave it a spiritual interpretation; declaring that there has never been but one true Passover, which our Saviour celebrated when he hung upon the cross: for that he then vanquished the adverse powers, and erected this trophy against the devil. In the same city of Alexandria, readers and chanters[4] are chosen indifferently from the catechumens and the faithful; whereas in all other churches the faithful only are promoted to these offices. I myself also, when in Thessaly, knew another custom. If a clergyman in that country, after taking orders, should sleep with his wife, whom he had legally married before his ordination, he would be degraded.[5] In the East indeed all clergymen, and even the bishops themselves, abstain from their wives: but this they do of their own accord, there being no law in force to make it necessary; for there have been among them many bishops, who have had children by their lawful wives during their episcopate. It is said that the author of the usage which obtains in Thessaly, was Heliodorus bishop of Trica in that country; under whose name there are

---

[1] Προσφέροντες. This expression is ambiguous, and may imply the *offering* of the consecrated elements *as a sacrifice*.

[2] ἡ παρασκευή. Holy Thursday, the fifth day of holy week, the day before Good Friday. See Bingham's Christ. Antiq. b. x. ch. ii. sect. 10.

[3] Τὸ ἀδύνατον (Rom. viii. 3).

[4] Ὑποβολεῖς. For the explanation of this name, which was given to the leaders of psalmody in churches, see Bingham's Christ. Antiq. b. iii. ch. viii. sect. 3.

[5] Upon the gradual introduction of celibacy among the clerical order, see Bingham's Christ. Antiq. b. iv. ch. v.; see also first Canon of the Council of Gangra, and Apostol. Canon li.

love books extant, entitled "Ethiopici,"[1] which he composed
in his youth. The same custom prevails at Thessalonica, and
in Macedonia, and Achaia. I have also remarked another
peculiarity in Thessaly, which is, that they baptize there on
the days of Easter only; in consequence of which a very
great number of them die without having received this rite.
At Antioch in Syria the site of the church is inverted; so
that the altar, instead of looking toward the East, faces the
West.[2] In Achaia and Thessaly, and also at Jerusalem, they
go to prayers as soon as the candles are lighted, in the same
manner as the Novatians do at Constantinople. At Cæsarea
likewise, and in Cappadocia, and the Isle of Cyprus, the
bishops and presbyters expound the Scriptures in the evening, after the candles are lighted. The Novatians of the
Hellespont do not perform their prayers altogether in the
same manner as those of Constantinople; in most things
however their usage is similar to that of the Catholic[3] Church.
In short, you will scarcely find anywhere, among all the sects,
two Churches which agree exactly in their ritual respecting
prayers. At Alexandria no presbyter is allowed to preach:
a regulation which was made after Arius had raised a disturbance in that Church. At Rome they fast every Saturday.[4]
154 At Cæsarea they exclude from communion those who have
sinned after baptism, as the Novatians do. The same discipline was practised by the Macedonians in the Hellespont,
and by the Quartodecimani in Asia. The Novatians in
Phrygia do not admit such as have twice married;[5] but

[1] Or the amours of Theagenes and Chariclea.

[2] It is laid down in the Apostolical Constitutions, (b. ii. ch. lvii.,) that the
fit and proper position of a church is that it shall look to the East. And
that such was the general, though by no means universal, custom is clear,
not only from this passage, but from Paulin. Ep. xii. ad Severum, who
says, "My church does not look towards the East, as the common custom is." See also Bonav. Rer. Liturg. b. i. ch. xx. n. 4, and Bingham's
Chr. Antiq. b. viii. ch. iii. sect. 2.

[3] τῇ κρατούσῃ, so called in a lower sense, as imperial and established.

[4] See note above. As Socrates wrote in the East, and for Greek readers,
it was unnecessary for him to add that the Greeks observed Saturday as
a festival.

[5] Διγάμους, Digamists, not in the sense we usually attach to the word,
of having two wives at the same time. A second marriage was always
regarded with disapprobation by the Church; and those who married
twice have always been held incapable of the priesthood. See Apostol.

those of Constantinople neither admit nor reject them openly, while in the Western parts they are openly received. This diversity was occasioned, as I imagine, by the bishops who in their respective eras governed the Churches; and those who received these several rites and usages, transmitted them as laws to posterity. It would be difficult, if not impossible, to give a complete catalogue of all the various customs and ceremonial observances in use throughout every city and country; but the instances we have adduced are sufficient to show that the Easter Festival was from some remote precedent differently celebrated in every particular province. They talk at random therefore who assert that the time of keeping Easter was altered in the Nicene synod; for the bishops there convened earnestly laboured to reduce the first dissident minority to uniformity of practice with the rest of the people. Now that differences of this kind existed in the first ages of the Church, was not unknown even to the apostles themselves, as the Book of *The Acts* testifies. For when they understood that the peace of the believers was disturbed by a dissension of the Gentiles, having all met together, they promulgated a divine law, giving it the form of a letter. By this sanction they liberated Christians from the bondage of formal observances, and all vain contention about these things; teaching them the path of true piety, and only prescribing such things as were conducive to its attainment. The epistle itself, which I shall here transcribe, is recorded in *The Acts of the Apostles*.[1] "The apostles and elders and brethren send greeting unto the brethren which are of the Gentiles in Antioch and Syria and Cilicia. Forasmuch as we have heard, that certain which went out from us have troubled you with words, subverting your souls, saying, Ye must be circumcised, and keep the law; to whom we gave no such commandment: it seemed good unto us, being assembled with one accord, to send chosen men unto you, with our beloved Barnabas and Paul, men that have hazarded their lives for the name of our Lord Jesus Christ. We have therefore sent Judas and Silas, who shall also tell you the same thing by mouth. For it

Canon, No. xvii., "He who has been twice married after Baptism . . . . cannot become a Bishop, Presbyter, or Deacon, or any other of the sacerdotal list."
[1] Acts xv. 23—29.

seemed good to the Holy Ghost and to us, to lay upon you
no greater burden than these necessary things: that ye abstain from meats offered to idols, and from blood, and from
things strangled, and from fornication; from which if ye
keep yourselves, ye shall do well. Fare ye well." These
things indeed pleased God: for the letter expressly says, "It
seemed good to the Holy Ghost to lay upon you no greater
burden than these necessary things." There are nevertheless
some who, disregarding these precepts, suppose all fornication
to be an indifferent matter; but contend about holy-days as
if their lives were at stake. Such persons contravene the
commands of God, and legislate for themselves, not respecting
the decree of the apostles: neither do they perceive that they
are themselves practising the contrary to those things which
God approved. We might easily have extended our discourse
respecting Easter, and have demonstrated that the Jews observe no exact rule either in the time or manner of celebrating
the paschal solemnity: and that the Samaritans, who are a
schism of the Jews, always celebrate this festival after the
equinox. But this subject would require a distinct and copious treatise: I shall therefore merely add, that those who
affect so much to imitate the Jews, and are so very anxious
about an accurate observance of types, ought to depart from
them in no particular. For if they have resolved on being
so correct, they must not only observe days and months, but
all other things also, which Christ (who was "made under
the law") did in the manner of the Jews; or which he unjustly suffered from them; or wrought typically for the good
of all men. Thus when he entered into a ship and taught:
when he ordered the Passover to be made ready in an upper
room: when he commanded an ass that was tied to be loosed:
when he proposed a man bearing a pitcher of water as a sign
to them for hastening their preparations for the Passover.
To be consistent, they must observe all these things, with an
infinite number of others of this nature which are recorded
in the Gospels. And yet those who suppose themselves to be
justified by keeping this feast, would think it absurd to observe any of these things in a bodily manner. No doctor, for
instance, ever dreams of going to preach from a ship—no person imagines it necessary to go up into an upper room, and
celebrate the Passover there—they never tie, and then loose

an ass again—and finally, no one enjoins another to carry a
pitcher of water, in order that the symbols might be fulfilled.
They have justly regarded such things as savouring rather of
Judaism than Christianity : for the Jews are more solicitous
about outward solemnities, than the obedience of the heart ;
and therefore are they under the curse, not discerning the
spiritual bearing of the Mosaic law, but resting in its types
and shadows. Those who favour the Jews admit the allegori-
cal meaning of these things ; and yet they pertinaciously contend about days and months, without applying to them a
similar sense : thus do they necessarily involve themselves
in a common condemnation with the Jews. But enough has
been said concerning these things. Let us now return to the
subject we were previously treating of, the subdivisions that
arose on the most trivial grounds among the schismatics, after
their separation from the Church. The Novatians, as I have
stated, were divided among themselves on account of the
feast of Easter, the controversy not being restricted to one
point only. For in the different provinces some took one view
of the question, and some another, disagreeing not only about
the month, but the days of the week also, and other unimportant matters ; in some places holding separate assemblies
because of it, in others uniting in mutual communion.

CHAP. XXIII.—FURTHER DISSENSIONS AMONG THE ARIANS
AT CONSTANTINOPLE.

BUT dissensions, arose among the Arians[1] also on this account. The contentious questions which were daily agitated
among them, led them to start the most presumptuous pro-
positions. For whereas it has been always believed in the
Church that God is the Father of the Son, the Word, it was
asked whether God could be called Father before the Son
had subsistence ? Thus from a denial of the main article of
faith, in asserting that the Word of God was not begotten of
the Father, but was created out of nothing, they deservedly
fell into absurd cavillings about a mere name. Dorotheus
therefore, whom they had sent for from Antioch, maintained

[1] See above, chap. xx.

that God neither was nor could be called Father before the Son existed. But Marinus, who had been summoned out of Thrace before Dorotheus, and was piqued at the superior deference which was paid to his rival, undertook to defend the contrary opinion. Their controversy respecting this term produced division, and each party held separate meetings. Those under Dorotheus retained their original places of assembly: but the followers of Marinus built distinct oratories for themselves, and asserted that the Father had always sustained that character, even when the Son was not. This section of the Arians was denominated Psathyrians, because one of the most zealous defenders of this opinion was Theoctistus, a Syrian by birth, and a cake-seller by trade. Selenas bishop of the Goths adopted the views of this party: he was of a mixed descent, a Goth by his father's side, and by his mother's a Phrygian, by which means he taught in the Church with great readiness in both these languages. This faction however soon quarrelled among themselves, Marinus disagreeing with Agapius, whom he himself had preferred to the bishopric of Ephesus. Their dispute was not about any point of religion, but they strove in narrow-mindedness about precedence, in which the Goths sided with Agapius. Wherefore many of the ecclesiastics under their jurisdiction, abominating the vain-glorious contest between these two, abandoned them both, and became adherents to the Homoousian faith. The Arians having continued thus divided among themselves during the space of thirty-five years, were reunited in the reign of Theodosius junior, under the consulate of Plintha the commander-in-chief of the army, the Psathyrians being prevailed on to desist from contention. They afterwards passed a resolution, giving it all the cogency of law, that the question which had led to their separation should never be mooted again. But this reconciliation extended no farther than Constantinople; for in other cities where any of these two parties were found, they persisted in their former separation.

CHAP. XXIV.—The eunomians divide into several
factions.

But neither did the Eunomians remain without dissensions:
for Eunomius[1] himself had long before this separated from Eudoxius, who ordained him bishop of Cyzicum, because that prelate refused to restore to communion his master Aëtius, who
had been ejected. But those who derived their name from him
were subsequently divided into several factions. For, first,
Theophronius a Cappadocian, who had been instructed in the
art of disputation by Eunomius, and had acquired a smatter-
ing of Aristotle's "Categories," and his "Book of Interpretation," having written some treatises which he entitled "On
the Exercise of the Mind," drew down upon himself the reprobation of his own sect, and was ejected as an apostate.
He afterwards held assemblies apart from them, and left behind him a heresy which bore his own name. Then Eutychius at Constantinople, from some absurd dispute, withdrew
from the Eunomians, and still continues to hold separate
meetings. The followers of Theophronius are denominated
Eunomiotheophronians; and those of Eutychius have the
appellation of Eunomieutychians. What those nonsensical
terms were about which they differed, I consider unworthy of
being recorded in this history, lest I should go into matters
foreign to my purpose. I shall merely observe that they
adulterated baptism: for instead of baptizing in the name of
the Trinity, they baptize into the death of Christ.[2] Among
the Macedonians also there was for some time a division,
when Eutropius a presbyter held separate assemblies, in consequence of a difference of opinion between him and Carterius. There are possibly in other cities sectarians which have
emanated from these: but living at Constantinople, where I
was born and educated, I propose to describe more particularly
what has taken place in that city; both because I have my-

[1] See above, b. iv. ch. vii. and xiii.
[2] Compare Canon Apost. l.: "If any Bishop or Presbyter does not
perform the one initiation with three immersions, but with one immersion
only into the death of the Lord, let him be deposed." So also Canon
Constant. vii.: "But the Eunomians, who baptize with one immersion
. . . . . . if they wish to be joined to the orthodox faith, we receive as heathens, and on the first day make them Christians."

self witnessed some of these transactions, and also because
the events which have there occurred are of pre-eminent importance, and are therefore more worthy of commemoration.
Let it however be understood that what I have here related
happened at different periods, and not at the same time.
Now if any one should be desirous of knowing the names of
the various sects, he may easily satisfy himself, by reading a
book entitled "Ancoratus," composed by Epiphanius bishop
of Cyprus: but I shall content myself with what I have
already stated. The public affairs were then thrown into
agitation from a cause I shall now refer to.

CHAP. XXV.—THE TYRANT EUGENIUS COMPASSES THE DEATH OF VALENTINIAN JUNIOR.

THERE was in the West a grammarian named Eugenius,
who after having for some time taught the Latin language,
left his school, and accepted an appointment at the palace,
being constituted chief secretary to the emperor. Possessing
a considerable degree of eloquence, and being on that account
treated with greater distinction than others, he was unable to
bear his good fortune with moderation. For associating with
himself Arbogastes, a native of Galatia Minor, a man of a
naturally ferocious and desperate character, who then had the
principal command of the army, he determined to usurp the
sovereignty. These two therefore agreed to murder the emperor Valentinian ; and having corrupted the eunuchs of the
imperial bed-chamber by the most tempting promises of promotion, they induced them to strangle the emperor in his
sleep. Eugenius immediately assumed the supreme authority
in the Western parts of the empire, and conducted himself
in such a manner as might be expected from a tyrant. When
the emperor Theodosius was made acquainted with these
things, he was exceedingly distressed, perceiving that his defeat of Maximus had only prepared the way for fresh troubles.
He however assembled his military forces, and having proclaimed his son Honorius Augustus, on the 10th of January,
in his own third consulate which he bore with Abundantius,
he again set out in great haste toward the Western parts,

leaving both his sons invested with imperial authority at
Constantinople. A very great number of the barbarians beyond the Danube volunteered their services against the
tyrant, and followed him in this expedition. After a rapid
march he arrived in the Gallias with a numerous army,
where Eugenius awaited him, also at the head of an immense
body of troops. They came to an engagement near the river
Frigidus, which is about thirty-six miles distant from Aquileia. In that part of the battle where the Romans fought
against their own countrymen, the conflict was doubtful: but
where the barbarian auxiliaries of the emperor Theodosius
were engaged, the forces of Eugenius had greatly the advantage. When the emperor saw the terrible slaughter made by
the enemy among the barbarians, he cast himself in great
agony upon the ground, and invoked the help of God in this
emergency: nor was his request unheeded; for Bacurius his
principal officer, inspired with sudden and extraordinary
ardour, rushed with his vanguard to the part where the barbarians were hardest pressed, broke through the ranks of the
enemy, and put to flight those who a little before were themselves engaged in pursuit. Another marvellous circumstance
also occurred. A violent wind suddenly arose, which retorted
upon themselves the darts cast by the soldiers of Eugenius,
and at the same time drove those hurled by the imperial forces
with increased impetus against their adversaries. So prevalent
was the emperor's prayer. The success of the struggle being
in this way turned, the tyrant threw himself at the emperor's
feet, and begged that his life might be spared: but the soldiery
beheaded him on the spot, as he lay a prostrate suppliant, on
the 6th of September, in the third consulate of Arcadius, and
the second of Honorius. Arbogastes, who had been the chief
cause of so much mischief, having continued his flight for two
days after the battle, and seeing no chance of escape, despatched himself with his own sword.

CHAP. XXVI.—DEATH OF THE EMPEROR THEODOSIUS.

THE anxiety and fatigues connected with this war threw
the emperor Theodosius into an ill state of health; and believ-

ing the disease which had attacked him would be mortal, he became more concerned about the public affairs than his own life, revolving in his mind the calamities in which the people are often involved after the death of their sovereign. He therefore hastily summoned his son Honorius from Constantinople, being principally desirous of setting in order the state of things in the Western parts of the empire. After his son's arrival at Milan, he seemed to recover a little, and gave directions for the celebration of the games of the Hippodrome on account of his victory. Before dinner he was pretty well, and a spectator of the sports; but after he had dined he became too ill to return to them, and sent his son to preside in his stead. On the following night he died, being the 17th of January, under the consulate of Olybrius and Probus, in the first year of the two hundred and ninety-fourth Olympiad. The emperor Theodosius lived sixty years, and reigned sixteen. This Book therefore comprehends the transactions of sixteen years and eight months.

BOOK VI.

THE PREFACE.

THE commission with which you charged me, O holy man of God, Theodore, I have executed in the five foregoing Books; in which, to the best of my ability, I have comprised the history of the Church from the time of Constantine. You will perceive that I have been by no means studious of style; for I consider that too great fastidiousness about elegance of expression might defeat the object I had in view.[1] But even supposing my purpose could still have been accomplished, I was wholly precluded from the exercise of that discretionary power of which ancient historians seem to have so largely availed themselves, whereby any one of them imagined himself quite at liberty to amplify or curtail matters of fact.

[1] See preface to the preceding book.

Moreover refined composition will by no means be edifying to simple-minded and unlearned men, who are intent merely on knowing what was really transacted, and pay not the least regard to beauty of diction.   In order therefore to render my production not unprofitable to both classes of readers,—to the learned on the one hand, whom no elaboration of language could satisfy to rank it with the magniloquence of the writers of antiquity, and to the unlearned on the other, whose understandings would be clouded by a parade of words,—I have purposely adopted a style, divested indeed of all affectation of sublimity, but at the same time clear and perspicuous.

Before however entering on our sixth Book, I must premise this, that in undertaking to detail the events of our own age I am apprehensive of advancing such things as may be unpalatable to many : either because, according to the proverb, " Truth is bitter ; " or on account of my not mentioning with encomium the names of those whom some may love ; or from my not lauding their actions.   The zealots of our Churches will condemn me for not calling the bishops " Most dear to God," " Most holy," and such like.   Others will be litigious because I do not bestow the appellations "Most divine," and "Lords," on the emperors, nor apply to them such other epithets as they are commonly assigned.   But since I could easily prove from the testimony of ancient authors,[1] that among them servants were accustomed to address their masters simply by name, without reference to their dignity or titles, on account of the pressure of business, I shall in like manner obey the laws of history, which demand a simple and faithful narration, unobscured by a veil of any kind.   My course will therefore be to record accurately what I have either myself seen, or have been able to ascertain from actual observers ; having tested the truth with unsparing labour, and by every means I could possibly command, where there was the least discrepancy of statement among the many parties consulted who professed to be intimately acquainted with these things.

[1] The comic writers, as Menander, Plautus, and Terence, for instance.

CHAP. I.—THEODOSIUS'S TWO SONS DIVIDE THE EMPIRE. RU-
FINUS IS SLAIN AT THE FEET OF ARCADIUS.

AFTER the death of the emperor Theodosius, his two sons.
undertook the administration of the Roman empire, Arcadius
having the government of the East, and Honorius of the West.[1]
At that time Damasus presided over the Church at imperial
Rome, and Theophilus that of Alexandria; John was bishop
of Jerusalem, and Flavian of Antioch; while the episcopal
chair at Constantinople or New Rome was filled by Nectarius,
as we mentioned in the foregoing Book. The body of the emperor Theodosius was taken to Constantinople on the 8th of
November in the same consulate, and was honourably interred
by his son Arcadius with the usual funeral solemnities.[2] On
the 28th day of the same month the army also arrived, which
had served under the emperor Theodosius in the war against
the tyrant Eugenius. When therefore, according to custom,
the emperor Arcadius met the army without the gates, the
soldiery slew Rufinus the Prætorian prefect. For he was
suspected of aspiring to the sovereignty, and of having invited
into the Roman territories the Huns, a barbarous nation, who
had already ravaged Armenia, and were then making preda-
tory incursions into other provinces of the East. On the very
day on which Rufinus was killed, Marcian bishop of the Novatians died, and was succeeded in the episcopate by Sisinnius, of whom we have already spoken.[3]

CHAP. II.—DEATH OF NECTARIUS AND ORDINATION OF JOHN.

A SHORT time after Nectarius[4] also, bishop of Constantinople died, on the 27th of September, under the consulate of
Cæsarius and Atticus. A contest thereupon immediately
arose respecting the appointment of a successor, some proposing one person, and some another: at length however it was

---

[1] See Gibbon, Decl. and Fall, chap. xxix.
[2] On the funeral ceremonies of the early Church, see Bingham's Christ.
Antiq. b. xxiii. ch. i. ii. &c.
[3] See b. v. ch. xxi.   [4] See b. v. ch. viii.

determined to send for John,[1] a presbyter of the Church at Antioch, who was very celebrated for his learning and eloquence.
By the general consent therefore of both the clergy and laity,
he was summoned to Constantinople by the emperor Arcadius;
and to render the ordination more authoritative and imposing,
several prelates were requested to be present, among whom
also was Theophilus bishop of Alexandria. This person did
everything he could to detract from John's reputation, being
desirous of promoting to that see Isidore, a presbyter of his
own Church, to whom he was greatly attached, on account of
a very delicate and perilous affair which Isidore had undertaken to serve his interests. The nature of this obligation I
shall now unfold. While the emperor Theodosius was preparing to attack the tyrant Maximus, Theophilus sent Isidore
with gifts and letters, enjoining him to present them to him
who should become the victor. In accordance with these injunctions Isidore, on his arrival at Rome, awaited there the
event of the war. But this business did not long remain a
secret; for a reader who accompanied him privately possessed
himself of the letters; upon which Isidore in great alarm returned to Alexandria. This was the reason why Theophilus
so warmly favoured Isidore. The court however gave the
preference to John: and when many had revived the accusations against Theophilus, and prepared for presentation to the
bishops then convened, memorials of various charges, Eutropius, the chief officer of the imperial bed-chamber, collected
these documents, and showed them to Theophilus, bidding
him choose between ordaining John, and undergoing a trial
on the charges made against him. Theophilus, terrified at
this alternative, consented to ordain John; who was invested
with the episcopal dignity on the 26th of February, under
the following consulate, which the emperor Honorius celebrated with public games at Rome, and Eutychian, then Prætorian prefect, at Constantinople. But since this John is
famous, both for the writings he has left, and the many
troubles he fell into, it is not proper that I should pass over
his affairs in silence: I shall therefore relate as compendiously
as possible of what extraction he was, with the particulars of
his elevation to the episcopate, and the means by which he

---

[1] Better known under his surname of Chrysostom, i. e. *Golden-mouth.*

was subsequently degraded; and finally, why he was more honoured after his death, than he had been during his life.

CHAP. III.—BIRTH AND EDUCATION OF JOHN BISHOP OF CONSTANTINOPLE.[1]

JOHN was born at Antioch in Syria-Cœle, of a noble family in that country, his father's name being Secundus, and that of his mother Anthusa. He studied rhetoric under Libanius the sophist, and philosophy under Andragathius. When he had already prepared himself for the practice of *Civil Law*, reflecting on the restless and unjust course of those who devote themselves to the practice of the Forensic Courts, he re-
156 solved to adopt a more tranquil mode of life. Following therefore the example of Evagrius, who had been educated under the same masters, and had some time before retired from the tumult of public business, he laid aside his legal habit, and applied his mind to the reading of the sacred Scriptures, frequenting the church with great assiduity. He moreover induced Theodore and Maximus, who had been his fellow-students under Libanius the sophist, to forsake a profession whose primary object was gain, and embrace pursuits of greater simplicity. Of these two persons, Theodore afterwards became bishop of Mopsuestia in Cilicia, and Maximus of Seleucia in Isauria. Being at that time ardent aspirants after perfection, they entered upon the ascetic
157 life, under the guidance of Diodorus and Carterius, who then presided over the monasteries. The former of these was subsequently elevated to the see of Tarsus, and wrote many treatises, in which he limited his expositions to the literal sense of Scripture, without attempting to explain that which was mystical.[2] But we must return to John, who was then living on the most intimate terms with Basil, at that time constituted a

---

[1] With this chap. compare Sozomen, b. viii. ch. viii.
[2] Θεωρίας. Literally, "contemplation;" here taken for the contemplative life, as opposed to the practical. It will hardly be necessary to adduce from Aristotle or Plato instances of the term in this sense, and of the kindred terms, θεωρεῖν, ἡ θεωρητική, as opposed to the lower or practical life (βιος πρακτικός).

deacon by Meletius, but afterwards ordained bishop of Cæsarea in Cappadocia. He was appointed[1] reader in the Church at Antioch by Zeno the bishop on his return from Jerusalem: and while he continued in that capacity, he composed a book against the Jews. Meletius having not long after conferred on him the rank of deacon, he produced his work "On the Priesthood," and those " Against Stagirius"; and moreover those also " On the Incomprehensibility of the Divine Nature," and "On the Women[2] who lived with the Ecclesiastics." After the death of Meletius at Constantinople, whither he had gone on account of Gregory of Nazianzen's ordination, John withdrew from the Meletians, without entering into communion with Paulinus, and spent three whole years in retirement. When Paulinus was dead, he was ordained a presbyter by Evagrius the successor of Paulinus. Such is a brief outline of John's career previous to his call to the episcopal office. It is said that his zeal for temperance rendered him stern and severe; and one of his early friends has admitted that in his youth he manifested a proneness to irritability, rather than to forbearance. Because of the rectitude of his life, he was free from anxiety about the future, and his simplicity of character rendered him open and ingenuous; nevertheless the liberty of speech he allowed himself was offensive to very many. In public teaching, the great end he proposed was the reformation of the morals of his auditors; but in private conversation he was frequently thought haughty and assuming by those who did not know him.

---

[1] ἀναγνώστης, "lector." On the order of "Readers" in the early Church, see Bingham, Christ. Antiq. b. ii. chap. v.

[2] Συνεισάκτοι. These were women who lived in the houses of the clergy as sisters, and exercised themselves in works of piety and charity. At a very early period, however, scandal seems to have arisen from this practice, and strong measures were repeatedly adopted by the Church for the suppression of the Syneisactæ. See Bingham, Christ. Antiq. b. xvii. ch. v. sect. 20; and Euseb. vii. c. xxx., where Paul of Samosata is deposed, among other reasons, for keeping these sisters in his house. See also the 3rd Canon of the Council of Nice.

CHAP. IV.—John renders himself odious to his clergy.
OF SERAPION.

Such being John's disposition and manners, he was led to conduct himself toward his clergy, after his promotion to the episcopate, with a measure of austerity beyond what they could bear: but his intention was in this way to discountenance any laxness of moral discipline among them. Having thus chafed the temper of the ecclesiastics under him, and incurred their displeasure, many of them stood aloof from him as a passionate man, and others became his bitter enemies. Serapion, whom he had ordained deacon, incited him to alienate their minds still more from him; and once in presence of the whole assembled clergy he cried out with a loud voice to the bishop —"You will never be able to govern these men, my lord, unless you visit them all with a rod." This speech of his excited a general feeling of animosity against the bishop, who not long after expelled many of them from the Church, some for one cause, and some for another. Those who were thus dealt with, as it usually happens when governors adopt such violent measures, formed a combination, and inveighed against him to the people. What contributed greatly to gain credence for these complaints was the bishop's always eating alone, and never accepting an invitation to a feast. His reasons for thus acting no one knew with any certainty, but some persons in justification of his conduct state that he had a very delicate stomach, and weak digestion, which obliged him to be careful in his diet; while others impute his refusal to eat in company with any one to his rigid and habitual abstinence. Whatever the real motive may have been, the circumstance itself was made a serious ground of accusation by his calumniators. The people nevertheless continued to regard him with love and veneration, on account of his valuable discourses in the Church, and therefore those who sought to traduce him, only brought themselves into contempt. How eloquent, convincing, and persuasive his sermons were, both those which were published by himself, and such as were noted down by shorthand writers as he delivered them, we need not stay to declare; but those who desire to form an adequate idea of them, must read for themselves, and will thereby derive both pleasure and profit.

[SOCRATES.]   x

CHAP. V.—JOHN DRAWS DOWN UPON HIMSELF THE DISPLEA-
SURE OF MANY PERSONS OF RANK AND POWER.   OF THE
EUNUCH EUTROPIUS.

As long as John attacked the clergy only, the machinations
of his enemies were utterly powerless; but when he proceeded to rebuke the nobles also with his characteristic
vehemence, the tide of unpopularity began to set against
him with far greater impetus, and the stories which were
told to his disparagement found many attentive listeners.
This growing prejudice was not a little increased by an
oration which he pronounced at that time against Eutropius,
the chief eunuch of the imperial bed-chamber, and the first
of all eunuchs that was admitted to the dignity of consul.
Desiring to inflict vengeance on certain persons who had
taken refuge in the churches, he induced the emperor to
make a law excluding delinquents from the privilege of
sanctuary, and authorizing the seizure of those who had
sought the shelter of the sacred edifices.[1]   But its author was
punished for this almost immediately; for scarcely had the
law been promulgated, before Eutropius himself, having incurred the displeasure of the emperor, fled for protection to
the church.   The bishop therefore, while Eutropius trembling
with fear lay under the table of the altar, mounting the pulpit 158
from which he was accustomed to address the people in order
to be the more distinctly heard, uttered the severest invective
against him: an act that excited general disgust, as it seemed
not only to deny compassion to the wretched, but to add insult
to cruelty.   By the emperor's order however, Eutropius,
though bearing the consulate, was decapitated, and his name
effaced from the list of consuls, that of Theodore his colleague
being alone suffered to remain as in office for that year.   John
is said to have afterwards used the same licence towards
Gaïnas, who was then commander-in-chief of the army;
treating him with excessive rudeness, because he had presumed to request the emperor to assign to the Arians, with
whom he agreed in sentiment, one of the churches within the
city.   Many others also of the higher orders, for a variety of
causes, were censured by him with the same unceremonious

[1] On the use of churches as asylums of refuge, see Bingham, viii. xi.

freedom, so that by these means he created many powerful
adversaries. Theophilus bishop of Alexandria had been
plotting his overthrow from the moment of his having been
compelled to ordain him; and concerted measures for this
purpose in secret, both with the friends who were around
him, as well as by letter with such as were at a distance. It
was not so much the boldness with which John lashed whatever was obnoxious to him, that affected Theophilus, as his
own failure to please his favourite presbyter Isidore in the
episcopal chair of Constantinople. Such was the state of
John's affairs at that time, mischief having thus threatened
him at the very commencement of his episcopate. But we
shall enter into these things more at large as we proceed.

CHAP. VI.—GAÏNAS THE GOTH ATTEMPTS TO USURP THE SO-
VEREIGN POWER, AND AFTER FILLING CONSTANTINOPLE WITH
DISORDER, IS SLAIN.

I SHALL now refer to some memorable circumstances that
occurred at that period, in which it will be seen how Divine
Providence interposed by extraordinary agencies for the preservation of the city and Roman empire from the utmost peril.
Gaïnas was a barbarian by extraction, who after becoming a
Roman subject, had engaged in military service, and risen by
degrees from one rank to another, until he was at length appointed generalissimo both of the Roman horse and foot.
When he had attained this lofty position, his ambition knew
no bounds short of rendering himself master of the Roman
empire. To accomplish this he sent for the Goths out of their
own country, and gave the principal commissions in the army
to his relations. Then when Tribigildus, one of his kinsmen
who had the command of the forces in Phrygia, had at the
instigation of Gaïnas broken out into open revolt, and was
filling that country with confusion and dismay, he took care
that the emperor Arcadius, who had not the slightest suspicion
of his treasonable designs, should depute him to settle matters
in the disturbed province. Gaïnas therefore immediately set
out, at the head of an immense number of the barbarous Goths,
on this pretended expedition against Tribigildus, but with the
x 2

real intention of establishng his own unjust domination. On reaching Phrygia he began to subvert everything; so that the Romans were suddenly thrown into great consternation, not only on account of the vast barbarian force which Gaïnas had at his command, but also lest the most fertile and opulent regions of the East should be laid desolate. In this emergency the emperor acted with much prudence, seeking to arrest the course of the traitor by address : he accordingly sent him an embassy with instructions to appease him for the present by every kind of concession. Gaïnas having demanded that Saturninus and Aurelian, two of the most distinguished of the senatorial order, and men of consular dignity, whom he knew to be unfavourable to his pretensions, should be delivered up to him as hostages, the emperor most unwillingly yielded to the exigency of the crisis ; and these two magnanimous personages prepared to die for the public good, and nobly submitted themselves to the emperor's disposal. They therefore proceeded towards the barbarian, to a place called the Hippodrome, some distance from Chalcedon, resolved to endure whatever he might be disposed to inflict ; but, however, they suffered no harm. The tyrant, simulating dissatisfaction, advanced to Chalcedon, whither the emperor Arcadius also went to meet him. Both then entered the church where the body of the martyr Euphemius is deposited, and there entered into a mutual pledge on oath that neither would plot against the other. The emperor indeed kept his engagement, having a religious regard to an oath, and being on that account beloved of God. But Gaïnas soon violated it, and instead of abandoning his purpose, was intent on carnage, plunder, and conflagration, not only at Constantinople, but also throughout the whole extent of the Roman empire, if he could by any means carry it into effect. The city was quite inundated by the barbarians, and the citizens were reduced to a condition almost like that of captives. Moreover a comet of prodigious magnitude, reaching from heaven even to the earth, such as was never before seen, presaged the danger that impended over it.[1] Gaïnas first most shamelessly attempted to make a seizure of the silver publicly exposed for sale in the shops : but when the proprietors, forewarned by report of his intention, abstain-

[1] Comp. Virg. Georg. i. 488, "Nec diri toties arsère cometæ." Comp. Æn. x. 272—274.

ed from exposing it on their counters, his thoughts were di-
verted to another object, which was to send an immense body
of barbarians at night to burn down the palace. Then indeed
God distinctly manifested his providential care over the city :
for a multitude of angels appeared to the rebels, in the form
of armed men of gigantic stature, whom the barbarians imagining to be a large army of brave troops, turned away from
with terror and amazement. When this was reported to
Gaïnas, it seemed to him quite incredible; for he knew that
the greatest part of the Roman army was at a distance, dispersed as a garrison over the Eastern cities. He sent therefore others for several successive nights, who constantly returned with the same statement, for the angels always presented
themselves in the same manner; whereupon he determined to
be himself a spectator of this prodigy. Then supposing what
he saw to be really a body of soldiers, who concealed themselves by day, and baffled his designs by night, he desisted
from his attempt, and took another resolution, which he conceived would be detrimental to the Romans; but the event
proved it to be greatly to their advantage. Pretending to be
under demoniacal possession, he went forth as if for prayer to
the church of St. John the Apostle, which is seven miles distant from the city. The barbarians who accompanied him
carried out arms with them, concealed in casks and other
specious coverings; which when the soldiers who guarded the
city gates detected, and would not suffer to pass, the barbarians put them to the sword. A fearful tumult thence arose
in the city, and death seemed to threaten every one; nevertheless the city continued secure at that time, its gates being
everywhere well defended. The emperor instantly proclaimed
Gaïnas a public enemy, and ordered that all the Goths who
remained shut up in Constantinople should be slain. Accordingly the day after the guards of the gates had been killed,
the Romans attacked the barbarians within the walls near the
church of the Goths, for thither such of them as had been left
in the city had betaken themselves; and after destroying a
great number of them, they set the church on fire, and burnt
it to the ground. Gaïnas being informed of the slaughter
of those of his party who were unable to get out of the city,
and perceiving the failure of all his artifices, left St. John's
church, and advanced rapidly towards Thrace. On reaching

the Chersonese he endeavoured to pass over from thence and take Lampsacus, in order that from that place he might make himself master of the Eastern parts.   As the emperor had immediately despatched forces in pursuit both by land and by sea, another miraculous interposition of Divine Providence occurred.   For while the barbarians, destitute of ships, were attempting to cross on rafts, and in vessels hastily put together, suddenly the Roman fleet appeared, and the west wind began to blow hard.   This afforded an easy passage to the Romans; but the barbarians with their horses, tossed up and down in their frail barks by the violence of the gale, were at length overwhelmed by the waves, and many of them also were destroyed by the Romans.   In this passage an incredible number of barbarians perished; but Gaïnas escaped thence and fled into Thrace, where he fell in with another body of the Roman forces, by whom he was slain, together with the Goths that attended him.   Let this cursory notice of Gaïnas suffice here.   Those who may desire more minute details of the circumstances of that war, should read "The Gaïnea" of Eusebius Scholasticus, who was at that time an auditor of [159] Troilus the sophist; and having been a spectator of the war, related the events of it in an heroic poem consisting of four books, which acquired for him great celebrity while the recollection of these things was fresh.   The poet Ammonius also has recently composed another description in verse of the same transactions, which he recited before the emperor in the sixteenth consulate of Theodosius junior, which he bore with Faustus.   This war was terminated under the consulate of Stilicho and Aurelian.   In the year following, Fravitus, a Goth by extraction, was honoured with the dignity of consul, to reward the fidelity and attachment he had evinced toward the Romans, and the important services he had rendered them in this very war.   On the 10th of April in that year there was a son born to the emperor Arcadius, Theodosius *the Good*. But while the affairs of the state were thus troubled, the dignitaries of the Church refrained not in the least from their disgraceful cabals against each other, to the great reproach of the Christian religion; for they were incited to tumult and reciprocal abuse by a source of mischief which originated in Egypt in the following manner.

CHAP. VII.—Dissension between Theophilus bishop of Alexandria and the monks.—Condemnation of Origen's books.

The question had been started a little before, whether God has a corporeal existence, and the form of man; or whether he is incorporeal, and without either the human or any other bodily shape? From this question arose strifes and contentions among a very great number of persons, some favouring one opinion on the subject, and others patronizing the opposite. The major part of the more simple ascetics asserted that God is corporeal, and has a human figure: but most others condemned their judgment, and contended that God is incorporeal, and void of all form whatever. This was the view taken by Theophilus bishop of Alexandria, who in the church before all the people inveighed against those who attributed to God a human form, expressly teaching that the Divine Being is wholly incorporeal. When the Egyptian ascetics were apprized of this, they left their monasteries and came to Alexandria; where they excited a tumult against the bishop, accusing him of impiety, and threatening to put him to death. Theophilus, aware of his danger, after some consideration had recourse to this expedient to extricate himself from it. Going to the monks, he in a conciliatory tone thus addressed them: "In seeing you, I behold the face of God." The fury of these men being a little moderated by this expression, they replied: "If you really admit that God's countenance is such as ours, anathematize Origen's book;[1] for some have drawn arguments from them in contrariety to our opinion. If you refuse to do this, expect to be treated by us as an impious person, and the enemy of God." "Do not be angry with me," said Theophilus, "and I will readily do what you require: for I myself also disapprove of Origen's works, and consider those who countenance them deserving of censure." Thus he succeeded in appeasing the monks at that time; and probably the whole matter would have been set at rest, had it not been for another circumstance which

---

[1] See Hieron. adv. Ruf. ii. vol. iv. p. 403. The opinions of Origen were formally condemned again in the second general council of Constantinople, A. D. 553.

happened immediately after. The monasteries in Egypt were under the superintendence of four devout persons named Dioscorus, Ammonius, Eusebius, and Euthymius : these men were brothers, and had the appellation of *the Long Monks* given them on account of their stature.   They were moreover no less distinguished for the sanctity of their lives than the extent of their erudition, and for these reasons their reputation was very high at Alexandria.   Theophilus in particular, the prelate of that city, loved and honoured them exceedingly : insomuch that he constituted Dioscorus, one of them, bishop of Hermopolis against his will, having forcibly drawn him from his retreat.   Two of the others he entreated to continue with him, and with difficulty prevailed upon them to do so, by the exercise of his episcopal authority : when therefore he had invested them with the clerical office, he committed to their charge the management of ecclesiastical affairs.   They, constrained by necessity, performed the duties thus imposed on them with credit to themselves ; nevertheless they felt severely the privation of philosophical pursuits, and such ascetic exercises as their new position rendered impracticable.   When however, in process of time, they observed the bishop to be devoted to gain, and greedily intent on the acquisition of wealth, believing this example injurious to their own souls, they refused to remain with him any longer, declaring that they loved solitude, and greatly preferred it to living in the city.   As long as he was ignorant of the true motive for their departure, he earnestly begged them not to leave him ; but when he perceived that they were dissatisfied with his conduct, he became excessively irritated, and threatened to do them all kinds of mischief.   Regardless of his menaces, they retired into the desert ; upon which Theophilus, who was evidently of a hasty and malignant temperament, raised a great clamour against them, and set in motion every contrivance likely to do them injury.   After this he viewed with jealous dislike their brother Dioscorus also, bishop of Hermopolis ; being extremely annoyed at the esteem and veneration in which he was held by the ascetics.   Aware however that these persons would be perfectly safe from his malevolence unless he could alienate the minds of the monks from them, he used this artifice to effect it.   He well knew that Dioscorus and his brothers, in their theological discussions with him, had often maintained that the Deity was incorporeal, and by no means had a human form; because, they argued, such a constitution would involve the necessary accompaniment of human passions, as Origen and other ancient writers have demonstrated. Now although Theophilus entertained the very same opinion respecting the Divine nature, yet to gratify his vindictive feelings, he did not hesitate to impugn what he and they had rightly taught: and by this means he succeeded in imposing upon the credulity of the sincere but ignorant monks, the greater part of whom were quite illiterate men. Sending letters to the monasteries in the desert, he advises them not to give heed either to Discorus or his brothers, inasmuch as they affirmed that God had not a body. "Whereas," says he, "the sacred Scripture testifies that God has eyes, ears, hands, and feet, as men have; the partisans of Discorus, being followers of Origen, introduce the blasphemous dogma that God has neither eyes, ears, feet, nor hands." Abusing the simplicity of these monks by this sophism, he stirred up a hot dissension among them. Such as had a cultivated mind indeed were not beguiled by this plausibility, and therefore still adhered to Discorus and Origen; but the more ignorant, who greatly exceeded the others in number, inflamed by an ardent zeal without knowledge, immediately raised an outcry against their brethren. A division being thus made, both parties branded each other as impious; the one side being reproachfully termed "Origenists," and the other "Anthropomorphitæ,"[1] between whom violent altercation arose, and an inextinguishable war. Theophilus, on receiving intimation of the success of his device, went to Nitra, where the monasteries are, accompanied by a multitude of persons, and armed the monks against Discorus and his brethren; who being in danger of losing their lives, made their escape with great difficulty. John bishop of Constantinople was ignorant meanwhile of the things that were doing in Egypt; but the eloquence of his discourses rendered him increasingly celebrated. He first enlarged the prayers contained in the nocturnal hymns, for the reason I am about to assign.

---

[1] For an account of this heretical sect, see Gibbon's Decl. and Fall, chap. xlvii.

CHAP. VIII.—The Arians and Homoousians practise nocturnal alternative hymns, a species of composition
ascribed to the martyr Ignatius, surnamed Theopho-
rus.[1] Conflict between the two parties.

The Arians, as we have said, held their meetings without
the city. As often therefore as the festal days occurred, that
is to say, the sabbath and Lord's-day[2] of each week, on which
assemblies are usually held in the churches, they congregated
within the city gates about the public piazzas, and sang responsive verses adapted to the Arian heresy. This they did
during the greater part of the night: and again in the morning, chanting the same responsive compositions, they paraded
through the midst of the city, and so passed out of the gates
to go to their places of assembly. But since they incessantly
made use of insulting expressions in relation to the Homoousians, often singing such words as these: "Where are they
that say three things are but one power?"—John, fearing
lest any of the more simple should be drawn away from the
Church by such kind of hymns, opposed to them some of his
own people, that they also, employing themselves in chanting
nocturnal hymns, might obscure the effort of the Arians, and
confirm his own party in the profession of their faith. John's
aim indeed seemed to be good, but it issued in tumult and
danger. For as the Homoousians performed their nocturnal
hymns with greater display, John having invented silver
crosses for them on which lighted wax-tapers were carried,
provided at the expense of the empress Eudoxia, the Arians,
who were very numerous, and fired with envy, resolved to
revenge themselves by a desperate attack upon their rivals.
This they were the more ready to do from the remembrance of
their own recent domination, and the contempt with which
they regarded their adversaries. Without delay therefore, on
one of these nights, they assailed the Homoousians; when

---

[1] This word, if written Θεοφόρος, denotes *a divine person, one whose
soul is full of God:* but Θεόφορος has a passive import, and implies *one
borne or carried by God.* This title is said to have been conferred on Ignatius, from his being the very child whom our Saviour *took up·in his
arms,* and set in the midst of his disciples. (Mark ix. 36.)
[2] τό τε σάββατον καὶ ἡ κυριακή. See Bingham, b. xx. chap. ii.

Briso, one of the eunuchs of the empress, who was leading the chanters of these hymns, was wounded by a stone in the forehead, and some of the people on both sides were killed. The emperor, incensed at this catastrophe, forbad the Arians to chant their hymns any more in public. We must however make some allusion to the origin of this custom in the Church 160 of singing hymns antiphonally. Ignatius, third bishop of Antioch in Syria from the apostle Peter, who also had conversed familiarly with the apostles themselves, saw a vision of angels hymning in alternate chants the Holy Trinity: after which he introduced the mode of singing he had observed in the vision into the Antiochian Church, whence it was transmitted by tradition to all the other Churches. Such is the account we have received in relation to these antiphonal hymns.[1]

CHAP. IX.—THEOPHILUS BISHOP OF ALEXANDRIA ENDEAVOURS TO DEPOSE JOHN BISHOP OF CONSTANTINOPLE.

NOT long after this, the monks, together with Discorus and his brothers, came from the desert to Constantinople. Isidore was also with them, once the most intimate friend of the bishop Theophilus, but then become his bitterest enemy, because of what I am about to mention. Theophilus being irritated against Peter, at that time the archpresbyter[2] of the 161 Alexandrian Church, determined to eject him; and as the ground of expulsion, he charged him with having admitted to a participation of the sacred mysteries, a woman of the Manichæan sect, before she had renounced her heresy. Peter in his defence declared, that not only had the errors of this woman been previously abjured, but that the bishop himself had sanctioned her admission to the eucharist: upon which Theophilus in a great rage, as if he had been grievously calumniated, affirmed that he was altogether unacquainted with the circumstance. To substantiate his statement, Peter summoned Isidore as one who could testify to the facts of the case. Isidore was then at Rome, on a mission from Theo-

[1] See Bingham's Christ. Antiq. b. xiv. ch. i.
[2] For an account of the duties belonging to this office, see Bingham's Christ. Antiq. b. ii. ch. xix. sect. 18.

philus to Damasus the prelate of the imperial city, for the
purpose of effecting a reconciliation between him and Flavian
bishop of Antioch, from whom the adherents of Meletius had
separated in detestation of his perjury, as we have already
observed.[1] When Isidore had returned from Rome, and was
cited as a witness by Peter, he deposed that the woman was
received by consent of the bishop, who himself had administered the communion to her : upon which Theophilus immediately
ejected them both.   Isidore therefore went to Constantinople
with Discorus and his brethren, in order to submit to the
cognizance of the emperor, and John the bishop, the injustice
and violence with which Theophilus had treated them.   John,
on being informed of their business, gave them all an honourable reception ; and admitting them at once to communion of
the prayers, only postponed their communion of the sacred
mysteries until their affairs should be examined into.   Whilst
matters were in this posture, a false report was carried to
Theophilus, that John had both admitted them to a participation
of the mysteries, and also taken them under his protection ;
wherefore he resolved not only to be revenged on Isidore and
Discorus, but also if possible to cast John out of his episcopal
chair. With this design he wrote to all the bishops of the
various cities, and concealing his real motive, ostensibly condemned therein the books of Origen merely : forgetting that
Athanasius, who preceded him long before, had, in confirmation
of his own faith, frequently appealed to the testimony and
authority of Origen's writings, in his orations against the
Arians.

CHAP. X.—Epiphanius bishop of cyprus convenes a synod
to condemn the books of origen.

He moreover renewed his friendship with Epiphanius
bishop of Constantia in Cyprus, with whom he had formerly
been at variance, having accused that prelate of entertaining
· low thoughts of God, by supposing him to have a human form.
Now although Theophilus was really unchanged in sentiment,
and had thus denounced the Anthropomorphite error, yet on
account of his hatred of others, he openly denied his own con-
[1] See above, b. v. ch. xv.

victions ; for he now professed to agree in opinion with Epiphanius, as if he had altered his mind.   He then urged him
by letter to convene a synod of the bishops in Cyprus, in
order to condemn the writings of Origen.   Epiphanius being
a person more eminent for his extraordinary piety than intelligence, was easily influenced by the crafty representations of
Theophilus : having therefore assembled a council of the bishops in that island, he caused a prohibition to be therein made
162 of the reading of Origen's works.   He also wrote to John
bishop of Constantinople, exhorting him to abstain from the
further study of Origen's books, and to convoke a synod for
decreeing the same thing as he had done.   When Theophilus
had in this ‚way wrought upon Epiphanius, whose devout character gave great weight to his proceedings, seeing his design
prosper according to his wish, he became more confident, and
himself also assembled a great number of bishops.   In that
convention, pursuing the same course as Epiphanius, he caused
a like sentence of condemnation to be pronounced on the
writings of Origen, who had been dead nearly two hundred
years : although this indeed was not his primary object, but
subsidiary to his purpose of revenge on Discorus and his
brethren.   John paid but little attention to the communications of Epiphanius or Theophilus, being intent on his own
ecclesiastical duties ; and while his celebrity as a preacher increased more and more, he wholly disregarded the plots which
were laid against him.   But as soon as it became apparent to
everybody that Theophilus was endeavouring to divest John
of his bishopric, then all those who had any ill-will against
John, combined in calumniating him.   Many of the clergy,
as well as of the persons of influence about the court, believing
that an opportunity was now afforded them of punishing John;
exerted themselves to procure the convocation of a grand
synod at Constantinople, despatching letters and messengers
in all directions for that purpose.

CHAP. XI.—OF SEVERIAN AND ANTIOCHUS : THEIR
DISAGREEMENT WITH JOHN.

THE odium against John Chrysostom was considerably increased by another cause.   Two bishops flourished at that time,

Syrians by birth, named Severian and Antiochus; the former of whom presided over the Church at Gabali, a city of Syria, the latter over that of Ptolemaïs in Phœnicia. They were both renowned for their eloquence; but although Severian was a very learned man, his pronunciation of Greek was defective, from his retaining somewhat of the Syriac accent. Antiochus came first to Constantinople, where he preached in the churches for some time with great zeal and ability; and having thereby amassed a large sum of money, he returned to his own Church. Severian hearing that Antiochus had enriched himself by his visit to Constantinople, determined to follow his example: he therefore exercised himself for the occasion, and having prepared a quantity of sermons, set out for the imperial city. He was most kindly received by John, whom at first he soothed and flattered, and was beloved and honoured by him; meanwhile his discourses gained him great celebrity, so that he attracted the notice of many persons of rank, and even of the emperor himself. It happened at that time that the bishop of Ephesus died, on which account John was obliged to go thither for the purpose of ordaining a successor. On his arrival at that city, finding the people divided in their choice, some proposing one person, and some another, and perceiving from the pertinacity of the contending parties that nothing but altercation was likely to ensue, he resolved quietly to end the dispute by preferring to the bishopric Heraclides, a deacon of his own, and a Cypriot by descent. As however the disorder was increased for awhile by clamours against this election, and allegations of the unfitness of Heraclides for the office, the settlement of this affair detained him a long time at Ephesus; during which Severian continued to preach at Constantinople, and daily grew in favour with his auditory. Of this John was not left ignorant, for he was continually made acquainted with whatever occurred by Serapion, of whom we have before spoken. To this person John had the greatest attachment, and had intrusted to him the entire charge of the episcopate, inasmuch as he was pious, faithful, extremely trustworthy, and very devoted to his interests. By him the bishop was aroused to a feeling of jealousy, by the assurance that Severian was troubling the Church. Having therefore, among other matters, deprived many of the Novatians and Quartodecimans[1] of their churches, he returned to Constan-

---

[1] See above, b. v. ch. xxii.

tinople, and resumed the care of the Churches under his own especial jurisdiction. But Serapion's arrogance was beyond all bearing ; for thus possessing John's unbounded confidence and regard, he was so puffed up by it, that he treated every one with contempt. And this contributed not a little to inflame the minds of the insulted parties against the bishop who patronized him. But between Serapion the deacon and Severian the bishop much dissension arose ; the former opposing Severian because he endeavoured to outshine John in eloquence, and the latter envying Serapion because of John's love for him, and the administration of the bishopric having been committed to him. While their minds were thus affected toward one another, an incident occurred which greatly increased their mutual enmity. On one occasion when Severian passed by him, Serapion neglected to pay him the homage due to his dignity, by retaining his seat instead of rising, as if to show how little he cared for his presence. Severian being indignant at this supposed rudeness and contempt, said with a loud voice to those present, "If Serapion dies a Christian, Christ has not been incarnate." Serapion took occasion from this remark to publicly incite Chrysostom against Severian ; for suppressing the first clause of the sentence, " If Serapion dies a Christian," he accused him of having asserted " Christ has not been incarnate ; " and this charge was sustained by several witnesses of his own party. The whole matter having afterward come under the cognizance of a synod, Serapion affirmed on oath that he did not see the bishop ; on which account those convened pardoned him, and entreated Severian to accept this excuse. John moreover, as some atonement to Severian, suspended Serapion from his office of deacon for a week, although he used him as his right hand in all ecclesiastical matters, in which he had great expertness. But Severian wished him to be not only divested of his diaconate, but excommunicated also, to which John would by no means consent : but going out of the council in disgust, he left the bishops to determine the cause, saying, "Do you decide as you think fit, for I will have nothing to do in the matter." The whole synod rose at these words, censuring the obduracy of Severian, and leaving the case as it before stood. From that time John admitted of no further intimacy with Severian, but advised him to leave the city, and return to his own country,

addressing him thus : — " It is inexpedient, Severian, that
you should so long absent yourself from your diocese, which
must now need the presence of its bishop.   Hasten back therefore to the Churches intrusted to your care, and neglect not
the gift with which God has endowed you."   He accordingly
departed.   But when this became known to the empress
Eudoxia, she severely reprimanded John, and ordered that
Severian should be immediately recalled from Chalcedon in
Bithynia, whither he had gone.   He returned forthwith ; but
John would hold no intercourse whatever with him, nor
could he be induced to do so by the mediation of any one.   At
length the empress Eudoxia herself, in the church called that
of *the Apostles*, placed her son Theodosius (who now so
happily reigns, but was then quite an infant) before John's
knees, and adjuring[1] him repeatedly by the young prince her
son, with difficulty prevailed upon him to be reconciled to 163
Severian.   In this manner was there an appearance of friendship renewed between these persons ; but they nevertheless
retained a rancorous feeling toward each other.   Such was the
origin of their mutual animosity.

CHAP. XII.—Epiphanius performs ordinations at constantinople without john's permission.

Not long after this, at the suggestion of Theophilus, the
bishop Epiphanius again comes from Cyprus to Constantinople,
taking with him a copy of a synodical decree by which, without excommunicating Origen himself, his books were condemned.   On reaching St. John's church, which is seven miles
distant from the city, he disembarked, and there held an assembly ; then after having ordained a deacon,[2] he entered Constan-

[1] Addressing him thus, " By this little child of mine, and your spiritual
son, whom I brought forth, and whom you received out of the sacred
font, be reconciled to Severian."
[2] The act of ordaining in another bishop's diocese was forbidden by
Apostol. Canon xxxv. : " Let not a Bishop dare to ordain beyond his
own limits, in cities and places not subject to him.   But if he be convicted
of doing so without the consent of those persons who have authority over
such cities and places, let him be deposed, and those also whom he has
ordained."   See also Canon xvi. of the Council of Nicæa.

tinople. In complaisance to Theophilus he declined John's courtesy, and instead of accepting accommodation at the episcopal palace, engaged apartments in a private house. He afterwards assembled all the bishops who were then in that capital, and producing his copy of the synodical decree condemnatory of Origen's works, recited it before them; but without being able to assign a better reason for this judgment, than that it seemed fit to Theophilus and himself to reject them. Some indeed subscribed this decree from a reverential respect for Epiphanius; but many refused to do this, among whom was Theotinus bishop of Scythia, who thus addressed Epiphanius:—"I choose not, Epiphanius, to insult the memory of one who ended his life piously long ago; nor dare I be guilty of so impious an act, as that of condemning what our predecessors by no means rejected: and especially when I know of no evil doctrine contained in Origen's books." Having said this, he brought forward one of that author's works, and reading a few passages therefrom, showed that the sentiments propounded were in perfect accordance with the orthodox faith. He then added, "Those who attempt to fix a stigma on these writings, are unconsciously casting dishonour upon the sacred volume whence their principles are drawn." Such was the reply which Theotinus, a prelate eminent for his piety and rectitude of life, made to Epiphanius.

CHAP. XIII.—THE AUTHOR'S DEFENCE OF ORIGEN.

BUT since many persons, imposed on by his detractors, have been deterred from reading Origen, as though he were a blasphemous writer, I deem it not unseasonable to make a few observations respecting him. Worthless characters, and such as are destitute of ability to attain eminence themselves, often seek to get into notice by decrying those who excel them. And first Methodius, bishop of a city in Lycia named Olympus, laboured under this malady; next Eustathius, who for a short time presided over the Church at Antioch; after him Apollinaris; and lastly Theophilus. This party of four revilers has traduced Origen, but on very different grounds, one having hatched one cause of accusation against him, and an-

[SOCRATES.] Y

other another; and thus each has demonstrated that what he has taken no objection to, fully has his sanction. For since one has attacked one opinion in particular, and another has found fault with another, it is evident that each has admitted as true what he has not cavilled at, giving tacit approbation to what he has not assailed. Methodius indeed, when he had in various places railed against Origen, afterwards, as if to disavow all he had previously said, expresses his admiration of the man, in a Dialogue which he entitled "Xenon."[1] But I affirm that [164] from the censure of these men, greater commendation accrues to Origen. For those who have sought out whatever they deemed worthy of reprobation in him, and yet have never charged him with holding unsound views respecting the holy Trinity, do in this way most distinctly attest his orthodox piety: and by not reproaching him on this point, they commend him by their own testimony. But Athanasius, the defender of the doctrine of consubstantiality, in his "Discourses against the Arians," continually cites this author as a witness of his own faith, interweaving his words with his own. Thus for instance: "The most admirable and laborious Origen," says he, "by his own testimony confirms our doctrine concerning the Son of God, affirming him to be co-eternal with the Father." Those therefore who load Origen with vituperation, overlook the fact that their maledictions fall at the same time on Athanasius, the eulogist of Origen. Having thus vindicated Origen, we shall return to the course of our history.

CHAP. XIV.—Epiphanius, admonished by John concerning his anticanonical proceedings, leaves Constantinople.

John was not offended because Epiphanius, contrary to the ecclesiastical canon, had made an ordination in his Church;[2] but invited him to remain with him at the episcopal palace. He replied that he would neither stay nor pray with him, unless he would expel Discorus and his brethren from the city, and with his own hand subscribe the condemnation of Origen's books. When John deferred the performance of these things,

[1] i. e. the house of entertainment for strangers.
[2] See above, chap. xii. and note.

saying that nothing ought to be done rashly before the decision of a general council, John's adversaries led Epiphanius to adopt another course. For they contrived that at the next assembly, which was to be held in the church named *The Apostles*, Epiphanius should come forth and before all the people condemn the books of Origen, excommunicate Discorus with his followers, and charge John with countenancing them. John, on being informed of these things, sent this message by Serapion on the following day to Epiphanius just as he entered the church: "You do many things contrary to the canons, Epiphanius. In the first place you have made an ordination in the churches under my jurisdiction: then, without my appointment, you have on your own authority officiated in them. Moreover, when heretofore I invited you hither, you refused to come, and now you allow yourself that liberty. Beware therefore lest, a tumult being excited among the people, even you yourself should incur danger therefrom." Epiphanius becoming alarmed on hearing these admonitions, left the church; and after accusing John of many things, he set out on his return to Cyprus. Some say that when he was about to depart, he said to John, " I hope that you will not die a bishop:" to which John replied, "I hope that you will not arrive at your own country." I cannot vouch for the truth of this report ; but nevertheless the event was correspondent to it in the case of both. For Epiphanius did not reach Cyprus, having died on ship-board after his departure ; and John a short time afterwards was driven from his see, as we shall show in proceeding.

CHAP. XV.—JOHN IS EJECTED FROM HIS CHURCH ON ACCOUNT OF HIS DISPRAISE OF WOMEN.

WHEN Epiphanius was gone, it was intimated to John that the empress Eudoxia had stimulated Epiphanius against him. And being of a fiery temperament, and of a ready utterance, he soon after pronounced a public invective against women in general, which the people considered was intended to apply indirectly to the empress. This speech was laid hold of by evil-disposed persons, and reported to those in authority, until at length it reached the empress ; who immediately complained of it to her husband, telling him that the insult offered to herself equally affected him. The emperor therefore authorized Theophilus to convoke a synod without delay against John; which Severian also co-operated in promoting, for he still regarded Chrysostom with aversion. In a little while therefore Theophilus arrived, accompanied by several bishops from different cities, who had been summoned by the emperor's orders. Those especially who had some cause of private pique against John flocked together; and all whom he had deposed in Asia, when he went to Ephesus and ordained Heraclides, did not fail to be present. It was arranged that they should assemble at Chalcedon in Bithynia. Cyrin was then bishop of that city, an Egyptian by birth, who said many things to the bishops in disparagement of John, denouncing him as an impious, haughty, and inexorable person, very much to the satisfaction of these prelates. But Maruthas bishop of Mesopotamia having accidentally trod on Cyrin's foot, he was so severely hurt by it as to be unable to embark with the rest for Constantinople, and was therefore obliged to remain behind at Chalcedon. Theophilus had so openly avowed his hostility to John, that none of the clergy would go forth to meet him, or pay him the least honour; but some Alexandrian sailors happening to be there, whose vessels had been laden with corn, greeted him with joyful acclamations. He refused to enter the church, and took up his abode at one of the imperial mansions called "The Placidian." Then a torrent of accusations began to be poured forth against John; for no mention was now made of Origen, but all were intent on urging a variety of criminations, many of which were ridiculous. Preliminary matters being settled, the bishops were convened in the suburbs of Chalcedon, at a place called "The Oak," and John was immediately cited to answer the charges which were brought against him. Serapion the deacon, Tigris the eunuch presbyter, and Paul the reader, were likewise summoned to appear there with him, for these men were included in the impeachments as participators in his guilt. John taking exception to those who had cited him, on the ground of their being his enemies, refused to attend, and demanded a general council. They repeated their citation four times in succession; and when he persisted in his rejection of them as his judges, always giving the same answer, they condemned him for contumacy, and deposed him without assigning any other cause for his deposition. This decision was announced towards evening, and incited the people to a most alarming sedition : insomuch that they kept watch all night, and would by no means suffer him to be removed from the church, crying out that his cause ought to be determined in a larger assembly. The emperor however commanded that he should be immediately expelled, and sent into exile. But as soon as John was apprized of this he voluntarily surrendered himself about noon, unknown to the populace, on the third day after his condemnation ; for he dreaded any insurrectionary movement on his account ; and was accordingly led away.

CHAP. XVI.—SEDITION ON ACCOUNT OF JOHN CHRYSOSTOM'S BANISHMENT. HE IS RECALLED.

THE people then became intolerably tumultuous ; and as it frequently happens in such cases, many who before were clamorous against him, now changed their hostility into compassion, and said of him whom they had so recently desired to see deposed, that he had been traduced. By this means therefore they were very numerous who exclaimed against both the emperor and the synod of bishops ; but they raged more particularly against Theophilus as the author of this plot. For his fraudulent conduct could no longer be concealed, being exposed by many other indications, and especially by the fact of his having communicated with Discorus, and those termed *the Long Monks*,[1] immediately after John's deposition. But Severian, preaching in the church, and thinking it a suitable occasion to declaim against John, said : "If John had been condemned for nothing else, yet the haughtiness of his demeanour was a crime sufficient to justify his deposition. Men indeed are forgiven all other sins : but 'God resisteth the proud,'[2] as the divine Scriptures teach us." These reproaches incensed the people still more ; so that the emperor gave orders for his immediate recall. Briso, a eunuch in the service of the empress, was therefore sent after him, who finding him at Prænetum, a commercial town situated over

---

[1] See above, ch. vii.   [2] James iv. 6.

against Nicomedia, brought him back toward Constantinople. When they reached Marianæ, a village in the suburbs, John refused to enter the city, and declared he would abide there, until his innocence had been admitted by a higher tribunal. His delay at that place increased the popular commotion, and caused them to break forth into very indignant and opprobrious language against their rulers. To check their fury John was constrained to proceed; and being met on his way by a vast multitude, who vied with each other in their expressions of veneration and honour, he was conducted immediately to the church, on reaching which the people entreated him to seat himself in the episcopal chair, and give them his accustomed benediction. When he sought to excuse himself, saying that he ought not to do so without an order from his judges, and that those who condemned him must first revoke their sentence, they were only the more inflamed with the desire of seeing him reinstated, and of hearing him address them again. Thus pressed, he resumed his seat, and prayed as usual for peace upon the people; after which, acting under the same constraint, he preached to them. This compliance on John's part afforded his adversaries another ground of crimination, although they took no notice of it at that time.

CHAP. XVII.—CONFLICT BETWEEN THE CONSTANTINOPOLITANS AND ALEXANDRIANS. FLIGHT OF THEOPHILUS AND THE BISHOPS OF HIS PARTY.

IN the first place then, Theophilus attempted to call in question the legitimacy of the ordination of Heraclides,[1] that thereby he might if possible find occasion of again deposing John. Heraclides was not present at this scrutiny; nevertheless they condemned him in his absence, on the charge of having unjustly beaten some persons, and afterwards dragged them in chains through the midst of the city of Ephesus. John and his adherents remonstrated against the injustice of passing sentence upon an absent person; but the Alexandrians contended that his accusers ought to be heard, although he was not present. A sharp contest therefore ensued between the

[1] See above, ch. xi.

Alexandrians and the Constantinopolitans, which led to blows,. whereby many persons were wounded, and some few killed. Theophilus, seeing what was done, instantly fled to Alexandria; and the other bishops, except the few who supported John, followed his example, and returned to their respective sees. After these transactions, Theophilus was degraded in every one's estimation: but the odium attached to him was exceedingly increased by the shameless way in which he continued to read Origen's works. And when he was asked why he thus countenanced what he had publicly condemned? he replied, "Origen's books are like a meadow enamelled with flowers of every kind. If therefore I chance to find a beautiful one among them, I cull it; but whatever appears to me to be thorny, I pass by, as that which would prick." But The-. ophilus gave this answer without reflecting on the saying of the wise Solomon,[1] that the words of the wise are as goads; and those who are pricked by the precepts they contain, ought not to kick against them. Soon after the flight of Theophilus, Discorus bishop of Hermopolis, one of those termed *the Long Monks*, died, and was honoured with a magnificent funeral, being interred in the church[2] at "The Oak," where the. synod was convened on John's account. John meanwhile was sedulously employed in preaching; and ordained Serapion, bishop of Heraclea in Thrace, on whose account the odium against himself had been raised. The following events occurred not long after.

CHAP. XVIII.—Of EUDOXIA'S SILVER STATUE.   JOHN IS EXILED A SECOND TIME.

THERE stood at this time a silver statue of the empress Eudoxia covered with a long robe, upon a column of porphyry supported by a lofty base, which had been erected so near the church named *Sophia*, that only half the breadth of the street separated them. At this pillar public games were accustomed to be performed; which John regarded from its proximity to

[1] Eccles. xii. 11.
[2] Μαρτυρίῳ. On the origin of this name as applied to churches, see Bingham's Christ. Antiq. b. viii. ch. i. sect. 8.

the church, as an insult offered to religion. Instead therefore
of representing to the emperor the impropriety of these exhibitions in such a place, and petitioning for their discontinuance,
he employed his ordinary freedom and keenness of tongue in
rebuking publicly those who tolerated them. The empress
was exceedingly piqued at this presumption of the bishop,
applying his expressions to herself as indicating marked contempt toward her own person: she therefore endeavoured to
procure the convocation of another synod against him. When
John was aware of this, he delivered in the church that celebrated oration commencing with these words: "Again Hero-
dias raves; again she is troubled; she dances again; and
again desires to receive John's head in a charger." This of
course exasperated the empress still more. Not long after
the following prelates arrived: Leontius bishop of Ancyra in
Asia, Ammonius of Laodicea in Pisidia, Briso of Philippi in
Thrace, Acacius of Beroea in Syria, and some others. John
presented himself fearlessly before them, and demanded an
investigation of the charges which were made against him.
But the anniversary of the birth of our Saviour having re-
curred, the emperor would not attend church as usual, but
sent Chrysostom an intimation that he should not communicate
with him, until he had cleared himself from those misdemeanours with which he stood impeached. When John's accusers
seemed to quail before his bold and ardent bearing, his judges,
setting aside all other matters, said they would confine their
examination to this one question, whether he had on his own
responsibility, after his deposition, again seated himself in the
episcopal chair, without being authorized by an ecclesiastical
council. On John's saying that he was reinstated by the decree of sixty-five bishops who had communicated with him;
Leontius objected that he had been condemned in a synod
composed of a much greater number. John then contended
that this was a canon of the Arians, and not of the Catholic 165
Church, and therefore it was inoperative against him: for
that it had been framed in the council convened against
Athanasius at Antioch, for the subversion of the doctrine of
consubstantiality. The bishops however would not listen to
this defence, but immediately condemned him, without considering that by using this canon they were sanctioning the
deposition of Athanasius himself. This sentence having been

pronounced a little before Easter, the emperor sent to tell
John that he could not go to the church, because two synods
had condemned him. Chrysostom therefore went there no
more ; but those who were of his party celebrated that feast
in the public baths which are named after Constantius, and
thenceforth left the church. Among his adherents were many
bishops and presbyters, with others of the clerical order, who
from that time holding their assemblies apart in various places,
were from him denominated *Johannites*. For the space of
two months, John refrained from appearing in public; after
which he was conveyed into exile by the emperor's command.
On the very day of his departure, some of John's friends set
fire to the church, which by means of a strong easterly wind [1]
communicated with the senate-house. This conflagration
happened on the 20th of June, under the sixth consulate of
Honorius, which he bore in conjunction with Aristænetus.
The severities inflicted on John's friends, even to the extent
of capital punishment, on account of this act of incendiarism,
by Optatus the prefect of Constantinople, who being a Pagan
was as such an enemy to the Christians, I ought I believe to
pass by in silence.

CHAP. XIX.—ORDINATION OF ARSACIUS AS JOHN'S SUCCESSOR.
INDISPOSITION OF CYRIN BISHOP OF CHALCEDON.

AFTER the lapse of a few days, Arsacius, the brother of
Nectarius who so ably governed the Church at Constantinople before John, was appointed to that see, although he was
then very aged, being upwards of eighty years old. During
his singularly mild and peaceful administration of the episcopate, Cyrin bishop of Chalcedon, upon whose foot Maruthas
bishop of Mesopotamia had inadvertently trodden, became so
seriously affected by the accident, that from mortification
having ensued, amputation was found necessary. Nor was
this abscission performed once only, but was required to be

---

[1] Ἀπηλιώτης, (from ἀπό and ἥλιος,) so called as coming from the
region of the sun's rising. " Ventus subsolanus." See Wessel. Herod.
viii. 188 ; Thucyd. iii. 23 ; Catull. Od. xxvi. 4.

often repeated : for after the injured limb was cut off, the gangrene so invaded his whole system, that he was compelled to submit to the loss of the other foot also. I have alluded to this circumstance, because many have affirmed that what he suffered was a judgment upon him for his calumnious aspersions of John, whom he so often designated as arrogant and inexorable. On the 30th of September, in the last-mentioned consulate, there was an extraordinary fall of hail of immense size at Constantinople and its suburbs. This also was declared to be an expression of Divine indignation on account of Chrysostom's unjust deposition : and the death of the empress only four days after the hailstorm, tended to give increased credibility to these reports. Others however asserted that John had been deservedly deposed, because of the violence he had exercised in Asia and Lydia, in depriving the Novatians and Quartodecimans of many of their churches, when he went to Ephesus and ordained Heraclides. But whether John's deposition was just, as his enemies declare, or Cyrin's sufferings were in chastisement for his slanderous revilings, whether the hail fell or the empress died on John's account, or whether these things happened for other reasons, or for these in connexion with others, God only knows, who is the discerner of secrets, and the just judge of truth itself. I have simply stated the reports which were current at that time.

CHAP. XX.—DEATH OF ARSACIUS, AND ORDINATION OF ATTICUS.

BUT Arsacius did not long survive his accession to the bishopric ; for he died on the 11th of November under the following consulate, which was Stilicho's second, and the first of Anthemius. In consequence of there being many aspirants to the vacant see, much time elapsed before the election of a successor : but at length, in the following consulate, which was the sixth of Arcadius and the first of Probus, a devout man named Atticus was promoted to the episcopate. He was a native of Sebastia in Armenia, and had followed an ascetic life from an early age : moreover in addition to a moderate share of learning, he possessed a large amount of natural prudence. But I shall speak of him more particularly here-after.[1]

CHAP. XXI.—JOHN DIES IN EXILE.

ON the 14th of September, in the following consulate, which was the seventh of Honorius and the second of Theo-166 dosius, John died in exile at Comanes. His love of virtue inclined him, as we have before observed, rather to anger than forbearance; and his personal sanctity of character led him to indulge in a latitude of speech which to others was intolerable. But what is most inexplicable to me is, how with a zeal so ardent for the practice of self-control and blamelessness of life, he should in his sermons appear to encourage licentiousness. For whereas by the synod of bishops repentance was accepted but once from those who had sinned after baptism;[2] he did not scruple to say, "Approach, although you may have repented a thousand times." For this doctrine, many even of his friends censured him, but especially Sisinnius bishop of the Novatians; who wrote a book condemnatory of this expression of Chrysostom's, and severely rebuked him for it. But this occurred long before.

CHAP. XXII.—OF SISINNIUS BISHOP OF THE NOVATIANS. HIS READINESS AT REPARTEE.

IT will not be out of place here, I conceive, to give some account of Sisinnius. He was, as I have often said, remarkably eloquent, and well instructed in philosophy. But he had particularly cultivated logic, and was profoundly skilled in the interpretation of the Holy Scriptures; insomuch that the heretic Eunomius often shrank from the acumen which his reasoning displayed. He was not simple in his diet; for although he practised the strictest moderation, yet his table

[1] See below, b. vii. ch. ii.
[2] Upon the Novatian doctrine and that of the Catholic Church, see above, b. iv. ch. xxviii.

was always sumptuously furnished. His habits were soft and delicate, being accustomed to clothe himself in white garments, and to bathe twice a day in the public baths. And when some one asked him why he who was a bishop bathed twice a day? he replied, "Because it is inconvenient to bathe thrice." Going one day from courtesy to visit the bishop Arsacius, he was asked by one of the friends of that prelate, why he wore a garment so unsuitable for a bishop? and where it was written that an ecclesiastic should be clothed in white? "Do you tell me first," said he, "where it is written that a bishop should wear black?" When he that made the inquiry knew not what to reply to this counter-query: "You cannot show," rejoined Sisinnius, "that a priest should be clothed in black. But Solomon is my authority, whose exhortation is, 'Let thy garments be white.'[1] And our Saviour in the Gospels appears clothed in white raiment;[2] moreover he showed Moses and Elias to the apostles, clad in white garments." His prompt reply to these and other questions called forth the admiration of those present. Again, when Leontius bishop of Ancyra in Galatia Minor had taken away a church from the Novatians, and afterwards came to Constantinople, Sisinnius went to him, and begged him to restore the church. But he received him rudely, saying, "Ye Novatians ought not to have churches; for ye take away repentance, and shut out divine mercy." To these and many other such revilings against the Novatians, Sisinnius replied: "No one repents more heartily than I do." And when Leontius asked him on what account? "That I came to see you," said he. On one occasion John, having a contest with him, said, "The city cannot have two bishops."[3] "Nor has

---

[1] Eccles. ix. 8.   [2] Luke ix. 29.

[3] The existence of two bishops in one city was forbidden by the 8th Canon of Nicæa. It was an ancient custom grounded on tradition from the apostles, that there should be only one bishop in a city. All attempts to consecrate a second bishop were condemned and resisted by the faithful. Thus when the emperor Constantius proposed that Liberius and Felix should sit as co-partners in the Roman see, and govern the Church in common, the people with one accord rejected the proposal, crying out, "One God, one Christ, one bishop." This rule, however, did not apply to the case of coadjutors, where the bishop was too old or infirm to discharge his episcopal duties. See Bingham's Christian Antiq. b. ii. ch. xiii.

it," said Sisinnius. John being irritated at this response, said, "You seem to pretend that you alone are the bishop." "I do not say that," rejoined Sisinnius; "but that I am not bishop in your estimation only, who am such to others." John being still more chafed at this reply, said, "I will stop your preaching; for you are a heretic." To which Sisinnius good-humouredly replied, "I will give you a reward, if you will relieve me from so arduous a duty." John being softened a little by this answer, said, "I will not make you cease to preach, if you find it so troublesome." So facetious was Sisinnius, and so ready at repartee: but it would be tedious to dwell further on his witticisms. The specimens we have given will serve to show what sort of a person he was. I .will merely add, that his uncommon erudition acquired for him the esteem and regard of the bishops who succeeded him; and that he was loved and honoured by all the leading members of the senate. He is the author of many works; but they are characterized by too great an affectation of elegance of diction, and a lavish intermingling of poetic expressions. On which account he was more admired as an orator than a writer; for there was dignity in his countenance and voice, as well as in his form and aspect, and every movement of his person was graceful. These advantages commended him to all the sects, and he was in especial favour with Atticus the bishop. But I must conclude this brief notice of Sisinnius.

CHAP. XXIII.—DEATH OF THE EMPEROR ARCADIUS.

NOT long after the death of John, the emperor Arcadius died also. This prince was of a mild and gentle disposition, and toward the close of his life was esteemed to be greatly beloved of God, from the following circumstance. There was at Constantinople an immense mansion, called Carya, because of a nut-tree in the court of it, on which it is said Acacius suffered martyrdom by hanging. A little chapel[1] was on that account built near it, which the emperor Arcadius one day thought fit to visit, and after having prayed there, left again. All who lived near this oratory ran in a crowd to see the

[1] Οἰκίσκος εὐκτήριος. See above, note on book i. chap. xix.

emperor; and some going out of the mansion referred to, endeavoured to pre-occupy the streets in order to get a better view of their sovereign and his suite, while others followed in his train, until all who inhabited it, including the women and children, had wholly gone out of it. No sooner was this vast pile emptied of its occupants, the buildings of which completely environed the church, than the entire mass fell. On which there was a great outcry, followed by shouts of admiration, because it was believed the emperor's prayer had rescued so great a number of persons from destruction. After this event, on the 1st of May, Arcadius died, leaving his son Theodosius only eight years old, under the consulate of Bassus and Philip, in the second year of the 297th Olympiad. He had reigned thirteen years with Theodosius his father, and fourteen years after his death, and had only then attained the thirty-first year of his age. This Book includes the space of twelve years and six months.

BOOK VII.

CHAP. I.—ANTHEMIUS THE PRÆTORIAN PREFECT ADMINISTERS THE GOVERNMENT OF THE EAST IN BEHALF OF YOUNG THEODOSIUS.

AFTER the death of Arcadius, his brother Honorius still governed the Western parts of the empire; but the administration of the East devolved on his son Theodosius junior, then only eight years old.[1] The management of public affairs was therefore intrusted to Anthemius the Prætorian prefect, grandson of that Philip who in the reign of Constantius ejected Paul from the see of Constantinople, and established Macedonius in his place. By his directions the imperial city was surrounded with high walls. He was justly esteemed the most prudent man of his time, and seldom did anything unadvisedly, but consulted with the most judicious of his friends respecting all practical matters; Troïlus the sophist

---

[1] See Gibbon's Decline and Fall, chap. xxxii.

was more especially his counsellor, who, while excelling in philosophical attainments, was not inferior to Anthemius himself in political wisdom. Almost all things were therefore done with the concurrence of Troïlus.

CHAP. II.—CHARACTER AND CONDUCT OF ATTICUS BISHOP OF CONSTANTINOPLE.

WHEN Theodosius thus in the eighth year of his age succeeded to the imperial authority, Atticus was in the third year of his presidency over the Church at Constantinople, and was become exceedingly eminent. For being, as we have before remarked,[1] distinguished alike for his learning, piety, and discretion, the Churches under his episcopate attained a very flourishing condition. He not only united those of his own faith, but also by his prudence called forth the admiration of the heretics, whom indeed he by no means desired to harass; but if he sometimes was obliged to impress them with the fear of him, he soon afterward showed himself mild and clement toward them. So assiduous was he as a student, that he often spent whole nights in perusing the writings of the ancients; and thus he became intimately acquainted with the reasonings of the philosophers, and the fallacious subtilties of the sophists. Besides this he was affable in conversation, and ever ready to sympathize with the afflicted: in short, to sum up his excellencies in the apostle's word, " He was made all things to all men."[2] Formerly, while a presbyter, he had been accustomed, after composing his sermons, to commit them to memory, and then recite them in the church; but by diligent application he acquired so much confidence as to be able to preach extemporaneously. His discourses however were not such as to be received with much applause by his auditors, nor to deserve to be committed to writing. Let these particulars respecting his talents, erudition, and manners suffice. We must now proceed to relate such things as are worthy of record, that happened in his time.

¹ See above, book vi. chap. xx.   ² 1 Cor. ix. 22.

CHAP. III. — Of THEODOSIUS AND AGAPETUS BISHOPS OF SYNADA.

THEODOSIUS bishop of Synada in Phrygia Pacata, was a violent persecutor of the heretics, of whom there was a great number in that city, and especially of the Macedonian sect, whom he sought if possible to root out of the country. This course he pursued not from any precedent in the orthodox Church, nor from the desire of propagating the true faith; but being enslaved by the love of filthy lucre, he was impelled by the avaricious motive of amassing money, by extorting it from the heretics. To this end he made all sorts of attempts upon the Macedonians, putting arms into the hands of his clergy; and employing innumerable stratagems against them, he delivered them up also to the secular tribunals.[1] But his annoyances were especially directed against Agapetus their bishop: and finding the governors of the province were not invested with sufficient authority to punish heretics according to his wish, he set out for Constantinople to petition for edicts of a more stringent nature from the Prætorian prefect. While Theodosius was absent on this business, Agapetus, who, as I have said, presided over the Macedonian sect, formed a wise and prudent resolution; and after communicating with his clergy, he called all the people under his guidance together, and persuaded them to embrace the Homoousian faith. On their acquiescing in this proposition, he proceeded immediately to the church, attended not merely by his own adherents, but by the whole body of the people. There having offered prayer, he took possession of the episcopal chair in which Theodosius was accustomed to seat himself; and preaching thenceforth the doctrine of consubstantiality, he reunited the people, and made himself master of the churches in that diocese. Soon after these transactions, Theodosius, in total ignorance of what had taken place, returned to Synada, bringing with him extended powers from the prefect. But on his going to the church and being forthwith unanimously expelled, he again betook himself to Constantinople, where he complained

---

[1] As to the limits of the secular power over ecclesiastics, and the cases in which the clergy were and were not exempt from their cognizance, see Bingham, book v. chap. ii.

to Atticus the bishop of the treatment he had met with, and the manner in which he had been deprived of his bishopric. Atticus, perceiving the advantage of this movement to the Church, consoled Theodosius as well as he could; recommending him to embrace with a contented mind a retired life, and thus sacrifice his own private interests to the public good. He then wrote to Agapetus, authorizing him to retain the episcopate, and bidding him be under no apprehension of being molested by Theodosius.

CHAP. IV. — A PARALYTIC JEW HEALED BY ATTICUS IN BAPTISM.

THIS was one important improvement in the circumstances of the Church, which happened during the ecclesiastic administration of Atticus. Nor were these times without the attestation of miracles. For a Jew who had been confined to his bed by paralysis for many years, and had been benefited neither by medical skill, nor by the prayers of his Jewish brethren, had recourse at length to Christian baptism, hoping that as it was the only means now left untried, it would prove to be the true remedy.[1] When Atticus the bishop was informed of his wishes, he instructed him in the first principles of Christian truth, and having preached to him the hope in Christ, directed that he should be brought in his bed to the font. The paralytic Jew receiving baptism with a sincere faith, as soon as he was taken out of the water found himself perfectly cured of his disease, and continued to enjoy sound health afterwards. Such was the miraculous power of Christ vouchsafed to be manifested even in our times; the fame of which caused many heathens to believe and be baptized. But the Jews who so zealously seek after signs, were not induced to embrace the faith by present miracles, notwithstanding the blessings they saw thus conferred by Christ upon men.

---

[1] Upon the miraculous effects which were attributed to Christian baptism, see the treatise of Tertullian, " De Baptismo," passim.

CHAP. V.—THE PRESBYTER SABBATIUS, FORMERLY A JEW,
SEPARATES FROM THE NOVATIANS.

NOT only did the Jews continue in unbelief after this
miracle, but many others also who were imitators of them
persisted in their impiety and rejected this evidence of Divine
power. Among these was Sabbatius, of whom mention has
before been made;[1] who not being content with the dignity of presbyter to which he had attained, but aiming at a
bishopric from the beginning, separated himself from the
Church of the Novatians under pretext of observing the Jewish Passover.[2] Holding therefore schismatic assemblies apart
from his own bishop Sisinnius, in a place named Xerolophus,
where the forum of Arcadius now is, he was guilty of an act
deserving the severest punishment.[3] Reading one day at one
of these meetings that passage in the Gospel where it is said,
"Now[4] it was the Feast of the Jews called the Passover,"
he added what was never written nor heard of before:
" *Cursed be he that celebrates the Passover out of the days of
unleavened bread.*" When these words were reported among
the people, the more simple of the Novatian laity, deceived by
this artifice, flocked to him. But his fraudulent fabrication
was of little avail to him, and issued in most disastrous consequences. For when shortly after, in conjunction with many
others, he kept this feast in anticipation of the Christian Easter,
a supernatural panic fell upon them, while they were passing
the night in the accustomed vigils, as if Sisinnius their bishop
were coming with a multitude of persons to fall upon them.
From the perturbation that might be expected in such a case,
and their being shut up at night in a confined place, they trod
upon one another, insomuch that above seventy of them were
crushed to death. On this account many deserted Sabbatius:
some however, holding his ignorant anticipative opinion,
remained with him. In what way Sabbatius, by a violation of

---

[1] Book v. ch. xxi.

[2] See note on b. i. ch. viii. x.

[3] Compare the well-known saying of St. Ignatius, μηδὲν ἀνεὺ τοῦ ἐπισ-
κόπου.

[4] This, like many other professed quotations from Scripture, is incorrectly cited: Luke xxii. 1 is most probably referred to.

his oath, afterwards managed to get himself ordained a bishop, we shall relate hereafter.[1]

CHAP. VI.—BISHOPS OF THE ARIAN HERESY.

DOROTHEUS bishop of the Arians, who, as we have said,[2] was translated by that sect from Antioch to Constantinople, having attained the age of one hundred and nineteen years, died on the 6th of November, in the seventh consulate of Honorius, and the second of Theodosius Augustus. He was succeeded by Barba, in whose time the Arian faction was favoured by possessing two very eloquent members, both having the rank of presbyter, one of whom was named Timothy, and the other George. The latter excelled in Grecian literature, and constantly had the writings of Aristotle and Plato in his hands:[3] the former had devoted himself more to the study of the sacred Scriptures, and was a great admirer of Origen; he also evinced in his public expositions of the Old Testament no inconsiderable acquaintance with the Hebrew language. Timothy had however formerly identified himself with the sect of the Psathyrians;[4] but George had been ordained by Barba. I have myself conversed with Timothy, and was exceedingly struck by the readiness with which he would answer the most difficult questions, and clear up the most obscure passages in the Divine oracles; invariably quoting Origen as an unquestionable authority in confirmation of his own sentiments. But it is astonishing to me that these two men should continue to uphold the heresy of the Arians; the one being so conversant with Plato, and the other having Origen so frequently on his lips. For Plato does not say that the second and third cause, as he usually terms them, had a beginning of existence; and Origen everywhere acknowledges the Son to be co-eternal with the Father. Nevertheless, although they remained connected with that sect, they purged it from some of its grosser corruptions, and raised it to a more tolerable condition, by abolishing many of the blasphe-

---

[1] See below, ch. xii.   [2] See b. v. ch. xii.   [3] See above, b. iii. ch. xvi.
[4] A title given to one of the sections of the Arian party. See above, b. v. ch. xxiii.

mies of Arius. But enough of these persons. Sisinnius
bishop of the Novatians, dying under the same consulate, was
succeeded by Chrysanthus, of whom we shall have to speak
by and by.

CHAP. VII.—CYRIL SUCCEEDS THEOPHILUS BISHOP OF ALEX-ANDRIA.

THEOPHILUS bishop of Alexandria having soon after fallen
into a lethargic state, died on the 15th of October,[1] in the ninth
consulate of Honorius, and the fifth of Theodosius. A great
contest immediately arose about the appointment of a successor, some seeking to place Timothy the archdeacon in the
episcopal chair; and others desiring Cyril, the nephew of
Theophilus. But although the former was supported by
Abundantius the commander of the troops in Egypt, yet the
partisans of Cyril triumphed, and on the third day put him in
possession of the episcopate, with greater power than his
uncle had ever exercised. For from that time the bishops of
Alexandria going beyond the limits of their sacerdotal functions, assumed the administration of secular matters.[2] Cyril
immediately therefore shut up the churches of the Novatians
at Alexandria; after which he took possession of all their
consecrated vessels and ornaments; and then stripped their
bishop Theopemptus of all that he had.

CHAP. VIII.—PROPAGATION OF CHRISTIANITY AMONG THE PERSIANS.

ABOUT this time Christianity was disseminated in Persia,
by means of the frequent embassies between the sovereigns of
that country and the Roman empire, for which there were continual causes. It happened that the Roman emperor thought
proper to send Maruthas bishop of Mesopotamia, who has
been before mentioned,[3] on a mission to the king of the Per-

[1] This chapter is out of chronological order : for Alaric took Rome in
410, A. D. See chap. x.
[2] Comp. chap. xi.   [3] Book vi. ch. xv.

sians: who perceiving this prelate to be eminently pious, treated him with great honour, and revered him as one who was indeed beloved of God. This excited the jealousy of the magi,[1] whose influence is considerable in that country, lest he should prevail on the Persian monarch to embrace Christianity. For Maruthas had by his prayers cured the king of a violent head-ache to which he had been long subject, and which the magi were unable to relieve. They therefore had recourse to this expedient in order to get rid of him. As the Persians worship fire, and the king was accustomed to pay his adorations in a certain edifice where a fire was kept perpetually burning; they concealed a man underneath the sacred hearth, ordering him to make this exclamation as soon as the king began his devotions: "Let the king be thrust out who is guilty of impiety, in imagining a Christian priest to be loved by the Deity." When Isdigerdes, for that was the king's name, heard these words, he determined to dismiss Maruthas, notwithstanding the reverence with which he regarded him. But this holy man, by the earnestness of his prayers, detected the imposition of the magi. Going to the king therefore, he addressed him thus: "Be not deluded, O king; but when you again enter that edifice and hear the same voice, explore the ground below, and you will discover the fraud. For the fire does not speak, but this pretended oracle proceeds from human contrivance." In accordance with this suggestion, the king went as usual to the place where the ever-burning fire was; and when he again heard the same voice, he ordered the earth to be dug up, where the impostor was found, who uttered the supposed words of the Deity. Indignant at the cheat which was thus attempted to be practised upon him, the king commanded that the tribe of the magi should be decimated.[2] After which he permitted Maruthas to erect churches wherever he wished; and from that time the Christian religion was diffused among the Persians. Maruthas being recalled for a while to Constantinople, was afterwards again sent as ambassador to the Persian court, when the magi sought by every possible means to prevent his having access to the king. One of their devices was to cause a most disgusting smell where

---

[1] μάγοι. The "wise men from the East," of whom we read in Matt. ii. 1, were probably of this caste, and well versed in Chaldean astrology.

[2] 'Απεδεκάτωσε, i. e. every tenth man put to death. See Dict. of Antiq. art. "Decimatio." Comp. Polyb. vi. 38; Liv. ii. 59; Tacit. Hist. i. 37; Cicero, Cluent. 46.

·the king was accustomed to go, and then accuse the Christians of being the authors of it. The king however, having already had occasion to suspect the magi, closely scrutinized the matter; and again detecting their deceptive tricks, he punished several of them, and held Maruthas in still higher honour. For the Romans as a nation he had much regard, and entered into an alliance with them. Nay, he was on the point of embracing the Christian faith himself, after witnessing another miracle which was wrought by Maruthas in conjunction with Abdas ·bishop of Persia: for these two by giving themselves to much fasting and prayer, had cast out a demon with which the king's son was possessed. But the death of Isdigerdes[1] prevented his making an open profession of Christianity. The kingdom then devolved on Vararanes his son, in whose time the treaty between the Romans and Persians was violated, as the sequel of this history will show.[2]

CHAP. IX.—BISHOPS OF ANTIOCH AND ROME.

DURING this period Porphyry received the episcopate of Antioch upon the death of Flavian:[3] and after him Alexander[4] was set over that Church. But at Rome, Damasus, having held that bishopric eighteen years, was succeeded by Siricius;[5] who, after presiding there fifteen years, left it to Anastasius: three years after Innocent was promoted to the same see, and was the first persecutor of the Novatians at Rome, many of whose churches he took away.

CHAP. X.—ROME TAKEN AND SACKED BY ALARIC.

ABOUT this time Rome was taken by barbarians;[6] for Alaric, who had been an ally of the Romans, and had rendered important services to the emperor Theodosius in the war against the tyrant Eugenius, having on that account been honoured with Roman dignities, was unable to bear his good fortune.

[1] A. D. 420.   [2] See below, ch. xviii.   [3] A. D. 404.
[4] A. D. 414.   [5] A. D. 385.
[6] For a full account see Gibbon's Decl. and Fall, ch. xxxi. See also Sozomen, b. ix. ch. vi.—ix.

He did not choose to assume imperial authority; but retiring from Constantinople he went into the Western parts, and laid waste all Illyricum. The Thessalonians opposed his march at the mouths of the river Peneus, whence there is a pass over Mount Pindus to Nicopolis in Epirus; and coming to an engagement, they killed about three thousand of his men. After this the barbarians that were with him destroyed every thing in their way, and at last took Rome itself, which they pillaged, burning the greatest part of the magnificent structures and other admirable works of art it contained. Having shared the booty among themselves, they put many of the principal senators to death by a variety of the most cruel tortures: but Alaric, in mockery of the imperial dignity, proclaimed one Attalus emperor, whom he ordered to be attended with all the insignia of sovereignty on one day, and to be exhibited in the habit of a slave on the next. After these achievements he made a precipitate retreat, a report having reached him that the emperor Theodosius had sent an army against him. Nor was this a groundless alarm, for the imperial forces actually arrived; but Alaric, terrified at the bare rumour, had already decamped. It is said that as this barbarian was advancing towards Rome, he was met by a pious monk, who exhorted him to refrain from the perpetration of such atrocities, and no longer to delight in slaughter and blood. To whom Alaric replied, " I am urged on in this course in spite of myself; for there is a something that irresistibly impels me daily, saying, *Proceed to Rome, and desolate that city.*" Such was the career of this person.

CHAP. XI.—BISHOPS OF ROME.

AFTER Innocent, Zosimus governed the Roman Church for two years: and after him Boniface[1] presided over it for three years. He was succeeded by Celestinus. This prelate took away the churches from the Novatians at Rome also, and obliged Rusticula their bishop to hold his meetings secretly in private houses. Until this time that sect had flourished exceedingly in the imperial city of the West, possessing many churches there, which were attended by large congregations.

[1] A. D. 418.

But envy attacked them also, as soon as the Roman episcopate, like that of Alexandria,[1] extended itself beyond the limits of ecclesiastical jurisdiction, and degenerated into its present state of secular domination.   For thenceforth the Roman bishops would not suffer even those who perfectly agreed with them in matters of faith, and whose purity of doctrine they extolled, to enjoy the privilege of assembling in peace, but stripped them of all they possessed.   From such tyrannical bigotry the Constantinopolitan prelates kept themselves free; inasmuch as they not only permitted the Novatians to hold their assemblies within the city, but, as I have already stated, treated them with every mark of Christian regard.

CHAP. XII.—OF CHRYSANTHUS BISHOP OF THE NOVATIANS AT CONSTANTINOPLE.

AFTER the death of Sisinnius, Chrysanthus was constrained to take upon him the episcopal office.   He was the son of Marcian, the predecessor of Sisinnius, and at an early age had a military appointment at the palace; but he was subsequently made governor[2] of Italy, and after that lord-lieutenant[3] of the British Isles, in both which capacities he acquitted himself with the highest credit.   Returning to Constantinople at an advanced age, with the desire of being constituted prefect of that city, he was made bishop of the Novatians against his will.   For when Sisinnius was at the point of death, he referred to him as a most desirable person to preside over the episcopate; and the people regarding this declaration as law, sought to have him ordained forthwith.   While he remained in privacy to avoid having this dignity forced upon him, Sabbatius, supposing a seasonable opportunity was now afforded him of making himself master of the churches, in thorough recklessness of the oath by which he had bound himself, procured his own ordination at the hands of a few undistinguished prelates.[4]   Among these was Hermogenes, who had been excommunicated with curses by Sabbatius himself on account of his blasphemous writings.   But this perjured procedure of

---

[1] See above, chap. vii.
[2] Ὑπατικὸς, Consularis.
[3] Βικάριος, Vicarius.
[4] See Bingham, b. ii. ch. xvi.

Sabbatius was of no avail to him: for the people, disgusted with his unsanctified ambition, used every effort to discover the retreat of Chrysanthus; and having found him secluded in Bithynia, they brought him back by force, and invested him with the bishopric. He was a man of singular modesty and prudence; and by his means the Churches of the Novatians at Constantinople were established and greatly augmented. He was the first prelate who distributed gold among the poor out of his own private property. From the Churches he would receive nothing but two loaves of the consecrated bread[1] every Lord's day. So anxious was he to promote the advantage of his own Church, that he drew Ablabius, the most eminent orator of that time, from the school of Troïlus, and ordained him a presbyter. Ablabius, whose sermons are remarkably elegant and full of point, was afterwards promoted to the bishopric of the Novatian Church at Nice, where he also taught rhetoric at the same time.

168

CHAP. XIII.—CONFLICT BETWEEN THE CHRISTIANS AND JEWS AT ALEXANDRIA: AND BREACH BETWEEN CYRIL THE BISHOP AND ORESTES THE PREFECT.

ABOUT this time the Jewish inhabitants were driven out of Alexandria by Cyril the bishop on the following account. The Alexandrians are more delighted with tumult than any other people: and if they can find a pretext, they will break forth into the most intolerable excesses; nor is it scarcely possible to check their impetuosity until there has been much bloodshed. It happened on the present occasion that a disturbance arose among the populace, not from a cause of any serious importance, but out of an evil that has become inveterate in almost all cities, viz. a fondness for pantomimic[2] exhibitions. In consequence of the Jews being disengaged from business on the sabbath, and spending their time, not in

[1] Ἄρτους Εὐλογιῶν, loaves of Benediction, i. e. offerings of the faithful, part of which was taken for the celebration of the Eucharist, and the rest allotted as food for the clergy.
[2] Ὀρχηστὰς, literally, "public dancers." For an account of the light in which theatrical shows were regarded in the early Christian Church, see Bingham, Christ. Antiq. b. xvi. ch. xi. 15, and the passages there mentioned.

hearing the law, but in theatrical amusements, dancers usually collect great crowds on that day, and disorder is almost invariably produced. And although this was in some degree controlled by the governor of Alexandria, yet the Jews were continually factious; and there was superadded to their ordinary hatred of the Christians, rage against them on account of the dancers. When therefore Orestes the prefect was publishing an edict in the theatre for the regulation of the shows, some of the bishop's party were present to learn the nature of the orders about to be issued. Among these was Hierax, a teacher of the rudimental branches of literature; one who was a very assiduous auditor of the bishop's sermons, and made himself conspicuous by his forward and noisy plaudits. When the Jews observed this person in the theatre, they immediately cried out that he had come there for no other purpose than to excite sedition among the people. Now Orestes had long regarded with jealousy the growing power of the bishops, and their encroachments on the jurisdiction of the civil authorities. Believing therefore that Cyril wished to set spies over his proceedings, he ordered Hierax to be seized, and publicly subjected to the torture in the theatre. Cyril, on being informed of this, sent for the principal Jews, and threatened them with the utmost severities, unless they desisted from their molestation of the Christians. These menaces, instead of suppressing their violence, only rendered the Jewish populace more furious, and led them to form conspiracies for the destruction of the Christians; one of which was of so desperate a character, as to cause their entire expulsion from Alexandria. Having agreed that each one of them should wear a ring on his finger, made of the bark of a palm branch, for the sake of mutual recognition, they determined to attack the Christians on a certain night: and sending persons into the streets to raise an outcry that Alexander's church was on fire, they thus drew the Christians out in great anxiety to save their church. The Jews immediately fell upon and slew them; readily distinguishing each other by their rings. At day-break the authors of this atrocity could not be concealed: and Cyril going to their synagogue, (which is the name they give their house of prayer,) attended by an immense body of people, took them away from them, and driving the Jews out of the city, permitted the multitude to

plunder their goods. Thus were the Jews, who had inhabited
the city from the time of Alexander the Macedonian, expelled
from it, stripped of all they possessed, and dispersed some in
one direction and some in another. One of them, a physician
named Adamantius, fled to Atticus bishop of Constantinople,
and professing Christianity, afterwards returned to Alexandria
and fixed his residence there. But Orestes the governor of
Alexandria viewed these transactions with great indignation,
and was excessively annoyed that a city of such magnitude
should have been suddenly bereft of so large a portion of its
population ; he therefore at once communicated the whole affair to the emperor. Cyril also wrote to him, describing the
outrageous conduct of the Jews ; and in the mean while sent
persons to Orestes who should mediate concerning a reconciliation : for this the people had urged him to do. And when
Orestes refused to listen to a word on the subject, Cyril ex-
169 tended toward him the book of the Gospels, believing that
respect for religion would induce him to lay aside his resent-
ment. When however even this had no pacific effect on the
prefect, but he persisted in implacable hostility against the
bishop, the following event afterwards occurred.

CHAP. XIV.—SEDITION OF THE MONKS AGAINST THE PREFECT
OF ALEXANDRIA.

SOME of the monks inhabiting the mountains of Nitria, of
a very fiery disposition, whom Theophilus some time before
had so unjustly armed against Discorus and his brethren,
being again transported with an ardent zeal, resolved to fight
valiantly in behalf of Cyril. About five hundred of them
therefore, quitting their monasteries, came into the city ; and
meeting the prefect in his chariot, they called him a Pagan
idolater, and applied to him many other abusive epithets.
Supposing this to be a snare laid for him by Cyril, he exclaimed that he was a Christian, and had been baptized by
Atticus the bishop at Constantinople. The monks gave but
little heed to his protestations, and one of them, named
Ammonius, threw a stone at Orestes which struck him on the
head, and covered him with the blood that flowed from the

wound. All the guards with a few exceptions fled, fearing to be stoned to death: but the populace, among whom the fugitive guards had mingled, running to the rescue of the governor, put the rest of the monks to flight, and having secured Ammonius, delivered him up to the prefect. Orestes immediately put him publicly to the torture, which was inflicted with such severity that he died under the effects of it: and not long after he gave an account to the emperors of what had taken place. Cyril on the other hand forwarded his statement of the matter also: and causing the body of Ammonius to be deposited in a certain church, he gave him the new appellation of Thaumasius,[1] ordering him to be enrolled among the martyrs, and eulogizing his magnanimity as that of one who had fallen in a conflict in defence of piety. This approval of Ammonius on the part of Cyril, met with no sympathy from the more sober-minded Christians; for they well knew that he had suffered the punishment due to his temerity, and had not lost his life under the torture because he would not deny Christ. And Cyril himself, being conscious of this, suffered the recollection of the circumstance to be gradually obliterated by silence. But the animosity between Cyril and Orestes did not by any means subside, but was kindled [2] afresh by an occurrence not unlike the preceding.

CHAP. XV.—OF HYPATIA THE FEMALE PHILOSOPHER.

THERE was a woman at Alexandria named Hypatia, daughter of the philosopher Theon, who made such attainments in literature and science, as to far surpass all the philosophers of her own time. Having succeeded to the school of Plato and Photinus, she explained the principles of philosophy to her [170] auditors, many of whom came from a distance to receive her instructions. Such was her self-possession and ease of manner, arising from the refinement and cultivation of her mind, that she not unfrequently appeared in public in presence of the

_____

[1] Θαυμάσιος, i. e. Admirable.
[2] Ἀπέσβεσε. This expression cannot be admitted, because it is opposed to the sense of the context; perhaps it should rather be, ἀνέφλεξε (ἀνὰ φλέγω, rursùs incendere).

magistrates, without ever losing in an assembly of men that dignified modesty of deportment for which she was conspicuous, and which gained for her universal respect and admiration. Yet even she fell a victim to the political jealousy which at that time prevailed. For as she had frequent interviews with Orestes, it was calumniously reported among the Christian populace, that it was by her influence he was prevented from being reconciled to Cyril. Some of them therefore, whose ringleader was a reader named Peter, hurried away by a fierce and bigoted zeal, entered into a conspiracy against her; and observing her as she returned home in her carriage, they dragged her from it, and carried her to the church called Cæsareum, where they completely stripped her, and then murdered her with shells. After tearing her body in pieces, they took her mangled limbs to a place called Cinaron, and there burnt them. An act so inhuman could not fail to bring the greatest opprobrium, not only upon Cyril, but also upon the whole Alexandrian Church. And surely nothing can be further from the spirit of Christianity than the allowance of massacres, fights, and transactions of that sort. This happened in the month of March during Lent,[1] in the fourth year of Cyril's episcopate, under the tenth consulate of Honorius, and the sixth of Theodosius.

CHAP. XVI.—THE JEWS COMMIT ANOTHER OUTRAGE UPON THE CHRISTIANS.

SOON afterwards the Jews renewed their malevolent and impious practices against the Christians, which drew down upon them deserved chastisement. At a place named Immestar, situated between Antioch in Syria and Chalcis, the Jews, while amusing themselves in their usual way with a variety of sports, impelled by drunkenness were guilty of many absurdities. At last they began to scoff at Christians and even Christ himself; and in derision of the cross and those who put their trust in the crucified One, they seized a Christian boy, and having bound him to a cross, began to

[1] Νηστειῶν οὐσῶν, literally, "while the fast was going on." See Bingham, b. xxi. ch. i.

laugh and sneer at him. But in a little while they became
so transported with fury, that they scourged the child until
he died under their hands. This brutal conduct occasioned
a sharp conflict between them and the Christians; and as soon
as the emperors were informed of the circumstance, they
issued orders to the governor of the province to find out and
punish the delinquents with the utmost severity. Thus
vengeance overtook the Jewish inhabitants of this place for
the wickedness they had committed in their impious sport.

CHAP. XVII.—Miracle at the baptism of a jewish
impostor.

About this time Chrysanthus bishop of the Novatians,
after presiding over the Churches of his own sect seven years,
died on the 26th of August, under the consulate of Monaxius
and Plintha. He was succeeded in the bishopric by Paul,
who had formerly been a teacher of Roman eloquence: but
afterwards abandoning this profession, had devoted himself to
an ascetic course of life; and having founded a monastery of
religious men, he adopted a mode of living very similar to
that pursued by the monks in the desert. In fact I myself
found him just such a person as Evagrius[1] describes these
recluses to be; imitating them in continued fastings, silence,
abstinence from animal food, and a very sparing use of oil
and wine. He was, moreover, particularly solicitous about
the wants of the poor; frequently visited those who were in
prison, and in behalf of many criminals interceded with the
judges, who readily attended to him on account of his eminent
piety. But instead of further enumerating the excellencies
that distinguished him, I shall content myself with mentioning
a fact well worthy of being recorded. A Jewish impostor,
pretending to be a convert to Christianity, had been often
baptized,[2] and by that artifice amassed a good deal of money.
After having deceived many of the Christian sects by this

[1] See Evagrius's Ecclesiastical History, b. iv. chaps. xxxv. xxxvi., &c.
[2] The iteration of baptism was always held to be a sacrilege, excepting
when any doubt existed as to the validity of the former baptism, when it
was allowed to be repeated conditionally.

fraud, and received baptism from the Arians and Macedonians, so that there remained no others on whom to practise his hypocrisy, he at length came to Paul bishop of the Novatians, declaring that he earnestly desired baptism, and requesting that he might obtain it at his hand. Paul commended the determination of the Jew, but told him he could not perform that rite for him, until he had been instructed in the fundamental principles of the faith, and given himself to fasting and prayer for many days.[1] The Jew, impatient of the long fasts which he most unwillingly was obliged to undergo, became the more importunate for his baptism; and Paul, not wishing to discourage him by longer delays now that he was so urgent, consented to grant his request, and made all the necessary preparations. Having purchased a white vestment for him, he ordered the font to be filled with water, and then led the Jew to it in order to baptize him. But by the invisible power of God, the water suddenly disappeared. The bishop and those present had not the least suspicion of the real cause, but imagined that the water had escaped by the ordinary channels underneath: these passages were therefore very carefully closed, and the font filled again. No sooner however was the Jew taken there a second time, than the water vanished as before. Then Paul, addressing the Jew, said, "Either you are a deceiver, or an ignorant person who has already been baptized." The people having crowded together to witness this miracle, one among them recognised the Jew, and identified him as having been baptized by Atticus the bishop a little while before. Such was the miracle wrought by the hands of Paul bishop of the Novatians.

CHAP. XVIII.—RENEWAL OF HOSTILITIES BETWEEN THE RO-
MANS AND PERSIANS AFTER THE DEATH OF ISDIGERDES.

ISDIGERDES king of the Persians, who had always favoured the Christians in his dominions, having died, was succeeded by Vararanes[2] his son. This prince, at the instigation of the magi, persecuted the Christians there with so much rigour, by inflicting on them a variety of punishments and tortures,

---

[1] See b. i. ch. viii.   [2] Βαραράνης. See above, chap. viii.

that they were obliged to desert their country and seek refuge
among the Romans, whom they entreated not to suffer them
to be completely extirpated. Atticus the bishop received these
suppliants with great benignity, and besought the emperor to
take them under his protection. It happened at the same time
that another subject of difference arose between the Romans
and Persians, both because the latter would not send back the
labourers in the gold mines who had been hired from among
the former; and also on account of their having plundered
the Roman merchants. The bad feeling which these things
produced, was greatly increased by the flight of the Persian
Christians into the Roman territories. For the Persian king
immediately sent an embassy to demand the fugitives, whom
the Romans were by no means disposed to deliver up; not
only as desirous of defending their suppliants, but also because
they were ready to do anything for the sake of the Christian
religion. They chose rather therefore to renew the war with
the Persians, than to suffer the Christians to be miserably
destroyed: the league was accordingly broken, and I must
now give some brief account of the fierce war that followed
thereupon. The Roman emperor first sent a body of troops
under the command of Ardaburius; who making an irruption
through Armenia into Persia, ravaged one of its provinces
called Azazene. Narsæus the Persian general marched against
him, but on coming to an engagement was defeated, and obliged
to retreat. Afterwards he judged it advantageous to make a
sudden irruption through Mesopotamia into the Roman territories, there unguarded, thinking by this means to be revenged
on the enemy. But Ardaburius being apprized of his design,
hastened the spoliation of Azazene, and then himself also
marched into Mesopotamia. Wherefore Narsæus, although
furnished with a large army, was prevented from invading
the Roman provinces; but arriving at Nisibis, a city in the
possession of the Persians situated on the frontiers of both
empires, he sent to Ardaburius, desiring that they might make
mutual arrangements about carrying on the war, and appoint
a time and place for an engagement. But Ardaburius said to
his messengers, "Tell Narsæus that the Roman emperors will
not fight when it pleases him." The emperor perceiving that
the Persian was mustering his whole force, made additional
levies to his army, and put his trust in God for the victory:

nor was he without immediate benefit from this pious confidence, as the following circumstance proves. As the Constantinopolitans were in great consternation, and apprehensive respecting the issue of the war, a vision of angels appeared to some persons in Bithynia who were travelling to that city on their own affairs, and bade them tell the people not to be alarmed, but pray to God in the assurance that the Romans would be conquerors, for that they themselves were appointed to defend them. Thus were not only the inhabitants comforted, but the soldiers also received fresh courage. The seat of war being transferred, as we have said, from Armenia to Mesopotamia, the Romans shut up the Persians in the city of Nisibis, which they besieged; and having constructed wooden towers, which they advanced by means of machines to the walls, they slew great numbers of those who defended them, as well as of those who ran to their assistance. When Vararanes the Persian monarch learnt that his province of Azazene had been desolated, and that his army was closely besieged in the city of Nisibis, he resolved to march in person with all his forces against the Romans: but dreading the Roman valour, he implored the aid of the Saracens, who were then governed by a warlike chief named Alamundarus. This prince accordingly brought with him a large reinforcement of Saracen auxiliaries, and exhorted the king of the Persians to fear nothing, for that he would soon reduce the Romans under his power, and deliver Antioch in Syria into his hands. But the event nullified these promises: for God infused into the minds of the Saracens a terrible panic, as if the Roman army was falling upon them; and finding no other way of escape, they precipitated themselves, armed as they were, into the river Euphrates, wherein nearly one hundred thousand of them were drowned. After this multitude had thus perished, the Romans, understanding that the king of Persia was bringing with him a great number of elephants, became alarmed in their turn; they therefore burnt all the machines they had used in carrying on the siege, and retired into their own country. What engagements afterwards took place, and how Areobindus, another Roman general, killed the bravest of the Persians in single combat, and by what means Ardaburius destroyed seven Persian commanders in an ambuscade, and Vitian, another Roman general, vanquished the remnant of the

[SOCRATES.]   2 A

Saracen forces, I believe I ought to pass by, lest I should digress too far from my subject.

CHAP. XIX.—OF PALLADIUS THE COURIER.

Now although the scenes of the transactions referred to, were in places very remote from the capital, yet the emperor received intelligence of what was done in an incredibly short space of time. For he had the good fortune to possess among his subjects a man endowed with extraordinary energy both of body and mind, named Palladius; who so vigorously managed the public conveyances, that he would reach the frontiers of the Roman and Persian dominions in three days, and again return to Constantinople in as many more. The same individual traversed other parts of the world on missions from the emperor with equal celerity: so that an eloquent man once said, not unaptly, "This man by his speed seems to contract the vast expanse of the Roman territories." The king of the Persians himself was astonished at the expeditious feats which were related to him of this courier: but we must not stay to give further details concerning him.

CHAP. XX.—A SECOND OVERTHROW OF THE PERSIANS BY THE ROMANS.

Such was the moderation with which the emperor used the advantage which God had given him, that he nevertheless desired to make peace; and to that end he despatched Helion, a man in whom he placed the greatest confidence, with a commission to enter into a pacific treaty with the Persians. Having arrived in Mesopotamia, at the place where the Romans for their own security had formed a trench, he sent before him as his deputy Maximin, an eloquent man who was the assessor of Ardaburius, the commander-in-chief of the army, to make preliminary arrangements concerning the terms of peace. Maximin, on coming into the presence of the Persian king, said he had been sent to him on this matter, not by the

Roman emperor, who was ignorant of the state of things, and thoroughly contemned the war, but by his generals. And when the sovereign of Persia would have gladly received the embassy, because his troops were suffering from want of provisions ; that corps among them which is distinguished by the name of *the Immortals*,[1] numbering about ten thousand of his bravest men, counselled the king not to listen to any overtures for peace, until they should have made an attack upon the Romans, who, they said, were now become extremely incautious. The king, approving their advice, ordered the ambassador to be imprisoned and a guard set over him; and permitted the Immortals to put their design upon the Romans into execution. They therefore, on arriving at the place appointed, divided themselves into two bands, with a view to surround some portion of the Roman army. The Romans, observing but one body of Persians approaching them, prepared themselves to receive it, not having seen the other division, in consequence of their suddenly rushing forth to battle. But just as the engagement was about to commence, Divine Providence so ordered it, that Procopius a Roman general with another part of the army appeared on the heights, who, perceiving their comrades in danger, attacked the Persians in the rear. Thus were they, who but a little before had surrounded the Romans, themselves encompassed, and in a short time utterly destroyed : and those who broke forth from their ambuscade, being next attacked by the Romans, were in like manner every one of them slain with darts. In this way was the mortality demonstrated of those who by the Persians were termed the Immortals; Christ having executed this vengeance upon that people, because of their having shed the blood of so many of his pious worshippers. The king of the Persians, on being informed of this overthrow, pretended to be ignorant of what had been done; and ordering the embassy to be admitted he thus addressed Maximin : "I agree to the peace, not as yielding to the Romans, but to gratify you, whom I have found to be the most prudent of your whole nation." Thus was that war concluded which had been undertaken on account of the suffering Christians in Persia, under the consul-

---

[1] Upon the subject of the Persian body-guard, called Ἀθάνατοι, see the account given by Herodotus, b. vii. chap. xxxi., and Baehr's note in loco.

2 A 2

ate of the two Augusti, being the thirteenth of Honorius, and the tenth of Theodosius, in the fourth year of the 300th Olympiad ; and with it terminated the persecution which had been excited in Persia against the Christians.

CHAP. XXI.—SINGULAR CHARITY OF ACACIUS BISHOP OF AMIDA TOWARD THE PERSIAN CAPTIVES.

A NOBLE action of Acacius bishop of Amida at that time greatly enhanced his reputation among all men. The Roman soldiery, in devastating Azazene, had taken seven thousand captives, whom they would on no account restore to the king of Persia: meanwhile famine began to rage among these unfortunates, a circumstance which greatly distressed that monarch. Their condition becoming known to Acacius, he thought such a matter was by no means to be trifled with ; having therefore assembled his clergy, he thus addressed them : "Our God, my brethren, needs neither dishes nor cups ; for he neither eats, nor drinks, nor is in want of any thing. Since then, by the liberality of the faithful, the Church possesses many vessels both of gold and silver, it behoves us to sell them, that by the money thus raised we may be able to redeem the prisoners, and also supply them with food." Having thus said, he ordered the vessels to be melted down, and from the proceeds paid the soldiers as a ransom for their captives, whom he supported for some time ; and then furnishing them with what was needful for their journey, sent them back to their sovereign. This extraordinary benevolence on the part of the excellent Acacius so astonished the king of the Persians, that he declared the Romans were determined to conquer their enemies as well by their beneficence in peace as by their prowess in war. He is also said to have been very desirous that Acacius should come into his presence, that he might have the pleasure of beholding such a man ; a wish which by the emperor Theodosius's order was soon gratified. After so signal a victory had through Divine favour been achieved by the Romans, many who were distinguished for their eloquence wrote panegyrics in honour of the emperor, which they recited in public. The empress herself also composed a poem in heroic verse : for she possessed a highly cultivated mind, being the daughter of Leontius the Athenian sophist, who had instructed her in every kind of learning. Atticus the bishop had baptized her a little while previous to her marriage with the emperor, and had then given her the Christian name Eudocia,[1] instead of her Pagan one of Athenaïs. Of the many who, as I have said, produced eulogiums on this occasion, some were stimulated by the desire of being noticed by the emperor ; while others were anxious to display their talents, being unwilling that the attainments they had made by dint of great exertion, should lie buried in obscurity.

CHAP. XXII.—VIRTUES OF THE EMPEROR THEODOSIUS JUNIOR.

BUT although I neither seek the notice of my sovereign, nor wish to make an exhibition of my oratorical powers, yet have I felt it my duty to record, without exaggeration, the singular virtues with which the emperor Theodosius is endowed : for I am persuaded that should I pass them over in silence, posterity would be defrauded of the knowledge of that which is calculated, as an illustrious example, to be eminently useful. In the first place then, this prince, though born and bred at a court, was neither stultified nor effeminated by the circumstances of his birth and education. He early evinced so much prudence, that he appeared to those who conversed with him to have acquired the wisdom and experience of advanced age. Such was his fortitude in undergoing hardships, that he would courageously endure both heat and cold ; fasting very frequently, especially on Wednesdays and Fridays,[2] from an earnest endeavour to observe with accuracy all the prescribed forms of the Christian religion. His palace was so regulated, that it differed little from a monastery : for he, together with his sisters, rose early in the morning, and recited antiphonal hymns in praise of the Deity. By this training he learnt the Holy Scriptures by heart ; and he would often discourse with the bishops on scriptural sub-

---

[1] Εὐδοκίαν, i. e. Benevolence: the word occurs frequently in the LXX., as equivalent to the more common form εὐδόκησις.

[2] Upon the observance of Wednesday as well as Friday as a fast-day in the early Church, see Bingham's Christ. Antiq. b. xxi. ch. iii.

jects, as if he had been an ecclesiastic of long standing. He was a more indefatigable collector of the sacred books and of the expositions which had been written on them, than even Ptolemy Philadelphus [1] had formerly been; while in clemency and humanity he far surpassed all others. The emperor Julian, although he professed to be a philosopher, could not moderate his rage against the Antiochians who derided him, but inflicted upon Theodore the most agonizing tortures. Theodosius, on the contrary, bidding farewell to Aristotle's Syllogisms, exercised philosophy in deeds, by getting the mastery over anger, grief, and pleasure.[2] Never has he revenged himself on any one by whom he has been injured; nor has he ever even appeared irritated. And when some of his most intimate friends once asked him, why he never inflicted capital punishment upon offenders? his answer was, " Would that it were even possible to restore to life those that have died." To another making a similar inquiry he replied, " It is neither a great nor difficult thing to put a mortal to death: but it is God only that can resuscitate by repentance a person that has once died." So habitually indeed did he practise mercy, that if sentence of death was passed upon a criminal, and he was conducted toward the place of execution, he was never suffered to reach the gates of the city before a pardon was issued, commanding his immediate return. Having once exhibited a show of hunting wild beasts in the amphitheatre at Constantinople, the people cried out, " Let one of the boldest Bestiarii encounter the enraged animal." But he said to them, " Do ye not know that we are wont to view these spectacles with feelings of humanity?" By this expression he instructed the people to be satisfied in future with shows of a less cruel description. His piety was such that he had a reverential regard for all who were consecrated to the service of God; and honoured in an especial manner those whom he knew to be eminent for their sanctity of life. The bishop of Chebron having died at Constantinople, the emperor is re-

---

[1] A name applied to him by *antiphrasis*, because he killed his brothers. It was by this king's command that the Old Testament was translated into Greek by the Seventy, thence called *The Septuagint*.

[2] It is said in his Ethics by Aristotle, even though a heathen, τέλος αὐτῆς οὐ γνῶσις ἀλλὰ πρᾶξις. How much more must this remark be true of the Christian religion as teaching the most pure morality on the highest sanctions.

ported to have expressed a wish to have his cassock of sack-
cloth of hair, which, although it was excessively filthy, he wore
as a cloak, hoping that thus he should become a partaker in
some degree of the sanctity of the deceased.   In a certain
year, during which the weather had been very tempestuous, he
was obliged by the eagerness of the people to exhibit the
usual sports in the Hippodrome; and when the circus was
filled with spectators, the violence of the storm increased,
and there was a heavy fall of snow.   Then the emperor made
it very evident how his mind was affected towards God;
for he caused the herald to make a proclamation to the people
to this effect: "It is better to desist from the show, and that
all should unite in prayer to God, that we may be preserved
unhurt from the impending storm."   Scarcely had the herald
executed his commission, than all the people with the greatest
joy began with one accord to offer supplication and sing praises
to God, so that the whole city became one vast congregation;
and the emperor himself, laying aside his imperial robes, went
into the midst of the multitude and commenced the hymns.
Nor was he disappointed in his expectation, for the atmosphere
suddenly resumed its wonted serenity; and Divine benevolence
bestowed on all an abundant harvest, instead of an expected
deficiency of corn.   If at any time war was raised, like David,[1]
he had recourse to God, knowing that He is the disposer of
battles, and by prayer brought them to a prosperous issue.
I shall here therefore relate, how by placing his confidence in
God he vanquished the tyrant John, after Honorius had died
on the 15th of August, in the consulate of Asclepiodotus
and Marian.   For I judge what then occurred worthy of
mention, inasmuch as there happened to the emperor's generals
who were despatched against the tyrant, something analogous
to what took place when the Israelites crossed the Red Sea
under the guidance of Moses.   My narrative must however
be brief, for the details, which I leave to others, would require
a special treatise.

---

[1] See the Book of Psalms, passim.

CHAP. XXIII.—TYRANNY OF JOHN AFTER THE DEATH OF THE EMPEROR HONORIUS. HE IS DESTROYED THROUGH THE PRAYERS OF THEODOSIUS JUNIOR.

THEODOSIUS being now sole ruler, concealed the death of the emperor Honorius as long as possible, amusing the people sometimes with one report and then with another. But he privately despatched a military force to Salonæ, a city of Dalmatia, that in the event of any revolutionary movement in the West there might be resources at hand to check it; and after making these provisional arrangements, he at length openly announced his uncle's death. In the interim, John, the emperor's chief secretary, not content with the dignity to which he had already attained, seized upon the sovereign authority; and sent an embassy to the emperor Theodosius, demanding to be recognised as his colleague in the empire. But that prince, after causing the ambassadors to be arrested, immediately sent off Ardaburius, the commander-in-chief of the army, who had greatly distinguished himself in the Persian war. He, on arriving at Salonæ, set sail from thence for Aquileia: but fortune was adverse to him as he then thought (although it afterwards appeared far otherwise); for a contrary wind having arisen, he was driven into the tyrant's hand. The capture of Ardaburius made the usurper more sanguine in his hope, that Theodosius would be induced by the urgency of the case to elect and proclaim him emperor, in order to preserve the life of this officer. And the emperor was in fact greatly distressed when he heard of it, as was also the army which had been sent against the tyrant, lest Ardaburius should be subjected to any rigorous treatment. Aspar, the son of Ardaburius, having learnt that his father was in the tyrant's power, and aware at the same time that the party of the rebels was strengthened by the accession of immense numbers of barbarians, knew not what course to pursue. But at this crisis the prayer of the pious emperor again prevailed. For an angel of God, under the appearance of a shepherd, undertook the guidance of Aspar and the troops which were with him, and led him through the lake near Ravenna: for in that city the tyrant was then residing, and there detained the military chief. Now no one had ever been known to have forded that lake before; but God then rendered that passable, which had hitherto been impassable. Having therefore crossed the lake, as if going over dry ground, they found the gates of the city open, and seized the tyrant. This event afforded that most devout emperor Theodosius an opportunity of giving a fresh demonstration of his piety towards God. For the news of the tyrant's being destroyed, having arrived while he was engaged at the exhibition of the sports of the Hippodrome, he immediately said to the people: " We will, if you please, leave these diversions, and proceed to the church to offer thanksgivings to God, by whose hand the tyrant has been overthrown." Thus did he address them; and the spectacles were immediately forsaken, the people all passing out of the circus singing praises together with him, as with one heart and one voice. And arriving at the church, the whole city again became one vast congregation, and passed the remainder of the day in these devotional exercises.

CHAP. XXIV.—VALENTINIAN PROCLAIMED EMPEROR.

AFTER the tyrant's death, the emperor Theodosius became very anxious as to whom he should proclaim emperor of the West. He had a cousin then very young, named Valentinian; the son of that Constantius who had been proclaimed emperor by Honorius,[1] and had died after a short reign with him, and of his aunt Placidia, daughter of Theodosius the Great, and sister of the two Augusti, Arcadius and Honorius. This cousin he created Cæsar, and sent into the Western parts, committing the administration of affairs to his mother Placidia. He himself also hastened towards Italy, that he might in person both proclaim his cousin emperor, and also, being present among them, endeavour to influence the Italians by his counsels not willingly to submit to tyrants. But when he reached Thessalonica, he was prevented from proceeding further by sickness; he therefore sent forward the imperial crown to his cousin by Helion a patrician, and he himself returned to Constantinople.

[1] See above, b. i. ch. xxxix., and b. ii. ch. i.

- CHAP. XXV.—CHRISTIAN BENEVOLENCE OF ATTICUS BISHOP OF CONSTANTINOPLE. HIS FOREKNOWLEDGE OF HIS OWN DEATH.

MEANWHILE Atticus the bishop caused the affairs of the Church to flourish in an extraordinary manner; administering all things with singular prudence, and inciting the people to virtue by his discourses. Perceiving the Church to be divided by the Johannists[1] assembling themselves apart, he ordered that mention of John should be made in the prayers, as was customary to ·be done of the other deceased prelates; by which means he trusted that many would be induced to return to the Church. His liberality was so great that he not only provided for the poor of his own Churches,[2] but transmitted contributions to supply the wants and promote the comfort of the indigent in the neighbouring cities also. On one occasion he sent to Calliopius, a presbyter of the Church at Nice, three hundred pieces[3] of gold with the following letter.

"Atticus to Calliopius—salutations in the Lord.

"I have been informed that there are in your city a great number of necessitous persons, whose condition demands the compassion of the pious. As therefore I have received a sum of money from him, who with a bountiful hand is wont to supply faithful stewards; and since it happens that some are pressed by want, that those who have may be proved, who yet do not minister to the needy—take, my friend, these three hundred pieces of gold, and dispose of them as you may think fit. It will be your care, I doubt not, to distribute to such as are ashamed to beg, to the exclusion of those who through life have sought to feed themselves at others' expense. In bestowing these alms I would have no distinction made on religious grounds; but feed the hungry, whether they agree with us in sentiment or not."

Thus did Atticus consider even the poor who were at a

---

[1] The adherents of the party of S. John Chrysostom. See above, b. vi. ch. iii.

[2] Ἐν . . . . παροικίαις, in the different parishes. See Bingham, b. v. ch. vi.

[3] Χρυσίνους. This is of indefinite value. (Στατῆρας may be understood. The value of a stater was 1l. 0s. 9d.)

distance from him. He laboured also to abolish the superstitions of certain persons. For he was informed that the Separatists from the Novatians, on account of the Jewish Passover,[1] had transported the body of Sabbatius from the island of Rhodes, where he had died in exile, and having buried it, were accustomed to pray at his grave. Atticus therefore caused the body to be disinterred at night, and deposited in a private sepulchre; after which those who had formerly paid their adorations at that place, ceased to do so, on finding his tomb had been opened. Moreover he manifested a great deal of taste in the application of names to places. To a port in the mouth of the Euxine Sea, anciently called Pharmaceus,[2] he gave the appellation of Therapeia;[3] because he would not have a place where religious assemblies were held, dishonoured by an inauspicious name. Another place in the vicinity of Constantinople he termed Argyropolis,[4] for this reason. Chrysopolis[5] is an ancient port situated at the head of the Bosphorus, and is mentioned by several of the early writers, especially Strabo, Nicolaus Damascenus, and the eloquent Xenophon in the sixth Book of his "Expedition of Cyrus;"[6] and again in the first of his "Grecian[7] History" he says concerning it, *That Alcibiades, having walled it round, established a toll in it, obliging all who sailed out of Pontus to pay tithes there.* Atticus, seeing the former place to be directly opposite to Chrysopolis, and very delightfully situated, declared the most appropriate name for it was Argyropolis, which was assigned to it from that time. Some persons having said to him that the Novatians ought not to be permitted to hold their assemblies within the cities: "Do you not know," he replied, "that they were fellow-sufferers with us in the persecution under Constantine and Valens?[8] Besides," said he, "they have stedfastly adhered to our creed: for although they separated from the Church a long while ago, they have never introduced any innovations concerning the faith."

[1] See above, chap. v. of this book. [2] Φαρμακία, i. e. "a poisoner."
[3] Θεραπείας, i. e. "service," "worship," or "healing:" for the word occurs in all three senses.
[4] The silver city. [5] The golden city.
[6] See Xenoph. Anab. b. vi. chap. vi. sect. 38.
[7] Ἑλληνικῶν. See b. i. chap. i. sect. 22. This happened in the year 411, A. C.
[8] See b. iv. chap. i.—vi.

Being once at Nice on account of the ordination of a bishop, and seeing there Asclepiades bishop of the Novatians, then very aged, he asked him how many years he had borne the episcopal office? When he was answered, fifty years: "You are a happy man," said he, "to have been exercised in so good a work for such a length of time." To the same Asclepiades he observed: "I commend Novatus; but can by no means approve of the Novatians." And when Asclepiades expressed his surprise at this strange remark, Atticus gave him this reason for the distinction. "Novatus has my approbation for refusing to communicate with those who had sacrificed, for I myself would have done the same; but I cannot praise the Novatians, inasmuch as they exclude laymen from communion for very trivial offences." Asclepiades answered, "There are many other 'sins unto death,' as the Scriptures term them, besides sacrificing to idols; on account of which even you ex-communicate ecclesiastics, but we, laymen also, reserving to God alone the power of pardoning them."[1] Atticus had more-over a presentiment of his own death; for at his departure from Nice, he said to Calliopius, a presbyter of that place: "Hasten to Constantinople before autumn if you wish to see me again alive; for if you delay beyond that time, you will not find me surviving." Nor did he err in this prediction; for he died on the 10th of October, in the 21st year of his episcopate, under the eleventh consulate of Theodosius, and the first of Valentinian Cæsar. The emperor Theodosius indeed was not at his funeral, being then on his way from Thessalonica, and did not reach Constantinople until the day after Atticus was interred. On the 23rd of the same month, Valentinian the younger was proclaimed Augustus.

CHAP. XXVI.—SISINNIUS IS CHOSEN TO SUCCEED ATTICUS.

AFTER the decease of Atticus, there arose a strong contest about the election of a successor, some proposing one person, and some another. One party was urgent in favour of a presbyter named Philip; another wished to promote Proclus, who was also a presbyter; but the general desire of the people

[1] For an account of the Novatians, compare b. iv. chap. xxviii.

was that the bishopric should be conferred on Sisinnius. This person held no ecclesiastical office within the city, but had been appointed to a presbyterate in a Church at Elæa, a village in the suburbs of Constantinople, where from an ancient custom the whole population annually assembled for the celebration of our Saviour's Ascension. His eminent piety, and above all his untiring efforts to promote the comforts of the poor even beyond his power, endeared him so much to the laity, that they procured his ordination on the last day of February, under the following consulate, which was the twelfth of Theodosius and the second of Valentinian. The presbyter Philip was so chagrined at the preference of another to himself, that he even introduced into his " Christian History" some very censorious remarks on this ordination. But as I cannot by any means approve of the temerity with which he has reflected on not only the ordination itself, but those also who ordained him, and more especially the lay partisans of Sisinnius, I deem it quite inadmissible to give the least countenance to his invectives by inserting any portion of them here : some notice however must be taken of his works.

CHAP. XXVII.—VOLUMINOUS PRODUCTIONS OF PHILIP, A
PRESBYTER OF SIDÈ.

PHILIP was a native of Sidè, a city of Pamphylia, which was also the birth-place of Troïlus the sophist, to whom he boasted himself to be nearly related. During his diaconate he was admitted to the privilege of familiar intercourse with John Chrysostom bishop of Constantinople. He was an exceedingly laborious student, and besides making very considerable literary attainments, formed an extensive collection of books in every branch of knowledge. Affecting the Asiatic style, he became the author of many treatises : for he wrote a refutation of the emperor Julian's works, and compiled a " Christian History," which he divided into thirty-six Books ; each of these Books occupied several volumes, so that they amounted altogether to nearly one thousand, and the mere argument.(or table of contents) of each volume equalled in magnitude the volume itself. In this composition, which he

has entitled not an "Ecclesiastic," but a "Christian History,"
he has grouped together abundance of very heterogeneous
elements, from the vanity of displaying the versatility of his
genius and the extent of his erudition: for it contains a
medley of geometrical theorems, astronomical speculations,
arithmetical calculations, and musical principles, with geogra-
phical delineations of islands, mountains, forests, and various
other matters of little moment. By forcing such irrelevant
details into connexion with his subject, he has rendered his
work a very loose production, useless alike, in my opinion, to
the ignorant and the learned; for the illiterate are incapable
of appreciating the loftiness of his diction, and such as are
really competent to form a just estimate, are disgusted with
his wearisome tautology. But let every one exercise his own
judgment concerning these books according to his taste. All
I have to add is, that he has sadly confounded the chronological order of the transactions he describes: for after having
related what took place in the reign of the emperor Theodosius, he immediately goes back to the times of the bishop
Athanasius; and this sort of thing is of frequent occurrence.
But enough has been said of Philip: we must now mention
what happened under the episcopate of Sisinnius.

CHAP. XXVIII.—PROCLUS ORDAINED BISHOP OF CYZICUM BY
SISINNIUS, BUT REJECTED BY THE PEOPLE.

THE bishop of Cyzicum having died, Sisinnius ordained
Proclus to the prelacy of that city. But while he was preparing to depart thither, the inhabitants anticipated him, by
electing an ascetic named Dalmatius. This they did in contempt of a law which forbad their ordination of a bishop, 172
without the sanction of the bishop of Constantinople:[1] but
they pretended that this was a special privilege granted to
Atticus alone. Proclus therefore continued destitute of the
presidency over his own Church, but his sermons acquired for
him celebrity in the Churches of Constantinople. We shall
however speak of him more particularly in an appropriate

[1] Suffragans were not allowed to be ordained without the consent of
their metropolitans. See Bingham, b. ii. ch. xvi. sect. 12.

place. Sisinnius survived his appointment to the bishopric scarcely two entire years, for he was removed by death on the 24th of December, in the consulate of Hierius and Ardaburius. For his temperance, integrity of life, and benignity to the poor, he was deservedly eminent; but his singularly affable and guileless disposition rendered him rather averse to business, so that by men of active habits he was accounted indolent.

CHAP. XXIX.—Nestorius promoted to the see of constantinople. his persecution of the heretics.

After the death of Sisinnius, such was the spirit of ambitious rivalry displayed by the ecclesiastics of Constantinople, that the emperors resolved that none of that Church should fill the vacant bishopric, notwithstanding the cabals of Philip's partisans, and the no less numerous votes in favour of the election of Proclus. They therefore sent for a stranger from Antioch whose name was Nestorius,[1] a native of Germanicia,[2] distinguished for his excellent voice and fluency of speech; qualifications which they judged important for the instruction of the people. After three months had elapsed, Nestorius therefore arrived from Antioch, being greatly lauded by some for his temperance: but what sort of a disposition he was of in other respects, those who possessed any discernment were able to perceive from his first sermon. Being ordained on the 10th of April, under the consulate of Felix and Taurus, he immediately addressed the emperor, before all the people, in these remarkable words: " Give me, my prince, the earth purged of heretics, and I will give you heaven as a recompence. Assist me in destroying heretics, and I will assist you in vanquishing the Persians." Now although this language was extremely gratifying to some of the multitude, who cherished a senseless antipathy to the very name of heretic; yet those, as I have said, who were skilful in predicating a man's character from his expressions, at once detected his levity of mind and violent temper, combined with an excessive love of vain-glory: inasmuch as he had burst forth into

[1] Gibbon's Decline and Fall, ch. xlvii.
[2] A city of Cilicia, on the western border of Syria.

such vehemence without being able to contain himself for the
shortest space of time; and to use the proverbial phrase,
"before he had tasted the water of the city," showed himself
a furious persecutor.   Accordingly, on the fifth day after his [173]
ordination, he determined to demolish the oratory in which
the Arians were accustomed to perform their devotions privately: an act that drove these people to desperation; for
when they saw the work of destruction going forward in their
edifice, they threw fire into it, which spreading on all sides
reduced many of the adjacent buildings also to ashes.   This
catastrophe created extraordinary tumult throughout the city,
and the Arians, burning to revenge themselves, made preparations for that purpose; but God, the Guardian of the city,
suffered not the mischief to gather to a climax.   Nestorius
however was from that time branded as an incendiary, not
only by the heretics, but by those also of his own faith.   Still
he could not rest there, but seeking every means of harassing
those who embraced not his own sentiments, he continually
disturbed the public tranquillity.   The Novatians also became
objects of his malignity, for he was incited to molest them in
every possible way, from the jealousy he felt towards Paul
their bishop, who was everywhere respected for his piety:
but the emperor's admonitions checked his fury.   With what
calamities he visited the Quartodecimans throughout Asia,
Lydia, and Caria, and what multitudes perished in a popular
tumult of which he was the cause at Miletus and Sardis, I
think proper to omit the description of.   The chastisement
inflicted on him for all these enormities, and for that unbridled
licence of speech in which he indulged himself, will be mentioned hereafter.

CHAP. XXX.—THE BURGUNDIANS EMBRACE CHRISTIANITY.

I MUST now relate an event well worthy of being recorded,
which happened about this time.   There is a barbarous nation
dwelling beyond the Rhine, denominated Burgundians, who
lead a very peaceful life, being almost all artisans, and supporting themselves by the exercise of their trades.   The Huns, by
making continual irruptions on this people, devastated their
country, and often destroyed great numbers of them.   In this

perplexity, therefore, the Burgundians resolved to have no
recourse to human aid, but to commit themselves to the protection of some god; and having seriously considered that the
God of the Romans mightily defended those that feared him,
they all with common consent embraced the faith of Christ.·
Going therefore to one of the Gallic cities, they requested the
bishop to grant them Christian baptism; who ordering them
to fast seven days, and having meanwhile instructed[1] them in
the elementary principles of the faith, on the eighth day
baptized and dismissed them. Becoming confident thenceforth, they marched against their invaders; nor were they
disappointed in their hope of Divine assistance. For Optar, the
king of the Huns, having died in the night from the effects of
a surfeit, the Burgundians attacked that people then without
a commander-in-chief; and although they were vastly inferior
in numbers, they obtained a complete victory, the Burgundians
being altogether but three thousand men, having destroyed no
less than ten thousand of the enemy. From that period this
nation became zealously attached to the Christian religion.
About the same time Barba bishop of the Arians died, on the
24th of June, under the thirteenth consulate of Theodosius
and the third of Valentinian, and Sabbatius was constituted
his successor.

CHAP. XXXI.—NESTORIUS HARASSES THE MACEDONIANS.

NESTORIUS indeed not only himself acted contrary to the
usage of the Church, but caused others also to imitate him in
this respect, as is evident from what happened during his episcopate. For Antony bishop of Germa, a city of the Hellespont,
actuated by the example of Nestorius in his intolerance of
heretics, began to persecute the Macedonians, under pretext of
carrying out the intentions of the patriarch. For some time
that sect endured his annoyance; but when Antony proceeded
to further extremities, unable any longer to bear his harsh
treatment, and becoming infuriated by despair, they preferred
the adoption of a cruel expedient to justice, and suborned two
men to assassinate their tormentor. When the Macedonians

[1] Κατηχήσας, catechised. See note on b. i. ch. viii. and b. vii.
ch. xvii.

had perpetrated this crime, Nestorius took occasion from it to
increase his violence of conduct against them, and prevailed on
the emperor to take away their churches.   They were therefore deprived of not only those which they possessed at
Constantinople, before the old walls of the imperial city, but
of those also which they had at Cyzicum, and many others
that belonged to them in the Hellespont.   Many of them
therefore at that time came over to the Catholic Church, and
professed the Homoousian faith.   But, as the proverb says,
"*drunkards never want wine, nor the contentious strife:*" and
so it fell out with regard to Nestorius, who, after having exerted himself to expel others from the Church, was himself
ejected on the following account.

CHAP. XXXII.—Of the presbyter anastasius, by whom
the faith of nestorius was perverted.

Nestorius had brought with him from Antioch a presbyter named Anastasius, for whom he had the highest esteem,
and whom he consulted in the management of his most important affairs.   This Anastasius preaching one day in the church
said, "Let no one call Mary *Theotocos:*[1] for Mary was but a
woman; and it is impossible that God should be born of a
woman."   These words created a great sensation, and troubled
many both of the clergy and laity; they having been heretofore taught to acknowledge Christ[2] as God, and by no means
to separate his humanity from his Divinity on account of the
economy of the incarnation.   This they conceived was inculcated by the apostle when he said, "Yea, though we have
known Christ after the flesh; yet now henceforth know we
him no more."[3]   And again, "Wherefore, leaving the word
of the beginning of Christ, let us go on unto perfection."[4]
While great offence was taken in the church, as we have said,
at what was thus propounded, Nestorius endeavoured to
establish the proposition of Anastasius, and in his desire to

[1] Θεοτόκον, i. e. mother of God.   Upon the whole controversy involved in
the word Θεοτόκος, see Hammond's Canons.   Notes on the Council of
Ephesus.
[2] Θεολογεῖν Χριστὸν.   [3] 2 Cor. v. 16.   [4] Heb. vi. 1.

shelter from reprobation the man for whom he had so exalted an
opinion, he delivered several public discourses on the subject,
in which he not only rejected the epithet *Theotocos*, but
involved the whole question in fresh grounds of controversy.
Then indeed the discussion which agitated the whole Church,
resembled the struggle of combatants in the dark, all parties
uttering the most confused and contradictory assertions.   The
general impression was that Nestorius was tinctured with the
errors of Paul of Samosata and Photinus, and was desirous of
foisting on the Church the blasphemous dogma that the Lord
is a mere man; and so great a clamour was raised by the
contention, that it was deemed requisite to convene a general
council to take cognizance of the matter in dispute.   Having
myself perused the writings of Nestorius, I shall candidly
express the conviction of my own mind concerning him: and
as, in entire freedom from personal antipathies, I have already
alluded to his faults, I shall in like manner be unbiassed by the
criminations of his adversaries, to derogate from his merits.   I
cannot then concede that he was either a follower of the
heretics with whom he was thus classed, or that he denied the
Divinity of Christ:[1] but he seemed scared at the term *Theotocos*, as though it were some terrible phantom.   The fact is,
the causeless alarm he manifested on this subject, just exposed
his grievous ignorance: for instead of being a man of learning,
as his natural eloquence caused him to be considered, he was in
reality disgracefully illiterate.   His conscious readiness of
expression led him to contemn the drudgery of an accurate
examination of the ancient expositors, and puffed him up with
a vain confidence in his own powers.   Now he was evidently
unacquainted with the fact, that in the First Catholic Epistle of
John, (iv. 2, 3,) it was written in the ancient copies, "Every
spirit that separates[2] Jesus, is not of God."   The mutilation
of this passage is attributable to those who desired to separate
the Divine nature from the human economy: or, to use the
very language of the early interpreters, some persons have

---

[1] But the question may be asked, How then does our author in the
next chapter make Nestorius himself declare, "I cannot term him God
who was but two or three months old."   It is difficult, and indeed impossible, to reconcile these two conflicting passages.

[2] Λύει.   In the Alex. MS. it is ὁμολογεῖ τὸν Ἰησοῦν, without the
Χριστὸν ἐν σαρκὶ ἐληλυθότα contained in the Greek copies now extant.

corrupted this Epistle, aiming at "separating the manhood of Christ from his Deity." But the humanity is united to the Divinity in the Saviour, so as to constitute but one person. Hence it was that the ancients, emboldened by this testimony, scrupled not to style Mary *Theotocos.* Eusebius Pamphilus, in his third Book of the Life of Constantine,[1] thus writes: " Emanuel submitted to be born for our sake; and the place of his nativity is by the Hebrews called Bethlehem. Wherefore the devout empress Helen adorned with the most splendid monuments the place where the Virgin Mother of God gave birth to her Son, decorating that sacred cave with the richest ornaments." Origen also, in the third volume of his Commentaries on the Apostolic Epistle to the Romans, gives an ample exposition of the sense in which the term *Theotocos* is used. It is therefore obvious that Nestorius had very little acquaintance with the old theologians, and for that reason, as I observed, objected to *that expression* only: for his own published Homilies fully exonerate him from all identification with Paul of Samosata's impious assertion of the mere manhood of Christ. In these discourses he nowhere destroys the proper Personality[2] of the Word of God; but on the contrary invariably maintains that He has an essential and distinct existence. Nor does he ever deny his subsistence as Photinus and Paul of Samosata did, and as the Manichæans and followers of Montanus have also dared to do. I can speak thus positively respecting Nestorius's opinion, partly from having [174] myself read his own works, and partly from the assurances of his admirers. But this idle contention of his has produced no slight ferment in the religious world.

CHAP. XXXIII.—DESECRATION OF THE ALTAR OF THE GREAT CHURCH.

WHILE matters were in this state, the church was profaned in the most outrageous manner. For the domestics of a man of quality who were foreigners, having experienced harsh treatment from their master, fled from him to the church, and ran up to the very altar with their swords drawn.[3] Nor could

[1] See b. iii. ch. xliii.   [2] Ὑπόστασιν. See note on b. i. ch. v.
[3] See Bingham, book viii. chap. xi.

they be prevailed upon by any entreaties to withdraw, so as not to impede the performance of the public services; but they obstinately maintained their position for several days, brandishing their weapons in defiance of any one who dared to approach them. At last, after having killed one of the ecclesiastics, and wounded another, they slew themselves. A person who was present at this desecration of the sanctuary, remarked that such a profanation was an ominous presage, and in support of his view of the matter, quoted the two following iambics of an ancient poet:

"For such prognostics happen at a time
When temples are defiled by impious crime."

Nor did succeeding events falsify these inauspicious forebodings: for there followed division among the people, and the deposition of the author of it.

CHAP. XXXIV.—SYNOD AT EPHESUS AGAINST NESTORIUS. HIS DEPOSITION.

SHORTLY after this, the emperor's mandate was issued directing the bishops in all places to assemble at Ephesus. Immediately after Easter, therefore, Nestorius, escorted by a strong body of his adherents, repaired to that city, and found many prelates already there. Cyril bishop of Alexandria made some delay, and did not arrive till near Pentecost; and Juvenal bishop of Jerusalem was not present until five days after that feast. While John of Antioch was still absent, those who were now congregated entered into the consideration of the question; and Cyril of Alexandria began a sharp skirmish of words, with the design of terrifying Nestorius, for whom he had a strong dislike. When many had declared that Christ was God, Nestorius said: "I cannot term him God who was two and three months old. I am therefore clear of your blood, and shall in future come no more among you." Having uttered these words he left the assembly, and afterwards held meetings with the other bishops who entertained sentiments similar to his own. Thus were those present divided into two factions. That section which supported Cyril, having constituted themselves a council, summoned Nestorius; but he refused to meet them until John of Antioch should arrive. They there-fore proceeded to the examination of the public discourses of Nestorius which had been the main subject of complaint ; and after deciding from a repeated perusal of them that they con-tained blasphemy against the Son of God, they deposed him.[175] This being done, the partisans of Nestorius constituted them-selves another council apart, and therein deposed Cyril himself, and together with him Memnon bishop of Ephesus. John bishop of Antioch made his appearance soon after these trans-actions ; and being informed of what had taken place, he pro-nounced unqualified censure on Cyril as the author of all this confusion, in having so precipitately proceeded to the deposition of Nestorius. Upon this Cyril combined with Juvenal to re-venge themselves on John, and they deposed him also. When Nestorius saw that the contention which had been raised was thus tending to schism and the destruction of communion, in bitter regret he cried out: "Let Mary be called Theotocos, if you will, and let all disputing cease." But although he made this recantation, no notice was taken of it ; for his deposition was not revoked, and he was banished to Oasis, where he still remains. Such was the conclusion of this synod, which was dissolved on the 28th of June, under the consulate of Bassus and Antiochus. John, when he had returned to his bishopric, having convened several prelates, deposed Cyril, who had also returned to his see: but being reconciled soon after, they mutually reinstated each other in their episcopal chairs. But the dissension which had been excited in the Church of Con-stantinople by the absurd garrulity of Nestorius, was by no means allayed after his deposition ; for the people were so agitated by divisions that the clergy unanimously anathema-tized him. For such is the sentence which we Christians are accustomed to pronounce on those who have advanced any blasphemous doctrines, in order that their impiety may be publicly exposed, as it were on a pillar, to universal execration.

CHAP. XXXV.—ELECTION OF MAXIMIAN TO THE EPISCOPATE OF CONSTANTINOPLE.

AFTER this there was another debate concerning the elec-tion of a bishop of Constantinople. Many were in favour of

Philip, of whom we have already spoken; but a still greater number advocated the claims of Proclus. And the votes of the majority would have determined the matter, had not some influential persons interfered, on the ground of its being forbidden by the ecclesiastical canon that a person nominated to one bishopric should be translated to another see.[1] The people believing this assertion, were thereby restrained; and about four months after the deposition of Nestorius, a presbyter named Maximian, who had lived an ascetic life, was elected to this episcopate. He was neither an eloquent man, nor at all disposed to trouble himself with the busy affairs of life; but had acquired a high reputation for sanctity, on account of having at his own expense constructed certain tombs for the reception of the pious after their decease.

CHAP. XXXVI.—THE AUTHOR'S OPINION OF THE VALIDITY OF TRANSLATIONS FROM ONE SEE TO ANOTHER.

BUT since some parties, by alleging a prohibition in the [176] ecclesiastical canon, prevented the election of Proclus, because of his previous nomination to the see of Cyzicum, I shall make a few remarks on this subject. Those who then presumed to interpose such a cause of exclusion, appear to me to have either been influenced by prejudice against Proclus to affirm what they knew to be untrue; or at the least to have been themselves completely ignorant both of the canons, and of the frequent and often advantageous usage of the Churches. Eusebius Pamphilus relates in the sixth Book of his "Ecclesiastical History,"[2] that Alexander bishop of a certain city in Cappadocia, coming to Jerusalem for devotional purposes, was detained by the people, and constituted bishop of that place, as the successor of Narcissus; and that he continued to preside over the Churches there during the remainder of his life. So indifferent a thing was it amongst our ancestors, to transfer a bishop from one city to another as often as it was deemed expedient. But to place beyond a doubt the fallacy

---

[1] See the 15th canon of Nicæa; the 21st of Antioch; and compare the 14th Apostolical canon.
[2] See chap. xi.

of the pretensions of those who opposed the ordination of Proclus, I shall annex to this History the canon which they cited
against him.   It runs thus :—" If[1] any one after having been
ordained a bishop should not proceed to the Church unto which
he has been appointed, from no fault on his part, but either
because the people are unwilling to receive him, or for some
other reason which casts no imputation on him ; let him be
partaker of the honour and functions of the rank with which
he has been invested, provided he intermeddles not with the
affairs of the Church wherein he may minister.   It is his duty
however to submit to whatever the synod of the province may
see fit to determine, after it shall have taken cognizance of the
matter."   Such is the language of the canon.   I shall now
show that this construction of its meaning is fully borne out
by abundant precedents of bishops having been translated
from one city to another to meet the exigences of peculiar
cases, giving the names of those bishops who have been so
translated.[2]   Perigenes was ordained bishop of Patræ: but[177]
inasmuch as the inhabitants of that city refused to admit him,
the bishop of Rome appointed him to the metropolitan see of
Corinth, on its becoming vacant by the decease of its former
bishop, where he presided during the rest of his days.   Gregory was first made bishop of Sasimi, one of the cities of
Cappadocia, but was afterwards transferred to Nazianzum.
Meletius, after having presided over the Church at Sebastia,
subsequently governed that of Antioch.   Alexander bishop
of Antioch translated Dositheus bishop of Seleucia, to Tarsus
in Cilicia.   Reverentius was removed from Arci in Phœnicia,
and afterwards translated to Tyre.   John was transferred
from Gordum, a city of Lydia, to Proconnessus, and presided
over the Church there.   Palladius was translated from Helenopolis to Aspuna ; and Alexander from the same city to
Adriani.   Theophilus was removed from Apamea in Asia, to
Eudoxiopolis, anciently called Salambeia.   Polycarp was transferred from Sexantapristi, a city of Mysia, to Nicopolis in

---

[1] Valesius contends that Socrates here adduces the eighteenth canon of
the synod at Antioch, instead of the twenty-first, which militates against
his view of the case.   The council of Antioch was held A. D. 341.
[2] Upon the sense in which we must understand the canons laid down
against the translation of bishops, see Bingham's Christ. Antiq. b. vi.
chap. iv. sect. 6.

Thrace. Hierophilus from Trapezopolis in Phrygia to Plo-
tinopolis in Thrace. Optimus from Agdamia in Phrygia to
Antioch in Pisidia ; and Silvanus from Philippopolis in Thrace
to Troas. Let this enumeration of bishops who have been
translated from one see to another suffice for the present, as I
deem it desirable here to give a concise account of him whom
I last mentioned. '

CHAP. XXXVII.—MIRACLE PERFORMED BY SILVANUS BISHOP
OF TROAS.

SILVANUS was formerly a rhetorician, and had been brought
up in the school of Troïlus the sophist ; but, aiming at perfection in the Christian course, he entered on the ascetic
mode of life, and threw aside the rhetorician's pallium.   Atticus bishop of Constantinople having afterwards ordained
him bishop of Philippopolis, he resided three years in Thrace ;
but being unable to endure the cold of that region from the
feebleness and delicacy of his frame, he begged Atticus to
178 appoint some one else in his place.   This having been done,
Silvanus returned to Constantinople, where he practised so
great austerities, that despising the luxurious refinements of
the age, he often appeared in the crowded streets of that
populous city shod with sandals made of hay.   Some time
having elapsed, the bishop of Troas died ; on which account
the inhabitants of that city came to Atticus concerning the
appointment of a successor.   While he was deliberating whom
he should ordain for them, Silvanus happened to pay him a
visit, which at once relieved him from further anxiety ; for
addressing Silvanus, he said : " You have now no longer any
excuse for avoiding the pastoral administration of a Church ;
for Troas is not a cold place : so that God has considered
your infirmity of body, and provided you a suitable residence.
Go thither then, my brother, without delay."   Silvanus
therefore removed to that city, where he performed a miracle
which I shall now relate.   An immense ship for carrying
burdens, such as they term *Platè*, intended for the conveyance
of enormous pillars, had been recently constructed on the
shore at Troas.   But every effort to launch this vessel proved
ineffectual ; for although many strong ropes were attached to

it, and the power of a vast number of persons was applied, all was unavailing. When these attempts had been repeated several days successively with the like result, the people began to think that the devil detained the ship; they therefore went to the bishop Silvanus, and entreated him to go and offer a prayer in that place, as they thought it could not be otherwise moved. He replied, with his characteristic lowliness of mind, that he was but a sinner, and that it pertained to some one more worthy to receive such grace from God as would relieve them from their difficulty. Being at length prevailed on by their continued entreaties, he approached the shore, where, after having prayed, he took hold of a rope, and exhorting the rest to vigorous exertion, the ship was by the first pull instantly set in motion, and ran swiftly into the sea. This miracle wrought by the hands of Silvanus, stirred up the whole population of the province to piety. But the uncommon worth of Silvanus was manifested in various other ways. Perceiving that the ecclesiastics made a gain of the contentions of those engaged in law-suits, he would never nominate any one of the clergy as judge: but causing the documents of the litigants to be delivered to himself, he summoned to him some pious layman in whose integrity he had confidence, and committed to him the adjudication of the case. Thus were all differences soon equitably settled; and by this procedure Silvanus acquired for himself great reputation from all classes of persons. We have indeed digressed pretty much from the course of our history; but yet it will not, we imagine, be unprofitable. Let us now however return to the place from which we departed. The ordination of Maximian on the 25th of October, under the consulate of Bassus and Antiochus, had the effect of reducing the affairs of the Church to a better ordered and more tranquil condition.

CHAP. XXXVIII.—MANY OF THE JEWS IN CRETE EMBRACE THE CHRISTIAN FAITH.

ABOUT this period a great number of Jews who dwelt in Crete were converted to Christianity, through the following disastrous circumstance. A certain Jewish impostor had the impudence to assert that he was Moses, and had been sent from heaven to lead out the Jews inhabiting that island, and conduct them through the sea: for he said that he was the same person that formerly preserved the Israelites by leading them through the Red Sea. During a whole year therefore he perambulated the several cities of the island, and persuaded the Jews to confide in his assurances. He moreover bid them renoumce their money and other property, pledging himself to guide them through a dry sea into the land of promise. Deluded by such expectations, they neglected business of every kind, despising what they possessed, and permitting any one who chose to take it. When the day appointed by this deceiver for their departure had arrived, he himself took the lead, and all following with their wives and children, they proceeded until they reached a promontory that overhung the sea, from which he ordered them to fling themselves headlong into it. Those who came first to the precipice did so, and were immediately destroyed, part of them being dashed in pieces against the rocks, and part drowned in the waters: and more would have perished, had not some fishermen and merchants who were Christians providentially happened to be present. These persons drew out and saved some that were almost drowned, who then in their perilous situation became sensible of the madness of their conduct. The rest they hindered from casting themselves down, by telling them the fate of those who had taken the first leap. When at length the Jews perceived how fearfully they had been duped, they blamed their own indiscreet credulity, and sought to lay hold of the pseudo-Moses in order to put him to death. But they were unable to seize him, for he suddenly disappeared: which induced a general belief that it was some malignant fiend,[1] who had assumed a human form for the destruction of their nation in that place.

CHAP. XXXIX.—PRESERVATION OF THE CHURCH OF THE NOVATIANS FROM FIRE.

A LITTLE while after this, the celebrity of Paul bishop of the Novatians, as a man beloved of God, was greatly increased.

[1] 'Αλάστωρ (this word is in Æschylus and Sophocles applied to *the Furies*).

For a terrible conflagration having broken out at Constantinople, such as had never happened before, by which the greater part of the city was destroyed, the fire consuming the public granaries, the Achillean bath, and everything else in its way, at length approached the church of the Novatians situated near Pelargus. When the bishop Paul saw the church endangered, he ran towards the altar, where he commended to God the preservation of the church and all that it contained; and he did not cease to pray not only for it, but also for the city. And God heard him, as the event clearly proved: for although the fire entered this oratory through all its doors and windows, it did no damage. And while many adjacent edifices fell a prey to the devouring element, the church itself was seen unscathed in the midst of the whole conflagration, triumphing over its raging flames. The fire was not extinguished until after it had been in active operation for two days and nights, and had burnt down a great part of the city: but the church remained entire, and, what is more marvellous still, there was not the slightest trace even of smoke to be observed either on its timbers or its walls. This occurred on the 16th of August, in the fourteenth consulate of Theodosius, which he bore together with Maximus. Since that time the Novatians annually celebrate the preservation of their church, on the 16th of August, by special thanksgivings to God. And both Christians and Pagans continue to regard that place with veneration as a peculiarly consecrated spot, because of the miracle which was wrought for its safeguard.

CHAP. XL.—PROCLUS SUCCEEDS MAXIMIAN BISHOP OF CONSTANTINOPLE.

MAXIMIAN having peacefully governed the Church during two years and five months, died on the 12th of April, in the consulate of Areobindus and Aspar. This happened to be on the fifth day [1] of the week of fasts which immediately precedes Easter. The emperor Theodosius wishing to prevent the disturbances in the Church which usually attend the election of a bishop, had made a wise provision for this affair; so that

[1] i. e. Thursday in Holy week.

before the body of Maximian was interred, he directed the bishops who were then in the city to place Proclus in the episcopal chair without delay. For he had already received letters from Cælestine bishop of Rome approving of this election, which he had forwarded to Cyril of Alexandria, John 179 of Antioch, and Rufus of Thessalonica; in which he was assured that there was no impediment to the translation to another see, of a person who had been nominated and really was the bishop of some one Church. Proclus being thus invested with the bishopric, performed the funeral obsequies of his predecessor: but it is now time to give some account of him.

CHAP. XLI.—EXCELLENT QUALITIES OF PROCLUS.

PROCLUS was a reader at a very early age, and assiduously frequenting the schools, became devoted to the study of eloquence. On attaining manhood he was in the habit of constant intercourse with Atticus the bishop, having been constituted his secretary. When he had made great progress, his patron promoted him to the rank of deacon, and subsequently to the presbyterate; after which, as we have before stated, Sisinnius ordained him bishop of Cyzicum. But all these things were done long before he was elected to the episcopal chair of Constantinople. In moral excellence he had few equals; for having been trained by Atticus, he was a zealous imitator of all that prelate's virtues. His patience, however, greatly exceeded that of his master, who occasionally exercised severities upon the heretics; for Proclus was gentle towards everybody, being convinced that kindness is far more effective than violence in advancing the cause of truth. Resolving therefore vexatiously to interfere with no heresy whatever, he restored in his own person to the Church that mild and benign dignity of character, which had so often before been unhappily violated. In this respect he followed the example of the emperor Theodosius; for as he had determined never to exercise his imperial authority against criminals, so had Proclus likewise purposed not to disquiet those who entertained other sentiments than his own on divine subjects.

CHAP. XLII.—EULOGIUM OF THE EMPEROR THEODOSIUS JUNIOR.

FOR these reasons the emperor had the highest esteem for Proclus. Indeed he himself was a pattern to all true prelates, and never approved of those who attempted to persecute others. Nay, I can confidently affirm, that in meekness he surpassed all those who have ever faithfully borne the sacerdotal office. And what is recorded of Moses in the book of Numbers,[1]— "Now the man Moses was very meek, above all the men which were upon the face of the earth,"—may most justly be applied to the emperor Theodosius. It is because of this, that God subdued his enemies without martial conflicts, as the capture of the tyrant John[2] and the subsequent discomfiture of the barbarians clearly demonstrate. For Divine aid has been afforded this most devout emperor in our times, of a similar kind to what was vouchsafed by the God of the universe to the righteous heretofore. I write not these things from adulation, but simply narrate facts such as everybody can attest.

CHAP XLIII.—CALAMITIES OF THE BARBARIANS WHO HAD BEEN THE TYRANT JOHN'S AUXILIARIES.

AFTER the death of the tyrant, the barbarians whom he had called to his assistance against the Romans made preparations for ravaging the Roman provinces. The emperor, being informed of this, immediately, as his custom was, committed the management of the matter to God; and continuing in earnest prayer, he speedily obtained what he sought, for the following disasters befell the barbarians. Rhougas their chief was struck dead with a thunderbolt. Then a plague followed which destroyed most of the men who were under him: and as if this was not sufficient, fire came down from heaven, and consumed many of the survivors. This series of supernatural catastrophes filled the barbarians with the utmost terror; not so much because they had dared to take up arms against a nation of such valour as the Romans pos-

---

[1] Num. xii. 3.   [2] See above, chap. xxiii.

sessed, as that they perceived them to be assisted by a mighty God. On this occasion, Proclus the bishop preached a sermon in the church which was greatly admired; in which he applied a prophecy out of Ezekiel[1] to the deliverance which had been effected by God in the late emergency. This is the language of the prophecy:—"And thou, son of man, prophesy against Gog the prince of Rhos, Misoch, and Thobel.[2] For I will judge him with death, and with blood, and with overflowing rain, and with hail-stones. I will also rain fire and brimstone upon him, and upon all his bands, and upon many nations that are with him. And I will be magnified, and glorified, and I will be known in the eyes of many nations: and they shall know that I am the Lord." This application of the prophecy was received with great applause, as I have said, and enhanced the estimation in which Proclus was held. Moreover the providence of God rewarded the meekness of the emperor in various other ways, one of which I shall now mention.

CHAP. XLIV.—MARRIAGE OF THE EMPEROR VALENTINIAN WITH EUDOXIA THE DAUGHTER OF THEODOSIUS.

HE had, by the empress Eudocia his wife, a daughter named Eudoxia, whom his cousin Valentinian, to whose care he had confided the empire of the West, demanded for himself in marriage. When the emperor Theodosius had given his assent to this proposal, they consulted with each other at what place on the frontiers of both empires it would be desirable that the marriage should be celebrated; and it was decided that both parties should go to Thessalonica (which is about half-way) for this purpose. But shortly afterwards Valentinian intimated by letter to Theodosius, that he would not give him the trouble of coming, for that he himself would go to Constantinople. Accordingly, having secured the Western parts with a sufficient guard, he proceeded thither on account of his nuptials, which were celebrated in the consulate of Isidore and Senator; after which he returned with his wife into the West. This auspicious event took place at that time.

[1] Ezek. xxxviii. 2, 22, 23.
[2] Russia, Moscow, Tobolsk. (Quoted from the Septuagint.)

CHAP. XLV.—THE BODY OF JOHN CHRYSOSTOM TRANSFERRED
TO CONSTANTINOPLE.

NOT long after this, Proclus the bishop reunited to the Church
those who had separated themselves from it on account of
bishop John's deposition; for he soothed the irritation which
had produced their schism, by the following prudent expedient.   Having obtained the emperor's permission, he removed
the body of John from Comani to Constantinople, in the
thirty-fifth year after his deposition.   And when he had
carried it in solemn procession through the city, he deposited it
with much honour in the church termed that of *The Apostles.*
By this means the admirers of that prelate were conciliated,
and again associated in communion with the other members of
the Catholic Church.   This happened on the 27th of January,
in the sixteenth consulate of the emperor Theodosius.   But
it astonishes me that the odium which has been attached to
Origen since his death, has not also fastened itself upon John.
For the former was excommunicated by Theophilus about two
hundred years after his decease; while the latter was restored [180]
to communion by Proclus in the thirty-fifth year after his
death ! This surely can only be accounted for by the difference of character in the two individuals who have acted in so
contrary a manner.   And men of observation and intelligence
cannot be deceived in reference to the motives and principles
which operate continually to produce anomalies such as these.

CHAP. XLVI.—DEATH OF PAUL BISHOP OF THE NOVATIANS,
AND ELECTION OF MARCIAN AS HIS SUCCESSOR.

A LITTLE while after the removal of John's body, Paul
bishop of the Novatians died, on the 21st of July, under the
same consulate; who at his funeral united, in a certain sense,
all the different sects into one Church.   For such was the
universal esteem in which he was held because of his rectitude
of life, that all parties attended his body to the tomb, chanting
psalms together.   But as Paul just before his death performed a memorable act, which it may be interesting to the

readers of this work to be acquainted with, I shall insert it here. And lest the brilliancy of that important deed should be obscured by dwelling on circumstantial details of minor consequence, I shall not stay to expatiate on the strictness with which he maintained his ascetic discipline as to diet even throughout his illness, without the least departure from the course he had prescribed for himself, or the omission of any of the ordinary exercises of devotion with his accustomed fervour. Conscious that his departure was at hand, he sent for all the presbyters of the Churches under his care, and thus addressed them: "Give your attention while I am alive to the election of a bishop to preside over you, lest the peace of the Church should hereafter be disturbed." They having answered that this affair had better not be left to them: "For inasmuch," said they, "as some of us have one judgment about the matter, and some another, we shall never agree to nominate the same individual. We wish therefore that you would yourself designate the person you would desire to succeed you." "Give me then," said Paul, "this declaration of yours in writing, that you will elect him whom I shall appoint." When they had written this pledge, and ratified it by their signatures, Paul, rising in his bed and sitting up, wrote the name of Marcian in the paper, without informing any of those present what he had inserted. This person had been promoted to the rank of presbyter, and instructed in the ascetic discipline by him, but was then gone abroad. Having folded this document and put his own seal on it, he caused the principal presbyters to seal it also; after which he delivered it into the hands of Marcus a bishop of the Novatians in Scythia, who was at that time staying at Constantinople; to whom he thus spake: "If it shall please God that I should continue much longer in this life, restore me this deposit, now intrusted to your safe keeping. But should it seem fit to Him to remove me, you will herein discover whom I have chosen as my successor in the bishopric." Soon after this he died: and the paper having been unfolded on the third day after, in the presence of a great number of persons, Marcian's name was found within it, when they all cried out that he was worthy of the honour. Messengers were therefore sent off without delay to bring him to Constantinople, who finding him residing at Tiberiopolis in Phrygia, brought him back with them by a pious fraud ;[1] whereupon he was ordained and placed in the episcopal chair on the 21st of August following.

CHAP. XLVII.—THE EMPRESS EUDOCIA GOES TO JERUSALEM.

MOREOVER the emperor Theodosius offered up thanksgivings to God for the blessings which he had conferred upon him; at the same time reverencing Christ with the most special honours. He also sent his wife Eudocia to Jerusalem, as she had bound herself by a vow to go thither, should she live to see the marriage of her daughter. The empress therefore, in her visit to the sacred city, adorned its churches with the most costly gifts; and both then, and after her return, decorated all the churches in the other cities of the East with a variety of ornaments.

CHAP. XLVIII.—THALASSIUS IS ORDAINED BISHOP OF CÆSAREA IN CAPPADOCIA.

ABOUT the same time, under the seventeenth consulate of Theodosius, Proclus the bishop undertook the performance of an act, for which there was no precedent among the ancient prelates. Firmus bishop of Cæsarea in Cappadocia being dead, the inhabitants of that place came to Constantinople to consult Proclus about the appointment of some one to succeed him. While Proclus was considering whom he should prefer to that see, it so happened that all the senators came to the church to visit him on the Saturday; among whom was Thalassius also, who had administered the government of the nations and cities of Illyricum. But notwithstanding the report of his being the person to whom the emperor was about to intrust the government of the Eastern parts, Proclus laid his hands on him, and ordained him bishop of Cæsarea, instead of his being constituted Prætorian prefect. In such a flourishing condition were the affairs of the Church at this time.

---

[1] Ἀγαθῷ δόλῳ. Similar, perhaps, to that which is mentioned and defended by Chrysostom in the first Book of his Treatise entitled "de Sacerdotio."

But I shall here close my history, praying that the Churches everywhere, with the cities and nations, may live in peace: for as long as peace continues, those who desire to become historians will find no materials for their purpose. And we ourselves, O holy man of God, Theodore, should have been unable to accomplish in seven Books the task we undertook at your request had the lovers of seditions chosen to be quiet. This last Book contains an account of the transactions of the last thirty-two years; and the whole history, which is comprised in seven Books, comprehends a period of 140 years. It commences from the first year of the 271st Olympiad, in which Constantine was proclaimed emperor; and ends at the second year of the 305th Olympiad, in which the emperor Theodosius bore his seventeenth consulate.

NOTES BY VALESIUS.

The Figures at the beginning of the Notes refer to corresponding Figures in the margin of the work.

BOOK I.

1. Page 1, line 8.—The meaning of Socrates is, that he will begin from the history of Arius, which Eusebius had but partly touched upon in his Life of Constantine : for Eusebius (he says) made it his business, in those books, to enlarge upon the emperor's praises, rather than to give an exact account of the ecclesiastical affairs. But he himself, resolving to commit to writing the affairs transacted in the Church, promises to give a more accurate account of the Arian heresy, and to begin his History from those things which Eusebius had either purposely omitted, or but slightly touched upon, as not conducive to his design. Indeed Socrates has not begun his History where Eusebius leaves off; for Eusebius continues his biography to the death of Constantine. But Eusebius has continued the series of his Ecclesiastical History only down to the tumults raised by Arius, and to those affairs which preceded the Nicene Council. If therefore we speak with respect only to the Ecclesiastical History of Eusebius, we may say that Socrates began where Eusebius ended. But if we take into account his books concerning the Life of Constantine, this will not be true.

2. P. 2, l. 5.—Socrates is here in an error, for Maximianus Herculius, who was otherwise called Maximian the Elder, was by Constantine's command slain in Gallia, A. D. 310. But Maximius Cæsar, two years after, being conquered by Licinius, died at Tarsus.

3. P. 2, l. 14.—Socrates repeats this in book vii. chap. xlviii., where he says that he began his History in the first year of the 271st Olympiad, the year in which Constantine the Great was proclaimed emperor. This Olympiad begins at the solstice of the year A. D. 305, being the year after the resignation of Diocletian. But Constantius did not die this year, but in the following, when he was the sixth time consul with Galerius Augustus.

4. P. 2, l. 16.—Socrates seems to have been of opinion, that Constantine and Maxentius began their reign in the same year that Diocletian and Maximianus Herculius resigned the empire. This also was the opinion of the author of the Chronicle of Alexandria, and of others who attribute the years of Constantius's reign to Constantine his son. And hence it is that Constantine the Great is reported to have reigned 32 years, whereas really he reigned but 30 years and 10 months.

5. P. 2, l. 23.—πάντα περιέπων. This passage must be understood in the qualified sense which we have given to it, for Galerius was not really chief and sole arbitrator of all things, as there were at the same time two other Augusti, Constantine in the Gallias, and Maxentius at Rome. But nevertheless he may be said to have exercised the supreme authority, because he was the senior Augustus, and was respected by the junior Augusti as a father. '

6. P. 5, l. 17.—Socrates here alludes to the soldiers' acclamations, who after a signal victory were wont to style their prince "Emperor," and "Augustus." The citizens did the same when the victorious prince made his entry into the city.

7. P. 7, l. 1.—Lucas Holstenius, in a dissertation upon this Epistle of Alexander, remarks that many interpreters have not well rendered these words, which they have generally translated thus : "whereas there is one body of the Catholic Church." He asserts, that the passage should rather have been thus rendered: "whereas the Catholic Church is one body, &c., or consists of one body." For Alexander alludes to St. Paul's Epistles, wherein the Church is frequently called Christ's body. (See Eph. i. 23, and other passages.)

8. P. 9, l. 40.—Prov. xviii. 4. So the Septuagint also words this text. But in the English authorized version of the Bible (which agrees with the Hebrew) it is rendered thus: "when the wicked cometh, then cometh also contempt."

9. P. 11, l. 27.—Valesius considers that Socrates is mistaken here; for he says that the Melitians did not side with the Arians till after the Council of Nicæa; being then solicited, by Eusebius bishop of Nicomedia, to cast scandalous aspersions upon Athanasius, as he himself testifies in his Second Apology against the Arians. If the Melitians had joined themselves with the Arians before the Council of Nice, the Fathers of that Council undoubtedly would not have treated them so leniently as they did.

10. P. 14, l. 7, 8.—In the MS. of Leo Allatius the passage is thus written : "It is neither decent, nor can it in any wise be believed a lawful thing, that so numerous a people of God (which ought to be governed by your prayers and prudence) should be at variance." Epiphan. Scholasticus followed the same reading; for thus he translates this place : "Tantum Dei populum, quem vestris orationibus et prudentiâ convenit gubernari, discordare nec decet, nec omnino fas esse credibile est."

11. P. 17, l. 20.—Gelasius Cyzicenus supposed that by these words the bishop of Constantinople was meant. He is supported by Nicetas, in his Thesaurus Orthodoxæ Fidei, book v. chap. vi., and Epiphanius Scholasticus in book ii. Histor. Tripart. On the other hand, Musculus (as is apparent from his rendering of these words) thought that the bishop of Rome was hereby meant: for he renders this place thus, "Romanæ autem civitatis Episcopus propter senium deerat," i. e. The bishop of Rome, by reason of his age, was absent. Valesius is of the same opinion with Musculus. For (in his Annotations on Eusebius's Life of Constantine, book iii. chap. vii.) he says, that at such time as this council was convened, Constantinople was not adorned with the name of The Imperial City. See Sozomen, book i. chap. xvi., and Theodoret, book i. chap. vii.

12. P. 17, l. 34.—The ancient writers are not agreed concerning the number of bishops that were at the Nicene Council. Eusebius, in his Life

of Constantine, book iii. chap. viii., estimates them at 250. Eustathius
affirms that they were about 270; but he says he had not cast up their
number exactly. The more constant and received account is, that there
sat in that synod 318 bishops; which is confirmed by Athanasius, in his
Epistle to the African Bishops, sub. init.; Hilarius, in his book against
Constantius; Jerome, in his Chronicon; and Rufinus. See Valesius's
notes on Eusebius de Vitâ Constant. book iii. ch. viii.

13. P. 18, l. 2.—Many senses may be given of these words. For first,
μέσος τρόπος may be taken for modesty and a courteous behaviour; supposing μέσῳ to be put for μετρίῳ. Secondly, the term may imply those
who were not the most eminent persons amongst the bishops for learning
or piety of life; but did not come much behind them. So the ancients
called those " medios principes ac duces," who were neither the best, nor
the worst, but between both. Lastly, this phrase may be used concerning
such as deserved to be praised on both grounds, namely, for their learning
and sanctity : and thus Sozomen interprets this place of Eusebius, as may
be seen from his History, book i. chap. xvi. See Valesius's notes on
Eusebius de Vitâ Constant. book iii. chap. ix.

14. P. 20, l. 9.—This Sabinus was bishop of the Macedonians in
Heraclea, a city of Thrace. He made a collection of the Synodical Acts,
of which Socrates frequently makes use in this History. But Socrates
reproves him in many places, both because he is unfaithful in his collection of those Acts, (studiously relating what conduced to the strengthening of his own heresy, and omitting the contrary,) and also because he
always exhibits feelings of irritation against the orthodox bishops. An
instance of which is this relation of Socrates, where he says that Sabinus
termed the Fathers of the Nicene Council ignorant and simple fellows.
But it is usual (adds Valesius) for heretics to calumniate the holy Fathers
and Doctors of the Church.

15. P. 21, l. 1.—The following Creed, says Valesius, is wanting in all
our MSS., viz. the King's, the Sfortian, and the Florentine ; but Christophorson (he adds) did very right in placing it here : for it is plain both
from Epiphanius Scholast., as also by the words which immediately follow
it, that it was placed here by the historian himself. But all the MSS.
omit it in this place, probably because it is repeated a little after in the
Epistle of Eusebius Pamphilus.

16. P. 22, l. 6.—Eusebius seems to affirm, that the emperor Constantine was the occasion of adding the word Homoöusios to the creed. But
this is very improbable. For Constantine was not so learned in theology,
being as yet but a catechumen. Eusebius therefore must be thus understood to say that the bishops judged that the word Homoöusios ought to
be added to the creed proposed by Eusebius Cæsariensis, and that Constantine confirmed their opinion. But Eusebius, who made it his business
to clear and excuse himself to those of his diocese, because he had subscribed that form of the creed published by the council, (as Athanasius
attests, in his book De Decret. Synod. Nicen., and in his book De Synod.
Arimini and Seleuciæ, designedly makes the business intricate, and
ascribes that to the emperor Constantine which should rather be ascribed
to the bishops.

17. P. 23, l. 4.—In this place, before the Nicene Creed, the Florentine
and Sfortian MSS. insert the words τὸ μάθημα. So the Greeks call the

creed, because the catechumens got it by heart. Thus Socrates, book
iii. chap. xxv., has these words, πιστεύομεν εἰς ἕνα θεὸν πατέρα παντο-
κράτορα, καὶ τὰ λοιπὰ τοῦ μαθήματος, "We believe in one God, the
Father Almighty, and the rest of the Articles of the Creed." See Leontius Bisantius, in his book De Sectis, p. 466.

18.   P. 27, l. 25.—'Ακριβὴς λόγος, the phrase that occurs here, imports
the rigour or extremity of the law; to which ἐπιεικεία (equity) is opposed.
The Fathers of the Nicene Council therefore say, that the synod dealt with
Melitius, not according to the rigour and extremity of the law, nor according to the exact rule and discipline of the Church, but by way of dispensation. For in the strictest sense of the law Melitius deserved no kindness
nor pardon, inasmuch as he challenged ordinations which in no wise belong
to him, and had made a schism in Egypt; as is evidently declared by the
words of this epistle, viz. "those that by God's grace have not been found
engaged in any schism." (Vid. infr.) By reason therefore of his rashness
and insolency, Melitius deserved to be deposed and excommunicated. But
yet the holy Fathers had a mind to treat him kindly, depriving him of all
power, and leaving him only the name of a bishop. Now many reasons
may be alleged why Melitius was thus kindly used. First, (as the holy
Fathers intimate in this epistle,) because they had before made use of
their sharpest severity and censure against Arius and his followers. Now
it was but just, that after so sad and heavy a sentence pronounced against
them, there should be a place afterwards left for clemency; especially,
since Melitius had been convicted of no heresy, but was only accused of
having made a schism. Secondly, there were many persons amongst the
Melitians who were good men, and eminent for the piety of their lives.
Lastly, they acted thus to promote peace, whereby the members of the
Church, which had been rent in sunder, might again cement and unite;
therefore the Nicene Fathers received the Melitians into communion. And
this is a most illustrious example of ecclesiastical dispensation.

19.   P. 27, l. 31.—Christophorson thought that by these words were
meant the presbyters ordained by Melitius. But Melitius ordained not
only presbyters and deacons throughout Egypt, but bishops also, and even
far more bishops than presbyters, as may be collected from the catalogue
which Alexander required of him after the Nicene synod; in which are
reckoned twenty-eight bishops of Melitius's party, but only five presbyters
and three deacons. This catalogue is extant in Athanasius' Second
Apology against the Arians. Since therefore Melitius had ordained so
many bishops, if the Nicene Fathers had made no determination concerning the bishops ordained by him, their sentence would have been imper-
fect; for they would have decreed what should be done with the presbyters ordained by Melitius, but would have made no mention of his bishops.
Hence these words must be taken in such a sense as to include both bishops
and presbyters, though Sozomen thinks otherwise. (See Sozomen, b. i.
chap. xxiv.)

20.   P. 27, l. 32.—In the first place, the synod decreed that the bishops
and clergy which had been ordained by Melitius, should be confirmed by
a more holy consecration, that is, that they should receive imposition of
hands from the bishop of Alexandria. For, as they had been ordained
without his consent, it was the pleasure of the synod that they should be
ordained by the bishop of Alexandria, according to the ancient usage, by

which it was customary, that all the bishops of the diocese of Egypt should be subject to the prelate of Alexandria. But the synod did not require the re-ordination of Melitius, because he had been rightly ordained before.

21. P. 28, l. 12.—We may remark that Melitius, as being the author of a schism, was more severely dealt with than his followers, the Melitians. For the Nicene Fathers deprived Melitius of all episcopal jurisdiction, and left him only the name of a bishop. But they permitted the Melitians to exercise their functions in the Church. That is, that the deacons should minister in the order of deacons, and that the presbyters should consecrate and baptize, as should also the bishops. They only took from them their power of voting in elections; a necessary precaution, lest the Melitians should clandestinely promote some men of their own party to the ecclesiastical preferments.

22. P. 29, l. 8.—Socrates elsewhere styles Melitius an arch-heretic. But neither the Nicene Fathers, nor Athanasius in his Second Apology, nor Epiphanius, accuse Melitius of any heresy; they only affirm that he was the author of a schism. But when the Melitians had afterwards joined themselves to the Arians, which happened after the Nicene synod and the death of Melitius, they turned their schism into a heresy, as Augustine writes concerning the Donatists. In this sense therefore Melitius may be termed an arch-heretic.

23. P. 32, l. 28.—See Eusebius's Life of Constantine, book iii. chap. xviii., where the Jews are styled " that most abominable society and confederacy." And so he adds that those Christians who celebrate Easter with the Jews, seem to be confederates in that wickedness which they committed against our Lord.

24. P. 33, l. 13.—As the Jewish Paschal Neomenia, or new moon, began from the fifth day of March, and ended on the third of April, hence it sometimes happened that their Passover began before the equinox, so that they celebrated two Passovers in one year, counting from the vernal equinox of one year to the vernal equinox of the year following. Ambrosius asserts the same in his Epistle to the bishops of Æmilia, where he relates that the Jews sometimes celebrated their Passover in the twelfth month, that is, according to the Latins and the Eastern Church. For the Jews never kept their Passover in their own twelfth month, but on the fourteenth day of their first month. But this celebration of their Passover twice in one year, which Constantine objects against the Jews, seems after all to be of little moment. For the Jews might have retorted the objection upon the Christians, namely, that they celebrated Easter twice in the same year. For, suppose Easter is this year kept on the 22nd of April, next year it must be kept sooner. And so there will occur two Easters amongst the Christians within the space of one year current. But this will not happen, if we reckon the year from the equinoctial cardo to the vernal equinox of the year following. See Epiphan. p. 824, edit. Petav., and Petav. Animadvers. p. 294, 295. See also Ægidius Bucherius de Paschali Judæorum Cyclo, chap. iii.

25. P. 35, l. 2.—By the term " dread of impending danger," Constantine alludes to the case of such Christians as through fear of persecution had neglected the Churches, or renounced the faith. The term unbelief belongs to the heathens, who had demolished the Churches, and divers ways vexed the Christians.

26.   P. 35, l. 18.—ráξις, the term here used, signifies, an office, or company of apparitors attending on a magistrate; i. e. a certain number of soldiers waiting on the judges : ἔπαρχοι are the prefects of the Prætorium, so termed because they were ἐπὶ τοῖς ἄρχουσιν, over the presidents and rectors of provinces.   Therefore ἐπαρχικὴ τάξις (the phrase here used) imports the office of the Prætorian prefecture, concerning which the reader can consult the Notitia Imperii Romani.

27.   P. 36, l. 1.—Concerning the Vicar-general or Rationalist (Catholicus) and his office, see Euseb. Eccl. Hist. b. vii. ch. x.   It may be here remarked that the term diocese (διοίκησις) began to be used in its ecclesiastical sense about the time of Constantine, as appears from his letters, and from some laws in the Cod. Theod.   See Eusebius's Life of Constantine, b. iv. ch. xxxvi.

28.   P. 36, l. 18.—Constantine here terms Licinius the public enemy, after whose destruction, he says, the sacred sepulchre of our Lord, which had been before concealed, was discovered.   Licinius was killed in the year of Christ 326, and in that very year, when Helena came to Jerusalem, the sepulchre of our Lord was found.   See Euseb. Vit. Const. b. iii. ch. xxx.

29.   P. 36, l. 34.—He means the temple built by the emperor Adrian on Mount Calvary, in honour of Venus ; which receptacle of Paganism was demolished by Helena, the mother of Constantine, and in its room was built a magnificent temple, at this day called The Temple of the Sepulchre.   A description of it is to be found in Sandys' Travels, b. iii. p. 125, &c. Lond. 1673.

30.   P. 37, l. 25.—The inner roofs of churches were commonly framed two ways.   For they were either beautified with arched or embowed roofs, or else painted with Mosaic-work.   Concerning the arched roofs, this letter of Constantine is an evidence.   Procopius bears witness to the use of the Mosaic-work, in his first book De Fabricis Justiniani, where he describes the temple of Sancta Sophia.   The arched roofs were usually adorned in two ways; for they were either gilded or painted.   This latter method was first invented by Pausias, as Pliny asserts, Hist. Nat. b. xxxv. ch. xi.

31.   P. 37, l. 37.—The reading must necessarily be προέθηκε, "He published."   For the Roman emperors usually proposed to public view those rescripts they wrote to the cities.   Therefore at the close of the rescript they added this word, " Proponatur," Let it be published.   So Constantine, when he had written many letters against Arius and his followers, commanded they should be proposed to public view in the Forum.   This letter was like an edict, and so it was requisite that it should be publicly read and promulgated by authority.

32.   P. 39, l. 4.—Sozomen relates the same story, book i. chap. xxii. But this story seems very improbable upon many accounts.   First, Because it is founded on the authority of no ancient writer.   Secondly, Because neither Socrates nor Sozomen say, of what city Acesius was bishop, which was very necessary to confirm the story.   Thirdly, Because it is not at all likely, that an heretical bishop would be summoned by Constantine to an ecclesiastical synod.   For if Constantine had sent for Acesius in order to restore peace and agreement to the Church, upon the same account he ought to have summoned the bishops of other heresies also to the Nicene Council.   Lastly, What Socrates says, that he

had this story from a very old man who was at the synod, seems altogether incredible. This person's name was Auxano, a Novatian presbyter, who was at the synod with Acesius, and lived until the reign of Theodosius junior, as Socrates says below, chap. xiii. Now from the Nicene synod to the beginning of Theodosius's reign is a period of 83 years. To this if we add 20, (for so old Auxano must needs have been when he was present at the council,) Auxano must necessarily have been above 100 years old when he told Socrates this story.

33. P. 40, l. 1.—It is to be observed that Rufinus says not a word of this speech of Paphnutius. (See his Eccles. Hist. book i. chap. iv.) But he relates that Paphnutius was one of the bishops in the parts of Egypt, and that he was present at the Nicene Council. A monastery is termed in Greek Ascetarium, that is, a place where the Ascetæ lived; concerning whom, and their course of life, see Euseb. Ecclesiast. Hist. book ii. chap. xvii.; book vii. chap. xxxii.

34. P. 43, l. 16.—This book of Athanasius is not now known to be extant. But it is probable that the names of the bishops who subscribed the Nicene Council were translated by Socrates out of that book. In the following line the term Παρασημείωσις imports the notation (or express declaration) of the time usually prefixed to all public acts. In the Greek collection of the canons the notation of the time is prefixed thus: "The canons of the 318 holy Fathers, convened at Nice, in the consulate of the most illustrious Paulinus and Julianus, on the 636th year from Alexander, on the nineteenth day of the month Desius, before the thirteenth of the calends of July."

35. P. 43, l. 20.—In the Greek collection also, it is supposed that the Council of Nice was assembled on the twentieth day of May. But in that case there would be too narrow a space of time left for the transacting of those affairs which Constantine accomplished after his victory over Licinius. For Licinius was subdued in the last engagement at Chalcedon, in September, A. D. 324, and after this Constantine made his entry into Nicomedia: later still, whilst he continued there, about to make his progress into the eastern parts, a messenger arrived, declaring to him the dissension of the Alexandrian Church, and of all Egypt, upon account of the opinion of Arius and the disturbances of the Melitians. And first he sent Hosius with his letters to Alexandria, to compose those differences by his authority. But Hosius, after staying a little while at Alexandria, returned to Constantine without effecting his business. All this could scarcely have been done in a shorter space of time than three months. Moreover, Constantine, perceiving the mischief to increase daily, resolved upon calling a general council of bishops, that he might thereby restore peace to the Church. Upon this account he despatched couriers throughout all the provinces, to convene the bishops at Nice in Bithynia. Supposing therefore that the couriers delivered the emperor's letters to every one of the bishops in the month of March, it is scarce credible that the bishops could come to Bithynia from the remotest regions, as well of the East as of the West, before the month of July: especially since they came by land, and not by water, as Eusebius states, De Vitâ Constant. book iii. chap. vi. See also Euseb. Life of Constant. book iii. chap. xiv.

36. P. 43, l. 24.—Socrates has observed no order here. For he says, that Eusebius and Theognis were recalled from banishment almost before

he has told us they were exiled. Sozomen, however, book i. chap xxi., relates that Eusebius and Theognis were banished by the emperor Constantine a little after the synod, and that other bishops were put into their sees; and in book ii. chap. xvi., he declares how they were recalled from their banishment. 'Baronius is mistaken in placing Eusebius' return from exile in the year A. D. 330, as also in asserting that Eusebius and Theognis were recalled from banishment after presenting to the bishops a libel of retractation. Compare Theodoret, Eccl. Hist. book i. chap. xx., where it is said, that the emperor banished them, because they entertained certain heretics, (probably Arians or Melitians,) whom he had commanded to be sent to his court from the city Alexandria, and held communion with them. For this reason Constantine ordered a synod of some bishops to be convened, by whom Eusebius and Theognis were condemned and deposed, after which the emperor banished them; as is expressly affirmed by Athanasius in his book De Synodis.

37. P. 44, l. 2.—By these words Eusebius seems to intimate, that he was condemned without being heard, and by a rash judgment or prejudice; to wit, because he had been condemned by the emperor, who was angry with Eusebius for several reasons, which are stated in Constantine's epistle to the Nicomedians: see Theodoret, ubi supr. It is to be observed, that what had really been done by the emperor, is attributed here to the bishops; for the emperor, and not the bishops, had recalled Arius from his exile. But writers usually speak thus; assigning that to the bishops, which was in reality the emperor's deed; and on the contrary, that to the emperor which the bishops did. So Socrates said above, that the Nicene synod forbad Arius to enter Alexandria; whereas this was the emperor's doing, as appears from his epistle.

38. P. 45, l. 3.—Socrates (as also Sozomen) is mistaken here in placing Alexander's death, and Athanasius's ordination, after the return of Eusebius and Theognis from exile. For Alexander, bishop of Alexandria, died within five months after the Council of Nice. (Comp. Theodoret, book i. chap. xxvi.) Alexander therefore must have died A. D. 325, and Athanasius was consecrated either at the latter end of the same year, or in the beginning of the next. The reader may here refer to Rufinus's Eccles. Hist. book i. chap. xiv., where this circumstance is added to the story; that the boys, upon Alexander's inquiry, confessed that some catechumens had been baptized by Athanasius, whom they had chosen bishop in their sports. Then Alexander, having demanded of those who were said to be baptized, what questions they had been asked, and what answers they had made, and also having examined him who had asked them the questions, found that all things had been done according to the rites of our religion; and, after holding consultation with his clergy, he ordered that those boys on whom water had been poured, after they had been perfectly questioned, and had returned complete answers, should not be re-baptized.

39. P. 46, l. 21.—Socrates borrowed this story out of Eusebius's Life of Constantine, book iii. chap. xxxiii. But he is mistaken in saying that the church which was built over our Saviour's sepulchre by Helena, or rather by Constantine, was called New Jerusalem. For Eusebius says no such thing: but he only alludes to the New Jerusalem, which is mentioned in St. John's Revelations.

40. P. 48, l. 4.—Philostorgius reports that the people used to come to this pillar with lighted tapers and worship it; but Theodoret appears to confirm the story in his Ecclesiastical History, book i. chap. xxxiv.

41. P. 49, l. 4.—This order of Constantine did not last long. For Julian commanded that the same cubit should be carried back again into the temple of Serapis, where it seems to have continued till the reign of Theodosius, and the demolishment of the temple itself. By the Christian banner mentioned below, he means the standard, or banner, which the emperor ordered to be made, in figure like to the cross that appeared to him in the face of the heavens. See above, chap. ii. .

42. P. 51, l. 1.— In this chapter Socrates has translated Rufinus, Eccles. Hist. book i. chap. ix., almost word for word; and calls those τόπους ἰδιάζοντας, which Rufinus has termed conventicula. Now conventicula are properly private places, wherein collects or short prayers are made; and from these places churches are distinguished, which belong to the right of the public, and are not in the power of any private person. It is to be observed that there are reasons for thinking that this conversion of the Indians by Frumentius happened in the reign of Constantius, and not of Constantine.

43. P. 53, l. 1.—Rufinus gives this story in his Eccles. Hist. book i. chap. x.; but he does not say that this child was the king's son, but the son of a certain woman of that country. He asserts that Bacurius, mentioned towards the end of this chapter as a petty prince of the Iberi, was a person of great fidelity, very studious of religion and truth; and that he did Theodosius the emperor great service in his war with Eugenius.

44. P. 56, l. 11.—It is most probable that the Manichæans adored the sun. Libanius relates the same concerning them, (book iv. Epist. 140,) where he commends the Manichæans, who were in Palestine (but suppresses their name) to Priscianus the president of Palestine. He speaks of them thus: "Those men who worship the sun without blood, and honour God with the second appellation, who chastise their belly, and account the day of their death to be gain; are found to be in many places, but are everywhere few in number. They injure no man, but are molested by some." By these words Libanius must mean the Manichæans; for they cannot be agreeably attributed to any other persons besides them. But he designedly omitted the mention of their name, because the name of the Manichæans was odious. Concerning the feigned fasts of the Manichæans see St. Cyril, Catech. Sect. vi. 18.

45. P. 58, l. 6.— This Archelaus, bishop of Mesopotamia, wrote in Syriac the dispute which he maintained against Manichæus, which was afterwards translated into Greek, and was in the possession of many persons, as Jerome attests, in his book De Scriptor. Ecclesiast. St. Cyril of Jerusalem has mentioned this dispute in his sixth Catechetical Lecture.

46. P. 59, l. 39.—It is hard to assign a reason why Socrates should join Montanus with Sabellius. For Montanus himself made no innovations in the doctrine of the Trinity, but followed the faith of the Catholic Church; as Epiphanius and Theodoret attest. Yet some of his disciples took away the difference of the persons, as Sabellius did; and hence it is, that in the Synodical Epistle of the Arian bishops at Sardica, Montanus is joined with Sabellius.

47. P. 61, l. 25.—What Socrates here says concerning the vacancy of

the see of Antioch for eight years, after Eustathius was deposed, is false. For immediately after Eustathius was ejected, and Eusebius of Cæsarea had refused that see, Paulinus, bishop of Tyre, was translated to that see, A. D. 329.   See Euseb. Eccles. Hist. book x. chap. i.

48. P. 62, l. 1.—This story concerning the Arian presbyter, whom Constantia Augusta recommended to her brother Constantine, Socrates probably borrowed out of Rufinus, book i. chap. xi. Eccles. Hist. But the story is to be viewed with suspicion, because Athanasius, who usually detects all the frauds of the Arians, has no where made mention of it, and also because the name of this presbyter is suppressed. But the authority of Rufinus is but small, for he wrote his History very carelessly, not from the records of affairs transacted, but from fabulous stories and relations grounded barely on report.

49. P. 64, l. 19.—Baronius relates that these affairs happened A. D. 329. But they more probably occurred in the following year, for they happened after Eustathius's deposition, when Eusebius and Theognius had returned from their exile. But what Baronius says, viz. that Constantine's letter concerning the re-admission of Arius into the Church, was written to Athanasius in the year of Christ 327, is a palpable mistake; and he dissents from Athanasius, whom notwithstanding he professes to follow in all things. For Athanasius relates, that soon after Constantine's letter, and Arius's repulse, the Melitians accused him of these crimes before the emperor.

50. P. 66, l. 8.—Considerable light is thrown upon this passage by Athanasius, who speaks thus in his Second Apologetic against the Arians: "Mareotis is a region of Alexandria. In that region there never was a bishop, or deputy bishop; but the Churches of that whole region are subject to the bishop of Alexandria. Each of the presbyters hath peculiar villages, (which are very great,) sometimes ten in number, or more." From these words it appears, that every village of Mareotis had not its particular presbyter; but that one presbyter governed ten villages and sometimes more. That village wherein Ischyras was, as being the least of all, undoubtedly had neither its peculiar Church nor presbyter. It is to be remarked that the epistle which all the presbyters and deacons of Mareotis wrote to the synod of Tyre, was subscribed by fourteen presbyters and fifteen deacons.

51. P. 71, l. 13.—This synodical epistle of the Jerusalem council is recorded in Athanasius's Second Apologetic against the Arians, and in his book de Synodis Arimini et Seleuciæ. In this epistle, the bishops, who had been convened there for the dedication of Constantine's church, attest that they had received into communion Arius and his followers, according to the emperor's command. Valesius is probably right in supposing that Arius, the arch-heretic, is not to be meant here, but another Arius, his name-sake, who had been condemned by Alexander bishop of Alexandria, together with Arius his ringleader. For Arius the arch-heretic died long before the Jerusalem synod.

52. P. 79, l. 21.—Concerning this gift, see Eusebius's Life of Constantine, book iv. ch. lxiii. Socrates borrowed the story out of Rufinus, Eccles. Hist. book i. chap. xi. But this story seems very improbable. For who can believe that the emperor Constantine, who then had many bishops about him, as Eusebius says expressly, and also grandees and

great officers, should make choice of one presbyter, and an unknown per-
· son too, to whom he might commit the keeping of his will, when he died?
There is greater probability in favour of the account given by Philostorgius, who says, that Constantine delivered his will to Eusebius of Nicomedia, by whom he had been baptized a little before.

BOOK II.

53. P. 83, l. 1.—Baronius in his Annals and others also relate that
Athanasius was recalled from banishment, A. D. 338, the year after the
death of Constantine, who, perceiving that prelate to be pressed on
every side by the calumnies of his adversaries, had for a time banished
him into the Gallias. But Valesius maintains that Athanasius was restored in the previous year, in which Constantine died. For Athanasius
· (in his Second Apologetic against the Arians, p. 805) relates, that he was
released from his banishment and restored to his country by Constantine the younger, who also wrote a letter in his behalf to the populace and
clergy of the Alexandrian Church. This letter Athanasius there recites:
the inscription of it is this, "Constantinus Cæsar, to the people of the
Catholic Church of Alexandria," and the letter is dated from Triers the
fifteenth day before the calends of July, which proves that Athanasius
was released from his exile soon after the death of Constantine the Great,
A. D. 337. For if he had been restored on the year following, then Constantine the younger would not have called himself Cæsar, but Augustus.
Nor would Athanasius have been restored by Constantine the younger,
but by Constantius, to whom was allotted the eastern part of the empire.
54. P. 84, l. 18.—Socrates is mistaken in placing the death of Alexander, bishop of Constantinople, in the year A. D. 340; and he is followed
in his error by Baronius. For the synod of the bishops of Egypt (which
was summoned to confute the calumnies brought against Athanasius by
the Eusebian faction) was convened in the year A. D. 339. But those
bishops expressly state in their synodic epistle, that at that very time
Eusebius had left Nicomedia, and had thrust himself into the see of
Constantinople. Now, if Eusebius had obtained the see of Constantinople
in the year of Christ 339, Alexander must necessarily be supposed to have
been dead before this year.
55. P. 85, l. 18.—There were two Churches of this name in Constantinople, the one called the Old, the other the New Irene. The Old Church
called Irene was contiguous to the Great Church, which was afterwards
named Sophia: it had no separate clergy, but the clergy of the Great
Church by turns ministered in it, as the emperor Justinian informs us
in his third Novel. In the old description of Constantinople, prefixed
to the Notitia Imperii Romani, this is called the Old Church, and is placed
in the second ward of the city together with the Great Church, but the
Church Irene (viz. the New Irene) is counted in the seventh ward. Socrates has made mention of the Old Irene above, book i. chap. xxxvii. It
is termed the Church of St. Irene, after the same manner that the Church
Sophia is called St. Sophia, not that there was a virgin or martyr called
by that name.
56. P. 87, l. 7.—Sozomen (Eccl. Hist. book iii. ch. vi.) explains
this passage in Socrates, where he speaks thus of Eusebius Emisenus:

" From his childhood, according to the custom of his own country, he learned the sacred Scriptures by heart." It is well known that the boys of Edessa got by heart the books of sacred Scripture, according to the usage of their ancestors; and indeed many ecclesiastical writers bear witness that the people of Edessa were most ardent lovers of the Christian religion.

57. P. 91, l. 7.—Socrates would seem to be mistaken here, for Eusebius of Nicomedia sent ambassadors to Pope Julius, to incite him against Athanasius, a long time before the Council at Antioch. But when the presbyters sent by Athanasius had confuted Eusebius's ambassadors in all points before Julius, at length Eusebius's messengers referred the decision of the whole matter to Julius. Julius therefore, according to the request of the ambassadors, wrote letters, both to Athanasius, and also to Eusebius and the rest of Athanasius's adversaries, inviting them to an ecclesiastical judicature at Rome. But this was done before the Council at Antioch, as Athanasius informs us in his Second Apologetic against the Arians, and Julius bishop of Rome, in his Epistle to the bishops convened in the Council of Antioch. This epistle of Julius Athanasius has inserted at the 739th page of his Works, edit. Paris, 1627. Sozomen, Eccl. Hist. book iii. chap. vii., has followed the mistake of Socrates.

58. P. 93, l. 1.—Socrates is mistaken here. For Gregory, who was created bishop of Alexandria in the synod of Antioch, held that bishopric six years, until the Council of Sardica, in which he was deposed and excommunicated, as it is related in the Synodical Epistle of that Council. And when he had survived this sentence about six months, he died, as Athanasius states in Epist. ad Solitar. Theodoret has corrected this mistake of Socrates and Sozomen, in book ii. of his Eccles. Hist. George was made bishop of Alexandria by the Arians long after Gregory, in the year of Christ 356.

59. P. 93, l. 12.—Socrates would seem to be in error in asserting that Paulus was at Rome at the same time that Athanasius was there. Marcellus bishop of Ancyra was at Rome together with Athanasius, as we are informed in Julius's letter to the Eastern bishops; which is also ascertained from Marcellus's Libel which he presented to Julius. But Julius speaks not a word concerning Paulus in his aforesaid Epistle; whom he would doubtless have mentioned, had he been then at Rome with Athanasius and Marcellus. He is also mistaken when he states that Athanasius returned at that time to Alexandria. For Athanasius did not go back to that city till after the Council at Sardica, that is, till after A. D. 348.

60. P. 97, l. 20.—The bishops who had been convened at Antioch at the consecration, having received the letter written by Julius to Eusebius of Nicomedia, in which he invited him and the rest of the Eusebians to Rome, in order to the having their cause discussed there on a set day, whereon a council was there to be held, detained Julius's messengers beyond the day appointed. Then, after they had held their synod, they dismissed the messengers, and gave them a letter to Julius. Upon receipt of which letter he wrote back that famous letter, which Athanasius has inserted in his Second Apology against the Arians, p. 739, &c., edit. Paris, 1627. In that letter Julius reprehends the insolency and pride which the Eastern bishops had used in their letters to him. But that which Socrates here adds, namely, that Julius complained because they had not invited him

to the synod, and that it was a canon of the Church, that nothing should be determined in the Church without consent of the bishop of Rome, is not to be found in that letter. Indeed, Julius complains in that epistle because the Eastern bishops, upon the receipt of his letter, wherein he invited them to the synod at Rome, had disregarded his invitation, and ordained Gregory bishop in the see of Athanasius. But he says not one word concerning this ecclesiastical rule or canon. Sozomen, however, Eccles. Hist. book x. chap. iii., says the same that Socrates does here.

61. P. 99, l. 26.—Athanasius, in his book de Synodis, says the same: his words are these: "Afterwards, repenting as it were [of what they had done], they again assemble a synod of their own party, three years after. And they send Eudoxius, Martyrius, and Macedonius of Cilicia, and some other persons with them, into the parts of Italy; who carried along with them a prolix [form of] faith." Baronius, in his Annals, says, that this second Council of Antioch was convened A. D. 344, but he would seem to be mistaken. For this expression of Athanasius [μετὰ ἔτη τρία, after three years] points rather to the fourth year than the third, for it denotes that three years were now past. Hence it is evident that that council (in which the large form of faith had been composed) was convened A. D. 345, not A. D. 344, as Baronius thinks.

62. P. 100, l. 29.—This was the opinion of the Arians. The Easterns explain this sentiment of theirs better hereafter, to wit, that the Father may be understood to have begotten the Son willingly, without compulsion.

63. P. 101, l. 32.—By these words the Eastern bishops mean, the heresy of Marcellus of Ancyra. The synodical epistle of the Eastern bishops at Sardica informs us of the nature of this heresy; for they write thus: "There hath risen up in our days one Marcellus of Galatia, the most execrable pest of all heretics, who, with a sacrilegious mind, and impious mouth, and a wicked argument, will needs set bounds to the perpetual, eternal, and timeless kingdom of our Lord Christ, saying that he began his reign 400 years since, and shall end it at the dissolution of this present world."

64. P. 102, l. 20.—The heresy of the Patropassians, or Patripassians, was very ancient and far diffused. Tertullian (Adv. Prax. chap. i. and ii.) charges this heresy upon Praxeus. The same was maintained by Hermogenes, whence they were termed Hermogenians. After whom Noëtus maintained the same opinion. (See Epiphan. Heres. 57.) From Noëtus they had the name of Noëtians; and from Sabellius, the disciple of Noëtus, they were called Sabellians. Priscillianus succeeded these in the same heresy; from him they had the name of Priscillianistæ. The sum and substance of this heresy thus propagated by these succeeding asserters of it, was this: they affirmed that there was but one person in the Deity, namely, the Father; that he only subsisted, and was the Maker of all things; that he not only came into the world, but was incarnate, and did all those things which we say were done by the Son. To exclude these heretics, the Aquileian Church added these two terms, "invisible" and "impassible," to the first article of the creed; showing by the first, that the Father was not incarnate, and by the second, that he was not crucified.

65. P. 103, l. 36.—This confession of faith (for so Athanasius calls it)

was presented by the ambassadors of the Eastern bishops to the Western prelates assembled at Milan. For some bishops, together with the presbyters of the Church of Rome, had gone thither to entreat Constans Augustus that he would write to his brother Constantius about the assembling of a general synod, in order to determine in an ecclesiastical judicature those dissensions which had been raised in diverse churches, as we are informed by Athanasius in his Apology to Constantius. Moreover, when the Easterns had presented this draught of the creed to those of the West, they requested them to subscribe it. But the Western bishops made answer, that, as to what belonged to the Articles of Faith, the Nicene Creed was to them sufficient, to which nothing was to be added, nor anything to be taken from it. And as concerning the condemnation of those heretics who were disallowed of in that confession, they requested the ambassadors of the Eastern bishops in the first place to condemn the Arian heresy. But upon their refusal to do so, the Eastern ambassadors, being angry, went away from the council. The Western bishops condemned the heresy of Photinus in that synod; but they pronounced no sentence against Marcellus, because he had before been judged clear from all manner of heresy in the Roman synod. Dionysius Petavius in his dissertation " de duplici Synodo Sirmiensi" has mistaken the year in which it was convened; for he says it was held A. D. 347, a little before the Council of Sardica. Baronius places this embassy of the Eastern bishops and the Council at Milan in the same year also. But Valesius adduces good reasons for believing that the Council of Milan must needs have been held A. D. 346.

66. P. 104, l. 19.—Athanasius does not say that about three hundred bishops of the Western Churches met at the Council of Sardica. He only says that those who were present at the Council of Sardica, or who subscribed the synodical epistle afterwards sent to them, together with those who before the Council at Sardica had written synodical epistles in his behalf, out of Phrygia, Asia, and Isauria, were in all three hundred and forty. This passage of Athanasius's occurs in his second defence against the Arians, p. 768, edit. Paris, 1627. Moreover, the same Athanasius (in his Epistle ad Solitar. p. 818) expressly asserts that the bishops who met at the Council of Sardica, as well those out of the Western as the Eastern parts, were no more than 170.

67. P. 105, l. 25.—The title of this work is " De Ecclesiastica Theologia adversus Marcellum;" it is in three books, which are at this day extant. Prefixed to them are two books entitled " Contra Marcellum," in which he reproves his design, malice, and envy. Eusebius, in the close of his second book against Marcellus, bears witness that he wrote these books by the order of those bishops who had condemned Marcellus in the synod of Constantinople. It is uncertain whether or no Socrates had ever seen those two former books against Marcellus, as he has made no mention of them.

68. P. 106, l. 12.—Socrates means those doxologies that occur at the end of Eusebius's sermons; which Eusebius always puts into this form: " Glory be to the unborn Father by his only begotten Son," &c. For example, in the end of his first book against Sabellius, these are his words: " Gloria uni non nato Deo," &c., i. e. " Glory be to the one unborn God, by the one only begotten God the Son of God, in one Holy

Spirit, both now, and always, and throughout all ages of ages.   Amen."
And so concerning the rest. Also, in the oration which Eusebius made at
the consecration of the church at Tyre, (see above, b. x. ch. iv.,) we
meet with the same form of speech; δι' οὗ αὐτῷ ἡ δόξα, &c., "by whom
be glory to him."   Further, it is manifestly known, that the Arians attributed this preposition *per quem*, "by whom," to the Son, with this
design, that they might make him subject to the Father.   See Theodoret
upon the first chapter of the First Epistle to the Corinthians.

69. P. 109, l. 5.—These words must have a favourable sense put
upon them, and are not to be understood as if Socrates meant to imply
that after the synod of Sardica the Western bishops held no communion
with the Eastern.   For in the synod of Sirmium (which was convened by
the Western bishops against Photinus two years after the synod at Sardica) the Western bishops sent their determinations to the Eastern, upon
account of preserving a communion; and the Eastern bishops wrote back
to them a reply.   The words of Socrates here must consequently be understood to mean that after the synod of Sardica the Western bishops observed a great deal of cautiousness in communicating with the Eastern.

70. P. 109, l. 16.—Athanasius relates the reason of this journey of his
to Rome in his second defence against the Arians; namely, that he might
take his leave of Julius the bishop, and the Roman Church, by whom he
had been so kindly entertained.   For he writes, that "upon receipt of
these letters he went to Rome, to bid the Roman Church and the bishop
farewell."

71. P. 109, l. 22.—Valesius regards this letter to Constantius as not
genuine. And this on three grounds; first, because Athanasius makes no
mention of this letter; secondly, because at that time Paul enjoyed his
bishopric, and was not present at the synod of Sardica; thirdly, because
Constantius in his first epistle to Athanasius says, that by a letter written
to his brother he has requested him to give Athanasius leave to return to
his see.

72. P. 117, l. 13.—This epistle of the Jerusalem synod is extant in
the second defence of Athanasius against the Arians, together with the
names of those bishops who subscribed to that synod.   But we may here
by the by take notice of the authority of the bishop of Jerusalem, who,
although he was no metropolitan, yet summoned the neighbouring bishops
to a synod, without the permission of the bishop of Cæsarea.

73. P. 117, l. 32.—Socrates speaks here concerning the ordinations
performed by Athanasius in Egypt.   For he says that was done after he
arrived at Pelusium, which is the first city of Egypt upon coming out of
Syria.   If this be so, the opinion cannot be maintained, that all ordinations, as well of bishops as of presbyters, throughout Egypt belonged to
the bishop of Alexandria.

74. P. 118, l. 9.—Eutropius gives the same account: for he says,
"Not long after, Dalmatius Cæsar was slain by a faction of the soldiers,
Constantius, his cousin-german by the father's side, suffering rather than
commanding it.   The allusion here is to the battle fought by night at
Singar, a fortress of Mesopotamia, wherein the son of Sapor king of Persia
was slain; but the Romans had a very great slaughter made amongst them.
See Amm. Marcellinus, b. xviii. p. 122, edit. Paris, 1636.   This engage-
ment happened A. D. 348.

75. P. 123, l. 33.—The same is recorded in Idatius's Fasti, after the consulate of Sergius and Nigrinianus, in these words : " During the consulate of these men, Constantius Gallus was created Cæsar on the Ides of March, and the sign of our Saviour appeared in the east, on the 28th of January." But the author of the Alexandrian Chronicle says that this sign was seen in the east, on the Nones of May, about the day of Pentecost ; and Socrates seems to confirm the same in this place. For he says, that this sign appeared in the east, when Gallus Cæsar entered Antioch. Now it is certain that Gallus was created Cæsar on the Ides of March in this year.

76. P. 124, l. 4.—It is not agreed amongst the learned, in what year the synod of Sirmium (wherein Photinus was deprived of his bishopric) was held. Socrates and Sozomen affirm it to have been celebrated after the consulate of Sergius and Nigrinianus, A. D. 351; in which year, by reason of the disturbances caused by the civil war, there were no consuls in the East ; but in the Western parts Magnentius Augustus was consul with Gaïso. Baronius is consequently wrong when he asserts, in his Ecclesiastical Annals, that that synod was convened in the year of Christ 357, when Constantius Augustus was the ninth time consul, and Julianus Cæsar the second time.

77. P. 124, l. 5.—The bishops here named by Socrates sat not in that synod of Sirmium, which was convened against Photinus, after the consulate of Sergius and Nigrinianus, in the year of Christ 351; but in that other synod, which was convened there when Eusebius and Hypatius were consuls, in the year of Christ 359, a little before the Council of Ariminum, which latter synod at Sirmium did also set forth that draught of the Creed, which was afterwards recited at Ariminum, before which the consuls' names were prefixed.

78. P. 125, l. 8.—At this place we follow the Sfortian MS. Valesius remarks that the draught of the Creed which was published in the synod of Sirmium against Photinus is approved of by Hilarius (in his book de Synodis) as being Catholic, but that Athanasius (in his book de Synodis Arimini et Seleuciæ) condemns and rejects it, in the same manner with the other Creeds composed by the Arians. Nor do Hilarius and Athanasius disagree with one another concerning this one form of the Creed, but about other draughts of it also ; for example, about the Antiochian draught. For Hilarius confesses that the Eastern bishops had good reason to compose new forms of the Creed, when new heresies arose against the Church. But Athanasius maintains that those new draughts of the Creed were craftily composed by the Arians, with a design to destroy the Nicene Creed. It should be added, that we must distinguish between the three synods of Sirmium, each of which published their form of the Creed. The first was convened against Photinus, in the year of Christ 351. The second was assembled in the year of our Lord 357, wherein the blasphemy of Hosius and Potamius was composed. The third was celebrated when Eusebius and Hypatius were consuls, in the year of Christ 359, wherein that Creed was drawn up which Marcus of Arethusa dictated.

79. P. 127, l. 1.—This Anathema is differently worded by all the authors in whom this Creed occurs. Valesius says, that he has published it according to the reading of the Florentine and Sfortian MSS. The

reading in Robert Stephens' is different from this ; and so is that in Athanasius de Synodis, p. 901. Hilarius has translated otherwise, as appears
from his version, at p. 339, edit. Paris, 1631. His words are these :
" Si quis dominum et dominum patrem et filium, quasi dominum a domino
intelligat : quia dominum et dominum duos dicat deos : Anathema sit."
The learned reader may take the liberty (as we have done) to follow
which copy he pleases.

80. P. 128, l. 1.—Athanasius in his book de Synodis writes in a like
strain ; " Having rejected all these things, as if they had invented better,
they promulge another Creed, which they wrote at Sirmium in Latin, but
it was translated into Greek." And Hilarius, in recording this Creed in
his book de Synodis, prefixes to it this title : " A copy of the blasphemy
composed at Sirmium by Hosius and Potamius." Valesius informs us
that the Potamius here mentioned was bishop of Lisbon, and at first a
defender of the Catholic faith, but that he was afterwards induced to corrupt the faith by the reward of a farm belonging to the emperor's revenue,
on which he had set his heart. Hosius of Corduba amongst the Churches
in Spain detected this man, and repelled him as an impious heretic. But
even Hosius himself, being summoned before the emperor Constantius on
the complaint of this Potamius, and terrified with threats, and being old
and rich, was fearful of banishment or proscription, and so yielded to the
impiety.

81. P. 129, l. 17.—Epiphanius relates, that Photinus, after he had
been condemned and deposed in the synod of Sirmium, (for so the reading must be, not " in the synod of Sardica,") went to Constantius, and
requested that he might dispute concerning the faith before judges nominated by him ; and that Constantius enjoined Basilius bishop of Ancyra
to undertake the disputation against Photinus, and gave leave that Thalassius, Datianus, Cerealis, and Taurus, who were Counts, should be
judges or auditors of that disputation. Amongst these Thalassius was
the chief person in favour and authority with the emperor, and was sent as
prefect of the Prætorium into the East together with Gallus Cæsar, A. D.
351. He died A. D. 353, in the sixth consulate of Constantius Augustus,
and in the second of Gallus Cæsar. Therefore it is clear that the synod
of Sirmium, and the disputation of Basilius against Photinus, cannot have
happened in A. D. 357, as Baronius asserts.

82. P. 129, l. 34.—Socrates apparently borrowed this passage out of
Athanasius de Synodis. But he is mistaken in one point, namely, in
assigning to the second form composed by Hosius and Potamius what
Athanasius had said concerning the third form of the Creed drawn up at
Sirmium. The passage in Athanasius is extant at p. 904 of the edition
so often here quoted. Petavius (in his Animadversions on Epiphanius,
p. 318) has followed this mistake of Socrates.

83. P. 133, l. 23.—Who these Ephectics were we may learn from
Diogenes Laertius. Philosophers (says he) were generally divided into
two sorts ; some were termed Dogmatici, who discoursed concerning
things as they might be comprehended ; others were called Ephectici, who
defined nothing, and disputed of things so as they cannot be comprehended.
Of these Ephectics (whom we may in English call Doubters) the Sceptics
were one species.

84. P. 134, l. 16.—We meet with the same number in Sozomen, book

iv. chap. ix. But as it is scarce credible that so great a number of bishops should have been convened at this Council of Milan, Valesius thinks that the copies of Socrates and Sozomen were false, and that instead of three hundred we should read thirty. In the Epistle of the Council of Milan sent to Eusebius bishop of Vercellæ, there are the names of thirty bishops only who consented to the condemnation of Athanasius, Marcellus, and Photinus. Amongst whom some Eastern bishops are recounted, as may be seen in Baronius' Annals, A. D. 355.

85. P. 134, l. 21.—The reading is the same in Sozomen, b. iv. ch. ix. But Baronius has long since remarked, that Alba is here put instead of Milan. For the latter, and not Alba, was the metropolis of Italy. And Dionysius, who then opposed Constantius and the Arians, was not bishop of Alba, but of Milan, as Athanasius asserts in his Epistle ad Solitar.

86. P. 135, l. 19.—Leontius bishop of Antioch had at first preferred Aëtius to the diaconate: but being afterwards reproved by Diodorus and Flavianus, because he had advanced to sacred orders a person who had been bred up in ill studies, and was an asserter of impious tenets, he divested him of his deaconship, as related by Theodoret, Eccles. Hist. b. ii. ch. xxiv. Eudoxius therefore, as soon as he had obtained the bishopric of Antioch, attempted to restore Aëtius to his former preferment.

87. P. 136, l. 20.—This third exposition of faith, as is remarked above, (b. ii. ch. xxx., note,) was not translated out of Latin; but was at first dictated in Greek by Marcus Arethusius. Athanasius, who has recorded this creed in his book de Synodis, does not say it was translated out of Latin; and yet, wherever he produces anything rendered into Greek out of the Latin tongue, his continual usage is to give the reader warning of it. Further, the last clause of this chapter is wanting in Robert Stephens's edition; nor are they in the version of Epiphanius Scholasticus.

88. P. 136, l. 22.—The title of the emperor prefixed before the exposition of faith at Sirmium, as extant in Athanasius, is as follows: " The most pious and victorious emperor Constantius Augustus, eternal Augustus," &c.; but Socrates, in his draught of the creed, has omitted these titles. Indeed Constantius so readily gave credence to such flatteries as these, that speaking of himself in his edicts and letters, he would sometimes assert his own eternity. This is attested by Amm. Marcellinus, who says that, "puffed up with an imaginary exemption from the lot of man, he departed so far from the path of right conduct as frequently to subscribe himself ' my eternity.' " The latter part of this Sirmian creed is given by Germinius in his epistle to Rufianus, Palladius, and others. The subscriptions of the bishops are extant in Epiphanius, in his book on the Semiarian Heresy, chap. xxii. The same form of the Sirmian creed is mentioned in the Exposition of the faith at Seleucia, which Epiphanius records in chap. xxv. of the same book, in these words, " Moreover, that that draught of the creed heretofore published at Sirmium in the presence of the piety of our emperor Constantius does exactly agree with this form of the creed, is very well known by them who have read that creed; which was subscribed by them that were then present, namely, Basilius, Marcus, Georgius bishop of Alexandria, Pancratius, Hypatianus, and most of the Western bishops."

89. P. 140, l. 8.—This letter of the synod at Rimini is extant in Latin, in Hilarius, amongst the fragments of his book de Synodis, page

451, edit. Paris, 1631 : but there is a considerable difference between the Greek version and the original Latin copy of this epistle. But this is usual with Greek translators, as often as they render Latin into Greek; as may be easily perceived from the emperor's rescripts which occur in Eusebius's Ecclesiastical History.

90. P. 145, l. 8.—From this passage we conclude, that the bishop of Constantinople had a right of ordaining throughout Hellespont and Bithynia, even before the council of Constantinople. The same is confirmed from the acts of Eudoxius bishop of Constantinople, who made Eunomius bishop of Cyzicum. Indeed, the bishops of Byzantium had a very great addition of authority and power, from the time that the emperor Constantine gave that city his own name, and ordained that it should be equal to the elder Rome. Also, Eusebius of Nicomedia, after his translation to that see, brought no small increase of jurisdiction to it. For he was the most powerful prelate of his own times.

91. P. 147, l. 25.—That which Socrates relates here, namely, that the Catholics prayed in the churches of the Novatians, seems incredible. In this matter Socrates was probably imposed upon by Auxano, who fixed upon all the Catholics what was perhaps done by some few Christians who were less cautious. For there is nothing more contrary to ecclesiastical discipline, than to communicate with heretics either in the sacraments or in prayer. But it is a mistake to conclude from this story that Socrates was a Novatian; on the contrary, it is evident from this passage that he was a Catholic. For in this chapter he frequently terms the Catholics "those of the Church," τοὺς τῆς ἐκκλησίας, and opposes them to the Novatians. Therefore it is clear that he looked upon the Novatians as external to the Church.

92. P. 149, l. 12.—At this place occurs no trivial difficulty. For the destruction of the city of Nicomedia happened when Datian and Cerealis were consuls, in the month of August, A. D. 358. But the Council of Seleucia was held in the month of September of the following year, in the consulate of Eusebius and Hypatius. These things therefore could not have happened in one and the same year. It seems therefore that the reading should be τῷ ἐχομένῳ ἐνιαυτῷ, "on the year following." Or if the common reading must be retained, we must understand our author's meaning to be, that the Council of bishops at Seleucia was held in the same year with the Council of Rimini.

93. P. 157, l. 1.—Before the emperor Constantius had made a prefect of the city at Constantinople, the province Europa (the chief city of which was Constantinople) was governed by a proconsul, as Socrates here attests. Athanasius mentions this proconsul in his Apologetic de Fugâ suâ, where he says that the emperor Constantius wrote letters to Donatus the proconsul, against Olympius bishop of Thracia. In the emperor Constantius's epistle also, which he wrote to the senate and people of Constantinople concerning the praises of Themistius, there is mention of this proconsul.

94. P. 157, l. 11.—The τάξεις were bodies or sodalities of officials or apparitors who attended upon the presidents and governors of provinces. It was their duty to collect the tribute from the inhabitants of the provinces, and to put in execution the orders of the president. Further, as all who had listed themselves in the soldiery, stood obliged by a military

oath, and enjoyed not a complete liberty, but were bound in a servitude, as it were, till such time as they were disbanded, so those officials who followed the civil service, were bound to this employment, as it were, and liable to the offices of their service; and their farms, as well as those of the decurions, were encumbered with these burdens, as is apparent from the Theodosian code.

95. P. 160, l. 18.—These words are not to be understood of all those who declined to frequent the Churches, but they must be joined to the foregoing words, and be meant of those persons who by the persuasion of Eustathius had separated themselves from the converse of their wives. Eustathius persuaded these men to avoid the Churches' assemblies, and not to communicate with other believers; but that, being as it were pure and perfect, they should participate of the sacred mysteries by themselves at home.

96. P. 161, l. 5.— Socrates makes the synod of Gangra, wherein Eustathius was condemned, to have been after that assembled at Seleucia, and after the Constantinopolitan synod. Sozomen (book iv. chap. xxiv.) places the synod of Gangra earlier than the Council of Antioch, which was held at the Dedication, A. D. 341. Indeed, Baronius (at the year of Christ 361) places the synod of Gangra in the reign of Constantine the Great. But he is confuted both by Socrates and Sozomen. For Socrates makes that synod to be later than the Seleucian and Constantinopolitan synod; and Sozomen places it after Eustathius's deposition, which was done by Eusebius bishop of Constantinople. Now Eusebius thrust himself into the see of Constantinople in the reign of Constantius. Basilius too makes no mention of the Council of Gangra. Hence it is manifest, that when Basilius wrote that epistle, which he did in Valens's reign, the Council of Gangra, wherein Eustathius was condemned, had not been held.

97. P. 161, l. 25.—Concerning the consecration of this church, it is recorded in Idatius's Fasti, that in Constantius's tenth and Julianus's third consulate, the great church at Constantinople was consecrated, on the fifteenth day before the kalends of March. Cedrenus, in his Chronicon, says this was the second consecration of this church. For it was first consecrated, says he, by Eusebius bishop of Constantinople. But being afterwards ruined, it was rebuilt by Constantius Augustus, and consecrated by Eudoxius.

98. P. 162, l. 7.—Meletius can scarcely have been translated from Sebastia in Armenia to the episcopate of Berœa. For Sozomen and Theodoret affirm that he was translated from Sebastia in Armenia to the see of Antioch, making no mention of his having been bishop of Berœa. Theodoret says only that, upon being promoted to the bishopric of Sebastia, and perceiving a contumacy in those under his charge, Meletius retired from thence to some other place. Then therefore he went to Berœa, as Valesius conjectures; but he did not preside over that city as bishop. This mistake of Socrates was perceived by Baronius, A. D. 360. But he is wrong in affirming that Meletius was translated from Berœa to Sebastia, not from Sebastia to Berœa. His name is written sometimes Meletius, sometimes Melitius. See Eusebius, Eccles. Hist. book vii. chap. xxxii.

99. P. 163, l. 8.—The term here used signifies adulterate, or counterfeit, by a metaphor taken from money which has a false stamp. So-

crates therefore calls the term Homoiöusios an adulterate name, because
it is corrupted from, and counterfeitly put instead of, Homoöusios,
which is, as it were, the key note of the true and uncorrupted Creed.
Further, the Acacians rejected as well the term Homoiöusios as Homoöusios, and retained only Homoios, i. e. "like the Father," and wholly ab-
horred the term Ousia, i. e. "substance."

100. P. 164, l. 15.—They had this name in regard they maintained
the Son to be made of nothing, or of things which are not. See Athanasius, p. 906, edit. Paris; whence Socrates borrowed these names for
these heretics.

101. P. 165, l. 2.—Maximus bishop of Jerusalem had at his death
ordained Heraclius to be his successor. But Acacius bishop of Cæsarea,
together with some other Arian bishops, slighting his ordination, substituted Cyril in the room of Maximus being now dead. This Cyril
degraded Heraclius from his episcopal dignity, and reduced him to the
degree of a presbyter, as Jerome relates in his Chronicon.

102. P. 166, l. 2.—It seems that the Arians asserted a tenet near of
kin to this of the Apollinarians. "Arius," says Athanasius de Adv. Christi,
"professes the flesh only to be the cover of the Deity, and asserts the
Word to have been in the flesh, in the stead of our inner man, that is, the
soul." In this opinion he was followed by Eunomius, as Theodoret informs us, Contr. Hæres. book v. chap. xi. But the Apollinarians differed
from him; for they distinguished (as we may see from this passage)
between the soul and mind of man, acknowledging that God the Word assumed a human body and a soul, (which Arius and his followers denied,)
but not the mind or spirit of man; the place of which was supplied,
they said, by the Word itself. This philosophical notion of making man
to consist of three parts, a body, a soul, and a mind, they borrowed from
Plotinus.

BOOK III.

103. P. 167, l. 6.—The statement of Socrates that Julian was proclaimed emperor in Constantinople, must not be understood as if this were
the first time of his being saluted emperor. For he had been proclaimed
in Gallia a long while before, whilst Constantius was alive. But, upon his
entry into Constantinople, he was declared emperor by the senate and
people of Constantinople, and took formal possession of the empire of
the East.

104. P. 168, l. 30.—Maximus of Epirus, or the philosopher of Byzantium, is mentioned by Suidas. He wrote concerning insoluble questions, and concerning numbers, as also a Comment upon Aristotle, which
he dedicated to his scholar, the emperor Julian. Now, if this be true,
Julius had two individuals of the name of Maximus his masters in philosophy, the one an Epirote or a Byzantine, the other an Ephesian.

105. P. 172, l. 3.—Gregory Nazianzen, in his former Invective against
Julian, confesses that the public manner of travelling and conveying of
necessaries from place to place was well rectified by Julian. For Constantius had impaired it much, by allowing the bishops every where the
use of it that they might come to the synods convened by him. But what
regulations Julianus made in this matter is hard to determine. And yet
we may conjecture from the words of Socrates that he put down travelling

by chariots, (which was called the Cursus Clavularis,) and that he adopted travelling on horse-back, upon horses provided for the public service. Johannes Lydus has treated at large de publico Cursu, in his book de Mensibus.

106.   P. 177, l. 5.—Eusebius and Lucifer were not the only persons who entered into a consultation about repairing the decayed state of the Church, and establishing the canon of faith; but other bishops beside them, who were at that time recalled from exile by Julian's edict: namely, Hilarius, Asterius, and the rest, as Theodoret remarks, b. iii. ch. iv., Eccles. Hist.   These prelates, with great zeal to the Catholic faith, took in hand to reduce heretics and schismatics to the path of truth, and recall them to their former concord.   Baronius relates, that Eusebius and Lucifer were commissioned with this legatine power by the Alexandrian synod.

107.   P. 178, l. 15.—Nicephorus, b. x. ch. ii., calls this person Cyrillus.   But in the Florentine and Sfortian MSS. he is termed Berillus. This emendation is confirmed by the version of Epiphanius Scholasticus. Berillus was not bishop of Philadelphia, as Socrates says here, but of Bostra (or of Bostri) in Arabia: he denied Christ to have been God before his incarnation, as Eusebius informs us, Eccles. Hist. b. vi. ch. xxxiii.

108.   P. 179, l. 2.—The Acts of the synod of Alexandria are not now extant; but it is evident, both from the synodical epistle which Athanasius wrote in the name of that council, and also from the fact that the great Athanasius was present at that synod, that what Socrates here says is false.   For, as to the synodical epistle, there occurs no such passage in it as this, "that the terms *ousia* and *hypostasis* are not to be used as often as we speak concerning God."   Nor would Athanasius ever have suffered that to have been determined in his synod, which manifestly contradicts the Nicene Creed; for in that creed the term *ousia* does occur.   Socrates seems to have been deceived by a passage in the synodical epistle, in which the terms *ousia* and *hypostasis* are not actually condemned: but this only is asserted, that it is more safe to use the terms of the Nicene Creed, than those of three hypostases and of one hypostasis.   Perhaps also Sabinus (whose collection Socrates had diligently perused) had led him into this mistake.

109.   P. 179, l. 11.—Some of the ancients were very cautious about acknowledging three hypostases in the Deity.   Particularly St. Jerome, who thought that the term hypostasis in this text signified "substantia:" and therefore in his version it is thus rendered, "figura substantiæ ejus," "the figure of his substance."   See Dr. Owen's account of this phrase, in his Exposition on the Hebrews, p. 55, &c., edit. London, 1668.

110.   P. 179, l. 15.—Irenæus Grammaticus was an Alexandrian, the scholar of Heliodorus Metricus, who by a Latin name was called Minucius Pacatus.   He wrote many books concerning the propriety of the Attic language.   For he compiled three books of Attic names, and as many more "de Atticâ consuetudine in dictione et in prosodiâ," which were alphabetically digested: he composed one book also de Atticismo, as Suidas relates in his Lexicon.

111.   P. 185, l. 31.—Socrates says, that Eleusius, Eustathius, and the rest of the Macedonians at this time, (that is, in the reign of Julian,) first made up a body of their own sect, and, having convened synods, confirmed

the creed of the Antiochian synod, and anathematized Acacius with his followers: and that when they were questioned by some, why they had communicated with the Acacians (whose creed they rejected) so long after the Seleucian synod; they made answer that, "the Western prelates erred in asserting the Homoöusian faith: the Easterns, being followers of Aëtius's opinion, professed the Son to be dislike the Father: but we, keeping the middle way, do affirm the Son to be like the Father according to his subsistence." This is Sophronius's answér. But that it may satisfy the question proposed, this must necessarily be understood, namely, "Since therefore the Acacians entertained the same sentiments, it need not be wondered at, that we have hitherto held communion with them." Acacius, it is certain, did profess the Son to be like the Father, in the same manner as the Macedonians did. See Sozomen, b. v. ch. xiv.

112. P. 186, l. 8.—The answer of the Macedonians, which Socrates has related above, is obscure enough; but the censure and reprehension of that answer which he now subjoins, seems much more obscure. The following seems to be the drift of the passage: the Macedonians were asked, why they dissented from Acacius, with whom they had before held communion. In their answer they blamed the Homoöusians and Aëtius. "This is nothing to the purpose," says Socrates. "For you were not questioned concerning Aëtius, but concerning Acacius; you merely sophisticate: for Acacius, as well as you, condemns Aëtius's opinion. Now, whereas you condemn Aëtius's opinion, you are not for that reason any whit less heretics. For by your own words you are convinced of novelty or heresy, whilst you assert the Son to be like the Father according to subsistence. Wherein you dissent as well from the Catholic followers of the Nicene Creed, who profess him to be of the same substance with the Father, as from the Arians, who assert him to be a creature, or unlike in respect of his substance." Theodoret (b. iv. Hæret. Fabul.) says that Macedonius asserted the Son of God to be every way like to the Father, and that he was the first who invented the term Homoiöusios. He was therefore one of the Semiarians, as well as Acacius.

113. P. 187, l. 14.—He means that Basilica which was in the fourth ward of the city of Constantinople. For this was simply and absolutely called the Cathedral. The other was termed the Theodosian Cathedral, which stood in the seventh ward of the city, as we are informed from the old description of that city. In the former Basilica therefore, the image of the public Genius of the city had heretofore been placed. For so these words of Socrates must be rendered. For the Greeks usually call that τόχη, which the Latins term Genius.

114. P. 194, l. 12.—Epimenides indeed predicted many things, partly to the Athenians, partly to the Lacedæmonians, and partly to the Cretans, as may be seen in Diogenes Laertius. But we never read that oracles were written by him. Suidas affirms that he wrote some mystical and expiatory poems, and some other obscure things; and these possibly may be styled oracles. Epimenides was a person well-skilled in lustrations and consecrations. (See Theophrastus, book vii. chap. x.) Hence it appears why Socrates termed Epimenides an Initiator.

115. P. 195, l. 4.—Οἱ μεταβολεῖς. So the Greeks in general term all small and minute merchants, because they barter their wares for a mean value. For μεταβόλλειν signifies to buy and sell for gain, and

μεταβολή imports a merchandizing trade, as Julius Pollux informs us, book. iii. chap. xxv. These traders are in Latin termed Cociones, Arilatores, and Dardanarii. But Nicephorus calls them παλινκαπήλους, whom Socrates here terms μεταβολεῖς; παλινκάπηλοι may in English be termed retailers, such as the Dardanarii heretofore were.

116. P. 196, l. 2.—Babylas succeeded Zabinus in the bishopric of Antioch, according to Eusebius, Eccles. Hist. book vi. chap. xx. The same author (book vi. chap. xxxix.) says that he died in prison; but Chrysostom (Lib. de S. Babyl. tom. ix. p. 669) tells us he was beheaded in Decius's reign. Where his body was first buried, is not known : but wherever it was, there it rested, till Gallus, Julian's brother, built a church over-against the temple of Apollo Daphnæus, (see Sozomen, book v. chap. xix.,) into which he caused S. Babylas's body to be translated. After this removal of it, mentioned in this chapter, it was entombed within the city of Antioch, in a church dedicated to his name and memory.

117. P. 200, l. 7.—Theodoret (Eccles. Hist. book iii. chap. xxv.) has recorded the following story of the death of Julian. It is reported, that upon the receipt of his wound, he filled his hand with blood, and threw it up into the air, and cried out, " O Galilean,"—so he termed our Saviour, and the Christians he called Galileans,—" thou hast overcome."

118. P. 201, l. 17.—Many of the ancients have undertaken to refute the writings of Porphyry and Julian against the Christians. Methodius, Eusebius, and Apollinaris wrote books against the former. Cyril wrote against Julian. The books of Cyril are still extant, but are not extraordinarily acute.

119. P. 204, l. 32.—In what books Origen has explained such passages in Sacred Writ as might trouble the readers, and has confuted fallacious arguments brought against the Christian religion, it is hard to assert. For in his books against Celsus, he has in no wise done this. Nor was it his design in that work to explain those passages in the Sacred Scripture which had any difficulty in them, but only to answer the objections of Celsus. Perhaps Socrates means the Stromata of Origen. For in those books Origen shows the congruity of the doctrines of our religion with those of the philosophers, as St. Jerome informs us in his epistle to Magnus the orator. In order to effect this, it was requisite for Origen to expound those places of Scripture which seemed to contradict the sentiments of the philosophers.

120. P. 206, l. 32.—He seems to mean the Taurobolia and Criobolia, after partaking in which the Pagans believed they were eternally regenerated, as the old inscriptions inform us. This whole ceremony is described at length by Prudentius, in the passion of Romanus the martyr, p. 255, &c., edit. Basil. It was in short thus: " The priest to be consecrated, being habited in his sacerdotal vestments, (adorned with a crown of gold, and wrapt about with a silken gown,) was put into a deep pit dug into the earth. Over this pit an altar made of planks was erected, through which many holes were bored ; upon this altar·a great bull was laid, adorned with garlands, and his horns were gilded: his breast they divided with a consecrated weapon. A stream of reeking blood gushing immediately out of the large wound, flowed upon the boarded altar, and running through the holes made therein, rained down upon the priest enclosed under the boards, who caught the shower of gore by putting his

head under the falling drops, wherewith he besmeared his garments and his whole body."

BOOK IV.

121. P. 216, l. 20.—Ammianus Marcellinus affirms that they revolted to the side of Valens, but he does not say that they were cut in sunder with saws. (See Amm. Marcellinus, book xxvi. p. 328, 329, edit. Paris, 1636.) He only states that the tribunes Florentius and Barchalba, after the fight at Nacolia, delivered Procopius bound to Valens, and that Procopius was immediately beheaded, and Florentius and Barchalba soon after underwent the same punishment. Philostorgius also relates that Procopius, was beheaded, and that Florentius, who delivered him to Valens, was burnt.

122. P. 217, l. 28.—Socrates has wrongly placed the promotion of Eunomius to the episcopate of Cyzicum in the reign of Valens Augustus. For Eunomius was made bishop of Cyzicum under the emperor Constantius, immediately after the synod of Seleucia, as Philostorgius affirms, (book v. chap. iii.,) and Theodoret, Eccles. Hist. book ii. chap. xxvii. and xxix.; and these two authors have recorded Eunomius's affairs with a far greater accuracy than Socrates. It is certain that Eunomius was banished by Valens, because he was reported to be a favourer of the tyrant Procopius. So unlikely is it, that he should have had the bishopric of Cyzicum then bestowed upon him. Sozomen has followed Socrates' mistake, Eccles. Hist. book vi. chap. viii.

123. P. 217, l. 34.—In civil and military offices some persons were actually employed in bearing of them, others were Vacantes, that is, persons that had the title of such an office, but were not actually concerned in the management of it; we may term them titular officers, who in the Code are said to be præcincti honore otiosi cinguli. So some tribunes are termed Vacantes in Amm. Marcellinus. After the same manner those bishops are termed Vacantes by Socrates, who had the bare name of a bishop, without a Church, without a clergy and people over whom they might preside. Of the same nature almost are those who now-a-days are styled bishops in infidel countries (in partibus Infidelium). Such therefore was Eunomius, when, being driven from Cyzicum, he resided with Eudoxius at Constantinople.

124. P. 218, l. 11.—Amm. Marcellinus relates that Valens laid siege to Chalcedon, during his war with Procopius. During the siege the inhabitants of that city reviled him from the walls, and contemptuously styled him Sabaiarius, small-beer-drinker. Sabaia (as Marcellinus describes it) was a small sort of liquor made of barley, very usually drank in Pannonia. In which country Valens was born, (see Socrates, book iv. chap. i.,) and therefore was, by way of reproach, called Sabaiarius, or Sabiarius. That this was the Pannonians' usual drink, Dio attests, lib. xlix., where he says, that the Pannonians fed upon a very mean diet, that they had very little wine or oil, and that barley and millet was their food and drink. See Amm. Marcellinus, book xxvi. p. 325, edit. Paris, 1636, and Valesius's notes thereon, p. 324.

125. P. 220, l. 13.—Sozomen mentions these baths, termed Constantianæ, Eccles. Hist. book viii. chap. xxi. They were in the tenth ward of the city of Constantinople, as we are informed from the old description of that city. Also Ammianus Marcellinus (book iii.) relates that Valens

built a bath at Constantinople, of the stones of the walls of Chalcedon, though others affirm that it was an aqueduct or conduit, and not a bath. Whatever it was, it was doubtless a very famous work; mention is made of it by Themistius, (in Oratione decennali ad Valentem,) and by Gregory Nazianzen in his twenty-fifth Oration; who very elegantly terms this aqueduct of Valens a subterraneous and aërial river. Valesius however thinks that we ought to read here not Constantiane but Carosianæ. For the baths called Constantiane were built by the emperor Constantius, as their name declares, but the Carosian baths were finished by Valens, and named Carosianæ from Carosia, the daughter of Valens, as Sozomen attests, book vi.

126. P. 220, l. 24.—Valesius gives several reasons for believing that Socrates is mistaken here, for that Valentinian the younger, who was born in the consulate of Gratianus and Dagalaïphus, was not the son of Valentinian, but of Valens Augustus. This mistake (in which error he is followed by Sozomen, book vi. chap. x.) most probably proceeded from his confounding together the two junior Valentinians, (one whereof was son to Valens, the other to Valentinian senior,) and so making but one person of two.

127. P. 221, l. 25.—Basil was made bishop of Cæsarea in Cappadocia A. D. 369, as Baronius has rightly observed. But Socrates seems to place his promotion to that bishopric somewhat earlier. For in his account at this place of those affairs that were transacted in Valentinianus's and Valens's second consulate, A. D. 368, he speaks of Basil as then bishop of Cæsarea, and Gregory of Nazianzum. But as to Gregory, Socrates is manifestly mistaken. For he was not at that time made bishop of Nazianzum by Basil, but of Sasimi; which bishopric he notwithstanding never entered upon, as he himself attests in his epistles.

128. P. 222, l. 6.—Baronius, at the year of Christ 365, reproves Socrates because he places this embassy of the Macedonians to Liberius bishop of Rome in A. D. 368, in which year Valentinian and Valens were the second time consuls. Baronius thinks that it was sent A. D. 365, and grounds his opinion on these two arguments especially. First, Eustathius with his companions was sent ambassador by the synod of Lampsacus. Now that synod was convened A. D. 365, seven years after the Seleucian synod, as Socrates attests. Secondly, if this embassy of the Macedonians were sent in A. D. 368, it would not have been sent to Liberius, but to Damasus. For Liberius died A. D. 367, in the consulate of Lupicinus and Jovinus; and in the same year Damasus entered upon that see. Valesius however assigns the embassy to the year 367, in which year Liberius died, about the beginning of September. Eustathius therefore might go to Liberius in June, and receive letters from him in August.

129. P. 226, l. 22.—Περίστασθαι, (the term here used,) signifies in this place "to decline," or "have an aversion for:" in which signification Lucianus uses it in Hermotimo. Langus and Christophorson render it abhorrere, "to abhor." This term occurs 2 Tim. ii. 16, where in the English version it is rendered "to shun."

130. P. 227, l. 8.—Sozomen tells us the same story, Eccles. Hist. b. vi. ch. xiii. But Baronius in his Annals, A. D. 370, reproves both these historians. For he maintains, that Eustathius bishop of Antioch was dead long before, in Constantius's reign. It is indeed scarce credible, that

Eustathius bishop of Antioch could live to these times. For as he was at the Nicene Council, which was held A. D. 325, we may suppose him to have been then in the forty-fifth year of his age. From this year to the third consulate of Valentinianus and Valens, (wherein Eustathius is said to have ordained Evagrius at Constantinople,) there are five and forty years. So that Eustathius must necessarily have been ninety years old, if he ordained Evagrius bishop in this year.

131. P. 232, l. 12.—This whole scene of that unhappy oracle, which some heathens had consulted that they might know who should succeed Valens in the empire, is set forth at length by Ammianus Marcellinus, in his 29th book. But it is difficult to assign the year wherein it happened. Baronius, in his Annals, places it A. D. 370. Valesius is of opinion, that it occurred A. D. 371, or at the beginning of the year 372. For Valens made his entry into Antioch at the end of summer, A. D. 371, and this conspiracy against Valens happened after his entry into the city of Antioch, as is manifest from Marcellinus.

132. P. 235, l. 7.—Παστάς, or (which has the same import) παστὸς, signifies a wedding-chamber, dining-room, or entertaining-room. See Stephens's Thesaur. Græc. Ling. in the word πάσσω. The translators of the Septuagint use this term in Joel ii. 16, and Psalm xix. 5, to express the Hebrew word חֻפָּה " chuppa ; " which was a tabernacle or tent set up on purpose for the performance of the solemnities usual amongst the Jews, in betrothing the man and woman.

133. P. 237, l. 25.—Jerome in his epistle to Ctesiphon against the Pelagians informs us, that Evagrius was an Origenist. Palladius (in Lausiaca) says Evagrius wrote three books. The first of these he calls Ἱερὸς, " The Saint : " the second Μοναχὸς, " The Monk ; " the third Ἀντιρρητικὸς, " The Refutation ; " which is against the frauds of the devil. Palladius terms that book of Evagrius " The Saint," which Socrates here calls " The Gnostic."

134. P. 239, l. 9.—Parembole is a village not far from Alexandria, near the lake Mareotis. Athanasius makes mention of it in his Second Apologetic against the Arians, where he produces the catalogue of presbyters, whom Meletius had in the city and within the territory of Alexandria. After mentioning of the presbyters and deacons of Meletius's party, which he had at Alexandria, he adds the name of Macarius, presbyter of Parembole. Parembole is also mentioned in the Notitia Imperii Romani, as being the quarters of the second Trajan legion under the command of the Comes of the military affairs throughout Egypt.

135. P. 244, l. 8.—Epiphanius Scholasticus and the other translators have rendered this place incorrectly, as if Antony the monk had come to Alexandria in the times of Valens Augustus. But Jerome informs us in his Chronicon, and in his Life of Hilarion, that Antony died in the reign of Constantius. But it is uncertain in what year of Constantius's empire Antony left the solitudes, and came down to Alexandria ; whether it was about the beginning of Constantius's reign, before the ordination of Gregorius the Arian, or rather after the synod of Sardica, and Athanasius's second restitution.

136. P. 245, l. 5.—Valesius considers that Socrates is wrong in asserting that Basil and Gregory, after they had finished the course of their learned studies at Athens, were hearers of Libanius the sophist at Antioch.

Gregory himself refutes this, in his poem concerning his own life; where he says, that he was in the thirtieth year of his age when he left Athens, and that his friends would have detained him at Athens, that he might be a professor of eloquence; (the same is attested by Rufinus, b. ii. ch. ix., Eccles. Hist.;) but that he fled secretly from thence, and went into his own country. Baronius says that Basil was preferred to the bishopric of Cæsarea, A. D. 369: and this he attempts to prove from Gregorius Nyssenus's testimony. Theophanes and Cedrenus, in his Chronicon, place the beginning of Basil's episcopate, A. D. 371. But the same authors affirm, that Basilius was yet but a presbyter in the eighth year of Valens : and Gregory Nazianzen says the same, that Basil was yet but a presbyter only of the Church of Cæsarea, when Valens, guarded with a party of heretical prelates, undertook an expedition against the churches of the East, which he hastened to deliver up to the Arians. Moreover Valens undertook this expedition against the orthodox in his own third consulate, that is, A. D. 370, as our Socrates does affirm : compare the 14th and 17th chapters of this 4th book.

137. P. 246, l. 3.—Socrates borrowed this out of Rufinus; who (in b. ii. ch. ix. Eccles. Hist.) writes thus: " But Gregory, being substituted bishop in his father's stead, at the town of Nazianzum, faithfully bore the storm of the heretics." And yet it is manifest, that Gregory was not made bishop, but coadjutor only to his own father Gregory, in the see of Nazianzum : and upon this condition too, than he should not succeed his father in that bishopric ; as he himself attests in his eighth oration, and in his poem concerning his own life. He was first constituted bishop of Sasimi by Basil the Great, who had been the first founder of this bishopric. From thence he was translated to the Constantinopolitan see, which he quickly left, and betook himself to Nazianzum, and governed that place as bishop, until, being wearied out with age and disease, he made choice of his own successor.

138. P. 246, l. 11.—This account differs from what the two Gregories, of Nazianzum and of Nyssa, relate concerning Basil. For they attest, that Basil was not brought before Modestus the prefect of the Prætorium at Antioch, but that this was done in the city Cæsarea. Sozomen therefore (Eccles. Hist. b. vi. ch. xvi.) has truly corrected the mistake of Socrates here, where he relates that Valens came from Antioch to Cæsarea, and ordered Basil should be brought before the tribunal of the prefect of the Prætorium. In the following words, " I wish you had not changèd yourself," Basil reproves Modestus, because from being a Catholic he was become an Arian, that he might please the emperor. We are indeed told by Gregory (in his funeral oration) that Modestus was an Arian.

139. P. 249, l. 21.—The Novatians boasted that the founder of their sect was a martyr ; and they wrote a book, the title of which was, The Martyrdom of Novatian. But this book, which was filled with fables, has long since been confuted by Eulogius bishop of Alexandria, in his sixth book against the Novatians. Moreover, in those Acts of his martyrdom, Novatian was not said to have suffered martyrdom, but only to have been a confessor of the faith of Christ. Before the time of Valens, the Novatians in Phrygia kept Easter at the same time the rest of the Catholics did.. After that it appears that they began to shun the communion and

society of the Catholics in this matter also. Besides the reason which Socrates assigns why the Phrygians more especially embraced the Novatian heresy, another too may be given. For Novatus, or Novatian, was by birth a Phrygian, and therefore it is no wonder that he had many followers of his own opinion in that province.

140. P. 250, l. 6.—Socrates has transcribed this following passage almost word for word out of Rufinus, Eccles. Hist. book ii. chap. xi. For he observes the same order that Rufinus does, after coupling together the ordination of Damasus and the promotion of Ambrose. But although Rufinus and Socrates have conjoined these two ordinations, as if they had been made at one and the same time, yet there was a great interval of time between each ordination. For Damasus entered upon the bishopric of Rome in the consulate of Lupicinus and Jovinus, in the year of Christ 367. But Ambrosius was promoted to the episcopate of Milan A. D. 374, as Baronius has observed.

141. P. 254, l. 10.—This speech of Themistius to Valens is extant in a Latin version by Duditius. The passage here alluded to by Socrates occurs in Duditius's version, at p. 508, where it is thus worded: " Wherefore, in regard God has removed himself at the greatest distance from our knowledge, and does not humble himself to the capacity of our wits; it is a sufficient argument, that he does not require one and the same law and rule of religion from all persons, but leaves every man a licence and faculty of thinking concerning himself, according to his own, not another man's liberty and choice. Whence it also happens, that a greater admiration of the Deity, and a more religious veneration of his Eternal Majesty, is engendered in the minds of men. For it usually comes to pass that we loathe and disregard those things which are readily apparent and prostrated to every understanding."

BOOK V.

142. P. 264, l. 24.—Socrates thought that Gregory had been translated from the bishopric of Nazianzum to that of Constantinople: which was the opinion of many others also. But Gregory never was bishop of Nazianzum; he was only his father Gregory's coadjutor in that bishopric, being sent for thither by his aged father, from the solitary retirement in which he had lived after accepting the bishopric of Sasimi, A. D. 371, as Baronius has remarked.

143. P. 268, l. 2.—The Constantinopolitan fathers hereby confer upon the bishop of Constantinople a precedency or primacy of honour only, but give him nothing of a metropolitan or patriarchal power or jurisdiction. This is evident, not only from the cautious expression of which the fathers of this synod make use, but also from these very words themselves, compared with the second canon of this Constantinopolitan synod. For in that canon the fathers had made a positive sanction, that a diocese should be governed by its bishops, or by a synod of all the bishops in the same diocese, and that the said bishops should exercise their ecclesiastical power in that diocese only; and that the bishops of the Thracian diocese should only govern the [ecclesiastical] affairs of their own diocese. Now Constantinople is situated in the Thracian diocese. And thus, by the order of this canon, Anatolius bishop of Constantinople is placed next after the legates of Leo bishop of Rome, in the subscriptions of the Council of

Chalcedon. See Concil. General, edit. Bin., Paris, 1636, tom. iii. pp. 452, 453. There occurs an eminent instance of this honour due to the Constantinopolitan bishop by virtue of this canon, in Synod. Chalced. Act. i. Vid. Concil. General, edit. Bin. ut prius, tom. iii. pp. 61, 62. See also Beveridge's Annotat. on the third Canon Concil. Constantinop., p. 95.

144.   P. 268, l. 12.—This is the first mention of Patriarchs in ecclesiastical history. But learned men differ much as to the time when these patriarchs were first constituted in the Christian Church. Valesius, in his notes on this chapter, and in his Ecclesiastical Observations upon Socrates and Sozomen, asserts that the patriarchal authority was confirmed by the sixth canon of the Nicene synod. This assertion is sufficiently confuted by Beveridge in his Annotat. upon that sixth canon, p. 52, &c.; in which passage, and also in his notes on the second canon of the Constantinopolitan Council, pp. 93, 94, Beveridge is of opinion that patriarchs were first constituted by this second œcumenical council held at Constantinople. Nevertheless, he grants, that most of those privileges which patriarchs afterwards challenged, were given them by other councils. Dr. Barrow's opinion is, that this diocesan or patriarchal form crept into the Church soon after the Nicene Council, without any solemn appointment, by a spontaneous assumption and submission." See his treatise on the Pope's Supremacy, p. 240, &c.

145.   P. 269, l. 3.—The Roman emperors who preceded Constantine the Great, committed the chief management of affairs in the civil state of the empire to one or at most to two prefects of the Prætorium. But Constantine introduced a new partition of the empire, and divided the management thereof amongst four prefects of the Prætorium : one of whom was prefect of the East, a second of Illyricum, a third of Italy, and a fourth of Gaul. Each of these prefects had several dioceses under them : every single diocese being a combination of different provinces together into one territory. In conformity with this model of civil government in the civil state, the regimen in the Church (which before had been metropolitical, when the provinces were independent on each other in ecclesiastical administrations) was adapted. The diocesan form of governance did probably creep into the Church in that interval of time between the Nicene and Constantinopolitan Councils. But it is certain that it was confirmed by the fathers convened in this second œcumenical synod, who decreed that the ecclesiastical dioceses should have the same limit with those of the state; and that it should be as unlawful for ecclesiastical persons to perform any office, or do any business, belonging to them, beyond that diocese wherein they were placed, as it was for the civil minister to intermeddle with any affair without the limits of his civil diocese. But, notwithstanding this diocesan form was brought into the Church, and thereupon patriarchal sees were erected; yet even after this time several provincial Churches had their ancient privileges confirmed to them, and remained independent of the patriarchal sees. For instance, the Cyprian Church was judged independent of the bishop of Antioch; and in like manner, Armenia was exempted from dependence on any patriarchate.

146.   P. 273, l. 3.—It cannot be inferred from this passage that Maximus was born in Britain. Zosimus (Hist. book iv.) says that he was a Spaniard. Gildas calls him " Germen Plantationis Britannicæ,"

[SOCRATES.]   2 E

"a branch of the Britannic plantation." Camden mentions him in his Britannia, (page 240, 241, edit. Lond. 1607,) where he quotes some verses out of Ausonius ; in which he is termed "Rutupinum Latronem," "the thief of Richborough." But Zosimus says that the embassy of Maximus was received by Theodosius, and that he acknowledged him as emperor, and admitted his statues, and ordered Cynegius, prefect in the Prætorium in the East, to declare to the people that Maximus was his colleague in the empire. This happened A. D. 384, in the consulship of Valentinian and Eutropius.

147. P. 279, l. 26.—Socrates has borrowed this out of Rufinus, Eccl. Hist. book ii. chap. xxix., but he has missed the meaning of Rufinus. For he does not say that it was predicted to the Pagans by other sacerdotal letters, that the temple of Serapis would be destroyed when that sign of the cross should appear ; he only says, that the Egyptians received this as a tradition from their ancestors, that the temples wherein they then worshipped should stand until that sign should come wherein there was life.

148. P. 281, l. 5.—Valesius states that among the Romans, bakers were called Mancipes, because they were Mancipati, or bound to the College of Bakers, and to the trade of making bread ; and refers the reader for further information to the eighteenth Law of the Theodosian Code de Pistoribus. But it is not probable that the Romans inflicted this sort of punishment upon adulteresses, for, after the time of Constantine, they always visited adultery with a capital punishment, as we are informed from the emperor's laws extant in both the Codes, Tit. ad Legem Juliam de Adulteriis. I omit the testimony of Amm. Marcellinus, book xxviii.

149. P. 281, l. 29.—The course of discipline in relation to penitence, as it was practised by the Fathers during the first and purest times, reformed open transgressors, by putting them into offices of open penitence, especially confession, whereby they declared their own crimes in the hearing of the whole Church, and from the time of their first convention were not capable of receiving the holy mysteries of Christ, till they had solemnly discharged this duty. During these times offenders in secret also, knowing themselves to be altogether as unworthy of admission to the Lord's table as the others who were withheld, and being persuaded that if the Church directed them in the offices of their penitence, and assisted them with public prayer, they would more easily attain what they sought, than by trusting wholly to their own endeavours ; and, having no impediment to stay them from it but bashfulness, which countervailed not the forementioned inducements, and besides, was greatly eased by that good construction which the charity of those times gave to such actions,—(wherein men's piety and voluntary care to be reconciled to God purchased them much more love than their faults were able to procure disgrace,)—these offenders in secret, I say, did not scruple to use some one of God's ministers, by whom the rest might take notice of their faults, prescribe them convenient remedies, and in the end, after public confession, all join in prayer to God for them. But, as professors of Christianity grew more numerous, so they waxed worse ; when persecution ceased, the Church immediately became subject to those mischiefs that are the product of peace and security, as schisms, discords, and dissensions ; faults were not corrected in charity, but noted with delight, and treasured up for malice

to make use of when the deadliest opportunities should be offered. Hereupon, as public confessions became dangerous and prejudicial to the safety
of well-minded men, and in diverse respects advantageous to the enemies
of God's Church; it seemed requisite first to some, and afterwards generally, that voluntary penitents should cease from open confession. Instead
of which, private and secret confession was usually practised, as well in
the Latin as in the Greek Church. The cause why the Latins made this
change of public confession into private, Leo the Great declares, in his
Decretal Epistles, Epist. lxxx., p. 148, 149, edit. Lugd. 1633. This alteration was made in the Greek Church, about such time as the heresy of the
Novatians arose, (as Socrates states here,) upon this occasion, the Church
resolving, contrary to the opinion of Novatus, or rather Novatianus, and
his followers, (concerning which see Euseb. Eccles. Hist. book vi. chap.
xliii.,) to admit the lapsed in the Decian persecution to communion, and
judging it fit, that before their admission, they, and all other voluntary
penitents in future, should do penance and make confession in private
only, (to the end that the Novatians might not take occasion from the
multitude of public penitents to insult the discipline of the Church, as
they usually had done,) constituted in every Church a penitentiary presbyter, whose office it was to receive the confessions and appoint the pen-
ances of secret offenders. So that if penitents in secret, being guilty of
crimes whereby they knew they had made themselves unfit guests for the
table of our Lord, sought direction for their better performance of that
which should set them clear, it was in this case the duty of the penitentiary to hear their confessions, to advise them the best way he could for
their souls' good, to admonish them, and to counsel them, but not to lay
upon them more than private penance. As for notoriously wicked persons
whose crimes were known, to convict, judge, and punish them was the
office of the ecclesiastical consistory. The office of the penitentiary was
continued in the Greek Church for the space of above some hundred years,
till Nectarius and the bishops of Churches under him begun a second alteration, abolishing even that confession which their penitentiaries heard in
private, upon the occasion which Socrates mentions here in this chapter.
See Hooker's Eccles. Polity, book vi. p. 332, &c., edit. Lond. 1666; also
Dr. Cave's Primitive Christianity, part iii. chap. v. On the other side of
the question consult Baronius, (Annals, A. D. 56,) Petavius, (notes on
Epiphanius, p. 225,) and Bellarmine. Sozomen (book vii. chap. xvi.)
tells us how a presbyter was to be qualified for the office of a penitentiary.
One of his qualifications was, that he ought to be ἐχέμυθος, "a person
that could hold his tongue;" from which it is plain that the confessions
made to him were private, and to be kept concealed. As to the Novatians
here mentioned, those heretics admitted no person to their communion
upon any repentance, who was once known to have sinned after baptism.
(See Euseb. Eccles. Hist. book vi. chap. xliii.) But this practice of theirs,
how fair soever their pretence might seem, made sinners not the fewer,
but the more close and obdurate.

150. P. 283, l. 5.—From this answer of Socrates to Eudæmon, it is
evident that the abolition of the penitentiary presbyter's office was disapproved by Socrates. Hence we may conclude that Socrates was no
Novatian, for the Novatians never admitted either of penitence, or of the
penitentiary presbyter. Besides, Socrates in this place terms the assembly

of the Homoöusians barely and simply "the Church," which he never would have done had he been a follower of the Novatian heresy.

151.   P. 287, l. 25.—Socrates is mistaken; for Polycarp did not suffer martyrdom in the reign of Gordian, but in that of Marcus Antoninus, as is manifest from Eusebius and other writers. It is certain, that Irenæus relates, in his third book against Heresies, (which he wrote during Eleutherius's presidency over the Roman Church, that is, in the times of Marcus Antonius,) that Polycarp had at that time suffered martyrdom. By the "some in Asia Minor," Socrates seems to mean the Syrians, Cilicians, and Mesopotamians, who kept Easter with the Jews before the Nicene Council, as Athanasius informs us in his epistle to the Africans. Those Eastern people therefore, concerning whom Socrates speaks, followed the Jews indeed, in observing the fourteenth day of the month next before the equinox; but they did not celebrate Easter on the same day on which the Jews kept it, but on the Sunday following. Wherefore Athanasius says, that they kept Easter at the same time with the Jews, but not on the same day, as his translator has ill rendered it.

152.   P. 289, l. 1.—Baronius, Eccles. Ann. a. d. 57 and 391, accuses Socrates of a double mistake, first, in asserting that the Romans fasted three weeks only in Lent before Easter; secondly, in asserting that in those three weeks, Saturdays were excepted, on which days the Romans fasted not.   As to the first, Socrates's opinion is defended against Baronius, by Halloixius in his Notes on the eleventh chapter of Irenæus's Life, p. 678. But the authority of Cassiodorus, who was himself a senator, consul, and prefectus prætorio in the city of Rome, goes directly to contradict him. There is also another ground for believing that what Socrates says concerning Saturday may be defended. For in the time of Pope Leo, the Romans did not fast on Saturdays in Lent; as is apparent from that pope's fourth sermon on the Lent Fast. The Venerable Bede also relates, that most people did not fast in Lent on Thursdays and Saturdays.

153.   P. 289, l. 25.—Περὶ συνάξεων. "Synaxis" is a word used by Christian writers in several senses. (1.) It is sometimes a general term, and contains all things usually done in the religious assemblies of Christians; in which sense we must suppose it to be taken here. (2.) The celebration of the Lord's supper is by a peculiar name termed "Synaxis." (3.) It is used so as to signify the Christian conventions or assemblies, without any respect had to the Eucharist. (4.) Synaxis is sometimes expressly distinguished from the celebration of the sacrament; in which sense Socrates uses it a little lower in this chapter, where he writes, "all things are performed which belong to the Church assembly, except the celebration of the Mysteries," or, the Eucharist. The reader will find good authorities assigned for all these significations of this term, by the learned Casaubon, Exercit. xvi. ad Annal. Eccles. Baronii, No. 42.

154.   P. 291, l. 23.—Petavius, in his Notes on Epiphanius, (Heresy of the Quartodecimans,) affirms that Socrates is mistaken here, and says, that the penitential canons of Basil the Great are sufficient to confute this error.   But it may be answered, that after Basil's death there was perhaps another usage observed in the Church of Cæsarea. For Socrates speaks of a rite then in use, when he wrote this History.

BOOK VI.

155. P. 301, l. 18.—Zosimus (book v.) relates that Alaric and the Goths, not the Huns, were invited by Rufinus to invade the Roman provinces. The same is asserted by Marcellinus in his Chronicon. But Sozomen (book viii. chap. i.) agrees with Socrates. Valesius reconciles the conflicting statements by supposing that Rufinus called in both those nations against the Romans, the Goths first, and afterwards the Huns.

156. P. 303, l. 10.—Sozomen agrees with Socrates in affirming that John Chrysostom did not practise the Civil Law. For they say that he went from the school of Libanius, when it was supposed he would have pleaded causes, and on a sudden betook himself to a retired life. Others however assert that for some time he pleaded causes: this seems to be intimated in an epistle by Libanius, where he is mentioned as studying the law, and is confirmed by the beginning of his first book de Sacerdotio, chap. i.

157. P. 303, l. 26.—Sozomen says the same of Diodorus bishop of Tarsus, namely, that he expounded the Sacred Scriptures, πρὸς τὸ ῥητὸν, literally, but avoided the more abstruse and mystical sense. Jerome, in his book de Scriptor. Eccles., says that his Comments upon the Apostle are extant, and many other pieces, which exhibit rather the style of Eusebius Emisenus, whose sense he has followed, though he could not imitate his eloquence, because of his ignorance of polite [or secular] learning. Jerome says that Diodorus has followed Eusebius Emisenus' sense, that is, his method in explaining the Scriptures. On the contrary, Theodoret (Hist. book iv.) compares his eloquence to a most limpid river; and Photius bears witness, that in his discourses he was clear and perspicuous.

158. P. 306, l. 20.—Hence it appears that the bishops did not usually preach to the people out of the pulpit. For Socrates remarks it as a singular fact, that Chrysostom being about to make an oration, he went up into the pulpit, that he might be the easier heard by the people. Bishops commonly preached standing on the steps of the altar.

159. P. 310, l. 20.—Advocates were formerly styled "Scholastici," as we are informed from the 74th and 76th Novels of Justinian's Institutes. Macarius, in his 15th Homily, writes thus, "He that desires to have a knowledge of legal matters, goes and learns the Abbreviatures. And when he has become the first there, he goes to the school of the Romans, where he is the last of all. Again, when he comes to be the first there, he departs to the school of the Pragmatici, where he is again the last of all, and a Novice. Then, when he is made a Scholasticus, he is Novice and the last of all the lawyers. Again, when he becomes the first there, then he is made a president or governor of a province."

160. P. 315, l. 7.—This must be a mistake, for Flavian and Diodorus were the first persons who in Constantius's reign divided the choir of singers at Antioch into two parts, and gave them David's Psalms, to be sung alternately, or by turns; this usage was first practised at Antioch, but afterwards spread over all the Churches of the world. Theodoret affirms this, Eccl. Hist. lib. ii. chap. xxiv.; and the antiphonal method of singing the Psalms seems to have been used at a much earlier date.

161. P. 315, l. 21.—So Arsacius, who succeeded Chrysostom in his

bishopric, is termed πρωτο-πρεσβύτερος, " chief presbyter," in the Acts of
the Synod " ad Quercum ;" and one Martyrius is styled πρωτο-διάκονος,
" chief deacon." Sozomen calls this Peter arch-presbyter. This is a
name of honour, not of seniority. For the bishops elected whom they
pleased out of the college of presbyters as arch-presbyters, as Liberatus
informs us in his Breviarium, chap. xiv.

162. P. 317, l. 9. — Socrates and Sozomen are mistaken in supposing that the Alexandrian synod, in which Theophilus condemned the
books of Origen, was held after that synod convened at Constantia by
Epiphanius. It is manifest that Theophilus first convened a synod at
Alexandria, and condemned the heresy above mentioned, A. D. 399. After
this Theophilus sent a synodical letter to all the bishops, and he wrote a
particular letter to Epiphanius, beseeching and entreating him to convene all the bishops of the island, condemn the same heresy himself,
and subscribe his synodical letter. This letter of Theophilus is extant in a
version preserved by St. Jerome.

163. P. 320, l. 16.—The ancients were accustomed to swear by their
children, and when they would earnestly entreat others, they besought
them by their own children, and whatever they accounted most dear.
So Virgil, "——oro per spem surgentis Iüli," Æn. vi. 364.

164. P. 322, l. 9.—Methodius wrote his books in the way of dialogues,
as is evident from his Convivium, and from his books concerning the resurrection, which he wrote against Origen, out of which books Epiphanius
produces some extracts. Of the same sort also was a dialogue entitled
Ξένων, or " the house of entertainment for strangers."

165. P. 328, l. 34.—Palladius tells us, that this very answer was
given by John Chrysostom's defenders, against the canon of the Antiochian
synod, namely, that that canon was made by the Arian bishops. But
Chrysostom's adversaries rejected this defence, asserting that canon to
have been made by the Catholic bishops. And when Elpidius, a bishop
of Chrysostom's party, urged them to subscribe the draught of the creed
then promulged by those bishops; they answered, in presence of the
emperor, that they were ready to subscribe it : but they put off that business to another time. Therefore, what must we determine concerning
this question? Athanasius indeed, in his book de Synodis, wholly rejects that Antiochian synod, together with its draught of the Creed, as having been held by the Arians with a design to subvert the Nicene Creed.
But Athanasius cannot be a sufficient witness in his own case, and to his
statement we oppose Hilary, then Pope Julius, and lastly, all the
Eastern and Western bishops, who have now at length by a general consent admitted that synod. Hilary, it is certain, fully admits it, in his
book de Synodis, and commends the form of the Creed drawn up there, as
both useful and necessary, on account of the heresies which sprang up
after the Nicene Council. Moreover, Pope Julius wrote a synodical
epistle to all the bishops who had been convened in that synod ; amongst
whom were Eusebius, Narcissus, Theodorus, and Maris. This synodical
epistle Athanasius records entire, vol. i. page 739, edit. Paris, 1626. In
the title and body of that letter, Julius terms them Beloved Brethren ;
which undoubtedly he would never have done, had he looked upon them
as Arians. Lastly, all the Easterns have acknowledged that synod to be
Catholic, and inserted its sanctions into the book of canons, soon after

John Chrysostom's times, as appears from the Council of Chalcedon. And at length the Western Church has by degrees admitted these canons. Notwithstanding, in John Chrysostom's times they might be rejected, since they had not then been received by a general consent of the whole Church, nor as yet admitted by the Roman Church. Pope Innocent, in his epistle to the Constantinopolitan Church, does not admit these canons. See Sozomen, book viii. chap. xxvi.

166. P. 331, l. 6.—Nicephorus adds, that the day whereon John Chrysostom died was dedicated to the exaltation of the Holy Cross. For so it was agreeable, that he who had passed his whole life under the cross, and had gloried in nothing but in the cross of his Lord, should be loosed from the frame of his body on that festival. The speech of Chrysostom mentioned in this chapter, occurs in none of the extant homilies of St. Chrysostom. And yet we have little reason to question the authority of Socrates, because he lived in the same times, and could have heard the sermons, as well of Chrysostom, as of Sisinnius bishop of the Novatians. This is one of the passages on account of which the adversaries of Socrates accuse him of leaning to the Novatian heresy: he certainly puts an unfavourable interpretation upon Chrysostom's saying, and also openly inclines to the side of Sisinnius bishop of the Novatian party.

BOOK VII.

167. P. 335, l. 13.—It is a question often disputed on both sides, whether it is lawful for Catholics, especially bishops, to persecute heretics. In the determination of this question Valesius considers that a distinction is requisite. For it is certain that on account of amassing money together, it is not lawful for Catholics to molest and vex heretics, though Theodosius bishop of Synnada at that time did so. Also to persecute them by criminal sentences, and to thirst after their blood, is in like manner unlawful, as Idatius and some other prelates of Spain did in their persecution of the Priscillianists. Notwithstanding, it is and always was lawful for Catholics, he adds, to implore the aid of princes and magistrates against heretics, in order to restrain them and keep them within the bounds of duty, lest they should behave insolently towards the Catholics, or insult and scoff at the Catholic religion. St. Augustine confesses that he once held that heretics ought not to be molested by Catholics, but that they were to be invited by mildness and quietness. But afterwards he altered his opinion, from a conviction that the laws of princes made against heretics, are useful to heretics themselves in order to their conversion. And he says that this was acknowledged by the Donatists themselves when they afterwards returned to the Catholic Church. For they affirmed that they should never have returned to the Church, but always have continued in their error, had they not been provoked and controlled as it were by those penalties contained in the Imperial Laws. The reader may refer, on this subject, to a most elegant passage in St. Augustine's forty-eighth Epistle to Vincentius; as also in his first book against Gaudentius, chap. xxiii.

168. P. 345, l. 10.—The loaves which the faithful offered for a sacrifice were termed "the loaves of benediction." Compare the fifty-ninth canon of the Council of Laodicea: "The bread of benediction ought not to be offered in Lent, except on the sabbath and on Sunday

only." Of these loaves some were taken for the Eucharist, the rest were
allotted for the food of the clergy by the bishop, who also took some of
them himself, as we are informed from this place. We must note further,
that Socrates says that he took the bread "from the Churches." For the
bishop had the full right to dispose at will of the oblations of all the
Churches which were under his own jurisdiction. See Gelasius's De-
cretals, chap. xxvii.

169. P. 347, l. 17.—Cyril held forth the book of the Gospels, that
he might conjure and earnestly beseech Orestes, prefect of Egypt, to be
reconciled with him. Socrates has remarked already, (see book vi. chap.
xi.,) that the ancients were accustomed to conjure and earnestly beseech
each other, by those things which they used to swear by. The usage of
the Christians was to swear by the Gospels, laying their hands on those
sacred books, or kissing them, as is done to our own day.

170. P. 348, l. 28.—At Alexandria there was formerly a school of
Platonic philosophy, over which, amongst others, Hierocles the philosopher presided. But the succession of this school is not to be deduced
from Plotinus, for the latter never taught philosophy at Alexandria.
Plotinus was indeed instructed in philosophy at Alexandria by Ammonius;
but he himself never kept a school there, but continued teaching at Rome
for the space of twenty-six years, until his death ; as Porphyry relates
in his Life. Hence Valesius proposes, instead of Plotinus, to read Ammonius ; unless it be supposed that the Alexandrian school had associated
Plotinus to themselves, as being the most eminent professor of the Platonic philosophy.

171. P. 364, l. 17.—It would seem to be inferred from this passage that
ecclesiastics in the Catholic Church, who had been excommunicated for
more enormous crimes, were cut off from the Church without all hope of
pardon, but that it was not so in the case of the laity. Laymen, who had
been separated from communion on account of public crimes, were restored to communion again by the remedy of penitence, at least once. But
to ecclesiastics who had been excommunicated, the door of penitence was
shut. For they were not admitted to public penitence, and they continued
therefore for ever excommunicated. For this reason ecclesiastics were
very rarely excommunicated ; but were either deposed, or suspended from
their office for some time, or at least reduced to a lay-communion. But
this runs counter to the first canon of the synod of Neocæsarœa, in which
the ecclesiastics who had committed fornication or adultery are driven
from communion, and brought to penitence. This passage, however,
may be explained otherwise also. For, from the time when Nectarius
abolished the penitentiary, all lay-men had a free power of communicating
left them ; nor was any one removed from communion on account of a
deadly crime, except ecclesiastics only.

172. P. 366, l. 27.—It is uncertain what law this was, and by whom it
was enacted. Valesius thinks that it was an Imperial law, whereby provision had been made that the inhabitants of Cyzicum should not ordain
themselves a bishop contrary to the consent of Atticus bishop of Constantinople. For if this had been a sanction made in a council of bishops,
Socrates would have used the term canon, rather than have called it a
law. After the death of Atticus, the inhabitants of Cyzicum disregarded
this law : for they said that that privilege had been granted specially to

Atticus, and did not belong to his successors. But they were mistaken ; for long before Atticus, the Constantinopolitan prelates had given bishops to the inhabitants of Cyzicum. For, in Constantius's time, Eudoxius bishop of Constantinople ordained Eunomius bishop of Cyzicum.

173.   P. 368, l. 4.—What the bishops, and especially the prelates of the greater Churches, said in their first sermon to the people, was very carefully observed among the early Christians. For from that sermon a conjecture was made as to the faith, doctrine, and temper of every bishop. Hence the people were wont to take particular notice of, and remember their sayings. A remark of this nature occurs above, book ii. chap. xliii., concerning the first sermon of Eudoxius bishop of Constantinople. And Theodoret and Epiphanius declare the same concerning the first sermon of Melitius to the people.

174.   P. 372, l. 26.—Socrates is mistaken here ; and while he reproves Nestorius, falls into the error of Eutyches, who thought that after the Hypostatic Union, there were not two natures, but only one nature in Christ. Unless we should say, that Socrates speaks here concerning persons, not natures. Socrates might be excused, if his words would admit of this sense ; but the words which he uses certainly signify natures rather than persons.

175.   P. 374, l. 5.—Evagrius and others deservedly blame Socrates in this place. We are informed from the Acts of the Synod of Ephesus, that when Nestorius had been condemned and deposed by the holy synod, and letters of deposition had been sent to him, he sent an account of what had taken place to the emperor Theodosius, complaining of the violence of his adversaries, and that they would not wait for the arrival of the Eastern bishops, who, it was said, would quickly be there. This account was subscribed by ten bishops of Nestorius's party. On the fifth day after, John bishop of Antioch arrived with the Eastern bishops. As soon as he understood what had been done, he assembled together the bishops, as well the Eastern prelates whom he had brought with him, as those ten who had subscribed the account of Nestorius, and deposed the bishops Cyril and Memnon. Nestorius himself was not present, because, having been condemned by an episcopal sentence, he had not been restored by the determination of a synod. But the bishops of his party, whom the sentence of the synod had in no wise touched, were present. Wherefore Socrates may be excused, if we say that these words, οἱ περὶ Νεστόριον, denote not Nestorius himself, but the bishops who were of his party, and had subscribed his relation. But in the other particulars Socrates cannot stand excused.

176.   P. 375, l. 16.—This is the eighteenth canon of the synod at Antioch. Socrates speaks of this synod above, book ii. chap. viii. ; and this very canon occurs at p. 447, tom. i. edit. Beveridge. But Socrates is mistaken in thinking that the bishops relied upon this canon, that they might exclude Proclus from the Constantinopolitan see. It is true indeed, that Proclus was one of the number who are meant in the aforesaid canon. For after he had been ordained bishop of Cyzicum by Sisinnius patriarch of Constantinople, he was not admitted by the inhabitants of Cyzicum, as Socrates has related before. But the bishops who were against Proclus's election did not rely upon this canon, but quoted the twenty-first canon of the same synod in confirmation of their own opinion ; the contents of

which are as follows : " A bishop ought not in any wise to remove from one see to another, neither rushing into it wholly on his own accord, nor forcibly compelled by the people, nor yet necessarily constrained by the bishops : but let him continue in that Church which God has at first allotted to him, nor let him remove from thence, agreeable to the previous determination made concerning this matter." Socrates therefore has mistaken between the eighteenth canon of the Antiochian synod and the twenty-first.

177. P. 376, l. 18.—Perigenes had been born and baptized at Corinth, the metropolis of Achaia : having afterwards been ordained, he continued presbyter of the same Church a long while with great integrity. Afterwards, when he had been promoted to the bishopric of Patræ by the bishop of Corinth, and the inhabitants of Patræ had refused to receive him, he was forced to return to Corinth. The bishop of that city dying not long after, the Corinthians requested he might be their bishop; and they made known their request to Boniface bishop of Rome. But Boniface would do nothing in that affair before he had received the letters of Rufus bishop of Thessalonica, who was deputed the vicegerent of the apostolic see throughout Achaia and Macedonia. He wrote therefore to him concerning this business, and afterwards, on receiving a reply from Rufus, he approved the election of Perigenes, and wrote a letter to him and the Corinthians.

178. P. 377, l. 16.—It is to be observed, that the ordination of the metropolitans of Thrace belonged at this time to the bishop of Constantinople. For the patriarchs of that city, by a certain singular privilege, ordained metropolitans. Hence it is, that Atticus patriarch of Constantinople, ordained Silvanus bishop of Troas, upon the request of the inhabitants of that city. For Alexandria Troas was the metropolis of Phrygia. This is in express words established by the twenty-eighth canon of the Council of Chalcedon, [tom. i. page 145, edit. Beveridge,] which treats concerning the privileges of the Constantinopolitan see : namely, that the metropolitans only of the Thracian, Pontic, and Asian diocese, should be ordained by the most holy Constantinopolitan see ; the decrees being first made by the common consent of the clergy and laity, and directed to the patriarch of Constantinople.

179. P. 381, l. 6.—Valesius has told us before, (see chap. xxxvi.,) that Rufus bishop of Thessalonica was deputed the vicegerent of the apostolic see, that is, Rome, throughout Achaia and Macedonia. He adds here, that he had the same vicegerency throughout Illyricum, as declared by the epistles of Innocent and Boniface bishops of Rome, which are to be seen in Lucas Holstenius's Roman collection. For the bishops of Thessalonica had that privilege from the times of Pope Damasus. Balsamo (in his comments on the synod in Trullo, page 359, edit. Paris, 1620) affirms, that the bishops of Thessalonica were formerly the legates of the Roman bishop; and that the bishop of Rome had a power of constituting legates in the Constantinopolitan patriarchate ; but he denies that he had a power of ordaining bishops. But Balsamo is mistaken; for those provinces, which then, when Balsamo wrote, were under the Constantinopolitan prelate, had formerly been under the bishop of Rome. See Beveridge's Synod. tom. i. page 154.

180. P. 384, l. 17.—By these words Socrates plainly discovers his

opinion, that these things are usually done through envy, or out of favour. For Socrates ascribes to the envy of Theophilus towards Origen, the condemnation of the latter so many years after his death. And, whereas John Chrysostom was brought back with honour into his own country, on the thirty-fifth year after his death, this event Socrates attributes to the love and benevolence of Proclus and the people of Constantinople. But Valesius rightly remarks, that although in affairs of this nature the affections of men have some influence, yet Divine justice and providence, whereby the Church is governed, always overrules them. Origen therefore, he adds, was condemned for his heterodox opinions; and John Chrysostom, being consecrated for his integrity of life and doctrine, continues in the Church to this very day.

THE END.

GENERAL INDEX.

performs ordinations there without leave of the bishop, 320; is admonished by him—his death, 323.

Epistle of Alexander, bishop of Alexandria, denouncing the Arian heresy, 6; from the Nicene synod, relative to its decisions, 26; from the emperor Constantine to the bishops and people, against the impiety of Porphyry and Arius, 31; to the Churches, relative to the Easter festival, 32; to Eusebius, and bishops of every province, respecting the building and maintenance of sacred edifices, 34; respecting the preparation of copies of the Holy Scriptures, 35; to Macarius, respecting the erection of a magnificent church on the site of the holy sepulchre, 36; of Julius, bishop of Rome, on behalf of Athanasius, 111; from Constantius, announcing the restoration of Athanasius, 115; to the laity, ib.; respecting the abrogation of all ecclesiastical enactments against Athanasius, 116; to the council of bishops at Rimini, 142; (second) from the synod of Rimini to the emperor Constantius, 143.

Epistles, from Constantius to Athanasius, recalling him from exile, 110.

Ethiopici, (see note,) 291.

Eucharist, the, variously celebrated, 290.

Eudæmon, a presbyter of the Constantinopolitan Church, counsels the abolition of the office of penitentiary presbyter, 282; Socrates' reply, 282, 283.

Eudocia, wife of the emperor Theodosius junior, fulfils her vow of going to Jerusalem, 386.

Eudoxia, the empress, endeavours to reconcile the bishops of Constantinople and Gabali, 330; her death, 330.

Eudoxius, bishop of Germanicia,

99; instals himself in the see of Antioch, 135; deposed, 156; promoted to the see of Constantinople, 161; his impious jesting, ib.; disturbs the Church of Alexandria, 228; his death, 229.

Eugenius (styled " the tyrant ") appointed chief secretary to Valentinian junior, whom he caused to be strangled, and assumed the supreme authority, 297; is defeated by Theodosius, and beheaded, 298.

Eunomians, the sect of, 12; dissensions among the, 296.

Eunomieutychians, the followers of Eutychius, ib.

Eunomiotheophronians, the followers of Theophronius, ib.

Eunomius, head of the sect of Eunomians, 134; appointed to supersede Eleusius in the bishopric of Cyzicum, 216, 217; his heretical principles, 217; seeks an asylum in Constantinople—specimens of his impiety, ib.

Euripides, 194.

Eusebius, surnamed Pamphilus, composes a History of the Church, 1; retracts his non-assent to the faith promulgated by the Nicene council, 22; his views of the faith, 22—24; copy of the Nicene creed, 24—26; undertakes to record the eminent doings of the emperor Constantine, 46; denies the accusation of Eustathius, and recriminates, 60; refuses the vacant bishopric of Antioch — his admirable conduct commended by the emperor Constantine, 61; his death, 84; a review of his writings, 105.

Eusebius, bishop of Berytus, takes possession of the see of Nicomedia, and defends Arianism, 6, 11, 12; defends Arianism before the council of Nice, 18; recalled from exile, 43; copy of his retractation, 44; returns to his heretical course, 58; conspires against Athanasius, 59; is translated to the vacant bishopric of Constantinople, 85; sends a deputation to Rome — his death, 91.

Eusebius, chief eunuch of the imperial bed-chamber, introduces Arianism into the palace, 82; put to death by the emperor Julian, 170.

Eusebius, bishop of Verceil, a city of Liguria, 134; exiled by Constantius, 135; recalled from exile — proceeds to Alexandria, 177; travels through the Eastern provinces to heal the distractions of the Church, 184, 185.

Eusebius, a consul, 149.

Eusebius Scholasticus, author of " The Gaïnea," 310.

Eustathius, bishop of Antiochia Magna, 43; accuses Eusebius Pamphilus — deposed, 60; various causes assigned, 61; ordains Evagrius to the see of Constantinople — he is banished by Valens, 229.

Eustathius, bishop of Sebastia, deposed for impious practices, 160; heads a deputation to the emperor Valentinian, 222; proceeds to Sicily, 227.

Eutropius, a presbyter among the Macedonians, 296.

Eutropius, chief officer of the imperial bed-chamber, under Arcadius—an oration against him, 306; incurs the emperor's displeasure—is decapitated, ib.

Eutychian, a monk of the Novatian Church, 41; miraculous effect attributed to his superior sanctity, 42.

Eutychius excommunicated, 156.

Eutychius, a teacher among the Eunomians at Constantinople, 296.

Euzoïus, a deacon, exiled—returns from exile, 63; recants, ib.; promoted to the see of Antioch, 162; attempts to depose Peter,

in order to instal Lucius, 233; his death, 256, 257.

Evagrius, bishop of Mytilene, deposed, 156; elected bishop of Constantinople by the Homoousian party — banished by the emperor, 229.

Evagrius, a disciple of two Egyptian monks both named Macarius, deacon of Constantinople — titles of the books he wrote—with extracts from his history, 236.

Evagrius, ordained bishop of Antioch on the death of Paulinus, 277.

Faith, the agreement at the Nicene council—number who signed and opposed it, 21; an exposition of, covertly to favour the Arian heresy, 88; a second, 89; an exposition of, drawn up and presented to Constans by bishops, 98; an elaborate exposition of the, promulgated by a synod of the Eastern bishops, 99; expositions of the, decreed by the synod of Sirmium, 124.

Famine, in Phrygia, 230; among the Persian prisoners, 356.

Fasting, days of, at Rome, 291.

Fasts, the author's opinion respecting, 288; the various modes of their observance, 289.

Felix, an Arian bishop, appointed to the see of Rome—expelled, 144.

Festival of Easter gives rise to distractions in the Church, 16.

Fidelis excommunicated, 156.

Fire from heaven consumes the tools with which the Jews were about to rebuild Solomon's temple, 198; destruction at Constantinople, 380.

Flaccilla, first wife of Theodosius the Great, 254; gives birth to a son, who is named Honorius, 274.

Flavian put into the see of Antioch, 269; rejected by the people, 277; his perjury and schism, ib.; his death, 342.

Franks, the, invade the Roman territories, 90; subdued by the consul Constans, 92.

Fravitus, a Goth, honoured with the office of consul as a reward for his fidelity, 310.

Fritigernes, chief of a division of the Goths, 255.

Frumentius visits India—aids in the dissemination of Christianity, 52; appointed bishop of India, *ib.*

Gaïnas, the Goth, commander-in-chief of the Roman army—seeks to usurp supreme authority—is met by Arcadius—they vow fidelity—violates his vow, 307; excites a tumult—is slain, 309, 310.

"Gaïnea," a book written by Eusebius Scholasticus, 310.

Gaius deposed by the synod of Rimini, 139.

Galerius, the surname of Maximian, 2.

Galla, second wife of Theodosius the Great, 253.

Gallus, kinsman of Constantius, invested with the sovereignty of Syria, 123; attempts innovations, 132; Constantius incensed at his conduct, causes him to be slain, *ib.*

George, bishop of Laodicea, 60; inducted into the see of Alexandria by the Arians, 93; commits horrible atrocities, 121; deposed, 156; burnt by Pagans, 174; his death resented by the emperor Julian, *ib.*

George, a learned Arian presbyter, 339.

Germinius deposed by the synod of Rimini, 139.

"Gnostic," title of a book written by Evagrius, 239.

Gnostic, a monk, views of, 239.

Gomarius, a rebel general, put to death by Valens, 215.

Goths invade the Roman territory, and, being defeated, embrace Christianity, 49; renew their attacks against Constantinople—are repulsed, 255; the Christianized, by simple views of truth, are led to reject the Arian heresy—become subjects of Valens, *ib.*; they return his clemency by hostile aggressions, 256.

Grata, daughter of Valentinian the elder, 253.

Gratian, a consul under the emperor Valentinian, 215.

Gratian, the emperor, grants freedom to all sects—creates Theodosius his colleague, 262; assassinated by Maximus, 273.

Gregory designated bishop of Alexandria, 88; his installation indignantly resented by the people, 91; ejected from the see of Alexandria, 93.

Gregory of Nazianzen, his sketch of the emperor Julian, 203; opposes the Arian heresy, 244; translated to the see of Constantinople, 265; refuses to continue in the see of Constantinople, *ib.*

Gregory the Just, his four virtues and their province, 239.

Gregory, brother of Basil, bishop of Cæsarea, 246.

Gregory Thaumaturgus, a disciple of Origen, celebrated for his knowledge of Divine truth, 247.

Gregory, three of the name, 247.

Hail of prodigious size viewed as indicative of God's displeasure, 221, 330.

Heathen temples in Alexandria demolished, 277, 278.

Helen, mother of Constantine, erects a magnificent church on the site of the holy sepulchre, 47; also at Bethlehem, and at Mount Ascension—her death, 48.

Heliodorus, a bishop of Trica, in Thessaly, 290.

Helion, a Roman, negotiates with the Persians, 355; conveys the imperial crown to Valentinian, 361.

Helladius, a Pagan grammarian of

Maximus the Novatian bishop of Nice, 249.

Maximus of Britain, causes Gratian to be assassinated, 273;' is admitted by Valentinian the younger as his colleague in imperial power, *ib.*; Theodosius puts him to death, 276.

Meletius (or Melitius) bishop of Sebastia, translated to Berœa—thence to Antioch—sent into exile by Constantius, 168; recalled by Jovian, 209; expelled by Valens, 213; his death, 269.

Melitians, their origin, they unite with the Arians, 11.

Melitius, bishop of Alexandria, deposed—becomes head of the sect called Meletians, 11; restored to communion by the Nicene council, 27.

Memnon, a bishop of Ephesus, 374.

Mendemus suffers martyrdom, 229.

Merobandes, a consul under Gratian, 273.

Meropius, a Tyrian philosopher, murdered, 51.

Methodius, bishop of Olympus in Lycia, author of "Xenon," 322.

Metrodorus, a philosopher, 51.

Metrophanes, a bishop of Constantinople, 76.

Milan, tumult at, 251.

Miracle, a, said to have been wrought through Christian baptism, 337; ascribed to Silvanus bishop of Troas, 377.

Miraculous healing of a child by a captive maid, 53.

Mithra, murderous rites in the temple of, unveiled, 173.

Modestus, the prefect, burns eighty pious ecclesiastics in a ship, 230.

Monasteries of Egypt, brief account of, 234; assailed by a military force—horrible excesses committed, 241.

Money-changers, (see note on this expression,) 193.

Monks of Egypt, their remarkable lives, 234; their sufferings, and Christian endurance, 242.

Monk, surnamed *the Long*, of Alexandria, 312.

Moses, a Saracen and monk, is, at the instance of Queen Mavia, ordained bishop of the Saracens, 257.

Names, many persons change their, to avoid death from suspicion, 232.

Narcissus, a Cilician bishop under Constantius, 98.

Narsæus, a Persian general, who commanded his country's forces against the Romans, 352.

Necromancy, practice of, 232.

Nectarius elected to the episcopate of Constantinople, 267; consulted by the emperor Theodosius as to the points of difference between the various sects, 270.

Neonas, bishop of Seleucia, ejected, 160.

Nepotian assumes the sovereignty of Rome—he is slain, 118.

Nestorius succeeds Sisinnius in the episcopate of Constantinople, 367; excites a tumult—persecutes the Novatians—Quarto-decimani unto death, 368; prevails on the emperor to deprive the Macedonians of their churches, 370; is ejected, *ib.*; deposed, and banished to Oasis, 374.

Nice, council of, summoned by Constantine—Eusebius Pamphilus's account of it, 17; names of bishops present at the council of, 43; period of the assembling of the council of, *ib.*

Nicene synod, did not alter the time of celebration of the Easter Festival, 292.

Nicocles, the Lacedæmonian, 168.

Nigrinian, a consul, 119.

Nilammon, a bishop, exiled under Constantius, 122.

Nile, superstitious views of its periodical overflowings, 49.

Theodosius, bishop of Philadelphia in Lydia, deposed, 156.

Theodosius, (a noble Spaniard,) elevated to share imperial power, 262; is baptized by the bishop of Thessalonica, 265; convenes a synod, 270; the Goths submit to him—proclaims his son Arcadius Augustus, *ib.*; secures to the Novatians the privileges enjoyed by other sects, 272; opposes the tyrant Maximus, 274; gains the victory—returns in triumph, 276; his remarkable clemency towards the senator Symmachus, *ib.*; demolishes the heathen temples in Alexandria, 278; confers great benefits on Rome, 280; reforms some infamous abuses, 280, 281; leaves Valentinian at Rome, and returns to Constantinople, 281; gives freedom to heretics, 283; favours the Novatians, *ib.*; defeats the regicide Eugenius, 298; sends for his son Honorius—dies, 299; his funeral obsequies, 301.

Theodosius jun. succeeds the emperor Arcadius, 334; his preeminent character, 357 — 359; proclaims his cousin Constantius emperor of the West, 361; convenes a synod at Ephesus, 373; his deserved eulogium, 382.

Theodosius, bishop of Synada in Phrygia Pacata, persecutes the Macedonians, 336; loses his see, 336, 337.

Theodulus, bishop of Chæretapi in Phrygia, deposed, 156.

Theodulus, a Christian who was cruelly martyred, 191.

Theognis, bishop of Nice, defends Arianism, 18; recalled from exile, 43; copy of his retraction, 44; abuses the emperor's clemency, 58; conspires against Athanasius, 59.

Theon, a philosopher of Alexandria, 348.

Theopemptus, a Novatian bishop, 340.

Theophilus succeeds Timothy at Alexandria, 274; induces Theodosius to demolish the temples, 277, 278; his acts, 315; flies from Constantinople, 327; his death, 340.

Theophronius, a Cappadocian and head of a sect, 296.

Theotinus, bishop of Scythia, defends Origen, 321.

Theotocos, disquisition on the term, 370.

Therapeia, a port in the Euxine Sea, called Pharmaceus, 361.

Thessalonica, singular custom among the clergy of, 291.

Thmuïs, a bishop, exiled under Constantius, 122.

Timothy succeeds Peter at Alexandria, 258; his death, 274.

Timothy, a learned Arian presbyter, 339.

Torture, horrible, inflicted upon Christian women, 146.

Transactions comprised in the last book, 387.

Troïlus, a sophist of prudence and judgment, 334, 335.

Tumult at Ancyra, 114.

Tyre, the council of, 67; summoned by the emperor, *ib.*

Ulfilas bishop of the Goths, 159.

Ulfilas translates the Scriptures, 255.

Unity between the Catholics and Novatians, 147.

Uranius, of Tyre, deposed, 156.

Urbanus suffers martyrdom, 229.

Ursacius conspires against Athanasius, 65; recants, 91; deposed, 139.

Ursinus, a deacon of Rome, 250.

Valens, bishop of Mursa, conspires against Athanasius, 65; recants, 91, 117; deposed, 139.

Valens raised to share the imperial dignity, 212; favours the Arians, *ib.*; resides at Constantinople—is intolerant and cruel, *ib.*; orders the walls of Chalcedon to be

JOHN CHILDS AND SON, BUNGAY.

Printed in the United States
105689LV00002B/17/A